Early Analytic Philosophy and the German Philosophical Tradition

Also available from Bloomsbury

Kant's Transition Project and Late Philosophy, by Oliver Thorndike
Portraits of Wittgenstein, edited by F.A. Flowers III and Ian Ground
The German Idealism Reader, edited by Marina F. Bykova
The History of Philosophical and Formal Logic, edited by Alex Malpass and Marianna Antonutti Marfori

Early Analytic Philosophy and the German Philosophical Tradition

Nikolay Milkov

BLOOMSBURY ACADEMIC
LONDON • NEW YORK • OXFORD • NEW DELHI • SYDNEY

BLOOMSBURY ACADEMIC
Bloomsbury Publishing Plc
50 Bedford Square, London, WC1B 3DP, UK
1385 Broadway, New York, NY 10018, USA
29 Earlsfort Terrace, Dublin 2, Ireland

BLOOMSBURY, BLOOMSBURY ACADEMIC and the Diana logo are trademarks of
Bloomsbury Publishing Plc

First published in Great Britain 2020
This paperback edition published in 2021

Copyright © Nikolay Milkov, 2020

Nikolay Milkov has asserted his right under the Copyright, Designs and
Patents Act, 1988, to be identified as Author of this work.

For legal purposes the Acknowledgments on p. ix constitute an extension
of this copyright page.

Cover design: Louise Dugdale
Cover image: © StudioM1 / iStock

All rights reserved. No part of this publication may be reproduced or transmitted
in any form or by any means, electronic or mechanical, including photocopying,
recording, or any information storage or retrieval system, without prior
permission in writing from the publishers.

Bloomsbury Publishing Plc does not have any control over, or responsibility for,
any third-party websites referred to or in this book. All internet addresses given in this
book were correct at the time of going to press. The author and publisher regret any
inconvenience caused if addresses have changed or sites have ceased to exist,
but can accept no responsibility for any such changes.

A catalogue record for this book is available from the British Library.

A catalog record for this book is available from the Library of Congress.

ISBN: HB: 978-1-3500-8643-2
PB: 978-1-3502-7797-7
ePDF: 978-1-3500-8644-9
eBook: 978-1-3500-8645-6

Typeset by Deanta Global Publishing Services, Chennai, India

To find out more about our authors and books visit www.bloomsbury.com and
sign up for our newsletters.

Contents

Preface	vii
Acknowledgments	ix

Part One Introductory Chapters

1	What Is Early Analytic Philosophy, and How to Write Its History?	3
2	What Is the Logical History of Philosophy?	15

Part Two Leibniz and Hegel

3	Leibniz's Project for *Characteristica Universalis* and the Early Analytic Philosophy	31
4	Making Sense of Hegel with the Help of Early Analytic Philosophy	41
5	Frege and German Philosophical Idealism	53

Part Three Hermann Lotze

6	Lotze and the Early Cambridge Analytic Philosophy	67
7	Russell's Debt to Lotze	81
8	Lotze's Concept of State of Affairs	96

Part Four Edmund Husserl

9	Edmund Husserl and Bertrand Russell, 1905–1918	111
10	Husserl's Theory of Manifolds in Relation to Russell and Wittgenstein	125
11	Wittgenstein's Indefinables and His Phenomenology	136

Part Five Two Neglected German Proto-analytic Philosophers

12	G. E. Moore and Johannes Rehmke	151
13	Leonard Nelson, Karl Popper, and Early Analytic Philosophy	166

Part Six Different Conceptions of Analytic Philosophy

14 Wittgenstein and the Vienna Circle versus G. E. Moore and Russell	181
15 Two Concepts of Early Analytic Philosophy	193
16 What Is Analytic Philosophy?	208
Notes	225
References	245
Index	272

Preface

I began to think about writing this book during my *séjour* as a Visiting Fellow at the Centre for Philosophy of Science, University of Pittsburgh, in 2005–6. While at Pittsburgh I had the opportunity to sit in on Mark Wilson's class on Scott Soames's history of analytic philosophy (2003),[1] and I attended seminars by Tom Ricketts on Frege and John McDowell on Wilfrid Sellars. What struck me above all was the profound influence that W. V. Quine has had on American philosophers and the central role that the problem of analyticity plays in that legacy. Quine's influence has led many American historians of analytic philosophy to choose the analytic/synthetic distinction as their starting point.

Breaking with this historical paradigm, the present book investigates the emergence and development of early analytic philosophy as an orientation to problems that originated within a particular historical context. Specifically, the study sheds light on the Germanophone roots of the early analytic philosophy associated with the Cambridge philosophers G. E. Moore, Bertrand Russell, and, later, Ludwig Wittgenstein. We shall find that many of the issues that preoccupied this school were familiar to the most renowned figures in the German philosophical tradition and addressed by them in profoundly original and enduringly significant ways.

The aim in these pages is to trace how particular problems and concepts that exercised the early analytic philosophers were closely connected with, and in many cases, hinged upon, the thinking of German philosophers and logicians of the first rank, from Leibniz to Lotze and Husserl, and even to thinkers conceived as antipodal to analytic philosophy, such as Hegel. Restricting itself mainly to these major thinkers, this study does not cover the relatedness of other important figures—such as Bolzano, Fechner, Herbart, von Helmholtz, Brentano, Ernst Mach, and Meinong to the early analytic philosophers. The two exceptions are Johannes Rehmke and Leonard Nelson, whose proto-analytic philosophy, unlike that of Bolzano, Brentano, and the rest, is little known, especially among Anglophone students of the movement.

The unheralded hero of the present study is Hermann Lotze. Still underappreciated, Lotze's philosophy stands out for how it successfully synthesizes elements of scientifically oriented German philosophy of the mid-nineteenth century with the thought of classical German idealism. Beyond being a seminal factor in the rise of analytic philosophy, Lotze's influence proved formative in phenomenology as well; his thinking informs key points of similarity between early analytic philosophers and Husserl, which I explore in Part Four of this book. Such a discussion is of particular historical value since for a considerable time, especially in the 1960s and 1970s, students of analytic philosophy and phenomenology regarded the two movements as antithetical. While, to be sure, recent years have seen growing recognition of the relation between these philosophical movements, a host of historically significant and also surprising connections remain to be disclosed and developed.

While seminally influential, however, German school philosophy (*Kathederphilosophie*) had a complex and in some respects problematic impact on nascent Cambridge analytic philosophy. This is only to be expected seeing that early analytic philosophy was embedded in different—in the British—philosophical tradition. As a result, the pioneers of the Cambridge school formulated positions that often stand at odds with those of analytic philosophy as it took shape in Germanophone authors. I discuss these differences in Part Six.

This study builds upon my work *English Philosophy in Context* which I originally defended as a *Habilitationsschrift* (second dissertation) at the University of Paderborn in 2009. Over the years, this work has matured and expanded through investigations into two important yet largely undeveloped and often misunderstood areas in the history of analytic philosophy. One is the history of logical empiricism (Milkov 2011, 2013a, 2015a)—my interest in it aroused during my stay in Pittsburgh. My investigation of this realm revealed that the Berlin Group around Hans Reichenbach, active between 1928 and 1933, which also included the young Carl Hempel, had a rather different orientation to the philosophy of science than that of the more famous Vienna Circle. Briefly put, the Berlin Group allied itself more closely with nineteenth-century German philosophy of science, in particular with Jakob Friedrich Fries and also with Leonard Nelson (Chapter 13). In consequence, unlike the Vienna Circle, the Berlin Circle did not champion positivism. This finding made it clear that logical empiricism is a kind of analytic philosophy that is patently different from the early analytic philosophy of G. E. Moore and Bertrand Russell (2013a: 26 ff.).

A second area of inquiry was the history of the German philosophy in the nineteenth century, with a particular focus on Hermann Lotze (Milkov 2010, 2017b). My studies in this field, in conjunction with other scholarship I published as two books on the history of early analytic philosophy in England (1997, 2003), have brought to light previously unrecognized yet historically consequential points of intersection and genealogical succession between the two philosophical movements.

Acknowledgments

Versions of each chapter, excepting the first, have earlier appeared in print in the following order: "A logical–contextual history of philosophy," *Southwest Philosophy Review* 27:1 (2011), 21–9; "A new interpretation of Leibniz's concept of *characteristica universalis*," in Hans Poser (ed.), *Einheit in der Vielheit, Proceedings of the 8th international Leibniz-congress*, Hannover, 2006, 606–14; "Frege and the German philosophical idealism," in Dieter Schott (ed.), *Frege: Freund(e) und Feind(e)*, Berlin: Logos Verlag, 2015, 88–104; "Lotze and the Cambridge analytic philosophy," *Prima philosophia* 13 (2000), 133–53; "Lotze's debt to Russell," *Studies in History and Philosophy of Science, Part A*, 39 (2008), 186–93; "Lotze's concept of 'states of affairs' and its critics," *Prima philosophia* 15 (2002), 399–414; "Russell and Husserl (1905–1918): The Not-So-Odd-Couple," in Peter Stone (ed.), *Bertrand Russell's Life and Legacy*, Wilmington (DE): Vernon Press, 2017, 80–104; "The formal theory of everything: explorations of Husserl's theory of manifolds (*Mannifaltigkeitslehre*)," *Analecta Husserliana* 88 (2005), 119–35; "What is Analytical Phenomenology?," *Analecta Husserliana* 59 (1999), 491–8; "G. E. Moore and the Greifswald objectivists on the given, and the beginning of analytic philosophy," *Axiomathes* 14 (2003), 361–79; "Karl Popper's debt to Leonard Nelson," *Grazer philosophische Studien* 86 (2012), 137–56; "L. Susan Stebbing's criticism of Wittgenstein's *Tractatus*," *Vienna Circle Institute Yearbook* 10 (2003), 351–63. I am grateful for permission to use material from these articles.

The material adapted from the works listed above has been corrected, revised, and recast to suit the unified aims of this new book, aims that took shape through several of my courses at the University of Paderborn, Germany. Those same aims served as the organizing theme of "Early Analytic Philosophy in Context," a graduate seminar that I offered in the Spring Term 2012 as the Bertrand Russell Visiting Professor at McMaster University, Ontario. Material that became part of this study was further developed in a course titled "Early Analytic Philosophy and the German Philosophical Tradition," which in Fall of 2018, I taught at the invitation of the University of St. Petersburg, Russia. Additionally, content from several of this book's chapters was presented at a number of professional meetings and workshops, to whose participants I owe a debt of thanks for valuable critical input and helpful suggestions. Thanks go also to all my colleagues, students, and friends who have encouraged and supported my work over the years, and in particular to Dr. Phillip Stambovsky (Fairfield University), who helped me improve the language of the book. I am also thankful to Mrs. Lilli Isabel Förster who did an excellent work of preparing the index. Most of all, however, I thank my wife Michaela—for her constant encouragement and inspiration.

Part One

Introductory Chapters

1

What Is Early Analytic Philosophy, and How to Write Its History?

1 Early Analytic Philosophy as Continuation of Mainstream German Philosophy

Nineteenth-century German philosophy and logic played a significant, yet still-insufficiently appreciated, role in the genesis of early analytic philosophy.[1] Hence any historically sound and adequately nuanced comprehension of the origins and character of analytic philosophy needs to be informed by detailed knowledge and fine-grained philosophical understanding of this influence.

Regrettably, until the mid-1960s there was little interest in tracing the relation between early analytic philosophy and the German philosophical tradition. Historians of philosophy regarded analytic philosophy simply as an outgrowth of British empiricism and Common Sense doctrine (Ayer 1936: 41). Reflective of this widely held view is Robert Ammerman's influential anthology of analytic philosophy (1965). Ammerman selected for inclusion mostly Anglophone philosophers. The two German figures he chose to include in the text, Rudolf Carnap and Carl Hempel, were represented only by the work they published in English while they taught in the United States. A most glaring (and telling) omission in the Ammerman collection is the absence of Ludwig Wittgenstein.

This situation was to change as a result of a series of developments in Anglophone philosophy, six of which are of particular significance: (i) Largely due to the persuasive powers of Michael Dummett, Anglophone scholars came to appreciate the substantial influence that Gottlob Frege exerted on the beginnings of analytic philosophy. This newly established historical factor had an increasing impact in the field, most notably in the wake of Dummett's monograph *Frege: Philosophy of Language* (1973). (ii) At the same time, studies appeared highlighting the formative influence that the thought of several leading Austrian philosophers had on analytic philosophy. Chief among these

Austrian thinkers were Bernard Bolzano and Franz Brentano and his school. (iii) Recent decades have witnessed a marked increase in scholarship that reassesses twentieth-century analytic philosophy. Among the most influential examples are monographs by Alberto Coffa (1991) and Michael Friedman (2000) that have pointed to the Marburg neo-Kantian, Ernst Cassirer as having exercised considerable influence over early logical empiricists. (iv) Another salient development is the growing debate over Edmund Husserl's impact on Rudolf Carnap's *Aufbau* program. This was initially traced in a paper by Verena Mayer (1991, 2016), then subsequently taken up in published essays by Jean-Michel Roy (2004) and T. A. Ryckman (2007), and ultimately in a volume by Guillermo Rosado Haddock (2008). (v) Along with these Husserl-related studies, other recent work on Carnap's *Aufbau* finds evidence of influence of the Germanophone philosophy on the early analytic philosophy both in the form of the Southwest neo-Kantian Heinrich Rickert's value theory (Mormann 2006a, 2006b) and in the empirical facet of Wilhelm Dilthey's philosophy (Damböck, 2012, 2016). (vi) Finally, the last few decades have seen scholarship disclosing evidence, hitherto largely neglected, of Hermann Lotze's legacy in early analytic philosophy (Gabriel 2002).

This book aims to transformatively advance these largely disparate efforts by developing a comprehensively unified account of early analytic philosophy as a movement that both inherited and transformed an entire spectrum of themes dealt with in mainstream German philosophy. This project challenges the widely held view that it was above all various schools of the so-called "continental philosophy" that genuinely reflected the legacy of mainstream German philosophy of the earlier period.

No doubt a decisive historical factor behind the decades-long failure to credit the role of German thought in the rise of analytic philosophy was the critical stance toward it prevalent in the English-speaking academy roughly from 1914 to 1970. This was to a great extent a function of bitter political and cultural conflicts that so largely infected the Zeitgeist of the epoch. The period was marked by sharply divided ideological parties and blocs—cosmopolitans against nationalists, liberals against conservatives, Germans against Britons and French. The split between analytic philosophy and continental philosophy emerged in this environment of sociocultural animosity and clashing ideologies. A major historical impetus of this development was the anti-German sentiments inflamed by the Great War (Akerhurst 2010). Anglophone scholars came to repudiate German philosophy as not only mistaken in principle but also imbued with dubious ideological undertones.[2]

It is long past time, however, to adopt a philosophically disinterested stance and to set the intellectual-historical record straight by articulating a theoretically balanced and comprehensive, ideologically unbiased account of this seminal current of twentieth-century Western philosophy. As a contribution to that end, the present book shows how the emergence of this philosophical movement represents the beginning of a transformation of mainstream German academic philosophy on British soil and, later, in America. We shall see how G. E. Moore, Bertrand Russell, and later also Ludwig Wittgenstein, the pioneering figures of analytic philosophy, inherited problems and doctrines that originated in German philosophical thought, and how they explored them along original lines in the language and theoretical idiom of a far different cultural and intellectual environment.

2 Competing Conceptions

As previously indicated, the present work is not the first to consider the history of analytic philosophy in the context of nineteenth-century German philosophy. But it expressly challenges the leading accounts by substantively revising the influential historical picture that they have retailed. This study opposes, in particular, five ways in which historians of philosophy have explained the relation of nineteenth-century German thought to analytic philosophy:

1) It rejects the assumptions of those studies that direct attention to Kant's analytic-synthetic dichotomy as something that early analytic philosophers putatively made central to their projects (Soames 2003, 2014/17). Many American authors in particular have made this the point of departure for their historical accounts (Hanna 2001) (see Chapter 15).
2) It opposes the recent trend, initiated by Robert Brandom and Paul Redding, to relate analytic philosophy to Hegel's grand philosophical *theories* (Redding 2007).[3] By contrast, the present investigation directs attention, particularly in Chapters 4 and 5, to selected elements of Hegel's *method* in order to show that they are related to early analytic philosophy in an important way.
3) Also challenged here is the thesis that Kevin Mulligan and Barry Smith have promulgated, one also championed by Dale Jacquette and Thomas Uebel, namely that the philosophy of Kant and that of the neo-Kantians have in principle nothing to do with analytic philosophy. Rejecting this supposition, the present study argues that Kant's philosophy introduced a

universe of ideas, some of which led to the flowering of modern forms of continental philosophy, and some to the emergence of formally rigorous, scientific philosophy, including analytic philosophy (Milkov 2013b).

4) The present work contests the view propounded by Alberto Coffa, Allan Richardson, and Michael Friedman that analytic philosophy was profoundly influenced by neo-Kantian thinking, particularly in its Marburg form (Friedman 1999; Richardson 1998). The chief objection to positing the mainstream neo-Kantians as historical antecedents of analytic philosophy is that the lead figures in both the Southwest and the Marburg schools were largely preoccupied with the philosophy of culture. As E. W. Orth has observed, neo-Kantianism "was closely connected with the emergence and spread of the concept of culture and had a typical culture-consciousness" (1994: 16; Flach 2007: 9–24; Damböck 2016: v). In this sense, it is a "philosophy of culture as a human product" (ibid.), a line of thought that early analytic philosophy at least dismissed as philosophically irrelevant. That said, however, it is beyond doubt that neo-Kantianism significantly contributed to the birth of analytic philosophy, above all, with the ways it perpetuated the logicalization of philosophy initiated by Kant (Milkov 2013b: § 5.1). Chapter 13 details this with reference to Leonard Nelson, a neo-Kantian and a neo-Friesian who defended a more realistic and objectivist view than his colleagues, and whose work had marked affinities with early analytic philosophy.

5) Lastly, this study questions Michael Dummett's claim that Frege alone introduced analytic philosophy as a kind of philosophy of language. After all, it is Russell who best lays claim to being the founder of modern analytic philosophy (Chapter 16: § 7), and he was not primarily a philosopher of language but a realist philosopher of the "external world" (Monk 1996a). Moreover, as will become clear in Chapter 5, there are elements in Frege that are not "analytic" in any sense consistent with Moore's and especially with Russell's concept of analytic philosophy. Among other things, such differences were to put Russell sharply at odds not only with Frege but also with Wittgenstein (Chapter 15; see also Milkov 2013, 2017).

3 A Brief Overview of the Proto-Analytic Philosophy

To help set the stage for the account of early analytic philosophy introduced in the chapters ahead, it will be well to profile the prehistory of analytic philosophy as it bears upon the historical lines of influence we shall identify and trace in the discussions to follow.

A defining moment of the prehistory of the early analytic philosophy was Kant's recalibration of Western philosophy by way of synthesizing logic with the rest of the field (Milkov 2013b). This recasting of different lines of philosophical study into one formal discipline, in order to achieve theoretical rigor (or "solid results"[4]) in philosophy, proved to be the source of an epochal enhancement of its heuristic power. A first result of this Kantian "formal turn" was that philosophers of widely different intellectual temperaments and theoretical interests became convinced that they could "improve on" Kant's system by developing it in their own way. The Kantian revolution inspired the projects of a diverse group of philosophers. They range from humanistic-oriented thinkers like Fichte, Hegel, and Schopenhauer to those such as Fries, Herbart, and Fechner, whose leading concerns were keyed to exact natural science and mathematics.

Further post-Kantian developments in the German academy proved to be antecedents of analytic philosophy. Less than a decade after Hegel's death Germanophone philosophical thinking took an objectivist turn, as it became obvious that many of Hegel's speculative claims and analyses were otiose or patently wrong or radically misconceived. First, in 1837, Bernard Bolzano published his *Wissenschaftslehre*, then in 1840, Adolf Trendelenburg saw into print his *Logical Investigations*, followed in 1841 and 1843 by the young Hermann Lotze who brought out his first ("lesser") *Logic* and first ("lesser") *Metaphysics* (see the next para.). In the following years (i.e., long before the birth of the neo-Kantianism) these and other Germanophone philosophers preoccupied themselves with ideas and themes which decades later would be identified as signature concerns of Cambridge analytic philosophy. The topics ranged from the proposition, objective content—both perceptual and conceptual—of knowledge, and intentionality, to the theory of logical forms, the objective nature of values and logical validity.

Without any doubt, the towering figure of the objectivist turn in German philosophy was Hermann Lotze (1817–1881). Lotze successfully synthesized components of exact, scientifically oriented philosophy with elements of classical German idealism. This explains why, like Kant, Lotze proved a major, if often unrecognized, influence on a plethora of *fin de siècle* philosophers and philosophical movements (Chapter 7: § 2). These ranged from phenomenology and Dilthey's life philosophy, to American pragmatism (Josiah Royce studied with Lotze in Göttingen), the so-called British "neo-Hegelians" (several of whom headed by Bernhard Bosanquet, translated Lotze's "greater" *Logik* (1874) and "greater" *Metaphysik* (1879) (Chapter 6: § 2)), and also early analytic philosophy.

One last point: today it is widely accepted that various schools of thought played a role in the genesis of analytic philosophy. However, few current students of the history of analytic philosophy are aware that German academic philosophy also produced a home-grown version of a proto-analytic philosophy: the Greifswald objectivism, associated with Johannes Rehmke, and the Göttingen neo-Friesian critical philosophy, whose chief exponent was Leonard Nelson. We shall probe, in Part Six, both of these schools of thought.

4 The Logocentrism of German Philosophy and the Emergence of the Early Analytic Philosophy

Analytic philosophy was launched by G. E. Moore and Bertrand Russell on the banks of the river Cam in the waning years of the nineteenth century (Hacker 1996: ix). It was characteristically a British–European product, which is to say that its principal sources of inspiration were ideas derived from the teachings of Berkeley, Hume, Leibniz, and Kant, as well as those of Plato and Aristotle. Before long, Wittgenstein was to join Moore and Russell in what they were convinced was nothing less than a philosophical revolution. It was Wittgenstein who ultimately strengthened the connection of this Cambridge initiative with the German logician and philosopher of mathematics Gottlob Frege. Prior to Wittgenstein's appearance on the scene, Frege had already exerted a considerable influence, partly via Peano, on Russell. Frege, in turn, was substantially influenced by the philosophical logic of Trendelenburg and, above all, of Lotze.

The development we took note in the preceding section, extending from the 1840s through the first decades of the twentieth century, induced the Cambridge philosophers to think along innovative analytic lines, albeit not before it underwent some "fine-tuning" (Chapter 12: § 3). The decisive factor that led to the emergence of analytic philosophy was the move to put logic at the center of thought. It was not, *pace* Scott Soames, merely Kant's idea of analyticity nor his distinction between analytic and synthetic truths that induced its birth; nor was it only the influence of Frege, Dummett's view, or Marburg neo-Kantianism, as Michael Friedman argues. Identifying as the definitive influence of yet another source, David Bell has sought to underscore the role Franz Brentano and his acolytes played in the birth of analytic philosophy (Bell 1999),[5] particularly their doctrine of the *a priori* truths (Smith 1994: 3).

Closer to the view introduced here on the roots of analytic philosophy is that of Hans-Johann Glock (1999), who stresses the shaping role that philosophical logic has played in German philosophy since Leibniz. It was this factor that differentiated German philosophy from both British philosophy, which historically was presented as conflating philosophy with empirical science,[6] and from the French, whose tendency was to assimilate philosophy with belles-lettres. Glock terms this logical spirit of German philosophy "logocentrism," which among other things caused its adherents to fight psychologism in philosophy. It was this logocentrism that proved to be more instrumental to the rise of analytic philosophy than any other factor. One result of this development was the rejection of naturalism. Moore, Russell, and Wittgenstein all propounded anti-naturalist positions.[7] That it was Frege who formulated the most radical criticism of naturalism has long since become common knowledge.

5 Middle and Late Analytic Philosophy

Among the most decisive shifts in the history of analytic philosophy in the direction of its recent forms was the rejection of logocentrism. This occurred over the course of about three decades. After 1950, analytic philosophy manifested a tendency, under the influence of W. V. Quine, to allegedly merge with natural science.[8]

Anticipations of this shift away from logocentrism were apparent as early as the 1940s, which saw the introduction of new currents of thought that justify distinguishing a discrete, "middle" phase of analytic philosophy. Its roots lie in early logical empiricism, with members of the Vienna Circle who (mis) interpreted the point of Wittgenstein's *Tractatus* as a book in philosophy of science, not as a treatise in philosophy of language. Its most celebrated form found expression in the newly formed discipline of analytic philosophy of science, initially understood as the "logic" of science. Without much ado, it abandoned the descriptive method of the early analytic philosophy and engaged itself instead with the problems of explanation in science (Popper 1934; Hempel and Oppenheim 1948) (see n. 15). This new philosophy commonly reinforced the impression that "analytic philosophy" was a specifically British movement (Carnap 1963: 28).[9]

The appearance in 1962 of Thomas Kuhn's famed *Structure of Scientific Revolutions* marginalized logocentrism in the philosophy of science. Then came the impact of John Rawls at start of the 1970s, which in place of logocentrism drew the attention of analytic philosophers to political theory.[10] The early forms of analytic philosophy faded from the scene with the advent of these influential new currents of thought. Quine, Kuhn, and Rawls were leading exemplars of doctrines that gave rise to "late" analytic philosophy.[11] The distinction here between early, middle, and late periods of analytic philosophy avoids the need to subscribe to Peter Hacker's widely controverted view that Quine's naturalistic revolution in analytic philosophy spelled the demise of the entire movement (Hacker 1996: 193 ff.). Be this as it may, analytic philosophy as pursued in its early years was unquestionably on the ropes by 1960, the year of Quine's *Word and Object*.[12]

The neglect of the clearly distinguishable successive trends in the development of analytic philosophy led to its distortive general accounts. Philosophers were led to attach the name "analytic philosophy" indiscriminately to the very different kinds of work and standpoints that characterized the three readily distinguishable periods of its development.

The consequences of failing to discriminate between different stages in the evolution of analytic philosophy when trying to grasp it synoptically is clearly seen in the example of Hans-Johann Glock's book *What is Analytic Philosophy?* Glock attempts to formulate a definition of analytic philosophy as we currently know it, without differentiating between the clear differences that unambiguously distinguish early, middle, and late phases of the movement.[13] As a result, he propounds the thesis that analytic philosophy is simply "a tradition that is held together *both* by ties of influence *and* by a family of partially overlapping features" (2008: 223). Furthermore, Glock portrays analytic philosophy as "made up of philosophers-at-a-time sharing certain features via chains of influence" (Pincock 2013: 10). Such a "definition" indicates nothing so much as that analytic philosophy was from the outset simply an innovative philosophical idiom—an unwarranted claim that has been in circulation for over thirty years now.

6 Descriptive Method of Exploring the History of Analytic Philosophy

As stated in the Preface, this book does not set out to detail a systematic account of the German influences on early analytic philosophers, nor of the latter's relation to German philosophy. Rather, the aim is to explicate interrelated topics and concepts that were of prime concern to philosophers in both traditions. The following chapters examine selected themes treated by leading German philosophers and logicians of the eighteenth and nineteenth centuries, and the first part of the twentieth century, and themes developed by the early analytic philosophers as well. Hence our concern here will be with issues such as the theory of forms, data, indefinables, and analysis from the diverse standpoints of philosophers with differing theoretical orientations. The advantage of this approach is that it elucidates a wide variety of topics that were of particular interest to the distinguished analytic philosophers—topics too often marginalized or disregarded in the literature.

What motivates the challenge, here, to the mainstream histories of analytic philosophy is the rich yield of a fine-grained investigation that targets from alternative perspectives topics formative of early analytic philosophy.[14] This historiographic method, one more attuned than those of the prevailing histories to the full spectrum of influences on the pioneers of the Cambridge analytic school, contributes a more informed and precise "logical geography" than any previous or more recent exposition of the ideas and concepts that gave shape to early analytic philosophy. In a significant move, this book takes its cue from the methodology of early analytic philosophy, which was more focused on descriptions than explanations.[15]

The result is an explication of the generative core concepts of early Cambridge analytic philosophy and their historical ramifications, this articulated as part of a comprehensive presentation (*übersichtliche Darstellung*) of the history of early analytic philosophy. Moreover, the selection of problematics addressed evinces no doctrinal bias. The aim is to present the pregnant subjects that preoccupied the early analytic philosophers, and to do so with a historical depth and precision that will deliver a more accurate picture of the history of early analytic philosophy. If the history outlined in these pages is not as cut-and-dried as the mainstream histories of analytic philosophy, the multifaceted story detailed here is more nuanced, wide-ranging and, we submit picture, historically truer to the development of analytic philosophy over the course of its first century.

As noted in the Preface, this study challenges above all the historiography of philosophy that assumes its most radical form in Scott Soames's previously cited story of the emergence and development of analytic philosophy (see also Chapter 15). What Soames retails is the history of the development of a single idea, "analysis," at the hands, successively, of Moore, Russell, Wittgenstein, the Vienna Circle, Ryle, Austin, Quine, and Kripke. Soames treats this notion as the overarching concern of analytic philosophy down through the decades. According to Soames, Moore, Russell, and the rest, each in turn corrected the work of predecessors while contributing new insights to the concept of analysis. Methodologically, Soames pretty clearly relates to Michael Dummett who likewise championed the view that analytic philosophy developed mainly in light of one basal idea, which is, according to Dummett, that philosophy of language is more fundamental than, and indeed is the sovereign referent of, every other philosophical genre.

In fact, Soames's approach exemplifies a variety of neo-Hegelian history of philosophy that clearly is at odds with the spirit of early Cambridge analytic philosophy, which advocated piecemeal, anti-holistic modes of inquiry. Paraphrasing Wittgenstein, we can say that instead of tracing the variegated themes that preoccupied early analytic philosophers over the course of their careers, historians of philosophy such as Soames have in general produced what are in essence monothematic accounts. They typically develop analyses from the standpoint of a single "leading" idea associated with a major figure in the history of philosophy, extrapolating from this keynote idea the entirety of the thinker's philosophical contribution.

7 Early Analytic Philosophy and the Progress in Philosophy

A further contribution that the present work makes to the historiography of early analytic philosophy is that it at once foregrounds genuine progress in the form of evolving thought in philosophy and makes explicit how such progress occurs. We shall see that various ideas of Plato and Aristotle that proved formative in early analytic thought were initially retrieved by Leibniz and Kant, underwent further development at the hands of Fries and Lotze, and were rethought once again, this time by Husserl and Russell.[16] A paradigm example is the varied history of the "context principle." It originated with Plato and Aristotle, was rediscovered by Kant, also employed by Hegel, reintroduced by Lotze, and enshrined in the thought of Frege.[17] Tracing such a pattern in the history of philosophical ideas has a precedent in Franz Brentano and Leonard Nelson, both of whom discussed "progress" and "regress" in philosophy along similar lines (Brentano 1998; Nelson 1962).

Championing the idea of progress in philosophy, Bertrand Russell launched the project of a new, "analytic" philosophy that would distinguish itself by its method of piecemeal advance. This philosophy would achieve its results step-by-step, in such a way that, if at some point one of its positions were to prove false, viable elements of discredited doctrine could be retained—just as in the exact sciences elements of refuted theories are commonly preserved (Chapter 16: § 3).

As in due course we shall see in detail, however, long before Russell's initiative, there were well-defined currents of philosophical thinking that progressed in this way. For example, in a manner similar to that of the new analytic method, German academic philosophy of the big nineteenth century introduced and developed concepts that survived the demise of the grand theories in which they originally figured (Part Three). Indeed, a variety of such surviving ideas were later recast by thinkers who operated with the quite different methodology of analytic philosophy. This supersession of historically successive philosophical contexts, whereby seminal ideas make their way through history, explains why philosophically formative ideas are often difficult to recognize. To make such ideas explicit is clearly a desideratum in a history of modern philosophy and a chief task of the present work.

In sum, this book brings to light the ways that a plurality of core concepts originating with German academic philosophy more generally crystalized in what we now identify as early analytic philosophy. Among other things, we shall discover that, for example, there are defining moments of relatedness between Hegel's dialectics and the method followed by the early analytic philosophers (Chapter Four). In this connection we shall see how the inner development of German academic philosophy, more generally, introduced concepts and lines of reasoning that later proved formative in analytic philosophy. The progress of these ideas was not always linear, though, nor was it always a function of a proximate influence. Time and again it happened that the same or similar ideas were simply rediscovered. A typical example is Bolzano's concept of "propositions in themselves" and the notion of "thought" advanced by Frege some fifty years later. There is no evidence that Bolzano either directly or indirectly influenced Frege on this point. It seems that Frege simply rediscovered Bolzano's idea.

Notwithstanding the emphasis on German thought, the present book's approach to the historiography of philosophy does not seek to advance any "back to German philosophy" movement. To the contrary, this work argues that the early analytic philosophy developed a persuasive and fruitful new method that helped to revivify philosophy. Moreover, many pregnant ideas initially mooted in the Germanophone philosophy in the big nineteenth century were fully explicated only by the founding fathers of analytic philosophy in Cambridge.

The "fine-tuning" of these ideas was an essential step in the development of early analytic philosophy as we know it and it was produced by Moore, Russell, and Wittgenstein. Elucidating the genealogical connections, as well as the less direct patterns of relation tying analytic philosophy to the German philosophy of the time, this study undertakes to contribute to a better and deeper understanding of both analytic philosophy and the Germanophone philosophy.

2

What Is the Logical History of Philosophy?

1 Do Systematic Philosophers Need a History of Philosophy as Part of Their Discipline?

Analytic philosophers often claim that the history of philosophy is scarcely of value for them. Michael Frede, for example, argues that "most of the history of philosophy is of no or little philosophical interest to us" (1988: 669). The same opinion is held by Calvin Normore (1990: 225) and Jorge Gracia, according to whom "philosophy is not necessarily dependent on its history" (1992: 118). To Gilbert Harman is attributed the catchphrase: "History of Philosophy: Just Say No!," which was allegedly sometime displayed on his office door at Princeton University (Sorell 2005: 44).

Apparently, what these authors mean with "us" here is not just "analytic philosophy" but any kind of philosophy which puts stress on advancing new arguments and theories instead of on discussing arguments and theories developed by past masters. In the German-speaking academy, non-historical philosophy is conventionally called "systematic philosophy" (see also Dummett 1975).

A first rejoinder to these authors is, ironically, historical: It is a well-known fact that radical, positive developments in the history of philosophy have in the past led to revolutions in systematic philosophy. Here are three examples:

1) The rediscovery of Aristotle's texts in Western Europe in the twelfth and thirteenth century transformed the philosophy of the time. Discussions of them stimulated the authors to explore new themes in philosophy. This development culminated in the imposing corpus of Aquinas's writings.
2) Despite the fact that he remained in shadow, there was one name that dominated the dramatic rise of the German university philosophy in the second half of the nineteenth century. This was Adolf Trendelenburg (Köhnke 1986) who, in the words of Rudolf Eucken, "introduced a

historical treatment of the problems, which combined the efforts of today with the work of the past millenniums" (1886: 114). It is this methodological revolution that in large measure set the stage for the golden age of the German school philosophy which reached its apogee with a line of thinkers from Frege, Wittgenstein, and Carnap to Husserl and Heidegger.[1]

3) A number of analytic philosophers introduced new themes of investigation after intensive studies in the history of philosophy. Roderick Chisholm and Michael Dummett, for example, inspired mountains of analytic literature on topics related to their studies, respectively, of Franz Brentano and Gottlob Frege.

This evidence, clearly substantiating the importance of the history of philosophy for systematic and analytic philosophy, discredits the stance of Frede, Normore, and Gracia referred to above.

2 How Does Analytic Philosophy Relate to the History of Philosophy?

R. G. Collingwood, in his *Autobiography* (1939), was one of the first to explicitly condemn the neglect by analytic philosophers of the history of philosophy. Against this reproach it can be pointed out that this neglect was not caused by the nature of analytic philosophy as such. Rather, it was because at the time the effort of analysts was concentrated on opening new horizons in philosophy and rejecting such old paths as they had followed thus far. To be more specific, the paramount interest of the analytic philosophy of the time was in logical analysis.

This point finds support in the fact that early analytic philosophers showed considerable historical interest from the very beginning. So, when faced with the task of writing down his New Philosophy in what came to be known as *The Problems of Philosophy* (1912a), Bertrand Russell did nothing but reread the classics: Plato, Descartes, Spinoza, Berkeley, Hume, Leibniz, and Kant. As a result, he wrote the book recurrently referring to them. The same can be said about G. E. Moore, the cofounder of analytic philosophy. He wrote two dissertations on Kant's ethic and the paper "Hume's Philosophy" (1909); in addition, he devoted two chapters in his 1910/11 lectures, *Some Main Problems of Philosophy*, to discussing Hume's arguments again.

Further, in the 1930s, the leading figure of the ordinary language philosophy, Gilbert Ryle, published two extensive papers in the field of history of philosophy: "Locke on the Human Understanding" (1932) and "Plato's *Parmenides*" (1939). In the 1950s and 1960s he wrote papers on Hume, as well as his remarkable book *Plato's Progress* (1966). J. L. Austin, another master of this philosophical movement in Oxford, edited Horace W. B. Joseph's *Lectures on the Philosophy of Leibniz* (1949), and wrote an extensive review of Jan Łukasiewicz's book on Aristotle's Syllogistic (1952).

The only early analytic philosopher whom one could properly charge with thorough neglect of the history of philosophy is Wittgenstein, whose notorious question—"What Does History Have to Do with Me?" (1979: 82)—became for some a slogan. *Pace* Hacker (1996), however, Wittgenstein is scarcely the founding father of analytic philosophy (see Chapter 16: § 6).

Analytic philosophy has shown an even more lively interest in its *own* nascent history, and this is from the very beginning. Three examples of its interest are:

1) Philip E. B. Jourdain began to investigate the history of the new philosophical movement as early as 1906, when he put questions to Russell concerning the history of his Theory of Descriptions (Grattan-Guinness 1977). Jourdain also wrote historical notes on Gottlob Frege. These inquiries resulted in Jourdain (1910/1912).
2) The very manifesto of the Vienna Circle (Neurath 1929) contained a historical section that lays out the chronicle of the movement. The first issues of *Erkenntnis* featured many articles on its history.
3) Gilbert Ryle repeatedly undertook to summarize the history of the analytic movement in philosophy (1949; 1971b). In the second half of the 1950s his pupils Urmson and Warnock, as well as Australia's John Passmore, authored extended studies of it (Urmson 1956; Passmore 1957; Warnock 1958).

The foregoing evidence discredits the claim that analytic philosophers neglect the history of philosophy. It suggests that the authors who criticize analytic philosophers for disparaging the history of philosophy have something different in mind. Apparently, they mean something like the method that Russell employed in his book on Leibniz (Russell 1900a; Ayers 1978: 42–6) and Strawson in his book on Kant (1966). In these works, Russell and Strawson, first, selectively discussed only those ideas of the respective authors which appeared "analytical enough" to them and ignored the others; secondly, they undertook to further develop these "analytical ideas." In other words, Russell and Strawson demonstrated an interest in historical figures of philosophy; however, they pursued this interest one-sidedly.

This same historical one-sidedness is also evident in G. E. Moore's method of "interpretative analysis" (Chapter 16: § 4.1), by means of which he undertook to determine, for example, what Berkeley really meant when he said that *esse est percipi*, maintaining that Berkeley intended something quite different from what he actually said. At the outset of this query, Moore declared that much of past philosophy is wrong, inasmuch as it contradicts "common sense." Moore's work was influential and many philosophers in Britain followed its lead. In a study of Hume, for example, Henry H. Price announces a modus operandi that clearly reflects the influence of Moore: "When he [Hume] makes mistakes, we must try to get him out of them, by suggesting alternatives which he might consistently have adopted. We must try to go behind his language, and when he is obscure... we must try to make him clear" (1940: 3).

However, although this "critical recycling" of classic philosophical texts was called the "Analytic Ideal" in the history of philosophy, the method was hardly restricted to practitioners of analytic philosophy. Indeed, the belief that the task of the historian of philosophy is to understand and articulate the ideas of past philosophers better than the latter themselves, had long informed the views of philosophers. Typical are the words of the neo-Kantian Wilhelm Windelband: "To understand Kant means to go beyond him" (1882: iv). Others, such as the German philosophers Schleiermacher, Fichte, A. W. Schlegel, as well as Wilhelm Dilthey, maintained that only part of any major earlier thinker's philosophy is of interest—the part that is close to their own philosophical intuitions. The rest was to be disregarded (Braun 1973: 223 n.). In other words, for many decades and centuries before analytic philosophy arrived on the scene, the historian of philosophy was held by many to be charged with separating the philosophical wheat from the chaff; what is "wheat" and what is "chaff" was determined by current philosophical interests.

3 Why Do We Need a History of Philosophy?— Or the Trouble With Philosophy as Such

At this stage of our analysis, we shall turn our attention to a problem with philosophy as such, namely that even philosophers of genius cannot, in principle, write down their completely finished story. They only suggest *steps* that their followers and interpreters explore and develop further in more articulated form. This characteristic feature of the greatest works of philosophical thought can be called the principle of "Indeterminatedness of Philosophy." It was best articulated by Dieter Henrich who has claimed that a newly discovered idea by a great philosopher can never be made clear enough at the first onset (1976: 9). The grasp of how it is constructed, that is, which element goes together with which in it, is a completely new problem that is to be solved by interpreters.

Exactly this latter problem is the proper subject of historians of philosophy, as we see it. They chart the maps of concepts and problems of earlier philosophical masters, in all their variation and provenance. In this sense the historians of philosophy investigate the worth of their great forebears in the discipline. They explore lines of thought in past philosophy which the masters themselves never explicitly pursued. Moreover, they also explicate the logic of the relationship between the ideas of a given philosopher and those of others.

Unfortunately, the more important the contribution of an author in philosophy is, such as that of Aristotle and Kant, the more nuanced and many-sided is his theory. Quite different lines of thought connect to one another. Furthermore, they are also connected with philosophical concepts and problems of other philosophers: friends and rivals.

In view of the foregoing, one can enumerate the tasks of the historian of philosophy as follows:

1) To explicate elements of different range and level of specific philosophical works.
2) To relate these elements in a logical net; to draw up their map (Chapter 15: § 8).
3) To relate them logically to the ideas of other philosophers: predecessors, contemporaries, successors—whether or not they are members of the philosopher's school or group.
4) To try to develop them further in their authentic sense.

4 The History of Philosophy as Systematic Philosophy

To sum up the results we have reached so far: the task of the historian of philosophy is to draw the map of the concepts, problems, ideas, and arguments raised in systematic philosophy and to track down the roots of the theories, concepts, and problems employed by the canonical figures of philosophy with the aim of tracing new logical connections between them. Consequently, the philosophical historian's task proceeds along two directions: (i) searching for origins (sources) of particular concepts, problems, and theories; (ii) reporting how other philosophers use these particular concepts and problems in their own different ways. The ultimate goal is to delineate with the greatest precision possible how the systematic philosophical problems and concepts, past and present, interrelate in formally determinate ways.[2]

In this sense, as practice of charting the map of problems and concepts originating with major thinkers, the discipline of the history of philosophy is systematic as well. Hence, it cannot stand opposed to systematic philosophy. Rather, we have two systematic philosophical disciplines, the first of which develops a system in one direction only, while the second investigates the connections of the theories and concepts of a particular philosopher with concepts and theories of selected predecessors and successors, including thinkers who champion alternative philosophical programs.

Historians of philosophy who are systematic, approach the thought of major figures of the past in ways sharply at variance with those of analytic philosophers, including Moore, Russell, Strawson, and Price.[3] The analytic philosopher typically selects a concept of an earlier thinker, say Peter Strawson's notion of presupposition, and tries to develop it further (Stalnaker 1973). The historian of philosophy, in contrast, strives to discover a net of logical dependencies in the writings of a particular philosopher, or of different thinkers, who utilized this concept or theory. Furthermore, as long as the historian is engaged in a synoptic enterprise such as charting the web of conceptual interrelations, he endeavors to investigate every nuance of the problems and concepts left by the philosopher under consideration—independently of the thinker's particular theoretical interest.[4] The task is comprehensively to reconstruct, in their full complexity, the ideas of the selected philosopher.

5 The History of Philosophy as Philosophical Propaedeutic

We should remark that the conception of the history of philosophy as mapping the configurations of interrelated concepts, problems, theories, and arguments which develop diachronically in logical implications is useful both to educate beginners in philosophy and to resuscitate the theoretical vigor of mature philosophers.

The results of such studies often take the form of philosophical dictionaries and encyclopedias. One could hardly claim that these are not of philosophical but rather of merely historical interest. It is true that their function is mainly propaedeutic. However, philosophical propaedeutic is an important element in the philosophy curriculum.

Here one should bear in mind that in the second half of the nineteenth century, philosophers widely believed that history of philosophy is relevant to philosophical propaedeutic. Further, it was generally accepted that the second pillar of philosophical propaedeutic is logic. Among other things, this explains why, exactly like in logic, in the history of philosophy there are no new truths. Indeed, instead of advancing new truths, logic teaches us to think correctly. Similarly, when we are confronted with a systematic philosophical problem, the history of philosophy helps us by providing a better orientation to it. To make use of an example of Gilbert Ryle's (1954: 96), both logic and history of philosophy are like military drills: they are not a part of the battle, but soldiers who perform them fight better in actual combat.

We can demonstrate this side of the history of philosophy by means of another of Ryle's examples. In the introduction to *The Concept of Mind*, Ryle points out that his aim "is not to increase what we know about minds, but to rectify the logical geography of the knowledge which we already possess" (1949a: 9). Among other things, philosophical maps make it possible to see a whole philosophical movement in perspective. The argument presented in these pages is that investigations in the history of philosophy aim at charting and improving such maps.[5]

This conception of the history of philosophy holds that in order to become good philosophers, philosophy students must be trained not only to advance new and original philosophical theses but also be able to orient themselves to the various possible solutions of the problem in order to determine which is the best one. There is no better means to this end than to study maps of genealogically and of logically interrelated concepts and theories supplied by the history of philosophy.

6 The History of Philosophy as the Study of the Logical Geography of Concepts

One way to develop history of philosophy as logical geography is to advance it as history of philosophical concepts. In order to illustrate this point, the present section briefly sketches it.

Wilhelm Tennemann (1710–1790) was perhaps the first to try to trace the logical development of one philosophical system into another. In this he was followed by Hegel, who saw past philosophers as struggling with problems, not simply as holding views. As Passmore put this, "[Hegel] paid very little attention to anything except the internal logical relations between theories" (1967: 228). This approach was best articulated in Windelband (1892) and was developed further by Nicolai Hartmann, who insisted that the proper subject of history of philosophy is philosophical problems (1910).

Hartmann, however, did not stop at that point. He knew that history of philosophy, which tracks down the logical connections between problems and theories, can easily become one-sided, losing sight of how philosophy develops in reality. The mischiefs of Hegel's history of philosophy exemplify these dangers best. Apparently, such considerations motivated Hartmann to look for a unit of investigation in the history of philosophy simpler than problems—and he found it in philosophical concepts. "Indeed," says Hartmann, "the 'concept' is, in a strict sense, a definable basic moment. It is reduced from the systematic problem—something like its abbreviation" (1910: 466). Metaphorically speaking, concepts are the atoms, and problems are the molecules of historical-philosophical inquiry. In this sense, Hartmann suggested a program for a history of philosophy that describes the ways that concepts develop diachronically in philosophy.[6] His hope was that this program would radically diminish the possibility of theoretical errors in this discipline.

What follows are two examples of how the history of analytic philosophy can be developed as history of concepts:

(i) In his review article of Carnap's *Meaning and Necessity* (1949), and especially in his paper "The Theory of Meaning" (1957), Gilbert Ryle was adamant that "the word-meanings do not stand to sentence-meanings as atoms to molecules" (1971b: 359). Indeed, while single words refer to objects, when in sentences, words denote only as parts of the whole. This is shown by the fact that the meanings of some words, in particular, those, which are only used in the context of a sentence, are learned in use only, not by direct acquaintance with what they supposedly denote.

In truth, this element of Ryle's philosophy of language was nothing but a vague formulation of the context principle—despite the fact that he did not call it that way at the time. He claimed that it was introduced by Plato, then revived by Kant; it was forgotten after that only to be rediscovered by Wittgenstein in the 1930s, and later adopted by Ryle himself, as well as by his friends the ordinary language philosophers. By contrast, Mill, Frege, Carnap, and, in a sense, also Russell and Wittgenstein of the *Tractatus* make no use of this principle, but rather of the "Fido"—Fido theory of meaning, according to which one name always corresponds to one object.

This history shows how difficult, tentative, and incremental is the process of determining the exact place on the philosophy-map where a concept employed by different influential thinkers belongs. Ryle strove mightily to trace down the historical development of the context principle but failed. This was done only by Michael Dummett in his paper "Nominalism" (1956). Dummett put the things in the right places saying that the context principle was (re)discovered by Frege, was randomly used by Russell and fully embraced by Wittgenstein, and then rediscovered by him—Dummett. In the light of this finding, Ryle's claim that Frege subscribed to the "Fido" is clearly mistaken. It also shows that philosophy exhibits both progress and regression (Chapter 1: § 7). So far as Ryle's general historical contention is defensible, it substantiates this fact: after the context principle was discovered by Plato, it was practically forgotten for over 2000 years, only to be independently introduced by Kant.

(ii) Not long ago, it was generally accepted that Moore was the philosopher who introduced the concept of "sense-data" in philosophy in his lectures "On Metaphysics," delivered in 1910/11, but published only in 1953 as *Some Main Problems of Philosophy*. In fact, however, the term was coined by Josiah Royce in 1882—under the influence of his German teacher in philosophy Hermann Lotze—and picked up by William James, after which Russell employed it in a number of manuscripts and articles he composed in the years 1896 through 1898. In the summer of 1898, however, Russell fundamentally rethought his philosophy and he dropped the term. Moreover, he forgot that he had used it altogether (Milkov 2001b). When in 1911, after another turn in his thinking, he encountered it in the manuscript of Moore's lectures "On Metaphysics," it struck him as a revelation. Subsequently, he adopted it as an epistemological term of art, for example, in his *The Problems of Philosophy* (1912a).

Above all, this story shows that the concept of "sense-data" is rather different from Hume's "impressions" with which it is often confused (Chapter 9: § 1.1).[7] It was introduced, above all, to indicate the objective content of perceptions under the influence of ideas laid out in Lotze's "greater" *Logic* (1874) and "greater" *Metaphysics* (1879). It deserves noting that parallel to the introduction of the idea of objective content of perceptions in philosophy, Lotze introduced the concept of "states of affairs" to signify the objective content of judgment (Chapter 8). The concept was adopted by his pupil Carl Stumpf, and developed later by both Husserl and Wittgenstein (Milkov 2015).

This chapter undertakes to remix Hartmann's program for a gap-free logicizing history of philosophy. In particular, we shall apply it not only to philosophical concepts but also to philosophical problems, arguments, and theories. In fact, the history-of-concepts approach is, if paradigmatic, only one example of framing a "logical history of philosophy."

7 What Is the Logical History of Philosophy?

In an astute paper (1999), David Bell has demonstrated that Moore's New Philosophy, called later "analytic," was formatively influenced by Franz Brentano through Moore's teacher George Stout. Neither Moore nor Russell discovered or invented it whole-cloth. To credit this influence on the philosophy of Moore-Russell is to appreciate how it arose concomitantly with the emergence of psychology as a discipline in its own right, more specifically the analytic psychology developed by Brentano. This historical fact changes its place on the logical map of philosophies and philosophers. Bell concludes that "we can gain an historical understanding of the form in which analytic philosophy emerged in Moore's early writings, on the basis of an understanding of the appropriate context" (1999: 201).

Suggestive as Bell's analysis in this paper is, his identification of this perspective as "historical understanding" is rather problematic. In the genealogy of the concept of "sense-data" described above (in § 6 (ii)), we saw that the concept originated with the move to assert objectivity of the content of mind, initiated already in the 1840s by Trendelenburg and Hermann Lotze. From this perspective, we saw the concept of "sense-data" in a connection that is radically different from its linkage with Humean "impressions." Apparently, this context of the concept "sense-data" is not merely historical; rather, it also reveals the relatedness of this theoretical construction with Lotze's conception that the mind has objective content. The task of the systematic historian of philosophy is just this: to place philosophical concepts and problems on a constantly adjusted map of their genealogical and logical development; or, to draw evermore detailed maps of what Ryle called "logical geography." In this case, the task is to connect the concepts of "sense-data" and "states of affairs" with the concept of the objective content of mind.

Seen this way, the project of this type of history of philosophy is to trace diachronically the steps in the construction of a philosophical theory. What may be called the *logical history of philosophy* thus investigates the logical context of problems and concepts of the philosophical masters of the past.

To make this project more readily comprehensible, we shall build on the discrimination already established in the literature between a philosophical history of philosophy and a non-philosophical history of philosophy. More specifically, we shall take the concept of a logical history of philosophy as a further development or major variant of the philosophical history of philosophy.

8 Keeping the Logical History of Philosophy Pure

One of the troubles with the history of philosophy today is that it mixes many methods of investigation into one. The different types of approaches to the great thinkers of earlier times range from the biographical and sociological, to the psychological and logical. This is connected with the fact that "great philosophers write under an enormous array of different pressures, many of them intellectual, some of them social or moral or emotional. All kinds of different currents come together in one person's mind" (Bennett 1988: 69). In recent years, a consensus was reached that all these approaches have the "right to exist": a philosophical work of a genius should be studied in many different ways.

The present work, however, makes a special effort to keep the logical history of philosophy clearly apart from all other historically cast orientations, and, when necessary, to distil points of logical context of historically seminal works from the biographical, sociological, and other material in which they are situated. The problem is that different approaches in history of philosophy often look very much alike, so that non-specialist would find them difficult to discriminate from each other.

One negative result of this circumstance is that systematic philosophers often blame the history of philosophy for flaws that are totally unrelated to logical studies. Conversely, historians of philosophy often decry a deficiency of "historical sense" on the part of the systematic philosophers when the latter probe the thought of major figures of the philosophical past. Systematic/analytic philosophers, so goes the argument, typically lack a "desire to achieve a historical understanding of the genesis of a text (the intentions of its author and its meaning for its original readers)" (Ayers 1978: 42). On this score Daniel Garber cautions that "if our only goal [is] philosophical truth, then history of philosophy may turn out to be marginal, if not altogether expendable" (Garber 1988: 31).

In contrast, we claim that systematic philosophers need "historical sense" also in cases when they only try to thematize previously unrecognized logical facets of the philosophers under study. What such logical history of philosophy stands to demonstrate is that even prima facie pure historical studies and discoveries in philosophy[8] have, above all, a logical point. Studies of this sort can serve as a means for unraveling logical connections among particular philosophical theories and concepts advanced in the past. Take, for example, the recent finding that in his formative years, Frege took part in the discussion group of the Jena mathematician Karl Snell, who was under the influence of Schelling and the German romantics (Chapter 5: § 1). This finding puts Frege's logic in a new theoretical—not just historical—perspective: it connects Frege's logic with ideas of the German Idealists.

In other words, the logical history of philosophy develops new historical facts and extracts from them heretofore overlooked logical connections. This means that what the traditional historians of philosophy call "historical understanding," is not simply historical. The systematic historian of philosophy derives from such understanding new logical perspectives on the chief figures of the philosophical past.

Another kind of non-philosophical history of philosophy is the so-called "sociological history of philosophy." Its objective is to investigate the social context of past philosophical theories and concepts. Despite some attempts to show that it is intrinsically philosophical (Kusch, 1995), when realized in its authentic form, it is not.[9] When he confronts such a study, the logical historian of philosophy will attempt to distil some facts of the logical context of philosophy which were by mere chance submerged in a sociological environment. This, incidentally, is what the sociologists of knowledge themselves often do—a case well illustrated in Randall Collins's book *The Sociology of Philosophies*. Despite its title and declared intent, it focuses attention on the "intellectual networks" of philosophers (1998: xviii), which, of course, are logical in nature.

9 Epilogue

It should be clear from the preceding sections that the objective of the logical history of philosophy is to draw a comprehensive, detailed map of the development of the philosophical concepts and theories, a map without omissions. Such philosophical history proceeds step by step and strives to reconstruct philosophy as a product of what amounts to a collective effort of thinkers who constitute a philosophical community. In this way, it radically departs from the Hegelian approach to the history of philosophy that aims at achieving a speculative logic of history of philosophy.

It is well to recall at this point that the conception of the history of philosophy as a discipline that draws the map of philosophical theories and concepts from time past agrees with Russell's understanding of the nature of "analytic philosophy"—although not with his approach to history of philosophy. Indeed, Russell rejected out of hand the heroic way of doing philosophy in which one philosopher tries to solve all problems at one stroke. Instead, he supported a step-by-step, incremental development of philosophical discourse. The results achieved in such a work are epistemologically proven and are often made by different thinkers and are thus rigorous (Chapters 1 and 16).

When properly carried out—as a logical history of philosophy—the history of philosophy can thus be of great value to analytic philosophers. What's more, it can serve as a *real* Analytic Ideal in the realm of history of philosophy in general.[10]

Part Two

Leibniz and Hegel

3

Leibniz's Project for *Characteristica Universalis* and the Early Analytic Philosophy

1 Leibniz's Idea of *Characteristica Universalis*

1.1 Philosophical Characteristic/*Characteristica Universalis*

The first variant of what became Leibniz's project for a new language was set out in a letter from Marin Mersenne to Descartes. In fact, Mersenne's idea was that of *pasigraphy*, a general language that helps one to understand all languages. In his reply to Mersenne of November 11, 1629, Descartes expressed interest for this project; however, he suggested a much wider variant of it: a project for *ideography* that mirrors human thoughts. This *ideography* would be connected with a *mathesis universalis* that could cast anything thinkable as a calculation. "The greatest advantage of such a language," said Descartes, "would be the assistance it would give to men's judgment, representing matters so clearly that it would be almost impossible to go wrong" (1977: 12–13; AT I: 81–2).

Descartes, however, ultimately repudiated this project as utopian. Such a language could be realized only if we could guarantee a certain order in reality. It would require that "all the thoughts which can come into [the] human mind must be arranged in an order like the natural order of the numbers" (ibid.). Moreover, "the order of nature would have to change so that the world turned into a terrestrial paradise." Descartes concluded that this "is too much to suggest outside fairyland" (ibid.).

In the Leibniz archives, an excerpt of Descartes letter is preserved together with Leibniz's commentary on it (A VI, 4: 1028–30; C: 27–8), attesting to the fact that he was quite familiar with these deliberations of Descartes. Leibniz, however, was more sanguine than Descartes about the practicability of the project. He was convinced that every science and discipline, and even every concept and thing, can have its own character. Moreover, Leibniz believed that elements of ideography, albeit in quite rudimentary form, already exist, and that the program for general ideography is not utopian. Thus "the model of a machine expresses the machine itself, the projective delineation on a plane expresses a solid, speech expresses thoughts and truths, characters express numbers, and an algebraic equation expresses a circle or some other figure" (1678: 207; A VI, 4: 1370). Another example of ideography is the language of logic with its forms (see § 5.1).

Leibniz further claimed that *characteristica universalis* must be modeled on mathematics. In particular, he had in mind the unique nature of numbers as precise characters that facilitate exact, algorithmic thinking. Other academic disciplines, as well as areas of public discourse, would benefit from establishing such languages in the future. This would make their subjects clear and distinct.

That said, Leibniz judged the universal characteristic to be more general, and also more important, than mathematics. In fact, mathematics—algebra and arithmetic—"are but shadows" of it (1678/9: 6; A VI, 4: 264), despite the fact that they are its best existing examples. It is important to stress that this was the first program for a single formal science since Aristotle introduced logic as a second formal discipline parallel to mathematics (Milkov 2013b: § 2).

1.2 "Let Us Calculate!"—Two Types of Analysis

Leibniz hoped that his project would help to solve any problem via calculation. In this way also, the dispute between the schools would become superfluous: "Our characteristic will reduce the whole [the disputing arguments] to numerical terms, so that *even reasons can be weighed*, just as if we had a special kind of balance" (1678/9: 9; A VI, 4: 269; emphasis added).

Perhaps the most interesting claim that Leibniz made about his project (we shall return to it in §§ 4 f.) was that it would be especially valuable in domains where we cannot directly apply precise arguments, those in which we advance by *conjecturing* and by estimating degrees. Such procedures are especially relevant in medicine, in court, military arts, and politics, where we *deliberate* on which way to follow (see § 3).

In this connection, Leibniz discriminated between two types of analysis. The most common type (Cartesian) analysis advances by leaps (*per saltum*) and is employed in algebra. It consists of "division of difficulty in several parts" (A VI, 3: 671). "The other [type of analysis] is special and far more elegant but less known"; Leibniz called it "'reductive' analysis" (1679: 233; A VI, 4: 544). Reductive analysis[1] is especially appropriate when we must resolve problems in practice by conjecturing. Occasionally, in *Ars inveniendi* in particular, Leibniz spelled out the difference between the two kinds of analysis, discriminating between the divisional analysis and combinatorics: "Analysis is a study which dissects the object with greatest possible exactness.... Combinatorics [, in contrast,] consists in that in order to explain an object, we add other objects" (A VI, 3: 429; C: 167). Creative scientists such as Galileo made use of combinatorics; the mathematician Descartes preferred the divisional analysis. In his philosophy, Leibniz, we should note, was above all interested in combinatorics, or in reductive analysis, not in analysis by leaps. The latter play important role mathematics.

1.3 The Turn in Leibniz's Conception of *Characteristica Universalis*

Around 1679 Leibniz started to class his *characteristica universalis* as "a certain new language that some people call Adamic language, and Jacob Böhme calls 'nature language'" (1678/9: 5; A VI, 4: 264). He also connected it with the language of Cabbala and with the *characteristica* of the "magicians."[2] Further Leibniz argued that "if we have an exact *language* (called also *Adamic* language), or, at least, a *really philosophical script* in which the concepts can be abridged to something like an *alphabet of human understanding*, then all that reason deduces from data could be found *by a kind of calculation*" (A VI, 4: 911).

In another formulation, Leibniz proposed "that one can devise a certain alphabet of human thoughts and that, through the combination of the letters of this alphabet and through the analysis of words produced from them, all things can both be discovered and judged" (1678/9: 6–7; A VI, 4: 265). This would be both a succinct and a more generalized analysis of human thoughts.

What was behind this turn in Leibniz's project for *characteristica universalis*? It appears that this new formulation of the idea of a universal characteristic was nothing more than Leibniz taking sides in the dispute of the second half of the seventeenth century between "Teutonic philosophy" (*philosophia teutonica*), on the one hand, and the "mechanic," or "excessively materialistic" philosophers, on the other. Leading figures of the latter school were Bacon, Descartes, Galileo, Hobbes, Hyugens, and Jungius who, in Leibniz's judgment, "having revived Archimedes's use of mathematics in physics . . . thought that everything in corporeal nature should be explained mechanically" (GP VII: 343).

From the historical-philosophical perspective, Leibniz rightly noted that the new philosophers formulated their method principally in opposition to the old scholastic method of pursuing knowledge through inference. Following Newton, Locke presented Baco's method systematically, thus developing it further. For him, perception, which is limited to the immediately existing reality, is the most important and fundamental source of knowledge. To oppose this tendency, Leibniz revived Aristotle's "substantial [or metaphysical] forms." In the wake of this turn, he introduced the term "metaphysical points" to identify the numbers.

The context of Leibniz's project for Adamic language comes more fully into view when one takes into account the fact that a century before Leibniz adopted it, the method of "mechanical philosophers" was already opposed by his fellow Saxonian Jacob Böhme. In Hegel's judgment, "for Jacob Böhme the contents of doing philosophy is intrinsically German, for what characterizes and specifies him, is the . . . Protestant Principle, which puts the mental world into its home [*Gemüt*] (into its concept) and contemplates, knows, and feels in its own self-consciousness all that which usually is outside" (1836: 301 f.). In short, this principle led Böhme to begin to consider reality as a concept, to embrace the belief that every subject investigated has its idiosyncratic laws of developing. Clearly, this idea was not far removed from Leibniz's dream for Adamic language can present every real thing and every concept.

2 Orthodox Interpretations of *Characteristica Universalis*

This section, reviews some interpretations of Leibniz's program for *characteristica universalis* that have appeared over the last 140 years. While they shed some light on what Leibniz's idea of *characteristica universalis* could be, it remains the case that after more than three hundred years the concept has not achieved the widespread application that its author had hoped for it.

2.1 The Program for Perfect Language

Frege was one of the first to reconsider Leibniz's project for *characteristica universalis*, understood as consisting of idiosyncratic characters.[3] Chemistry and mathematics already took this way. Similarly to Leibniz's program for *characteristica universalis*, Frege's program for conceptual notation was ideographic: a means for the graphical representation of ideas, or concepts. More specifically, Frege's idea was that the conceptual notation should serve for "perspicuous representation of the forms of thought" (1881: 89). The perspicuity of the symbolism was to be achieved through appropriate spatial relations of the symbols, which is what Frege was aiming for when he invented his eccentric symbolism (Milkov 1999: 43).

In this connection, Frege criticized Boole's logic for not thematizing the content of logical formulae.[4] In "Boole's Logical Calculus and the Conceptual Notation" (1881) Frege observed that while Boole's project aimed to develop a technique or skill that would help solve logical problems automatically (logical laws were transformed by Boole into algorithms), he was interested in the content of a logical formula, that is, in the connection of the latter with the being. In "On the Aim of the Conceptual Notation" (1882/3) Frege was even more explicit:

> My aim was different from Boole's. I did not wish to present an abstract logic in formulas, but to express a content through written symbols in a more precise and perspicuous way than is possible with words. In fact, I wished to produce, not a mere *calculus ratiocinator*, but a *lingua characterica* in the Leibnizian sense. (1882/3: 90–1)

The idea of perfect symbolism (of "logically perfect language") was also prominent in Wittgenstein's *Tractatus*. In fact, the objective of the book was to present such a symbolism (Milkov 2017). In 6.122, Wittgenstein reached the conclusion that in such a symbolism "we can in fact recognize the formal properties of propositions by mere inspection of propositions themselves." This view closely followed—through Frege's mediation—Leibniz's doctrine of *characteristica universalis*, according to which "a complex chain of proof is to be fixed in one single formula, so that one could grasp the proof in a single glance" (Peckhaus 1997: 31).

This genealogic connection throws some light on further similarities between Leibniz's and Wittgenstein's programs: (i) Leibniz's "*ars characteristica* is the art to build, and order, symbols, in such a way that these are in same relations as the thoughts which they represent" (ibid.: 32). In the same way, Wittgenstein claimed that "in 'aRb' 'R' is not a symbol, but that 'R' is between one name and another symbolizes" (1979: 109). (ii) Like Leibniz, Wittgenstein maintained that besides letters and numbers, characters can be also figures, pictures, or models. (iii) In typical Leibnizian manner, Wittgenstein asserted that when we construct graphically correct symbols, all the problems of logic are *eo ipso* resolved. In this sense, "we cannot make mistakes in logic" (5.473). (iv) Finally, also in Leibnizian spirit (A VI, 4: 959), Wittgenstein embraced the principle *simplex sigilum veri* (5.4541).

2.2 Ontological Characteristic:[5] Wittgenstein's *Tractatus*

As we saw in Section 2.1, Descartes claimed that if natural order is not guaranteed, the project for *characteristica universalis* would be a doomed.[6] In what could pass for an effort to make Leibniz's project viable, Wittgenstein met precisely this requirement. In the *Tractatus*, he asserted that the world consists of facts that, in turn, consist of objects. Wittgenstein claimed further that objects are "formal concepts" (4.1272). This suggests that Tractarian ontology was logico-ontology: it was the flip side of Wittgenstein's new, "perfect" symbolism. On this score the *Tractatus* secured a complete congruence between symbolism and the world that Descartes had thought impossible.

More concretely, in Wittgenstein's Tractarian ontology objects are primitives or indefinables (Chapter 11: § 2.5). We can see the world—any aspect of it—as combinations of these building blocks. For example, when we see a blue spot in a particular visual field, we can analyze it to blue qualities of a certain size and a certain shape—that is, to a certain combination of objects, interwoven in a certain way (Milkov 2001).

Apparently, this ontology is in perfect harmony with the conceptual notation based on primitive symbols, the combination of which yields all other symbols: a conceptual notation close to the one Leibniz dreamed of.

3 Alternative Interpretations

More than three centuries after Leibniz proposed his plan for *characteristica universalis*, contemporary interpreters judge that it "appears as a more or less unattainable goal" (Rutherford 1995: 227). As we already saw, however, it is a notion that philosophers have repeatedly tried to revive;[7] and this is also the aim of the present chapter, in pursuit of which it makes a rather free interpretation of Leibniz. But then Leibniz himself, as we saw in Section 2, advanced an alternative, even competing, conception of *characteristica universalis*.

Leibniz's principal hope for his *characteristica universalis* was that it would be especially helpful in fields where conjectures prevail—above all in "propositions of civil or natural history, in the art of investigating natural bodies and thinking persons, and, especially, in public life, in medicine, in jurisprudence, in military art and in state governing" (A VI, 4: 913).

The present interpretation of Leibniz's project starts with this question: What can help in such cases best? Apparently, the answer is: Judicious intuitions (skills, or Cartesian *bona mens*—Milkov 1992) that we further verify in reality. The sort of encyclopedia of universal characters that would best help develop judicious intuitions is a *compendium of forms* (Milkov 2004a: § 4). As we shall see in what follows, the writings of Moore and Russell provide illustrations that underwrite this view.

3.1 Moore and Russell

Like Leibniz, Moore insisted that mistakes in ethics have the same roots as mistakes in mathematics: "Certain it is that in all those cases where we found a difference of opinion, we found also that the question had not been clearly understood. . . . It is as with a sum in mathematics" (1903a: 145). The key is rightly to pose the question; then one may readily calculate the correct answer.[8] The only difference between ethics and mathematics, in this respect, is that ethics is much more complex and so, the calculation required is much more complicated.

In fact, central to early analytic philosophy is the idea that if we could eliminate all conceptual confusions we would see the truth and agree on it and hence reach the point at which we could "calculate" (Milkov 1997, i: 196). Russell, for example, developed this notion by way of the claim that rigorous (analytic) philosophy examines the subject under consideration with the help of the forms, or models, it establishes.[9] Such philosophical-logical models can be collected in a special "dictionary," or encyclopedia, as Leibniz had in view (A VI, 3: 430; C: 169). But only when they are fully articulated we can examine the subject under consideration without vagueness or misunderstanding. Explicitly, Russell advanced this program in two forms: (i) In *Our Knowledge of the External World*, where he insisted that the new symbolic logic introduced such fruitful hypotheses, which can be most helpful in investigating different problems of *academic interest* (1914: 68; 1918: 85; see Milkov 2004a: § 4). In other places Russell insisted that forms can be suggested not just by logic but also by rigorous philosophy in general. In particular, he spoke about epistemic, propositional, factual forms, as well as forms of objects (Milkov 2003: 71–75). (ii) In *The Problems of Philosophy*, where he claimed that training in rigorous philosophy can also be helpful for discussing matters of *public interest* (Russell 1912a: Chapter 15).[10]

3.2 A Digression on Plato

Long before Moore and Russell, Plato introduced peirastic dialectic as the discipline most helpful in gaining wisdom. First of all, it tests, or examines, the interlocutor's beliefs and arguments. Apparently, it is not a theory but an application of trained skill, or practical intuition.[11] That is why, as Plato wrote in his seventh letter, its knowledge cannot be put into words, whereas knowledge of the other sciences can be. The skill of the peirastic dialectician simply supports the ability to better assess the arguments and facts under consideration. The dialectician is wiser than other academics, scientists, and intellectuals in general exactly in this sense (*Rep.*, 534e). The practitioner of dialectic examines a number of alternative solutions of the problem under analysis and decides which one is the most appropriate.

This examination, or conjecturing (cf. Leibniz's "balancing"), is a kind of calculation of well-established facts and arguments.[12] It is also a procedure similar to Leibniz's reductive analysis, or combinatorics (cf. § 1.2).

In his early dialogues, Plato elaborated manuals for Art of Discourse. In fact, they were nothing but *verbatim* reports of selected eristic matches, especially popular in Athens of the time. This practice was based on the belief that "tried argument-sequences can be learned by heart and studied for their strength and weakness, and the successful ones can, *en bloc*, become parts of the common repertoire of all who may ever debate the same thesis" (Ryle 1966: 198).[13] In a sense, they were similar to chess training. Chess players are typically drilled by memorizing patterns of different combinations, which can later be used in related situations. In the same way, Plato believed that memorizing different forms of dialectical argumentation is an irreplaceable instrument for philosophical training. This gives us firm ground to interpret Plato's manuals as the first pieces of Leibniz's *Encyclopedia*.

Unfortunately, in his later years, namely in *Republic*, Plato came to reconceive dialectics as a search for special truths, or "super axioms" (Milkov 2013b: § 2.1). Eventually, in and after *Philebus*, he replaced this discipline with his theory of forms, in the sense of general *laws*, from which we can make deductions about the particulars, and adopt the view that forms pertain to a special realm that is truer and more exact than reality.

4 New Interpretation of Leibniz's Project

Having summarized certain relevant philosophical practices of Moore, Russell, and Plato, we will now interpret Leibniz's discipline of *characteristica universalis* as resulting in a compendium or an encyclopedia of selected particular forms. To be more explicit, we speak of a toolbox of *particular* or specific *forms* which supplies "a priori (which is to say: non-inductive) knowledge relating to certain fundamental structures in a wide range of different spheres of objects" (Smith 1997: 586). We mean here forms of everything: of mental attitudes, of material objects, of propositions, of intentions, of scientific theories (Chapter 11: § 3.4). Importantly enough, the knowledge of particular forms is not only *a priori* but also synthetic in the sense that these forms are first to be discovered in a process of analysis.

Typical examples of such forms are: (i) some philosophical ideas, for example, Hermann Lotze's discovery of values and their connection to logic (Chapter 7), Franz Brentano's (re)discovery of intentionality,[14] J. L. Austin's (re)discovery of speech-acts (see Mulligan 1987), or the logical forms Russell described in *Mysticism and Logic* (§ 3.1); (ii) some philosophical arguments. Examples include the argument from illusion, the problem of other minds, the private language argument, the problem of the rule-following, etc.

As Friedrich Waismann put it, "[These] are not so much questions, as tokens of profound uneasiness of mind" (1956: 449). Discussions of such puzzles teach us to rightly calculate different options in problematic situations. The forms in such cases are simply different moves made in the process of discussing such puzzles. In fact, what unifies diverse versions of analytic philosophy is nothing but "a common repertoire of analytic techniques and a rich fund of instructive examples to draw upon" (Beaney 2013: 26).

The use of encyclopedia or compendia of such forms is intrinsically informal; it is a science-cum-practice activity—the science is the collection of forms, and the practice is their application, or verification. This explains why it is best applied in such disciplines as medicine, jurisprudence and military arts. Contrary to the conception of Plato's forms, however, the forms of the *characteristica universalis*, as here conceived, have no existential import. They are simply models of reasoning that help to find the best solution for every specific situation which we encounter either in practice or in theory.[15]

It needs to be stressed that this project is not utopian, elements of it already used in practice.[16] For example: (i) in every new case the judge consults the "forms" of legal codes; (ii) in the process of diagnosing patients, physicians consult medical dictionaries and encyclopedias.

4.1 Arguments in Defense of This Interpretation

This interpretation of Leibniz's project of *characteristica universalis* is supported, first of all, by the fact that he himself initially realized his program for universal conceptual notation as, in the sense of Frege-Dummett, a contextual "calculus of truths," not of individuals.[17] Indeed, Leibniz's initial idea of a universal characteristic, first articulated in his 1666 dissertation "Art of Combinations," was that "just as there are predicaments [categories] or classes of simple notions, so ought there be a new genus of predicaments in which propositions themselves or complex terms might also be set out in a natural order" (1678/9: 6; A VI, 4: 265).

Secondly, Leibniz insisted that *characteristica universalis* must help to reach "proofs beyond quantities." Helpful to this purpose are the forms of the logicians, but also what he had called the substantial, or metaphysical forms, or the metaphysical proofs of the degree and intensity of forms (A VI, 4: 910).

Thirdly, Leibniz often expressed rather catholic views as to what *characteristica universalis* can achieve. In difficult cases it would simply help to choose the most reasonable alternative. Of course, nobody can guarantee that it will be the winning position; it is just more probable that it will be (A VI, 4. 913–14).

Finally, this interpretation also explains how philosophical education proceeds. When studying the classics of philosophy, we usually learn different models of reasoning, or what Leibniz called different metaphysical forms. We often master these models without realizing which ones they are exactly and who their originator was (in the same way in which we use different techniques of, say, skiing, without exactly knowing who devised them and when). Similarly, using the corpus of a well-selected *characteristica universalis*, or a proper thesaurus of philosophical discoveries, arguments, and paradoxes of the past, we achieve the skills of correct thinking that form the basis of a good philosophical education (Milkov 1992).

4

Making Sense of Hegel with the Help of Early Analytic Philosophy

G. F. W. Hegel's philosophy is notoriously difficult to classify. The interpreters agree that it is monumental and important. Regrettably, few agree about what makes it so and also what exactly one can do with it as a philosophical resource. This perplexity is reflected in the fact that, in contrast to Italian and an evermore embattled cohort of British idealists, Hegel was not a significant factor in German academic philosophy of the time.[1] While we are familiar with the distinguished neo-Kantian movement, there was no comparable neo-Hegelian movement in the German academy. Moreover, as we shall see in Chapter 6, the British "neo-Hegelians," with the possible exception of J. E. M. McTaggart, were not really Hegelians. As a matter of fact, Hegel was much more influential among the young German intellectuals and revolutionaries of the time, the best known among them being Karl Marx, than among academic philosophers. One of the objectives of this chapter is to more accurately locate Hegel's place in the history of philosophy. The approach we shall take to this challenging but long-needed undertaking—we shall compare Hegel's philosophy to seminal figures and schools of early analytic philosophy—is unorthodox, yet it yields a number of surprising and historically significant findings.

We begin the investigation here with brief discussions of Hegel's relatedness to Wittgenstein, Frege, and the ordinary language philosophy. We shall conclude with a more extended analysis of the similarities of Hegel's *method* with that of the most distinguished exponents of early analytic philosophy.

1 Hegel in the Context of Philosophy of His Time

Prior to commencing the body of the analysis, it will be helpful to identify some hallmarks of Hegel's philosophy that are often overlooked.

Above all, Hegel's program can be seen as a reaction against the rising proto-analytic philosophy connected with the names of Leibniz, Wolff, Lambert, and Kant (each of them had keen interest in philosophy of mathematics)—and against the formalization of philosophy. Philosophy must not only control other philosophers and intellectuals, serving as "intellectual police," but also deliver new content.

But one can also put this point the other way around. In a sense, Hegel followed the tradition, as it began to take its modern shape in Leibniz and Kant, of the logicization of philosophy. He, however, transformed Kant's logic, making it a logic of content, as radically as Kant transformed Aristotle's syllogistic, making it much more formal. To be more explicit, whereas Kant rewrote the syllogistic into "transcendental logic" (Milkov 2013b), Hegel took things a step further with the introduction of his "speculative logic" (which we take up in § 4). This was a task of reconceiving the old conception of logic. The latter is "a fully ready [but] well-entrenched, one may even say ossified, material, and the task is to make it fluid again" (*Sc. log.*, 12.5). Importantly enough, exactly like Aristotle and Kant, Hegel insisted that he was the sole originator of "his" new kind of logic.

One can gain an alternative perspective on Hegel's revolution in philosophy if one compares it to the similar advances made by other German philosophers: turning back for inspiration and ideas to the philosophy of antiquity. First, Leibniz declared that the new modern philosophy—that of Descartes and John Locke—is too mechanistic and so looked back to Aristotle's "substantial forms" and *causa finalis*. Then Kant rediscovered the ancient dialectics. Hegel too found support for his new philosophy in the ancient world (Heidegger 1960). After Hegel, Franz Brentano returned to the scholastics and to Aristotle again, in particular, to the concept of intentionality. A generation later, Heidegger rediscovered, first, Aristotle, and then the pre-Socratic philosophers and grounded his philosophy of human being (*Sein*) on their ideas.

2 Hegel and Wittgenstein

One way to better understand Hegel's place in the history of philosophy is to treat him as Wittgenstein's opposite—and so, as counterposed to the early analytic philosophy—in relation to the subject matter of philosophy. Roughly, Hegel founds his theoretical explorations in points where Wittgenstein's *Tractatus* ends and at what Wittgenstein called "the mystical":[2] in the Absolute and in

Hegel's peculiar realm of "truth." As Hegel himself put it, "The true, however, is what is itself infinite, and it cannot be expressed or brought to consciousness in finite terms" (*Enc.*: § 28). Like Heidegger in the next century, Hegel maintained that science is interested in "correctness," not in truth. What is problematic with this conception is that Hegel's examples of truth, understood this way, came only from the realm of culture: "true friend," "true artwork," "true/untrue (failed) state." It is unclear how it could apply to the realm, for example, of cosmology.

No wonder about this position of Hegel, however, since, according to him, the core of philosophy is religion. To be more explicit, for Hegel, both religion and philosophy concern the "truth,"[3] the thing humans appreciate most, as distinguished from mere technical "correctness." Wittgenstein's interest was rather opposite: he was only interested in language, world, and logic.

Hegel further maintained that we can call philosophy the religion of the Spirit (*des Geistes*). That is how and why philosophy is different from sciences: philosophy is a kind of "spiritual" exploration of nature. It is a speculative thinking. Furthermore, Hegel held that speculative thinking can be also called mystical thinking. Indeed, "the mystical (taken as synonymous with the speculative) is the concrete unity of those determinations that count as true for the understanding only in their separation and opposition" (§ 82). It opposes the principle of abstract identity.

Despite this clear disparity between Hegel and Wittgenstein, however, they do have something in common also in this direction. In particular, according to 6.122 of Wittgenstein's *Tractatus*, "In a suitable notation we can in fact recognize the formal properties of propositions by mere inspection of the propositions themselves." In another place we have shown that this conception of the Tractarian Wittgenstein can be seen as the other side of his understanding of the mystical (Milkov 1987, 2004). Indeed, both cogent works of art, good life and also perfect logical notation help to see the things "together with the whole logical space" (1979: 83), not in a discursive way. The same can be said about the mystical—"the feeling of the world as a limited whole" (6.45).

What Wittgenstein shares with Hegel is also the all-pervasiveness of logic. To be sure, according to the early Wittgenstein, "logic seemed to have a peculiar depth—a universal significance. It lies quasi at the basis of all sciences. The logical investigation explores the essence of all things" (*PI*: § 89). Similarly, to Hegel, logical forms are "the ground existing in and for itself, of everything. . . . This form of syllogistic inference is a universal form of all things" (*Enc.*: § 24, A).

3 Hegel and Frege

Having referred to clear similarities between Hegel's and Wittgenstein's logical philosophy, we may find it helpful next to also consider a few points at which Hegel's logic was close to that of Frege's.[4]

Above all, exactly like by Frege, concepts are the main subject of Hegel's philosophy (see § 4). Furthermore, exactly as Frege did later, Hegel maintained that natural languages cannot express the subtlety of logical forms (Käufer 2005). Logic needs a more sophisticated language—another thing is that the new languages introduced by Hegel and Frege are radically different. Besides, similarly to Frege later, Hegel maintained that "the universal factor of the concept is not merely something common [to several things]" (*Enc.*: § 163). The judgment is not a combination of concepts. The concept itself is "essentially *one* [a unity] and the moments contained in it are not to be considered as diverse sorts" (§ 166).

But the similarity between Hegel's and Frege's understandings of concepts goes a step further. Hegel held that "in nature it is the organic life, which corresponds to the stage of the concept. Thus, for example, the plant develops itself out of its seed" (§ 161). In a like manner, in his *Foundations of Arithmetic*, Frege held that arithmetical definitions contain in themselves all ordinal numbers, similarly to how seeds contain the trees, and not as beams are contained in a house (1884, § 88).

Following Kant, Hegel also supported the context principle later adopted by Frege: "The various species of judgment are to be considered not merely as an empirical manifold, but instead as a totality determined by thinking. One of Kant's services is to have provided some validation of this demand" (*Enc.*: § 171). Hegel also opposed the psychological divisions of concepts into clear, distinct, and articulate (§ 165). He can be thus considered one of the forerunners of anti-psychologism in logic. We would like to remind the reader that today Frege is considered as the greatest champion of anti-psychologism.

4 Hegel and the Ordinary Language Philosophy

In recent years, the modus operandi of Hegel's philosophy has been often seen as conceptual analysis. Some maintain that, according to Hegel, "an essential part of what it is to grasp a conceptual content, and to be able to apply it correctly to an object, consists in mastering its connections with the concepts it entails, and with the concepts that entail it." Francesco Berto, the author of these lines (2007: 19), further holds that the product of Hegel's conceptual analyses is a kind of "conceptual geography." This readily calls to mind the fact that the method of conceptual analysis is the basic approach of the early analytic philosophy as well, in particular, of the Oxford ordinary language philosophers who practiced it in the form of connective analysis (Strawson 1992: Chapter 2) (Chapter 16: § 4.1). The task of such analysis is to critically assess and rectify the "logical geography" of concepts (Ryle 1949a: 10).

To make more sense of Hegel's understanding of philosophy as consisting of conceptual analyses, we need to understand that his conceptual analyses were mainly elucidations of the knowledge we acquire in sciences and in practical life. Apparently, what Hegel meant when he introduced this method was that in logic we investigate the achieving of "truth" in physics, biology, etc. The point, as we have noted, is that the products of science and mathematics are in Hegel's view not true—not really. They are simply correct. Scientific theories are to be elucidated by the speculative logic. They can become true only after such examination.

This explains why Hegel, in a way similar to Wittgenstein many years later, approached philosophy not as a doctrine but as a process of realizing already available modes of knowledge. That is why, in Hegel's *Logic*, "the propositions of paragraphs appear not as theses but as truisms: they don't need additional grounds of what we do when we read something and at that think and understand something" (Stekeler-Weithofer 1992: 105). That is also why at the end of the day Hegel maintained, like Wittgenstein a century later, that "the business of philosophy consists merely in bringing explicitly to consciousness what has been valid for humanity since antiquity with respect to thinking. Philosophy thus does not establish anything new" (*Enc.*: § 22).

The correlation of Hegel's philosophy of concepts and Oxford connective analysis is disclosed by the critical attitude of the ordinary language philosophers to formal logic. According to Gilbert Ryle, formal logic exercises control over philosophical understanding and is helpful in training human reason. However, it cannot, in his view, immediately help to solve philosophical problems. To this purpose, a kind of informal logic that examines the logical forces of concepts can be more helpful (1954: 114 ff.). Peter Strawson, in his turn, opposed to formal logic a specific logic of language. The former investigates the logical power of concepts and phrases. The two logics are alternatives and neither is subordinate to the other. When correctly employed, they can illuminate each other (1952: 231).

If, however, Hegel's logic is, in a sense, close to that followed by the ordinary language philosophy, why are they traditionally considered radically at variance? The answer attaches to two cardinal differences between Hegel's and Oxford's conceptual analyses:

1) First of all, Hegel's conceptual analyses are developed in an encyclopedic system that, he insisted, is finite and also closed. Mainly this insistence on a closed encyclopedic system elicited a strong antipathy toward Hegel by the majority of twentieth-century philosophers, and not just by the exponents of the analytic school (White 1957). This also constitutes the principal difference between Hegel's conceptual analysis and that of the Oxford ordinary language philosophy. As with a geographical exploration, the objective of the latter was not to produce a closed logical system. It made case conceptual analyses instead and was in principle open to new logical discoveries.

2) Joining the "linguistic turn" in philosophy, Oxford conceptual analysts didn't speak about the world as such. They explored the one and only world of concepts (or language), independently of how concepts evolve in science or mathematics. Be this as it may, some of the analysts were convinced that conceptual investigation can yield fruitful results in science. J. L. Austin, in particular, tried to make available the data of theoretical humanities (Milkov 2003: 105).

5 Hegel's Dialectic and the Method of the Early Analytic Philosophy

Recent decades have seen several attempts to exploit the relatedness between the early analytic philosophers and Hegel. Some thirty years ago, Peter Hylton (1990) and Nicholas Griffin (1991) investigated the apprenticeship of Bertrand Russell with neo-Hegelians. Twenty-five years later, the direction of interest changed. Scholars such as Paul Redding and Angelica Nuzzo have sought a connection between Hegel and analytic philosophy, following the lead of Robert Brandom and John McDowell. According to Redding (2007) and Nuzzo (2009), Hegel can be seen as a theorist of concepts. Moreover, they find that Hegel's understanding of concepts is close to that of early analytic philosophers (see § 4). The approach we are following in this section of the chapter is different. As distinguished from the studies of such parallels, the focus of the present text concentrates upon the relatedness of the *methods* employed by the early analytic philosophers and by Hegel. This is a hitherto unexplored line of inquiry. The goal is to open a new perspective both in the history of the early analytic philosophy and in Hegel studies. The concern in what follows is not with the genealogical connection between these two theoretical orientations, but rather with their kinship.

5.1 Hegel and the Eliminativist Method of Early Analytic Philosophy

The official story has it that the early analytic philosophy was developed in opposition to Hegel's dialectic. Whereas analytic philosophers strived to fix the *exact* terms and boundaries of logic, ontology, and epistemology, Hegel was interested in the *transition* of terms, concepts, and objects in other concepts and objects. Despite the fact that this story seems to be correct and convincing (as far as it goes), there are also striking similarities between Hegel's method of dialectic and the method of the early analytic philosophers. For one thing, the latter typically deployed the economic method of elimination. The early G. E. Moore would demonstrate how one step in philosophical analysis also performs—accomplishes ipso facto—a side-task, most economically killing two birds with one stone. The following presents nine examples of this approach: (i) I know a class of sense-data and I ipso facto know their object; (ii) I know the existence of an object and ipso facto know the existence of its sense-data; (iii) I know the words of a proposition and I ipso facto know its meaning; (iv) I believe a proposition and I ipso facto understand it; (v) I apprehend a proposition and ipso facto apprehend the fact about which it is; (vi) I apprehend directly sense-data and am ipso facto aware of the proposition that I perceive it directly; (vii) I apprehend directly sense-data and ipso facto apprehend the proposition that it exists; (viii) I have an immediate knowledge of a proposition and I can ipso facto immediately know the resulting proposition; (ix) in the case that I can prove that there are two things in the world, I can ipso facto also prove that there are two things outside me (Milkov 1997, i: 210). In all these cases a superfluous duplication of terms is eliminated.

Russell's "eliminativist philosophical method" (Landini 2007: 21) originated as a method of interpretation, or of paraphrases. Its result was abolishing numbers, relations, classes, propositions, propositional functions, and also objects of the external world as entities. Following Moore's and Russell's lead, in the *Tractatus* Wittgenstein eliminated logical constants, logical types, and epistemological subjects. He did not subsequently abandon but actually deepened this approach in *Philosophical Investigations*. (We return to this point in § 5.4.)

The principal finding of this section is that the method of eliminating, characteristic of the early analytic philosophy, was not merely a product of the method of analysis. It was also related to aspects of the Hegelian type of dialectic—this in the sense that it exhibited marked affinities with Hegel's teachings on immediacy and mediacy in ontology, epistemology, and logic. Importantly enough, Hegel introduced an approach in philosophy that has till now received considerably less attention than it warrants (Butler 2011). Characteristic of it is the varying relatedness of the elements of a whole into one other. In short, it "consists in constructing 'immediacies' that connect one [item] with another and thus make the process of constituting the composition of the whole" (Holz 1990: 399). Its advantage is that it secures the most economic type of connection between the entities of mereological unities, as well as the most economic type of connection between them and the unities. On this count, Hegel's method can help engender a highly efficient form of eliminativism.

In a first book on the history of analytic philosophy, the present writer termed the distinguishing feature of this approach "analytic immediacy" (Milkov 1997, i: 41 f.).[5] This was demonstrated to be characteristic of all Cambridge early analytic philosophers, including John Wisdom (Milkov 2019a). Tellingly, however, Frege did not subscribe to this approach (ibid.: 123),[6] and it is even less characteristic of what today is called "late analytic philosophy." The latter mainly focuses on exactness, not on eliminativistic reconstruction.[7]

5.2 Hegel's Ontology/Logic and His Method

As just noted, Hegel's ontology and logic explored the connection of the individuals (particulars) of a whole with one other, as well as with the whole itself. Wholes are unities of individuals that "bound to one another [and] are in fact not alien to one another but instead only moments of *one* whole, each of which, in its relation to the other" (*Enc.*: § 158).[8] In such cases Hegel spoke about mediation, or of dialectical immediacy (Milkov 1997, i: 86). An appropriate mediation can bring about the most economical connecting of the elements in a unity. It can thus help sponsor a highly efficient form of eliminativism, which is neither causal nor a relation of ontological dependence. Hegel held mediation to be the "glue" that binds the elements of the unity together, without being itself an element (see § 6.3). A notable implication of the conception of dialectic immediacy applied as a method is the comprehensive inner connection of the all elements of the totality: every element in it is connected with every other in the whole as well as with the whole as such.

It deserves mention that Hegel's critique of the simple immediacy was mainly exercised in his epistemology and was directed against the empiricists John Locke, David Hume, and F. H. Jacobi. It was a fight against the "given." Hegel argues that epistemological immediacy always already involves mediacy in itself since it takes place between two poles: subject and object. Evidently, pure immediacy is impossible. As Andreas Arndt has remarked, "The immediacy, as Hegel understood it, is not only *mediated* immediacy but is also a source, a *mediating* immediacy" (2004: 23). A prime example of dialectical immediacy is Hegel's concept of "sublation." According to it, one can understand the spirit not as reduced to nature but "only insofar as it contains in itself nature as sublated" (*Enc.*: § 96). Also in ordinary language, "sublation" means two things:

> By "*aufheben*" we understand on the one hand something like clearing out of the way or negating, and we accordingly speak of a law, or instance, or an institution as having been "*aufgehoben*." On the other hand, however, *aufheben* also means something like preserving, and in this sense we say that something is well taken care of." (Ibid.)

Similarly, Russell's eliminativism is not identical with reductionism. The core of his "philosophical project [is] that [it] is not just *reductivist* (like Frege's) but *eliminativist* [see n. 6]. Numbers are not 'reduced' to classes but 'eliminated' as mere logical fictions. Talk of numbers is nevertheless shown to be logically legitimate" (Beaney 2016: 245).

5.3 What Is Analytic Immediacy?

Not only Russell but also all early analytic philosophers followed a method related to Hegel's dialectics. Apparently, that method was developed in the context of the pursuit of "economy of thought" that was a major trend in philosophy of the *fin de siècle*, although it remains unwarrantably neglected in the literature. It is best known from the works of Ernst Mach, but William James and Edmund Husserl actively pursued it as well: this movement was not limited to a single philosophical school or tradition. The specific claim here is that the early analytic philosophers, G. E. Moore, Russell, and Wittgenstein, developed the vague principle of "economy of thought" into, what can be called, the much clearer and more powerful "principle of analytic immediacy." One is reminded here that Russell called his method "logical analysis" only faute de mieux.

Perhaps the finest illustration of this approach is Moore's quasi-Hegelian ontology developed around the concepts of "organic unity" as advanced in his *Principia Ethica* (1903a). In *The Principles of Mathematics* (1903) Russell, in his turn, defended the "unity of propositions" that he opposed to the logic based on the "aggregate" of terms. The elements of both unities, organic and propositional, preserve their identity only because they are reciprocally related to one another and also to the whole. Precisely this relation is what constitutes their "glue"—the nature of wholes is not something mechanical (Chapter 8: § 3.1). The connection between the elements of the unity is not produced in the way the connection keeping together the members of a chain is produced.

Symptomatically enough, the late analytic philosopher Graham Priest defends an opposite position. Like Moore and Russell, he claims that "unities are more than just the sum of their parts." The parts must also be appropriately related. In contrast to Moore and Russell, however, according to Priest, merely relating them is insufficient for unifying them. There must be something else that makes them one, something akin to an Aristotelian form. Priest calls this an object "gluon" which is a "contradictory entity" (McIntosh 2016: 130). The early Wittgenstein, in contrast, saw the glue in the whole not as entity but as a product of the *way* in which its elements are related to one another (Milkov 2019). Moreover, he tried correctly to express this understanding, borrowing from one of Husserl's acolytes, Adolf Reinach, the concept of "state of affairs" (*Sachverhalt*) (McGuinness 2002: 171 f.). According to Wittgenstein, the "general propositional form" is *es verhält sich so und so* (*Tractatus*, 4.5).[9] Literally translated this means "The things correlate to one another in a certain way" (Chapter 6: § 8.1). It brings to expression the effective relation between the elements of the whole, as well as their relation to the whole per se.

It remains to be said that the method of Wittgenstein's analysis is intrinsically a dynamic process (an activity, "not a body of doctrine," 4.112) whose objective is to achieve a clearer vision of the subject under scrutiny in several steps. The very verbal noun Wittgenstein uses in the *Tractatus*—*Sachverhalt*—indicates the dynamic, the processive.[10] Similarly, according to Hegel's dialectics, every concept transforms into another concept. The transformation is realized by way of *explicating* aspects of the initial concept (*Enc.*: § 84). Significantly, this explication makes the initial concept more precise.[11] The relatedness of the practice of analysis as developed in the early analytic philosophy to Hegel's dialectic is also revealed by the fact that some leading analytic philosophers, Rudolf Carnap, for example, also called the practice of analysis *explication* (1947: 4).

5.4 Wittgenstein's Radical Analytic Immediacy

Wittgenstein pursued a really Hegelian fight against the naïve mediacy and for dialectical immediacy in logic, ontology, and epistemology. In this respect he was much more radical than Moore or Russell. Moreover, there is an essential difference between the eliminativist method adopted by Russell and that followed by the Tractarian Wittgenstein. This difference stands out in sharp relief when one compares Russell's logic and his philosophy of language with those of the *Tractatus*.

Russell's logical atomism was based on the idea of a "logical skeleton," elaborated in *Principia Mathematica*, on which the data of experience are to be fleshed out. In the *Tractatus*, however, Wittgenstein does not employ the skeleton metaphor, and this for good reason. His logical forms are directly—immediately—embedded in the one and only one world of facts. In this way, he effectively bracketed the Russellian logical skeleton. To be more explicit, in the Tractarian philosophy of language, the elements of propositions (symbols, names) stick together on their own, without a mediating moment,[12] thanks to their logical profile (shape) alone. Logical constants (which do not represent) or some other quasi-logical objects external to them have nothing to do with the unity of propositions.

Moreover, an austere quasi-ontology corresponds to the austere Tractarian conceptual notation. Just as the propositions are concatenations of names, without logical objects that connect them together, so the Tractarian objects that build up states of affairs do not cohere with the help of a mortar, or any other kind of *tertium quid* (Wittgenstein 1973: 23). In states of affairs objects cohere to one another without mediation, thanks to their formal profile (to their topology) alone.

This understanding led Wittgenstein to claim in the *Tractatus* that the logically correct conceptual notation alone—the conceptual notation that eschews intermediary elements—makes all superfluous entities in logic, such like logical objects, disappear (Milkov 2017). Another consequence of this conception was Wittgenstein's contention (already cited in § 2, above) that "in a suitable notation we can in fact recognize the formal properties of propositions by mere inspection of the propositions themselves" (6.122). We don't need the mediation of concepts or proofs to this purpose; we don't need any form of inference. In this way Wittgenstein achieved a most radical form of eliminativism.

It remains to be noted that Wittgenstein's method in *Philosophical Investigations* can be seen as nothing but further development of the method of analytic immediacy he introduced in the *Tractatus* (Milkov 1992). In his later work, Wittgenstein argued that when we learn a language, or a calculus of mathematics, we do not learn rules "by heart" (it is just another *tertium quid*) that we later follow in practice. We are simply *trained* in this or that way to use the language or the calculation; the result is that we accept them. In fact, "my [whole] life consists in my being content to accept many things" (1969: § 344).

What follows from this position is that Wittgenstein later didn't abandon the early analytic method of doing philosophy as some commentators have claimed in our day. On the contrary, he profoundly deepened it. In fact, the whole "mystery" of the later Wittgenstein consists in the fact that he radically extended the power of what we have called here the method of analytic immediacy, introduced by G. E. Moore and Bertrand Russell. Now logic was dissolved in language games that are situated in practices of life. That is why instead of logic, Wittgenstein came to speak about grammar. A notorious problem endemic to much traditional philosophy is that, under the influence of language, it reifies concepts used in thinking about mind and thinking itself. Hegel was a towering exception here. Long before Wittgenstein, Hegel criticized the view that *mind* is a *thing* (*Enc.*: § 34).[13]

6 Differences between Hegel and the Early Analytic Philosophy

Given so many similarities between Hegel and the early analytic philosophy why are they usually considered fundamentally opposed? To make a long answer short, Hegel's main—radical—difference with early analytic philosophy was his fight against "solid results." As we shall see in Chapter 16: § 3, however, achieving "solid results" is the main objective of analytic philosophy. In contrast, to Hegel only bad philosophy holds that "the True consists in a proposition which is a fixed (*festes*) result, or which is immediately known [without a process]" (*Phen.*, § 40).

In truth, however, this pivotal difference between Hegel and the early analytic philosophy only reflects the fact that Hegel radically changed the subject matter of modern philosophy, which became now the infinite and the mystical (§ 2). At the same time, at the center of his attention moved problems of *conditio humana*, namely problems of human being, culture, and society. In this way he laid the groundwork for what later received the name "continental philosophy" (Chapter 16: § 5.2).

5

Frege and German Philosophical Idealism

1 Frege and the German Idealists

The received view has it that analytic philosophy emerged in reaction to the German idealists, above all Hegel, and their British epigones (the British neo-Hegelians). According to Bertrand Russell, German idealism failed to achieve solid results in philosophy. The distinguished analytic philosopher Michael Dummett saw Gottlob Frege as a key figure in the concerted effort to throw off idealism: "In the history of philosophy Frege would have to be classified as a member of the realist revolt against Hegelian idealism" (1967: 225).

This chapter establishes that while Frege too sought "solid" results in Russell's sense (Chapter 16: § 3), and on that count qualifies as analytic philosopher, he nonetheless took a radically different view than did Russell. Frege never spoke against Hegel, Schelling, or Fichte.[1] What's more, like the German idealists, his sworn enemy was empiricism as paradigmatically exemplified, for Frege, by John Stuart Mill (Bertrand Russell's godfather). By contrast with empiricism, which he, exactly like Hegel, regarded as "shallow," Frege stated that "the basis of arithmetic lies deeper, it seems, than that of any of the empirical sciences" (1884: § 14).[2]

Beyond targeting empiricism, Frege actually integrated elements of German philosophical idealism into his logic. When one takes into account the scholarly milieu in which Frege pursued his formative studies, the readiness with which he did this is not difficult to explain. Frege served his philosophical apprenticeship in an academic environment dominated by German idealists. He attended the University of Jena in the 1870s, where the faculty was organized into three informal clubs: one was led by the mathematician Karl Snell, the philosopher Kuno Fischer headed a second group, and the zoologist and popular philosopher Ernst Haeckel oversaw the third club. Frege belonged to Snell's "Sunday Circle" which met until 1880. Through the mediation of philosophy professor

Karl Fortlage, however, this group, "influenced by Schelling and the German Romantics," maintained close contact with Kuno Fischer's group, in which the thought of Kant and Hegel predominated (Kreiser 2000: 13; Sluga 1984: 321). Add to this that Snell was the teacher and intellectual guide of Frege's professor and mentor Ernst Abbe (Snell's son-in-law) and it should come as no surprise that Frege attached high importance to his participation in the "Sunday Circle."

The first Anglophone scholar to point out what Frege's thought owes to nineteenth-century Germany philosophy was Hans Sluga (1980).[3] Sluga argued that Frege followed the philosophical-logical tradition originating with Leibniz and Kant, and which Adolf Trendelenburg and Hermann Lotze developed significantly just prior to and into Frege's time. Sluga has identified this current of philosophical thought as the tradition of "classical German philosophy." About the same time, a philosophical historian writing in German, Gottfried Gabriel, did much to bring this tradition to light, casting Frege as neo-Kantian (1986).

Advancing beyond Sluga and Gabriel, the present chapter reveals that through the mediation of Trendelenburg and especially of Lotze, many elements of German idealism found their way into Frege's logic and philosophy. Indeed, albeit clearly intending to transform the philosophy of the time, Trendelenburg and Lotze, while often critical of Hegel, were not anti-Hegelian. Rather, their objective was *to reform* German idealism.

Under Hegel's influence Trendelenburg, senior to Lotze by fifteen years, began to explore thinking as a process. As a result, he changed the very architecture of the received philosophical logic. As Volker Peckhaus explains, "The traditional [Aristotelian] core, the theory of inferences, with syllogistics at its center, was pushed into the background. The new core was the theory of judgment" (2009: 16). Lotze, for his part, was an openly eclectic philosopher (Chapter 6: § 2) who, while renouncing Leibniz, undertook to systematize the most pregnant thoughts of Kant, Hegel, Fichte, and Schelling (Milkov 2010).

What needs to be borne in mind here is that Trendelenburg and Lotze influenced Frege along fundamentally different lines. Following formative ideas of Leibniz (Chapter 3: § 2.1), Trendelenburg looms as a defining influence in Frege's effort to formulate an artificial language that can better express our thoughts, something Frege first presented in the *Concept Notation* (1879). Lotze's impact becomes evident immediately after that when Frege was to make philosophical sense of his *lingua characterica*. As we shall see, through the course of this discussion German idealism exerted a formative influence on Frege in both his early and late philosophical development.

That said, the received view is nonetheless accurate in that there were many respects in which Frege and the German idealists were antipodal. Above all, Frege stressed discursive exactness as opposed to "dialectical transition" from one "characterization or formula" into another (Hegel 1830: § 81). Moreover, he did not hesitate to marry mathematics and philosophy: Frege was convinced that philosophy could thereby make mathematics more precise. The classical German idealists, by contrast, as well as their distinguished successors such as Trendelenburg and Lotze, counted themselves "pure philosophers" and so refused on principle to incorporate logical or mathematical formulas in their theoretical explorations (Chapter 9: § 2.2).

All of this led Frege scholars to conclude that Frege was a philosophical logician who was radically anti-Hegelian. As has already been adumbrated, however, Frege borrowed many elements of the philosophy of the German idealists. In what might otherwise strike one as paradoxical, these elements proved instrumental, we shall see, to Frege in achieving rigor and exactness in logic.

2 Anti-mechanicism, Pro-organicism

We have noted that while the classical Aristotelian logic started with concepts, went on to treat judgments (propositions), and ended with inferences, Frege's post-Trendelenburgian logic commenced with judgments (1883: 94)—and he had good reasons for this.

What Frege most opposed is the so-called "aggregative" conception of judgments. The mainstream logicians of his time conceived of judgments as complexes of concepts.[4] They "found it difficult to distinguish between a combination of terms which constitutes a judgment and one which constitutes merely a complex concept" (Sluga 1975: 483). Frege directed his criticism against these "mechanical logicians," most notably George Boole, who considered thinking a process of pure calculation. Frege found that Boolean logic "represents only part of our thinking; [but] the whole can never be carried out by a machine or be replaced by a purely mechanical activity" (1880/81: 35).

This opposition to mechanistic logic has a long tradition in German philosophy. It originated with Leibniz who held that in their analytic predilections, Descartes and Locke went too far. As a corrective, Leibniz reintroduced ideas of Aristotelian metaphysics (Chapter 3: § 1.3). The German idealists employed analogous argumentation, as did Hermann Lotze.

Against the mechanistic logicians, Frege advanced a kind of "logical organicism" (Gabriel 2008: 121 ff.). This found expression in the fact that, similarly to the German idealists, he regularly used biological metaphors in his logic. The following enumeration of Frege's recourse to such metaphors over the years makes manifest his unswerving commitment to logical organicism:

1) In "Boole's Logical Calculus and the Conceptual Notation" Frege maintained that the starting point of his logic is the event of judging. Judging is a process that organically connects the parts of the concept. We can discriminate the elements of the concept as discrete individuals only after the concept is already constructed (1880/81: 17, 19).
2) In *Foundations of Arithmetic* Frege held that arithmetical definitions contain in themselves all ordinal numbers, similar to how seeds contain the trees, and not as beams are contained in a house (1884: § 88).
3) In *Basic Laws of Arithmetic* Frege compared arithmetic with a tree "that unfolds in a variety of methods and axioms, while the roots go in the depth" (1893: xiii).
4) Four years later Frege declared that our "thought is not an association of ideas—no more than an automaton . . . is a living being" (1897a: 145).
5) Seventeen years beyond that we find him asserting that science "must endeavor to make the circle of improvable primitive truths as small as possible for the whole of mathematics is contained in these primitive truths as in a kernel [*Keim*].[5] Our only concern is to generate the whole of mathematics from this kernel" (1914: 204–5).

3 Frege's Two Types of Analysis

To grasp the role of Frege's "logical organism" one needs to recognize that he employed two concepts of analysis. First, following Kant, Frege regarded knowledge in arithmetic as analytic in the sense that we derive it, *deduce* it, from definitions and general laws by logical means (1884: § 3): we shall refer to this as "analysis$_1$." Frege determined, however, that Kantian derivation (deduction) is also *synthetic*, in the sense that it creates something new, and he drew attention to this point in *Foundations*: "The conclusion we draw from it [the definition] extended our knowledge, and ought therefore, on Kant's view, to be regarded as synthetic; and yet they can be proved by purely logical means, and are thus analytic" (§ 88).

Frege's position, we should note, stands clearly opposed to the view, widely accepted (for example, by Hume) prior to the ascendancy of post-Kantian German idealism, that analytic judgments are epistemologically sterile. Also Wittgenstein, lacking Frege's background in idealism, would call analytic judgments "tautological."

The second type of analysis (call it "analysis$_2$") is *decompositional* in nature. The difference between analysis$_1$ and analysis$_2$ becomes patent when one revisits the previous example of the plant. A plant, to which Frege relates the particular numbers, is synthesized (or analyzed$_1$) in a process of photo*synthesis*. We may decompose it, subject it to analysis$_2$, only afterward, anatomizing it in order to determine, for instance, its composition. The living, existing plant, however, cannot as such undergo analysis$_2$.

While Frege's analysis$_2$ correlates with the scientific analysis, say, in chemistry, his analysis$_1$ is close to the growth and self-maintenance (synthesis) that distinguish biological organisms. Regrettably, many Fregeans uncritically adopted the received judgment that the master was an "analytic philosopher" pure and simple. As a consequence they did much to play down the pivotal difference between the two alternative senses of "analysis" with which Frege operated, when they didn't simply ignore it.

An additional factor that militates against properly understanding Frege on this score is that he was, without question, also an adept at analysis$_2$. He maintained, for example, that logicians have the task of isolating what is logical from psychology and language and doing so in the same way that scientists undertake to isolate the elements of chemistry (Chapter 15: § 2). There is more to Frege's position, however, since "even when we have completely isolated what is logical in some form or phrase from the vernacular or in some combination of words, our task is still not complete. What we obtain," observes Frege, "will generally turn out to be complex; we have to analyze this, for here as elsewhere we only attain full insight by pressing forwards until we arrive at what is absolutely simple" (1880: 6).

In short, the method of decompositional analysis plays a substantial role in Frege's philosophical logic. This sort of analysis became especially prominent in his thought five years after he published his *Conceptual Notation* (Gabriel 2008: 123 f.), in particular, when he discovered that numbers are objects and when concepts began to serve a defining role in his logic (Weiner 2004: 70). These developments notwithstanding, analysis$_1$ prevailed over analysis$_2$ in Frege's thinking. It is of more than passing interest that this tendency finds a parallel, as we shall see, in the prime role of quantification theory over propositional calculus in his logic (see § 8).

4 "Saturatedness": Chemical or Biological Metaphor?

The standard account has it that Frege borrowed from chemistry the metaphor "saturated/unsaturated" which he employs to characterize the relation between function and argument (Potter 2010: 13). On this matter, as with those noted in the preceding section, commentators have simply presumed that Frege was an "analytic" philosopher—whatever they take this notion precisely to mean. Is this view correct?

Before probing the meaning of "saturated [*gesättigt*]" as Frege utilized it, one should be aware that the metaphor in question derives not from chemistry but from biology: the German term "*satt*" ("full up") applies to organisms when their striving or desire to eat is satisfied. Be this as it may, scholars invoke this biological term across a wide range of non-biological disciplines: from epidemiology and demography to economics (a market can be "saturated") and mathematics. In chemistry "saturation" is understood as "the point at which a solution of a substance can dissolve no more of that substance"[6]—which is to say it means the achieving of a final stable state by one mass individual as a result of a dynamic process.

Frege, however, conceived the notion of being *gesättigt* along completely different lines. He held that in logic "the argument does not belong with a function, but goes together with the function to make up a complete whole [*vollständiges Ganzes*]" (1891: 140). In other words, Frege's concept and object are *two* individuals that fuse in order to build up the "organic unity" of a thought—like two cells that merge in order to constitute a germ (see n. 5): one of the "*ungesättigt*," the other one capable to make the first one "*satt*." Frege held that we invariably subvert such a thought, once formulated, by subjecting it to analysis$_1$. Similarly, he maintained that we do not construct a concept by subsuming the subject under the predicate. Rather, concept's different elements (its "characteristics [*Merkmale*]") grow together (*wachsen zusammen*)—are synthesized—so as to form ("build") it.

In an unpublished-in-his-lifetime review of Arthur Schoenflies's book *The Logical Paradoxes of Set-theory*, Frege noted, "The unsaturatedness of one of the components is necessary, since otherwise the parts do not hold together. Of course two complete wholes can stand in a relation to one another; but then this relation is a third element—and one that is doubly unsaturated" (1906: 177). In light of this position it comes as no surprise that when he read Wittgenstein's *Tractatus*, Frege questioned: "What is the thing that binds [the objects in a state of affairs]" (2011: 53)? To Frege's way of thinking such a connection should be a kind of concrescence (*Zusammenwachsen*) of the two (or more) objects into one.[7]

This judgment reflects Frege's view that one of the purposes of the function/argument and concept/object distinction is to replace the idea that the content of a sentence is composed of constituents that are merely subsumed in one complex. Indeed, the Booleans had "assumed concepts to be pre-existent and ready-made and judgments to be composed from them by aggregation" (Sluga 1987: 85). Frege, on the other hand, taught that concepts and propositions are to be synthesized, *created* (§ 3). This idea of "creation" simply does not obtain when one takes "saturation" in the chemical sense: no creation occurs in chemical saturations.

5 Life

Beyond Frege's recourse to the "saturation" metaphor, his organicism appears in a number of other forms. Perhaps the most significant instance stands at the very center of his philosophical logic, namely in the idea that thinking—the subject matter of logic—is to be understood as embedded in human life.[8]

When we are awake, we cognitively react to the events and situations of the external world, thus making judgments. Moreover, in judgments we advance (*fortschreiten*), asserts Frege, from a thought to its truth-value. This is the case since when we judge in *real life*, we are, as Frege puts it, "serious." In other words, in real life we know that matters have irreducibly practical import and that ultimately our survival is at stake when it comes to judging matters correctly. In contrast, when we *play*, we are not, in Frege's view, serious—we are not preoccupied with real life.[9] In play, our sentences accordingly have no truth-value. What they betoken is simply the exercise of our free will. In such cases what we produce is merely a series of *obiter dicta*, not propositions.

We can see now why judgment played a central role in Frege's logic. We know Frege's claim in "On Sense and Meaning" that judgment "is something quite peculiar and incomparable" (1892: 165). Judgment is such because it is the event, the step that intrinsically connects logic to life. Frege went on to claim that when we make judgments, we strive for truth. Moreover, this striving is the "motor" that connects logic with the world: "It is the striving for truth that," as he put it, "drives us always to advance from the sense to the thing meant" (163).

It is evident from the foregoing that, like Hegel's logic and that of Lotze, Frege's logic is markedly anthropocentric in character.[10] Frege argued that logic

6 Logical Voluntarism

Besides championing organicism in his philosophy of logic, Frege asserted that to make a judgment is to make a choice between opposing values, between truth and falsehood. The judgment *acknowledges* the truth of the content. "We grasp," he declares, "the content of a truth *before* we recognize it as true, but we grasp not only this; we grasp the opposite as well. When asking a question we are *poised [schwanken wir]* between opposite sentences" (1880: 7; emphasis added) until we decide, in an act of will, its truth-value.

Frege's terms "before" and "poised" show that judgments are processes.[11] More precisely, a judgment is an act of inquiring whether a thought be true or false. It is based on our intuition—on the feeling that our thoughts constitute either a correct or a mistaken assessment of reality. Frege maintained, moreover, that the process of "accepting one of [the truth-values] and rejecting the other is one act" (1906a: 185): an act of exploration, one followed by an act of decision.

Frege's activist view of judgment proved of fundamental importance in his logic, and gives us leave to speak of a Fregean "logical voluntarism." This logical voluntarism found expression in Frege's claim that assertoric force is one of the constitutive elements of our articulation of a judgment[12]—a position that reveals another facet of Frege's debt to German idealism, particularly to the philosophy of J. G. Fichte: it has clear connection with human free will.[13] Wittgenstein, who in contrast to Frege had, as we've noted, no idealist background, promptly rejected this thinking as Frege gave expression to it in his logical symbolism: "Frege's 'judgment stroke' '⊢'" declared Wittgenstein, "is logically quite meaningless" (1922: 4.442). Russell, in his turn, maintained that "the vehicles of truth and falsehood" are our beliefs (1921: 139), not our will.

Significantly, Frege was convinced that this voluntarism does not contradict the objectivity of logic that he defended. His conviction on this head appears to derive from the fact that his Conceptual Notation was a language (*lingua characterica*) and so intrinsically connected with Being, understood as an absolute singularity.[14] From this it follows, on Frege's view, that when two persons judge a situation "seriously," in his sense, they make the same judgment. In other words, the "seriously" secures the objectivity of judgments—a position that Michael Dummett saw fit to label as "realist."

7 Logic of Content

Beyond its other debts to German idealist thinking, Frege's logic also paralleled Hegel's project for a logic of content that opposed the formal logic of the Kantian type. Frege articulated his logic of content along two lines:

1) As already mentioned, in *Conceptual Notation* (1879) he sought to establish a *lingua characterica*, not just a *calculus ratiotinator*. This program undertook to present the thinking process in a transparent way, one that would yield a "perspicuity of presentation" (*Übersichtlichkeit der Darstellung*) of it (1882: 88).[15]

Frege simply aimed to replace inconvenient, ordinary language that develops spontaneously and that manifests many defects, as measured against his new language. He was convinced that his new language would prove to be a vehicle in which our thought finds its true articulation. Arguably, this project had its roots in *philosophia teutonica*[16] that followed the "Protestant principle which put the world of mind into its own home, so that it contemplates, knows and feels what otherwise lies beyond it, in its own terms" (Hegel 1836: 826–7) and doesn't investigate it from outside, through quasi-objective principles. This impelled Frege to investigate thinking according to its own laws, and not with the help of formalist schemes.[17]

In order to present our thinking in its true form, Frege employed the relation of logical signs in two dimensions, something that resulted in his complex Conceptual Notation. As Frege saw it, "the spatial relations of written symbols on a two-dimensional writing surface can be employed in far more diverse ways to express inner relationships than the mere following and proceeding in one-dimensional time, and this facilitates the apprehension of that to which we wish to direct our attention" (1882: 87; see Milkov 1999).

This original approach to logic made feasible the allegedly impossible marriage between this formal discipline and in-depth philosophical exploration. With its help Frege circumvented logicians like Boole, Grassmann, Jevons, and Schröder, all of whom failed to connect logical forms with philosophical content (88). But he also left behind the traditional German philosophers, including those who were well versed in mathematics and logic, like Hermann Lotze and Edmund Husserl, who strictly adhered to the dogma not to incorporate what are merely formal tools as substantive components of philosophical development (Chapter 9: § 2.2).

2) The second line along which Frege developed his logic of content, beginning in *Conceptual Notation*, was that of logical semantics, which he treated as "judgeable content." In the early 1890s he further developed formal semantics by introducing the idea of the sense of a proposition. This innovation anchored Frege's logic in the world and thus categorically differentiated it from the constructs of the formal logicians. Indeed, his Conceptual Notation was not only logic but also a language that is intrinsically connected with Being (see n. 14.) understood as an absolute singularity, and also with life.

8 Intensional Logic

Frege's logic is intensional in that in it a *function* ranges over every *argument* that falls under it, and a *concept* defines every *object* that falls under it (Gabriel 2008: 120): "The concept has a power of collecting together far superior to the unifying power of synthetic apperception" (1884: § 48). And this is not because the objects are spatial or temporal parts of concepts. It follows, rather, from the circumstance that the objects obey the "laws" of concepts. The essential point to note here is that the dependence relation is not immediate or intuitive—it is not realized because of inclusion in the volume of the whole. Rather, it is abstract: it is a quasi-Newtonian dependence "from a distance."

The intensional stance that distinguishes Frege's logic also governs the relation between propositional and predicate calculus. As van Heijenoort has noted, "in Frege's system the propositional calculus subsists embedded in quantification theory.... In that system the quantifiers binding individual variables range over all objects" (1967: 325).

A similar line of thought had earlier appeared in the German idealists, according to whom the Idea (the "Absolute") determines the characteristics and behavior of all individuals that fall under it with necessity of a law. One way to appreciate the singular nature of this conception is to compare it to the idealist aspect of Spinoza's thinking, which pictures "individuals as mere accidents of substance" (Inwood 1992: 304).

The fact that German idealist thought-determinations philosophically substantiate Frege's new logic should hardly be surprising given that some of his contemporaries who lacked his comprehensive background in German idealism,

Carl Stumpf, for example, also elaborated a radically anti-psychologist and anti-Millian philosophy of arithmetic, but one which was based on mereological logic (Stumpf 1870). Of course, we would not deny that main inspirations of Frege's logic were Cauchy and Weierstrass, not Hegel or Schelling (Grattan-Guinness 1985/86).

Significantly, the absolute primacy that Frege's logic of quantifiers accorded the function and the concept introduced a new emphasis on the role of individuals in logic—indeed, the power of the general term makes it possible to fix the parameters of the particular that falls under it with signal exactness. It was in this way that Frege foregrounded the problematic of reference, which was to become defining topic of twentieth-century philosophy of language.

Frege's intensional first-order logic has been subjected to considerable criticism on this point. A prominent recent commentator, Barry Smith, dismisses it as "fantology" (2005). While no one would deny that first-order logic has great expressive and inferential power, it lacks the resources to treat objects of the real world, such as universals, types, processes, and, we might add, mereological entities. Smith objects that its "universe of discourse consists of particular items" (of individuals) only (2008: 110). In fact, Frege's first-order logic is of use only in mathematics, the objects of which are typically not situated in space and time. For object of the real world, on the other hand, one must have recourse to an alternative to predicate logic, namely a logic of terms.

Over the years, Frege accorded increasing significance to the role of intensions in logic. In "Function and Concept" he replaced the naïve function-argument logic of *Conceptual Notation* with logic of "course-of-value" (*Wertverlauf*) of concepts. As the very name of this logic suggests, in contrast to the positions of the parts that constitute mereological wholes, the position of an individual (or argument) in a course-of-value is intrinsically indeterminate: it is "floating"—a factor that Frege symbolized with a curve—until it is identified. Correspondingly, in his epistemology Frege spoke about "course-of-images" (*Vorstellungsverlauf*) (1882: 83, 87) that can be determined only through his Conceptual Notation. Apparently, the indeterminateness of the general (the "absolute") was Frege's leading theoretical stance.

Russell readily embraced Frege's new logic, particularly the idea of "denoting phrases."[18] He regarded the latter as a pivotal innovation because denoting phrases can indicate infinite collections of individuals with the help of singular (intensive) concepts; and they can do this precisely because their denotation is undetermined. Russell was convinced that this "discovery" resolves the paradox of infinity.[19] However, it was not long before Russell detected another paradox: the paradox of classes. Apparently, Frege's logic simply led Russell to relocate paradox from one domain, the realm of infinity, to another, the realm of classes that range over infinite number of individuals (Milkov 2017). In other words, the paradox of classes was a consequence of embracing class-concepts that range over infinite numbers of individuals.

Over the last hundred years or so it has turned out that the most effective way to address the "paradox of classes" is to accept multitudes that do not fall under a class-concept that ranges over them.[20] In other words, the paradoxes disappear when we abandon those ideas in Frege's logic that were supported by the philosophy of the German idealism.

Part Three

Hermann Lotze

6

Lotze and the Early Cambridge Analytic Philosophy

1 Lotze, Not Hegel, Lies at the Bottom of Cambridge Analytic Philosophy

Conventional wisdom has it that the early philosophy of Moore and Russell was under the strong sway of the British "neo-Hegelians." Yet, those historians who investigate the British "neo-Hegelians" of 1880–1920 in detail, call attention to the fact that the latter were anything but mere epigones of Hegel: William Sweet made this point in regard to Bosanquet (1995: 39–60), Geoffrey Thomas in regard to Green (1987: 45–54), and Peter Nicholson in regard to Bradley (1990). Finally, Nicholas Griffin has shown that Russell from 1895–8, then an alleged neo-Hegelian, "was very strongly influenced by Kant and hardly at all by Hegel" (1996: 215).

These facts are hardly surprising, if we keep in mind that the representatives of the school of T. H. Green—Bradley, Bosanquet, W. Wallace, R. L. Nettleship— were called "neo-Hegelians" only by their opponents. As it turns out, that term had little descriptive value from the outset. Indeed, the four students of Green "had some knowledge of Hegel, and a good deal more of Kant. The fact of their having this knowledge was used by their opponents . . . to discredit them in the eyes of a public always contemptuous of foreigners" (Collingwood 1944: 16). The "neo-Hegelians" themselves categorically repudiated the application.

Scholars well versed in German philosophy of the nineteenth century find the claim that mainstream British philosophy of 1870–1910 was "Hegelian" rather puzzling. Historically speaking, after 1840, there was scarcely any German academic philosopher of importance who would have openly declared that he was Hegelian. (Prominent exception was the historian of philosophy Kuno Fischer (see Chapter 4: n. 1).) The principal reason for this was that in the 1840s, a host of new scientific discoveries revealed that many of Hegel's speculations were simply mistaken and Hegelianism in strict sense was consequently judged a spectacular flop. The question thus arises as to whether the leading philosophers in Britain were so ill-informed about this development that between 1870 and 1910 in Germany they embraced Hegelianism as their philosophical credo? There is evidence to establish that this was not the case. In 1877, for example, Wilhelm Wundt had informed his British colleagues in the newly founded *Mind* (old series) that the Hegelian school had "at the present day the fewest thoroughgoing adherents [in Germany]" (1877: 511).

Be this as it may, it is beyond any doubt that early Cambridge analytic philosophy developed under massive Teutonic influence. One of the first historians of contemporary philosophy to notice this was John Passmore. In *Hundred Years of Philosophy* Passmore devoted considerable space to the philosophy of Christoph Sigwart, Rudolf Herman Lotze, Johan Friedrich Herbart, and Friedrich Ueberweg. Lamentably, the books coverage of these thinkers was only "a residue of a much more expanded account which Arthur Prior had persuaded [him] to castrate" (Passmore 1995: 194).

The present chapter will establish that Rudolf Hermann Lotze (1817–1881) was not just one among many other powerful German philosophers from about 1880–1920 whose ideas and doctrines played a formative role in the thinking of colleagues in Britain. He was clearly the leading figure among them.

2 Why Are the British Idealists Believed to Be Hegelian?

If, however, the leading *fin de siècle* British philosophers were not really Hegelian but Lotzean, why were they called exactly so? Mainly for three reasons: The first being that Lotze himself can easily be interpreted as a Hegelian. The issue is the method of eclecticism to which Lotze subscribed. Indeed, from the very beginning, his slogan was: "When we cannot necessarily join one of the dominating parties, we [shall . . .] stay in the middle via free eclecticism"[1] (1843: 1). This method meant that Lotze adapted to his purpose the ideas of different philosophers, above all of Kant, Fichte, Schelling, and also Hegel, distilling what he took to be the most valuable among them and formulating them in an exact form. This also explains the manifest presence of Hegel's ideas in Lotze's writings.

Secondly, G. F. Staut and James Ward (Moore's and Russell's teachers at Cambridge) were widely believed to be Hegelian. In truth, though, they were under the direct influence of Lotze.[2] This is shown by the fact that Lotze was one of the philosophers set for examinations at Cambridge between 1890 and 1910.

Indeed, Moore later remembered that Ward encouraged him "to read pieces of Lotze's *Metaphysics* and to write essays on these pieces [which] then ... [Ward] discussed privately with [him]" (1942: 17). Furthermore, toward the end of this period, C. D. Broad won the Burney Prize with an essay on Lotze's Philosophy of Religion (Kuntz 1971: 57).

Thirdly, the philosophers who most influenced the young Moore and Russell through reading, the putatively neo-Hegelian Bradley and Bosanquet, were also strongly under Lotze's sway. This should be no surprise since their teacher, Thomas Hill Green, was so enthusiastic about Lotze that in 1880 he started a major project to translate Lotze's *System of Philosophy* into English; this included Lotze's "greater" *Logic* (1874) and "greater" *Metaphysic* (1879).[3] After Green's untimely death two years later, this project was continued by a team under the guidance of Bosanquet. Besides Green and Bosanquet, A. C. Bradley (brother of F. H. Bradley), R. L. Nettleship, and J. Cook Wilson contributed to translation and editing of Lotze's work. (The other—the real British "neo-Hegelian" who directly influenced Moore and Russell—J. M. E. McTaggart, born in 1866—was too young to take part in this translation.) The two volumes appeared in English in 1884. At the same time, in Cambridge James Ward and Henry Sidgwick were instrumental in preparing the translation of Lotze's three volumes of *Microcosm* by Elisabeth Hamilton and E. E. Constance Jones. This translation appeared in 1885.

Given the immersion in Lotze of Russell's philosophy teachers at Cambridge, one can understand why Russell, who was for years under the impression that he was a "neo-Hegelian," was shocked when in June 1897 he first read Hegel in the original (Chapter 7: § 6). He found that Hegel's writings substantially deviated from his own standard of exactness. In fact, what he liked in the "neo-Hegelians" were mainly some points of Lotze's philosophical logic assimilated in their writings, as well as the Lotze-style relationism. We shall consider both of these facets of Lotze's influence in the next section.

3 Lotze's Influence on the British Philosophers

Lotze influenced the British idealists mainly in two directions—by introducing philosophical logic and by underlining the importance of relations:

1) *Philosophical Logic.* As Agnes Cuming long ago noted, what Bradley and Bosanquet adopted from German philosophy was, above all, some ideas from Lotze's philosophical logic:[4] "Their treatment of the problems of logic is almost a continuation from the point at which the German writer left off" (1917: 165).

In general, the significance of Lotze's philosophical logic was widely appreciated in Europe in the early years of the twentieth century. Thus in 1912 Heidegger called Lotze's *Logic* "the basic book in modern logic" (1978: 23 n.). A few years later, the neo-Kantian Bruno Bauch wrote, "Of everything that has followed in the area of logic from Hegel to the present day, there is nothing that has surpassed Lotze's logical achievements in value" (1918: 45). We must keep in mind that in the 1910s Bruno Bauch was a colleague of Frege in Jena, and one of his few admirers. This, however, did not hinder him from appreciating Lotze as the most prominent among the logicians.

With the rapidly growing predominance of symbolic logic of the new "analytic philosophy," awareness of the importance of Lotze's logic declined perceptibly after 1920, and to such an extent that in the early 1960s the name of Lotze rated not so much as a footnote in *The Development of Logic* of William and Martha Kneale (1962), still one of *the* standard historical texts.

One of the reasons for the radical decline of interest in Lotze's logic is that, as often occurs in philosophical logic, the original ideas that it contributed were anonymously assimilated (Milkov 2013b: § 6). This means that because they are technical they are often absorbed like an anonymous meme, without being necessarily connected with the person who advanced them. This explains why Bradley, a man who, by all accounts, was strongly influenced by some ideas from German philosophy, "had no high opinion" of German philosophy as such (Taylor 1925: 7).

Moreover, the innovations in this rapidly developing field of logic spread very quickly and were widely accepted in a short time. A typical example in this respect is the context principle, rediscovered by Lotze as early as in the 1840s.[5] Vehemently criticized by J. S. Mill, "the slogan 'Only in the context of a proposition [or judgment] do words have meaning' . . . [became] an Anglo-Hegelian commonplace" after 1875, assumed also by Green and Bosanquet (Manser 1983: 62).

Apparently, the main reason philosophers lost interest in Lotze's logic was that a new paradigm of theoretical reasoning emerged in the 1920s, the main characteristic of which was the schism between continental and analytic philosophy. Suddenly, many important achievements of the late-nineteenth-century philosophy lost their significance or were recast in new forms and terms.

2) *Relationism*. The second defining component of Lotze's thinking that had a seminal influence on the British philosophers was his relationism. To be sure, before Lotze, relations were "neglected as largely subjective, and of dependent or related becoming" (Kuntz 1971: 38). After Lotze's "objectivist turn" (Chapter 7: § 2), relations gained a central position in philosophy.

In Britain Lotze's translator T. H. Green adopted the view that reality is relational and he was first to make relations a core theme of philosophical discourse.[6] F. H. Bradley sought to confute Greens's Lotzean metaphysical thesis. Indeed, a major thrust of *Appearance and Reality* (1893) was a "general criticism of relations" and the demonstration that they are only appearances. Some years later Russell rehabilitated Lotzean relationism when he abandoned monistic idealism for atomistic realism.

4 Lotze and the Logicalization of Philosophy

Lotze held that "after centuries of philosophical work it is impossible to suggest new ideas" (Becher 1929: 51). That is why he saw his task as an examination of the old ideas in philosophy from new perspectives, which is also how he conceived his programmatic eclecticism. Thus, Lotze aimed to give a new meaning to some specific philosophical ideas introduced in philosophy after 1781—the year Kant's first *Critique* was published. In an original move, he essayed to recast these notions as problems of logic. In this way, Lotze continued the logical turn in metaphysics started by Kant, which eventually made metaphysics a formal science (Milkov 2013b).

Lotze's innovative method introduced—or at least revived—a number of seminal philosophical concepts which are still widely discussed today. Among the most consequential of them is the concept of value in logic—its most notorious successor was the concept of truth-value; the context principle; the objective content of judgment, a concept that was later developed by Brentano in the idea of radical distinction between subject and object of knowledge (Milkov 2018); the notion of state of affairs (*Sachverhalt*) (Chapter 8), a signal element in the philosophy of both Husserl and Wittgenstein; and the idea that perception features objective content: its most notorious successor was a concept that Russell would later transmogrify into that of sense-data (Milkov 2001b).

Lamentably, Cambridge analytic philosophers failed to adopt another pregnant idea propounded by Lotze (one that he actually borrowed by Schleiermacher and Trendelenburg). This was "the objective [scientific, or analytic] study of the earlier achievements in philosophy" (Stumpf 1910: 166), the detailed, minute study in history of philosophy (Chapter 2). The Cambridge program for many decades lacked a rigorous and comprehensive historical component. This situation began to charge only in the late 1960s, thanks above all to the influence of Michael Dummett's books on Frege's philosophy and logic (1973, 1981, 1991).

Many concepts today mainly associated with Frege's name were actually introduced, or revived, by Lotze. (Frege attended at least one of Lotze's lectures in Göttingen, on philosophy of religion and, as it is clear from "17 Key Sentences on Logic," he industriously explored Lotze's *Logic* [Sluga 1980: 45].) The special concerns of this present book, however, preclude an investigation of Lotze's influences on Frege (Gabriel 1984, 1989a, 1989b, 2002), a complex topic that calls for monograph study of its own. The focus in the sections ahead is on how Lotze's extensive logicalization of philosophy influenced three leading figures of the early Cambridge analytic philosophy: Russell, Moore, and Wittgenstein.

5 Lotze's Connectionism

Lotze's philosophy suggested a form of "connectionism"—connectionism not in the sense of the contemporary philosophy of mind but in the sense of the "general inner connection of all reality," of "the connection passing throughout all reality" (1879: §§ iii, iv). The ontological points of the universe—the substances (the things, the objects)—are nothing but the tying knots (*die Kraftpunkte*) of different systems of such connections. Lotze related them "to optical instruments which reflect . . . not convertible beams in a direction which they themselves cannot follow" (1841: 232).

The central concept in Lotze's connectionist ontology is *relation*. Lotze was convinced that it is the category of relation that unites all philosophical theories. Moreover, he embraced this thesis because he believed that "all who search for truth of any sort, believe in an order of things" (Kuntz 1971: 26).[7]

In the literature Lotze's connectionism was described in a variety of ways. P. G. Kuntz, for example, presented Lotze's metaphysics as a Theory of Order. To be more specific, Kuntz took Lotze to be interested not in formal order, but in concrete, "actual series, networks of series, causal regulations, analogies, and processes that are encountered, not merely thought" (1971: 29). Other authors insisted that Lotze's "philosophy is essentially an analysis of the concept of mechanism of the nature" (Höffding 1896, ii: 571); that is, of the concept of all-embracing causal connection, whereby the particulars of our experience are related to all other elements by way of lawful connection.

6 Lotze and Russell

6.1 Overview

That connectionism and Lotze-style relationism lies at the bottom of Russell's project for New Philosophy is clearly seen in Russell's *The Principles of Mathematics*. Indeed, a Lotzean subtitle "A Study of Order" could properly be applied to the title, given its focus on the order in space (Part VI) and the order in time (Part VII). The only leading theme of the work that was not explicitly discussed by Lotze is the order in mathematics. The reason for this is simple. While Lotze maintained that logic is setting up the foundations of mathematics (for him "mathematics develops as a branch of general logic," so that "the fundamental ideas and propositions of mathematics have their systematic place in logic" (1874: § 18)[8]), he was against the formalization of logic. Lotze saw in it an "addiction of thinking" which is attractive not because of the value of the scientific results themselves but because of the exactness of the results to which it leads (1843: 2).[9] For this position he was severely criticized early on by Russell in *An Essay in the Foundations of Geometry* (1897a: 96).

6.2 Lotze's general influence on Russell[10]

That Russell was much more neo-Lotzean than neo-Hegelian in the last years of the nineteenth century is clearly seen from the following facts:

1) The thinking of the philosophers who directly influenced Russell most in this period—Helmholtz, Stumpf, Erdmann—was significantly impacted by Lotze, not by Hegel. Moreover, Russell subscribed to many of the ideas of Lotze's ancestors Herbart and, ultimately, Kant.

2) Russell already embraced Bradley's anti-psychologism in his first printed review (1895).[11] We must remember, however, that the father of the criticism of psychologism was Lotze (Gabriel 1989b: ix),[12] not Bradley. Actually, Lotze's anti-psychologistic views were already mature by 1841–43 (in his "lesser" *Logic* and "lesser" *Metaphysics*), before Bradley was even born.

3) Russell embraced the relationism that, as we already have seen, was also central to T. H. Green and F. H. Bradley. In fact, Russell adopted the view of "space as relational and of spatial figures as relations" already in *An Essay in the Foundations of Geometry* (Russell 1897a: 96).

6.3 Russell's Supposed Disagreement with Lotze

It is true that Russell rejected certain of Lotze's core theses, as the two salient examples that follow illustrate. However, he did so without fully grasping the German philosopher's position.

1) Russell's most general disagreement with Lotze's concerned the latter's alleged doctrine that the points are factual—not absolute. As a consequence, Russell charged, Lotze did not accept autonomous relations but claimed that relations are functions of the points between which they stand. Russell contended that this view arose "from neglect to observe the eternal self-identity of all terms and logical concepts, which alone form the constituents of propositions" (1903: § 426).

    Lotze's actual position on this matter was not, however, as one-sided as Russell represented it to be. Ontologically, Lotze *did* assume that external relations have priority over the things they connect. As a result, he adopted a form of atomism, something recognized by many commentators who read Lotze as an atomist, for example, Harald Höffding (1896, ii: 574 ff.) and Anthony Manser. On Manser's reading, Lotze assumed that "what is complex in our mental life must be constructed out of simple atoms" (1984: 309).[13]

2) A second example that illustrates how Russell's criticism trades on an oversimplified representation of Lotze's thinking concerns the question: "Are there absolute points of space and moments of time?" Lotze claimed that the things are "at least participants in immutable independent being, and present the fixed points to which is attached, in whatever way, the varying course of events" (1856/64, iii: 466; 1885, ii: p. 579). Their independence as fixed points of the ontological discourse is at hand, however, only "up to the moment of their [of individual things] being again perceived by us. This being perceived is itself nothing but a new relation which is added to, or dissolves, the old ones" (ibid.: 467, 580).

All in all, it can be said that to Lotze the priority of things over the relations in which they enter is epistemological, while the priority of the relations over the things is ontological: "In order to think the existence of things [as different from perceiving them] one must grasp [them as independent]" (1856/64, iii: 471; 1885, ii: 584). However, this does not mean that they *are* independent. In this sense, Lotze observed that "the existence of everything presupposes the existence of some other to which it must be related" (ibid.: 472, 585). Things, to Lotze's way of thinking, are in the net of these potential relations, in a "vault [*Gewölbe*] of mutually related things," or nodes in a "tissue of orders."

6.4 Lotze's Dialectics

Lotze's position on the holism/atomism controversy may at first seem unclear, but only if one fails to understand his peculiar method he himself called "dialectical" (1841: 320).[14] This explains why, as Kuntz observed, "there are some passages [in Lotze's writings] in which he does seem conscious of the contradictions and [nevertheless] attempts to mediate between the two [positions]," not to eliminate one of them (1971: 34).

Some authors appreciate these traces of Hegel's dialectics in Lotze's writings. Eduard von Hartmann complains that "there are scarcely a 'yes' by Lotze, which is not sublated at another place by a 'no'" (1888: 147). Yet other philosophers, George Santayana was one of them, turned attention to the fact that despite the apparent contradictions, Lotze's system remained astonishingly consistent. How can this be?

The point is that Lotze did not replicate Hegel's dialectics *mot à mot*—he developed it further. Specifically, Lotze enriched it through the method of eclecticism (see § 1). In Lotze's hands, Hegel's dialectics is refined as a method of resolving philosophical dilemmas. To be more explicit, Lotze maintained that the conflicting philosophical conceptions often correspond to different philosophical perspectives. This is the key to grasping the seemingly contradictory aspects of Lotze's own philosophy. Thus, as Santayana discerned, the idealist monism of his system is rather "psychological, it is a personal manner of reading things, a poetic intuition of the cosmic life" (1889: 155). At the same time, Lotze subscribes to an atomism in science.

Especially intriguing—but also tricky—is the fact that Lotze often unfolded different faces of his apparently conflicting intuitions in the course of one and the same investigation. Thus he consciously commenced his ontological studies with pluralistic realism only to end them with monistic idealism.

The use of the dialectical method made Lotze—similarly to Wittgenstein later[15]—a "slippery fish." His position is characteristically difficult to state and also hard to criticize. For this reasons it is perhaps not surprising that Russell misinterpreted Lotze's theory of space.

7 Lotze and Moore

As already mentioned in Section 1, similarly to Russell, G. E. Moore knew Lotze's work very well. Hence, it does not come as a surprise that in many respects the philosophies of Lotze and Moore show affinity.

7.1 Relatedness of Philosophical Approaches

Moore's thought most resembles that of Lotze with respect to the following four features of the latter's approach in philosophy:

1) An abiding concern of Lotze's was to keep his systematic views consistent with common sense (*die gewöhnliche Meinung*). That this was the guiding principle of his philosophy is today scarcely recalled.
2) Lotze was convinced that "the logical reasoning is nothing but a critical elucidation, or working-up, of the ordinary course of presentations" (1843: 66).
3) Lotze's understood his approach as one that clears up language-usage and common sense, for example, of the word "is."
4) The very stance of Lotze's philosophy was down-to-earth realism, directed against any form of speculation.

Beyond issues of a general philosophical orientation, Lotze was also close to Moore with respect to some key particulars of theory, something quite evident, for example, in Moore's program in *Principia Ethica* for finding a logical solution to ethical problems.

Moreover, Moore would eventually, like Lotze, conceive his system of metaphysics to be based on data and their interconnections, albeit Lotze said nothing about the nature of the data themselves—for him they were "indefinables" (Höffding 1896, ii: 578) (Chapter 11). This term was extensively used by Moore, starting with *Principia Ethica*, where he accepted as indefinables good and bad (1903a: 5), and finishing with the introduction of the term sense-data in epistemology (Chapter 12).

7.2 Moore's Theory of Judgment

A more specific line of theoretical influence of Lotze on Moore[16] can be traced in Moore's Relational Theory of Judgment as advanced in the paper "On the Nature of Judgment," in which he introduced the following definition: "A proposition is a synthesis of concepts, together with a specific relation between them" (1899: 64).

Such formulations make it evident that Moore's Relational Theory of Judgment is little more than a paraphrase of Lotze's theory of a judgment's content as an interrelation of things or elements of facts (*sachliches Verhalten*). According to this conception, a judgment expresses a relation (*Verhältnis*) between the contents of two presentations; that is, a relation between two factual pieces of reality which are the content of the judgment. To understand a sentence is to understand a "factual relation of presented contents" (*sachliches Verhältnis der vorgestellten Inhalte*) (Chapter 8).

The theory grew out of Lotze's critique of substance/attribute metaphysics. In place of the latter, he spoke of "tying up [*Verknüpfung*] of the multiple until [receiving] the general" of the "substance" already in his "lesser" *Logic* (1843: 85). Later on, Lotze spoke of supplementing (*Ergänzung*)[17] the elements in a substance and of substances' assistance (*Förderung*) of the elements (1879: § 70).[18]

That Lotze embraced a relational theory of judgment is attested by his claim that the copula "connects the general and the particular in the concept only in so far as it keeps them apart" (1843: 86). He called their connection (*Verknüpfung*) "logical relation": it is a logical form. By contrast, the connection between substance and accident is a "metaphysical relation" (88) (Chapter 8).

Moore's Relational Theory of Judgment was later developed by Russell into a Multiple Relation Theory of Judgment.[19] After 1905, Russell effectively deconstructed his (of 1900–3) and the Moorean propositions completely, reducing them to their terms plus the interrelation between the terms. Russell's theory, nevertheless, preserved the relational character of judgments, which was the core of Moore's theory. According to Russell, the belief or judgment (J) is a relation between the subject (S), the form (F), and the objects of judgment or belief ($x_1, x_2, \ldots x_n$). He symbolized the relation of judgment or belief this way: J ($S, F, x_1, x_2, \ldots x_n$) (1913: 144). Of particular interest here is that Russell's symbol largely replicated Lotze's formula of composed "true wholes," $M = \varphi$ (A B R), where φ presents the kind of connection between its elements A, B, and R (R is the sum of all implicit elements of M). What Lotze's formula lacks is Russell's subject S.

8 Lotze and Wittgenstein

The influence of Lotze on Wittgenstein was rather indirect—it was exercised from above through his teacher Russell. An additional bridge to Lotze was possibly Samuel Alexander with whom Wittgenstein stayed in contact while in Manchester (1909–11), before moving on to Cambridge. Alexander's *Space, Time and Deity*, in particular, delivered as Gifford Lectures (1916–18), betrays a considerable Lotzean influence. Still another possible conduit of Lotzean influence on Wittgenstein was William James, whose *Varieties of Religious Experience* Wittgenstein is known to have read.[20]

Finally, and of utmost importance, is Lotze's influence on Wittgenstein via Frege. This took the form of Frege's bid to introduce the act of will in logic relative to the concept of asserting propositions (Chapter 5). Given that the present chapter restricts itself to Lotze's impact on early Cambridge analytic philosophy, the topic of Lotzean elements in Frege's thinking must be put off for another occasion. Having in mind this restriction, one can detect the shaping power of Lotze's thinking in Wittgenstein's work principally in terms of three philosophical themes.

8.1 States of Affairs and General Logical Form

The most salient legacy of Lotze's thought in Wittgenstein's early work is the latter's employment of the concept of "states of affairs" (*Sachverhalte*) as basic concept in logic and ontology. As we are going to show in Chapter 8, this concept was introduced in philosophy by Lotze. Wittgenstein in the *Tractatus* defines states of affairs as "a combination of objects" that "fit into one another like the links of a chain" (1922: 2.01, 2.03). Lotze defines them as "a concatenation of objects" (1879: § 117).

In the *Tractatus* Wittgenstein also claims that all the various combinations of basic forms of objects (which are indefinables [Chapter 11] and form the "substance of the world," 2.021) give rise to an infinite number of states of affairs. Further, elementary (atomic) states of affairs are concatenated in complex states of affairs, in the same way in which objects and forms of objects are concatenated in states of affairs. The concatenations in complex states of affairs are a kind of tying up of logical forms of individual states of affairs.

Wittgenstein's propositions, however, are a combination of forms. Among other things, the employment of the same principle of compositionality in states of affairs, propositions, and complex propositions explains the otherwise enigmatic claim in the *Tractatus* that there is just one logical constant (Milkov 2001: 404). There is no logical constant active *between* atomic propositions and another logical constant (or some other logical operator) active *in* atomic propositions. This one logical constant is employed in the one and only one general form of propositions which is "what all propositions by their very nature, had in common with all another" (5.47). The general logical form reads: "The things hang together soandso [*es verhält sich so und so*]"[21] (4.5) and denotes how things stand in relation to all other things.

It is astonishing how close this claim of Wittgenstein is to that of Lotze. Indeed, Lotze's first principle—"that the determination of every existing thing depends on its position in a multitude" (substance, whole, states of affairs)—was also founded on the "general logical form of composition of series" (Misch 1912: xxxii). Exactly like Wittgenstein in the *Tractatus*, Lotze assumed that there is one pattern of composition in both mind and matter.[22]

8.2 Panpsychism

Lotze maintained that "the law that makes the substantial unity of a thing is an individual law; it is conceived on the analogy of human character, or of aesthetic unity like melodies" (Santayana 1971: 183). This position makes it understandable why the elements of the states of affairs in Lotze's microcosmology "take care [*kümmern sich*]" of one another (1879: § 69); they have "fate [*Schicksale*]" and "sensitivity [*Reizbarkeit*]" (§ 70). These concepts are clear elements of the doctrine of panpsychism.[23]

A closer look at Wittgenstein's Tractarian microcosmology, according to which "I am my world (the microcosm)" (5.63) reveals that it contains a chain of assumptions, all of which clearly have panpsychic implications:

1) In 1916 Wittgenstein discussed the expression: "As I can infer my spirit (character, will) from my physiognomy, so I can infer the spirit (will) of each thing from its physiognomy"[24] (1979: 84). Similarly, he maintained that the facts have features "in the sense in which we speak of facial features." These are their prototypes (1922: 4.1221). Panpsychic elements are also to be discerned in language: "Every word has a different character in different contexts, [but] at the same time there is one character it always has: a single physiognomy. It looks at us" (1953: 81).
2) Furthermore, the later Wittgenstein held that every animal natural kind has its own physiognomy. Since animals, in opposition to things, are

active, the idiosyncrasy of their physiognomy finds expression in the idiosyncrasy of their life. Thus every animal natural kind has a peculiar form of life. There is a human form of life, a lion form of life, and so forth.

3) Viewed from a more abstract perspective, each *individual* of a specific animal natural kind has its own form of life. Consequently, since life and world are one (1922: 5.641), the inner content of such "primitive" form of life is a microcosm (the micro-world); its outer limit is a macrocosm (the macro-world). This position practically echoes Lotze's concept of microcosm (Milkov 2006, 2017b).

8.3 Logic, Ethics, and Aesthetics Have One Source

In the *Tractatus*, ethics, aesthetics, and logic have their roots in the experience *sub specie aeternitatis* in which we see the objects under scrutiny as limited wholes. In logic such a whole is the "perfectly" analyzed logical situation that finds expression in a correct (perfect) formula; in aesthetics the "perfect work of art"; in ethics the "good life" (Milkov 2004). These wholes are contemplated; they can be shown, not articulated. They are ineffable (Chapter 11).

The common source of ethics, aesthetic, and logic is the fact that they all advance products which have value. This conception of Lotze was further developed by the Southwest neo-Kantians, especially by Wilhelm Windelband, who was his closest student. Windelband set out, in contrast, that the knowing of the world do not occur *sub specie aeternitatis*. We have such knowledge only of things that have value, not merely an existence (1883: 343).

This is exactly what Wittgenstein discovered on October 7, 1916 (1979: 83). We see *sub specie aeternitatis* the work of art, the good life, and the perfect logical symbol.

7

Russell's Debt to Lotze

1 Russell: Hegelian or Lotzean?

Many of today's historians of analytic philosophy find the early philosophy of Moore and Russell to be much more Hegelian than previously believed. Thomas Baldwin, for example, speaks of "a Hegelian origin of analytic philosophy" (1991: 49). What is even more striking is that Russell himself, between 1894 and 1899, insisted that he was "a full-fledged Hegelian. . . . Wherever Kant and Hegel were in conflict, [he] sided with Hegel" (1959: 42).

We can explain this belief of Russell and his exegetes with reference to the fact that Russell's notion of Hegelianism was communicated to him mainly by his oldest friend and tutor in Cambridge, John McTaggart, and in particular, by McTaggart's first book, *Studies in Hegelian Dialectic*, which was published precisely when Russell took his first steps in articulating his own philosophy—in 1896.[1] In fact, however, McTaggart's study of Hegel was far from being truly Hegelian. Arguably, "no one has ever been convinced that the Hegel he described exists outside McTaggart's fertile imagination" (Passmore 1966: 76).

This observation substantiates the starting claim of the chapter, which is that the influence of Hegel on Russell was rather vague and general. We can trace it mainly through three elements of Russell's thought:

1) The project for a dialectical transition from one science to another and for an encyclopedia of sciences. The idea was that, when they are developed in isolation, sciences are incomplete and enmeshed in contradictions; this incompleteness can be overcome only through a dialectical transition to a broader science.
2) Russell's penchant for paradoxes that, among other things, helped him to discover the paradox of classes (Milkov 2003: 56).

3) Russell's main task as a philosopher was set out in Hegelian terms: he strove to solve some of the problems of Hegel's (bad) logic and mathematics—to put it aright with the help of ideas from Cantor and Weierstrass.

This, however, was a very loose form of Hegelianism indeed. It only set up the general direction of Russell's philosophy, its broad shape, not its content. The thesis of this chapter is that with respect to content, the influence of the Hermann Lotze was much more powerful. Briefly stated, Lotze gave Russell both the specific themes and problems of his philosophy, as well as theoretical means to deal with them.

One sees this borne out by the prominent role of Lotze's thinking in all three books of Russell's theoretical philosophy from the turn of the century: *An Essay on the Foundations of Geometry* (1897a), *A Critical Exposition of the Philosophy of Leibniz* (1900a), and *The Principles of Mathematics* (1903). In the *Essay*, in particular, a special section is dedicated to the analysis of Lotze's philosophy of space, which is more extensive and more developed than the sections dedicated to other philosophers and mathematicians. In *Leibniz*, Lotze, not Bradley, is the most frequently quoted nineteenth-century philosopher. Further, the only philosopher of the same century to whom Russell dedicates a whole chapter in the *Principles* was Lotze again: in chapter LI, Russell discussed Lotze's theory of space and substance.

2 The Main Characteristics of Lotze's Philosophy: Objectivism and Relationism

In order to grasp those elements of Lotze's philosophy which gave it the power to influence Russell, one must appreciate that Lotze was a key figure in the philosophy of the time. He influenced practically all the world-philosophies of the late nineteenth and early twentieth century: (i) the British idealists (Chapter 6: § 1); (ii) Husserl's Phenomenology (Hauser 2003); (iii) William James's Pragmatism (Kraushaar 1938/1939); (iv) Dilthey's philosophy of life (Orth 1984); and (v) the neo-Kantians (Gabriel 1989a: xii).[2] What was the reason for the phenomenal influence of his philosophy? In order to answer this question, we shall first briefly review some key stages in Lotze's intellectual development.

Lotze advanced the principles of his philosophy as a very young man. He published his "lesser" *Logic* and "lesser" *Metaphysics* in 1841 and 1843 at the age of twenty-four and twenty-six, respectively. Of special importance is that these two books were the third installment of an anti-Hegelian, objectivist movement in German-speaking Europe, which first began in 1837, when Bolzano issued his *Wissenschaftslehre*. Three years later, in 1840, Trendelenburg published his *Logische Untersuchungen* (Chapter 1: § 3). Later on, when a new surge of philosophical objectivism crested again in the 1870s, Lotze used the opportunity to restate his position in his "greater" *Logic* (1874) and his "greater" *Metaphysics* (1879).

Georg Misch articulated the objectivism of Lotze's philosophy this way (1912: xxv): closely following Trendelenburg, Lotze advanced a philosophy that did not start from the subject-object opposition. Trendelenburg abolished the dualism between subject and object in philosophy, referring to the concept of movement which is common to them both. Lotze went further: he suggested uniting the order between all objects and terms, which is the "universal inner connection of all reality" (1879: § iii). Especially important in Lotze's theory of order is the concept of relation. His often repeated ontological motto was: "It belongs to the notion and nature of *existence* to be related"; or "to exist" means "to be related" (1885: 587).[3] We can call this conception of his *relationism* (Chapter 6: § 3, (ii)).

Lotze's motive for accepting relationism as central to philosophy was his metaphysical—indeed, anthropological—belief that "all who search for truth of any sort, believe in an order of things" (Kuntz 1971: 26). To postulate the primacy of order and relations in ontology was to assume that nature is a cosmos, not chaos. Furthermore, since man thinks in series—indeed, thinking is an activity of relating,—he can be seen as a *microcosm*. This conclusion impedes Lotze to jointly study microcosm and macrocosm, a conviction which found expression in his three-volume book on *Microcosm* (1856/64, 1885; Milkov 2017b).

In general, the anthropological stance is central to Lotze's philosophy. Not in sense that he introduced anthropology into philosophy, though—in fact, anthropology was discussed long before Lotze. Lotze introduced the idea that the fundamental metaphysical and logical problems are to be discussed and answered in terms of human beings with their perceptual and rational characteristics (Milkov 2006: 50; 2010: § 2 (d)).

3 Lotze's Promotion of Philosophical Logic

Lotze's objectivist predisposition was coupled with another key feature of his as a philosopher: he was scientifically oriented. His credo was that no philosophical theory should contradict scientific results. This is hardly a surprise if we keep in mind that Lotze earned the *venia legendi* (a license to teach at German universities based on a second dissertation) both in philosophy and in medicine. In his medical writings, and above all in the programmatic *Allgemeine Pathologie* of 1842, he rejected vitalism—in any of its forms—more radically than anyone before him.

Lotze was not a lonely pioneer, however, in embracing the scientific orientation in German philosophy. In this he followed his teacher and friend G. T. Fechner (1801–1887). Already before these two philosophers, scientific philosophy had also been embraced by Hegel's contemporaries Jacob Friedrich Fries (1773–1843)[4] and Johann Friedrich Herbart (1776–1841).[5] What distinguished Lotze in this connection was the way he used to reconceive particular problems of the philosophy of German idealism, recasting them into a refined, science-friendly form.

To cut a long story short, Lotze's chief accomplishment on this score was to compress the problems of generations of philosophers—above all some anthropological problems of German idealism—into logically strict theses and theories. A typical example is his approach to studying thinking: Lotze married thinking to valuing (to value) and becoming; he taught that logic pursues the valuing, psychology pursues the becoming. This means that the same subject, thinking, in this case, can be investigated from two radically different sides. One can investigate its validity—this is what (philosophical) logic does—or one can investigate its development—this is done by psychology.

This new approach of Lotze's made ethics a rigorous discipline on the one hand, and enriched logic on the other; in other words, it made the old metaphysics an exact, formal discipline and logic more philosophical. One of the motives for embracing this method was Lotze's conviction that if we present different, often seemingly contradictory systems in a formal way, then their contradictoriness vanishes (Misch 1912: xxii). The point is that the formal presentation of philosophical theories eliminates their subjective side; and it is mainly subjective aspects that makes philosophical theories animus.[6]

The introduction of this approach to philosophy led to radical changes in philosophical practice. In particular, Lotze started to investigate philosophical problems bit by bit, piecemeal, so that a later discovery of a mistake in his investigation did not make his overall philosophy false.[7] Lotze's piecemeal philosophical method advanced a number of concepts and theories, some of which he introduced and some that he merely revived. Many of these ideas are still widely discussed today. Here are some of them: (i) the concept of value in logic (its best known successor was the concept of truth-value[8]); (ii) the context principle;[9] (iii) the idea of concept/judgment as a function;[10] (iv) the metaphoric of *coloring* expressions and of *saturated-unsaturated* expressions;[11] (v) the objective content of perception or the concept of the given (its best known successor was the concept of sense-data [Chapter 12]); (vi) the objective content of judgments (state of affairs) (Chapter 8).

In short, Lotze introduced a whole bundle of philosophical-logical problems and theses of philosophical logic that could be further investigated in isolation, independently of his system. On this score he instructed his readers to regard his philosophy as "an open market, where the reader may simply pass by the goods he does not want" (1874: 4). Among other things, this characteristic of Lotze's writings made him the most "pillaged" philosopher of the nineteenth century (Passmore 1966: 51). Many later philosophers adopted his ideas without referring to their origin in his philosophical work.

Russell, in particular, as we shall see, was a significant beneficiary of Lotze's original approach. While Russell adopted some discoveries of Lotze's philosophical logic, he rejected Lotze's overall philosophical system. Typical in this respect is the central role relations play in Russell's philosophy, as well as the objective content of judgments (propositions) (see § 7) and of sense perceptions (sense-data).

4 The Principle of Teleomechanism

In the previous section we discussed the general outlines of Lotze's influence on Russell's philosophy. The ensuing sections trace this influence in more concrete terms.

The first principle of Lotze's philosophy was that all processes and movements—physical, biological, psychological, bodily, social, ethical, cultural—are accomplished in a way that can best be described as mechanical. This assumption helped Lotze to eschew references to "deep" causes which were typical of Hegel's speculative philosophy. At the same time, however, Lotze insisted that this Principle of Mechanism is not the final solution in science—it is merely a notion employed for the purpose of better understanding of the processes of our environment. Moreover, since the Principle of Mechanism cannot solve all problems, it clearly indicates—even delineates—that "higher and essential being" that transcends its purview.

Lotze specified further that the Principle of Mechanism can be understood as the way in which purposes are realized in the world. However, it does not specify what these purposes really are. The Principle of Mechanism is simply a method of research; it is not an *explanation* of life and mind. Indeed, our ideas of forces and natural laws of science do not explain how things really work in nature. To understand this, we must connect them to the realm of the "highest," that is, to anthropology—to those elements of the living person's knowledge without which they cannot grasp the world (1886: 306).

It is precisely the realm of higher and essential being that brings us to a position from which to understand the processes in these mechanisms (305). Lotze himself called this conception, combined with the Principle of Mechanism, "teleomechanism." Briefly, the method of "teleomechanism," or of "teleological idealism," is to seek the truth in some teleological connection. At the same time, Lotze insisted that scientists should investigate elements of the highest being only when they reach problems of foundations.[12] Before this point, the mechanism is sine qua non for understanding the world and its construction (*der Weltbau*). There is no exception from this rule.

The principle of teleomechanism shapes the logic, metaphysics, and science through what Lotze calls *idealities*, which serve as concepts of orientation to us. Among them there are ethical values, logical validities, and aesthetic worth. In science and metaphysics a central role is played by the idealities of spatial and temporal order, the principle of atomicity and the aforementioned relationism. As we shall see presently (in § 8), Russell adopted the latter group of idealities from Lotze.

5 Lotze's First Impact on Russell (1896)

The first metaphysical (anthropological) concept that Russell embraced as central to his philosophy under Lotze's influence was that of spatial and temporal order. In the *Essay of the Foundations of Geometry*,[13] Russell explored it at length and found Lotze's discussion of space and time "excellent in many respects" (1897a: § 85).

Most fundamentally, Russell adopted Lotze's idea that in order for thinking to be possible at all, its objects must be complex:[14] they must consist of clearly different elements. Indeed, a simple thing, argued Russell, "is unthinkable, since every object of thought can only be thought by means of some complexity" (1896a: 564). That complexity can be achieved only when referring to individuals (terms), which are different from any other individual.

Russell finds differentiation to be a key element of perception itself. In perception, there must be "at least one 'principle of differentiation,' an element, that is, by which the things presented are distinguished as various" (1897a: § 128).[15] Russell called this element "a form of externality." His argument here was similar to his argument in defense of complex objects of thinking. The objects of perception must be complex since in order to perceive them, we must differentiate these parts; and in order to differentiate, and then relate them, they must be external one to another.

For human beings, forms of externality, space, and time are of paramount importance. These are forms of intuition which make our knowledge as such possible. They are given to us *a priori*, and so are most fundamental.[16] This was a central assumption of Russell's early philosophy, and it brought with it a considerable stress on the concepts of space and time in all periods of his philosophical development. The latter point was underlined by Paul Hager, who insisted that "space and time theories are absolutely central to Russell's philosophy" (1994: xii), so that when Russell revised his philosophy, this involved, as a rule, a change in his position on space and time.

Furthermore, Russell discriminated between empty space and spatial order. More specifically, he understood empty space as the possibility of the relations between and in spatial figures, which secures their form of externality (1897a: § 197). Because this space is a mere possibility, he accepted that it is absolutely empty; it is also conceptual and *a priori*.

The empty space is differentiated through matter. The unit of differentiation is the atom, which is part of the matter. The atoms are unextended in the sense that they have no spatial characteristics; they are points which are connected through spatial relations to other atoms. Straight lines, planes, and volumes are spatial relations between two, three, and four atoms, respectively.

Questions about "parts of space, or spatial figures, arise," says Russell, "only by reference to some differentiating matter, and thus belong rather to spatial order than to empty space" (§ 204). The spatial order of matter is different from empty space. Roughly, spatial order is an aggregate of spatial relations that are immediately presented to us.

Our suggestion is that this theory of space is evidence of the influence of (at least) two ideas of Lotze's on Russell. First of all, Russell's distinction between empty space and spatial order followed Lotze's discrimination between extension and place/moment, which appears already in his "lesser" *Metaphysics* (1841).[17] Second, and more specifically, Lotze claimed that extension refers to an infinite multiplicity of possible directions; only a place in space and a moment in time make these possibilities actual reality (Pester 1997: 110).

This conception of Lotze's was, in fact, motivated by his objectivism (§ 2): by his wish to preserve the objective character of space, in opposition to Kant's claim that space is a form of subjective intuition.[18] In particular, Lotze's argument was that if space is only our private form of intuition, to which there is no analogue in the objective world, as Kant claimed, then other beings may have other spaces; these spaces, however, can be never presented to us—not as spatial relations (1841: 232 ff.; 1888: 195 ff.). Lotze further claimed that space and its objective counterpart have the same multiplicity. This makes it possible to learn something from subjective intuition about "the manner in which what appears to us as space *must* appear to any beings with our laws of thought" (Russell 1897a: § 86).

Russell was impressed with this argument of Lotze's and adopted the view of empty space as conceptual precisely in order to preserve the objective character of our knowledge of space. Indeed, Kant's claim that space is intuitive leads to radical subjectivism about space.[19]

Another idea of Lotze's which Russell followed in the *Essay* was his atomism. In fact, Russell defended a Lotzean-style atomistic philosophy of science already when reviewing Hannequin (1896b). Lotze, incidentally, introduced this conception of atomism in his philosophy of space and time around 1840, when criticizing Jacob Fries's notion that matter is interplay of powers (2003: 85 ff.). According to Lotze,

1) Atoms are the ultimate building blocks of the universe: they are idiosyncratic and remain unmodified in all compositions in which they come. Lotze's atoms are thus different from the atoms of antiquity that were understood as last elements of reality which have different forms but the same substance (1856/64: 39; 1885: 34).
2) Atoms are "punctual" (*unräumlich*), without extensions. After all, extension is possible only where there are many points which can be easily identified and differentiated (1879: § 188 ff.; Milkov 2006: 35; 2017b: § 3.5).

Russell embraced both facets of Lotze's atomism.

6 Lotze's Second Impact on Russell (1897)

After Russell put his *Essay* into print in October 1896, he traveled for three months to the United States where he lectured at the Bryn Mawr and John Hopkins universities. Later he remembered: "Contact with academic Americans, especially mathematicians, led me to realize the superiority of Germany to England in almost all academic matters" (1967: 197). Back in Britain, he read (in German) Hegel's *Wissenschaft der Logik* for the first time (in March 1897) only to find that it radically deviated from his own standards of exactness. Looking for a new philosophical inspiration, Russell read Lotze's *Metaphysics* once again in May 1897.

The first fruit of this new reading of Lotze's was not late in coming; it found expression in the paper "Why Do We Regard Time, But Not Space, as Necessarily a Plenum?" (1897b) that Russell wrote in June 1897. Nicholas Griffin speaks of it as "in many ways an enigmatic little paper": its brevity belies its importance (1991: 331). The paper does not appear so enigmatic, however, if one reads it with the knowledge that Russell wrote it under Lotze's influence. This is clear, among other things, from the notes "Can We Make a Dialectical Transition from Punctual Matter to the Plenum?" (1897c), written immediately before the paper, in which Russell refers expressively and positively to Lotze.

In "Why Do We Regard Time, But Not Space, as Necessarily a Plenum?" Russell tried a new start in philosophy, laying more stress on the logical discussion of metaphysical problems and drawing up in this way a program that he was to realize in full only in the *Principles*. For the first time Russell distinguished between two concepts of space and time: (i) as consisting of relations; (ii) as adjectives to the absolute. Russell also insisted that, for logical reasons, space and time need to be treated in the same way: either as relational or as adjectival. In addition, he claimed that, if accepted, "an adjectival treatment of space and time would imply that both space and time were plena and that monism was true. On the other hand, a relational treatment would entail that space and time were punctual and that pluralism was true" (Griffin 1991: 328–9). In short, with this claim Russell assumed that "the question whether space and time are relational or adjectival will decide the issue of monism versus pluralism" (331). Finally, the paper also outlined the conception that relations are irreducible to properties, and this makes monism problematic; indeed, the very formulation of the question of relations or adjectives tacitly implies as much (Imaguire 2001: 69).

Characteristically, the paper offered no solution to the problems it raised. It did something more important though: it outlined the logical scheme in which Russell was to discuss the problems of space and time, monism and pluralism, for years to come.

7 Lotze's Third Impact on Russell (1898)

Early in 1898 Russell experienced an even stronger influence of Lotze than the first and the second time. A central claim of this chapter is that this influence was largely responsible for Russell's turn of 1898, when he, in his own words, abandoned British idealism and monism for (Platonic) realism and pluralism.

Here is the whole story delivered in some detail. In the Lent Term (January–February) 1898, Russell attended McTaggart's lectures on Lotze.[20] Russell's notes from these lectures survived, and are deposited at the Humanities Research Centre, University of Texas at Austin. Although McTaggart laid special stress on Lotze's metaphysics, the surviving twenty-four pages of notes (on lectures IV to XVI) present Lotze's philosophy in full: logic, metaphysics, psychology, philosophy of religion, motion and matter, atomism. The lectures gave Russell an opportunity to thoroughly acquaint himself with the overall system of Lotze's philosophy—also with its anthropological part.

The changes in Russell's thinking, caused by this third encounter with Lotze's ideas, can be easily discerned in the manuscript "An Analysis of Mathematical Reasoning," which he started to write on April 1, 1898. Most notably, in the paper's introduction, Russell adopted an idea which later became leading in the *Principles*: "Whatever can be a logical subject I call a *term*" (1903: § 47). Terms are all those things which can be counted (see § 8); they have a being. This idea became the cornerstone of Russell's new theory of propositions, which many authors consider the kernel of his philosophy (Imaguire 2001; Stevens 2005).[21] Lotze's influence on Russell traces to Lotze's assertion that judgments have an objective content—they relate things (*sie verhalten Sachen*) which differ one from another with necessity (Misch 1912: lviii) (Chapter 8).

An idea radically different from "being" is that of "existence," which is a predicate. If a term has this predicate, it is called an *existent*. The basic class of existents is composed of the various parts of space and time: places and moments. Being "forms of externality," places and moments are different from other existents, more specifically, from the things which are in them (Russell 1898: 171). This conception, in fact, was nothing but the theory of absolute space and time which was to characterize Russell's philosophy before he met Wittgenstein.[22] On this view, space and time are series of absolute moments and places; the real particular moments and places are *in* the absolute ones (Milkov 2005).

The decision to subscribe to the absolute theory of space and time was further evidence for the groundbreaking changes in Russell's philosophy in April–June 1898, immediately after he attended McTaggart's lectures on Lotze. More specifically, it shows Russell's new theory of judgment as theoretically underpinning his theory of space and time.[23] Indeed, the conception that judgment consists of substantially different elements served as a model for the conception that space and time consist of substantially different moments/places.

In brief, what was new in "An Analysis of Mathematical Reasoning" was the insistence that the terms are immutable and eternally self-identical, and that they are the constituents of judgments/propositions (Griffin 1991: 297 f.). In the preface to the *Principles* Russell called this position "pluralism which regards the world . . . as composed of an infinite number of mutually independent entities, with relations that are ultimate, and not reducible to adjectives of their terms or of the whole which these compose" (1903: xviii). The only thing that he did not elaborate there was the theory of relations (see § 8).

Immediately after Russell heard McTaggart's lectures on Lotze, in March 1898, he started to study Whitehead's *A Treatise on Universal Algebra* and in April, Dedekind's *Nature and Meaning of Numbers* (*Was sind und was sollen Zahlen?*). After that he ceased to believe that mathematics investigates quantities; instead, he adopted the view that it investigates "extensive magnitudes" and their structures.[24] This turn faced Russell with the task of laying "the philosophical foundations of a theory of manifolds" (Griffin 1991: 280) (Chapter 10). It should be clear, however, that the intensive examination of Lotze in January and February helped Russell most to change his position in the philosophy of mathematics. To be more specific, Russell did this with the help of his new theory of judgment, which was eventually transformed into a new theory of propositions.

We see, then, that in the first half of 1898 Russell underwent two turns. On the one hand, he abandoned the Kantian transcendental approach to mathematics and adopted the view that mathematics is reducible to logic. This shift commenced when Russell read Whitehead and Dedekind in March–April 1898 and ended in the beginning of July the same year, after his exchange of thoughts with Couturat and Poincare in an intensive correspondence (Milkov 2003: 49). On the other hand, with his theory of propositions and the method of analysis of propositions, Russell's philosophy took a turn to Platonic realism. It was in this respect that the influence of Lotze proved decisive. It is essential to stress that the second turn was supportive of the first one, in the sense that it philosophically underpinned the theory of manifolds (classes) which was central to the first turn.[25] How it did this will be discussed in the next section.

8 Russell Follows Lotze's Philosophical Logic

In Section 4 we saw that Russell followed Lotze in assuming that idealities are indispensable in philosophy. In this section we shall consider how two such idealities—individuals and series—first made their appearance in Russell's philosophy in the spring of 1898.

(i) *Individuals*. It is well known that in the *Principles*, as well as in *Principia Mathematica*, Russell advanced a program for a symbolic language which is governed by a "philosophical grammar." This language has logically simple names and a strict syntax. This program also entails an ontology, whereby "there are 'things' [individuals] which have properties and have, also, relations to other 'things'" (1959: 158). Things are not the sum of their properties.

Russell had, in fact, embraced these principles in chapter I of "An Analysis of Mathematical Reasoning," where he insisted that each term is identical with itself and different from all other terms. He called this kind of difference "difference of being" (1898: 168). "It is," notes Griffin, "the kind of difference that numeration depends upon, and it is in virtue of their difference of being that all terms can be counted" (1991: 280). Lotze, for his part, introduced an idea very close to Russell's "difference of being" already in *Mikrokosmus* (1856/64: 474).

This notion was arguably nothing less than a fundamental metaphysical (and anthropological) principle incorporated into Russell's logical symbolism. Russell adopted it only because he was convinced that it alone can explain how human knowledge functions. In other words, Russell's individuals, which gives orientation to his *calculus universalis*—Russell's counterpart of Lotze's mechanism—pertained to the Lotzean "highest and essential being."

(ii) *Series*. Russell held that the concept of individuals also helps to explain series;[26] this is important since series are the means by which we can best clarify mathematics, physics, and other sciences. Russell put special stress on the fact that the rejection of individuals, for example, in the form of rejection of the identity of indiscernibles, would make counting impossible.[27] Indeed, "if *a* and *b* have all their properties in common, you can never mention *a* without mentioning *b* or count *a* without at the same time counting *b*, not as a separate item but in the same act of counting" (1959: 115). Counting is only possible when the elements counted are different, and so they form a series. What is more, the rejection of the identity of indiscernibles would make measurement of magnitudes impossible. Indeed, for measurement to be possible at all, each unit-quantity must be different from all the others.

There are different kinds of series, such as numbers, points in space, moments in time, and causal series of events. Across such domains, Russell claimed that the construction of series—in space, time, colors, numbers—depends upon mutual incompatibility or a real difference in the constitutive elements (individuals). He thus insisted that the elements of the series must not only be related to one another but also differ from one another, and this in such a way that even indiscernibles should not be conceived as identical. Russell's final claim was— he made it explicitly only in "The Classification of Relations" (1899)—that this requirement can be only achieved if there is an asymmetric transitive relation between the individuals of every serial order.

9 Russell Misinterprets His Own Philosophical Development

Russell produced many documents that recount how his philosophy developed. Unfortunately, they were often misleading. We note one such misinterpretation at the beginning of this chapter. Russell always stressed that in the period from 1896 to 1898 he was a neo-Hegelian. The evidence, however, suggests otherwise. Furthermore, he reported that "towards the end of 1898" he and Moore rebelled against both idealism and monism. The latter claim is clearly false: "Russell," as Griffin rightly observes, "was always a pluralist" (1991: 306), also in the *Essay on the Foundations of Geometry*. Moreover, Russell's claim that in 1898 he rejected idealism is at least controversial: Russell's turn was from a transcendental idealism to Platonic realism which, strictly speaking, is idealistic too. As the analysis we made in Sections 7 and 8 make clear, there are sound reasons to rename Russell's 1898 turn a "turn towards a new theory of judgment/propositions."

In the present section we are going to see how misleading Russell's recollections are concerning when he exactly made his dramatic turn to a new theory of judgment/proposition, and also who impelled him to take it. Russell's answer was that (i) it happened in the second half of 1898 (ii) under Moore's influence.

First thing to note is that this claim contradicts what Moore himself wrote on this issue: he only spoke about "mutual influence" between Russell and himself (1942: 15) in elaborating closely related theories of judgment that were later developed in a joint theory of propositions.

But how did Russell and Moore come to their closely related positions? By way of answer, we shall point to the fact that Moore derived his realist theory of judgment from Franz Brentano and his acolytes (Bell 1999). This, however, is not the end of the story. Brentano's theory of judgment, in its turn, only remixed Lotze's realistic theory of judgment (Milkov 2018). This point was already underlined by Georg Misch: "Brentano agrees with Lotze in the crucial point that judgment—through the thinghood [*Sachlichkeit*]—refers to reality"[28] (1912: xvii). As we already have seen, Russell, for his part, borrowed his theory of judgment directly from Lotze.

Russell doubtless tells the truth when he reports experiencing a revelation in November 1898, when he first read Moore's "On the Nature of Judgment," in which Moore spelled out his relational theory of judgment. Russell only misinterpreted the reasons for this: he did not learn that theory from Moore, but rather saw in it his new theory of judgment from April–June 1898 expressed in a most clear and precise way.

This claim can be underpinned with two more facts previously cited in the literature:

1) There is "an unmistakable similarity of approach between the '[An] Analysis [of Mathematical Reasoning]' and these works of Moore ['The Nature of Judgment' and his second dissertation]. Yet Russell had written the 'Analysis' before he read Moore's Fellowship dissertation of 1898" (Griffin and Lewis 1990: 159)—Russell read it in November 1898. Moreover, "the theory of judgment in the 'Analysis' is very much more elaborate than that in either Moore's second dissertation or 'On the Nature of Judgment'" (160).

   Drawing the ineludible implication from these facts, Nicholas Griffin declares that Moore's two dissertations of 1897 and 1898, as well as his paper "On the Nature of Judgment," could not be the source of the changes in Russell's logic in April 1898 (1991: 298 f.). Unfortunately, Griffin did not investigate other possible sources—for example Lotze—which may have prompted the change of Russell's mind: despite the fact that Griffin was the first to note that "Russell had a Lotzean phase in 1897–8" (1991: 37 n.).

2) Russell met Moore in 1898 for discussion first on May 10, that is, when a good deal of "Analysis" was already written. Moreover, some published letters of Russell's make it clear that in these discussions it was Russell who brought ideas to Moore, not vice versa: "[Russell was] talking mainly to Moore, who seemed on the whole inclined to assent to what [he] had to say" (Griffin and Lewis 1990: 159). The same at their second discussion on June 18: "He [Moore] was not at all discouraging" to what Russell told him (160).

8

Lotze's Concept of State of Affairs

1 Hunting States of Affairs

Sachverhalt, usually translated as state of affairs (see § 7), is one of the few terms in philosophy which began to be widely used only in the twentieth century, mainly through the works of Edmund Husserl and Ludwig Wittgenstein. Husserl employed the term extensively in *Logical Investigations* (1900/1) (Mulligan 1989; Rosado Haddock 1991), as well as in *Formale und Transzendentale Logik* (1929), and Wittgenstein in *Tractatus logico-philosophicus* (1922). Determining who first introduced the concept as a philosophical term of art, and in exactly what sense, is consequently of considerable interest. Indeed, several attempts have been made to establish the term's philosophical provenance.

Perhaps the first "hunter" to try to trace down the term was Carl Stumpf. He suggested that the term "state of affairs" originated with Franz Brentano (1924: 240). Some two decades later Paul Linke set out that this was Carl Stumpf himself (1946: 46). As we just have seen, Stumpf himself knew nothing about this.

In recent years, the term's philosophical origin has been further investigated by Barry Smith. At first, he held that the concept appeared in Stumpf's lectures from 1888, "and its first appearance in philosophical print has been in 1900 in Husserl's *Logical Investigations*" (1978: 33; Mulligan 1985: 145). A dozen years later he claimed that the term was introduced by Julius Bergmann in his *Allgemeine Logik* published in 1879 (1990a: 128). Next Smith discovered that as a philosophical term, state of affairs was mentioned for the first time in Rudolf Hermann Lotze's *Logic* (1874) (1992a: 1104).[1] But he maintained that it became a central concept only in Bergmann's *Allgemeine Logik* (1879), meaning the objective element which corresponds to the judging intellect. By 1994, Smith was convinced that "the term is introduced by Stumpf to designate the immanent content of a judgement.... The earlier use of state of affairs by Lotze and the German logician Julius Bergmann did not, it seems, have any influence" (1994: 87 n.).

In what follows, we shall see that the term and the concept of "state of affairs" were introduced by Lotze in his *Logic* (1874) and by nobody else. It will become clear, as well, that Lotze used this term with a meaning which laid the foundations for its later use by Stumpf, Husserl, and also by Wittgenstein. While it is true that Stumpf, Alexius Meinong, Husserl, and other phenomenologists made use of the term to denote the specific ontology of judgments as opposed to facts, this modification was not essential to the authentic meaning of the concept of state of affairs as introduced by Lotze. For what is more, the phenomenologists' notion of state of affairs has a meaning logically reducible to that of Lotze's notion.

2 States of Affairs as the Objective Content of Judgments

But what was Lotze's concept of state of affairs? In order to answer this question, we should first track down its history in his thought.

From the very beginning of his career as a philosopher, Lotze's saw his task as that of Plato in the *Theaetetus*: to secure knowledge which is to be extracted, and separated, from perception. He maintained that the main characteristic of knowledge is that it is valid and so is true. This means that only knowledge presents the things as they really are—and, in fact, that is what is expected from thinking as a result. The difference between perception and knowledge (thinking) can be formulated this way: whereas knowledge asserts different ideas which belong together (*zusammengehören*), perception (as well as imagining, daydreaming, etc.) involves the adding of ideas to one another by accident: they *greaten zusammen*.

Let us put this point in other terms. The perceiving mind, asserts Lotze, presents "kaleidoscopically" a multiplicity of contingent pictures (*Bilder*) (1843: 72) (Milkov 1992). Only then comes thinking, which consists in going through the ideas which perception finds together for a second time, producing in this way *Nebengedanken*, or secondary thoughts. The latter connect only those ideas which they find belong together intrinsically, that is, which are intrinsically connected in reality. This is how knowledge comes about.

But how it can be that the judgment connects the ideas in the same way in which objects are connected in reality? In order to answer this question, we must bear in mind that Lotze's judgment does not denote an interrelation of ideas (*Vorstellungen*), but rather interrelation of things. So his state of affairs is nothing but the objective (*sachliche*) interrelations (*Verhalten*) of real things as presented in the judgment (Df.1). In turn, the minimal (atomic) objective interrelations of things are nothing but a possible content of judgments.

For Lotze, then, thinking consists of producing justifiable thoughts that are secondary thoughts. These are satellite thoughts that accompany the kaleidoscope of the stream of consciousness making part of it *knowledge*. Knowledge is nothing but presenting the things, as they are in reality, in our judgments.

3 The Formal Structure of States of Affairs

3.1 Substances: The Composition of the Ontological Glue

Trying to specify the nature of states of affairs in Lotze's philosophy, we must, above all, have in mind that for him the forms of logic and epistemology have only a secondary meaning which is dependent on the ontological forms.

According to Lotze's ontology, the world consists of relations and substances. The elements of a substance (or a whole) connect with one another in a reciprocal relation C, and in certain order (*Folge*) F, which excludes all other orders. The same is also the structure of the minimal composite unity, the state of affairs— and this is the second definition of state of affairs (Df.2). If we call the whole of the state of affairs (the substance) M, and its elements A, B, and R, we can denote the substance with the formula $M=\varphi(A\ B\ R)$, where φ stands for the connection between the elements, A and B are determinate elements, and R is the sum of all implicit elements (1879: § 70).[2]

The elements of the substance (the whole) effect themselves reciprocally. They are in a *reciproca tantum* relation to one another.[3] Lotze states in this connection that the elements of the whole mutually exercise one another *effectus transeunt*, which is the opposite to the *effectus immanens*. In other words, all the elements of the whole exercise on one another a kind of minimal effect.[4]

Here are some elucidations on this point. Lotze's terms in German here are *transeuntes Wirken* and *immanentes Wirken*. Now, *transeuntes Wirken* is usually translated (see Lotze 1885) as "transeuter action." In his critique of Lotze in *The Principles of Mathematics* Russell calls *effectus immanens* and *effectus transeunt* "immediate" and "mediate action" (1903: 452). Yet, "action" in German is *Handlung*. And what Lotze has in mind here is neither *Handlung* nor *Verursachung* (causing), but rather effecting, which, however, does not lead to physical changes in the objects of the substance but to some kind of minimal internal changes which, nevertheless, are essential for the substance. Most importantly, they produce the "ontological glue" (Armstrong 1978, i: 113–16;

Vallicella 2000; Priest 2014) that keeps the elements of the states of affairs together in it. In short, *effectus transeunt* (or "action in passing," "cursorily action") is the minimal effect A exercises on B in the substance M, and B on A, thanks to which they stay in M. Through it, the isolated, autonomous elements of the substance became interdependent.

3.2 Relations: States of Affairs as Particular Case of States-of

The main idea of Lotze's ontology is that there are different systems of relations in the world, every one of which gives rise to what may be called different "states of something."[5] The systems of relations in the world are of miscellaneous kinds, every one of which has its specific coordinates. Here are two of them:

- the system of geometrical relations;
- the system of colors.

These two nets of relations are necessary to the world of the real, but not to the world of art, or to the spiritual world of men, or to other forms of life (to the lion's form of life, etc.). Of course, there are also other kinds of relation-nets (1856/64, iii: 461–2; 1885, ii: 575). From the perspective of the cognizing subject, Lotze singles out two in particular:

- that of perception; this net is the universe of what he calls "local signs" (*Localzeichen*);
- that of judgments and concepts; this net is the universe of interrelations of objective things (*sachliche Verhalten*).

Lotze conceived states of affairs (*Sachverhalte*) to be only one element in a particular nexus of relations—that of judgments and concepts (Df.3).

Moreover, the *sachliche Verhalten* themselves take different forms. There are:

1) relations of extension (*Raumverhältnisse*; 1879: §§ 114, 132);
2) relations of places—Lotze often speaks of *Lagenverhältnisse* (§ 77);
3) of relations of weight; and
4) *Wunschverhalt* can be added to them (Mulligan 1985: 145).

4 Non-structural Characteristics of Lotze's States of Affairs

Besides their extensional characteristics, Lotze's states of affairs manifest three typical intensional (non-structural) traits: judgments as examining their contents, judgments as posting the truth of their content, and judgments as counterparts of values.

4.1 Judgment as Examining Its Content

Lotze's "secondary thoughts," to turn now back to them, are nothing but taking "a critical stand towards a combination of ideas" (Df.4). This is how Julius Bergmann understood them in his *Allgemeine Logik*. The same view informs the thinking of Lotze's pupil Wilhelm Windelband, who stressed that the secondary thought "is not merely an expression of a relation of presentations, but rather a critical attitude of the consciousness to such [a relation]" (1884: 170).

Some German authors have noted that this idea is nothing but a modified form of Hegel's method of dialectical self-development (*Selbstentwicklung*) of the truth (Misch 1912: xxvii). Perhaps it would be more correct to say that Lotze's secondary thoughts are incorporation into logic of the old idea of Plato-Aristotle of peirastic (examining) of the subject, the proposition, or the fact under scrutiny (Milkov 2013b: § 1).

To be sure, the kernel of Lotze's method of examining lies in the conviction that we somehow grasp, in a vague form, what we intend to find in our analysis.[6] More precisely, Lotze finds an "inner regularity of the content sought-after, [that] being unknown yet, is not open to us in specific realistic definitions of thought. However, being present in the form of opinion, it really has . . . the defensive force to negotiate what is not suitable to her" (1841: 33). Thanks to this ability, we can assert, in our secondary thoughts, that the connection of ideas that lie before us in our perception is either true or false.

4.2 Two Other Intensional Characteristics of Lotze's States of Affairs

Lotze's concept of content of judgment (*Urteilsinhalt*) has two other dimensions which have nothing to do with their structural characteristics.

1) Lotze identified state of affairs with affirmation of judgments. He held that the being of judgment consists in its affirmation (*Bejahung*), or positing (*Setzung*) (Df.5). This conception was connected with a variant of the context principle: "The affirmation of a single notion has no meaning which we can specify; we can affirm nothing but a judgment in which the content of one notion is brought into relation with that of another" (1856/64, iii: 469; 1885 ii: 582). Later, this point was articulated

by Frege so: the judgment acknowledges the truth of its content; only this acknowledgment makes the combination of ideas a judgment. In other words, the judgment is an acceptance, or assumption of a content as true, or rejecting it as false (1976: 127).

2) In addition, the content of judgment also stands, correlatively, as the counterpart of the concept of *value* (Df.6)—this is another term that introduced in logic. More specifically, he held that whereas the idea (*Vorstellung*) happens, the content of judgment is valid (1874: § 316). Concepts have meaning (*Bedeutung*), but not value. They acquire a value only through the proposition in which they occur (§ 321).

The conception that judgment has value was also embraced by Frege. In contrast to Lotze, however, and also to Wittgenstein, this logician threw aside the extensional understanding that the content of the atomic judgments are also combinations (*Verkettungen*) of objects. This explains why Frege never made use of the concept of states of affairs.

Following Herbart, and developing further the idea of content of judgment, Lotze also explored the idea of the *given* (*Gegebene*) in philosophy, understood as an "experienced content of perception," as distinguished from the content of judgment. The given *is*; it is opposed to both what *happens* (e.g., changes) and the *validities* (propositions, judgments). The transition between these three is impossible. Lotze thus made a radical distinction between *genesis* and *being*; between *happen* and *is*. In this way he set out a philosophical approach that was further explored by Frege and Wittgenstein (Chapter 15: § 2).

5 Two Critics of Lotze's Judgment

5.1 States of Affairs as Objective Content of Judgment

Lotze's judgments, as we have seen, secure knowledge and so build upon the world of perception, rendering it epistemologically articulate. Some of the commentators on Lotze, however, unwarrantably neglect this point. Barry Smith, for example, asserts that Lotze stuck to the old "combinatory theory" of ideas.

But this theory was explicitly rejected by Lotze, who wrote in his "lesser" *Logic*: "Already Kant has noticed that judgment is a such only when its segments pertain together, thanks to the necessary unity of apperception by the synthesis of multiplicity" (1843: 87). From the time of Johann Friedrich Herbart and

Adolf Trendelenburg, this was a standard argument in antinaturalistic theories of knowledge. This criticism was also taken up by Christoph Sigwart and Wilhelm Wundt, among others. In the words of Hans Sluga, all of them "accuse empiricism of a genetic fallacy, of trying to substitute a historical account of the origin of some belief for a reasoned justification or proof of it" (1980: 55 f.).

The difference between ideas that "meet at random" (*zusammengeraten*) in our mind and ideas that intrinsically "belong together," or "tie together" (*Zusammenknüpfen*), is so radical in Lotze that it is difficult to understand why a commentator such as Smith fails to take account of it. Such an egregious lapse becomes less of a mystery, perhaps, if we consider the views of another philosopher who somewhat like Smith tries to prove that Lotze was not the man who invented the "logic of knowledge"—Michael Dummett. To be sure, in a sense, Smith and Dummett try to demonstrate the same thing, namely, that philosophers, whose early formation was significantly influenced by Lotze, developed their own doctrines from scratch. Barry Smith was anxious to demonstrate this in regard to Brentano and his pupils, and Michael Dummett in regard to Frege. Indeed, Dummett is convinced that Lotze failed "to make any distinction between what occurs in a stream of consciousness and what occurs in thinking" (1991: 71). Hence, Lotze, allegedly, did not realize that thoughts are neither ideas nor combinations of ideas.

Nothing can be further away from the truth. Lotze introduced the term "state of affairs" in his second ("greater") *Logic* (1874) expressly to denote the objective content of thought. He thought that a judgment expresses a relation (*Verhältnis*) between the content of two presentations; that is, a relation between two objective parts of reality. To understand a sentence is to understand an "objective relation of presented content" (*sachliche Verhältnis der vorgestellten Inhalte*). The content of Lotze's judgment would thus appear to be at least as objective as the Fregean thoughts.

Perhaps Dummett is misled by addressing this point of Lotze on the basis of Bernard Bosanquet's translation in the English edition of *Logic* (1874) of Lotze's *Nebengedanke* as "auxiliary notion," which Dummett ameliorates to "auxiliary thought." In truth, *Nebengedanke* are not thoughts which are "auxiliary," that is, helping the ideas. Rather, they are "second wave" judgments which check whether the first conform to reality. They are "secondary thoughts" which convert *ideas* into *knowledge*.

Dummett insists that in the first of Frege's "Seventeen Key Sentences on Logic"—"The connections [of ideas] which constitute the essence of thinking are of a different order from associations of ideas" (1979: 174)—Frege tries to correct Lotze on this point (1981: 523). In truth, here Frege merely echoes Lotze. Apparently, this interpretation of Dummett is again due to incorrect translation: this time of *Zusammenknüpfen* of ideas into "combination of ideas." The German term, however, means "tying ideas up."

All this can be supported by the fact that to Lotze ideas which are only connected together—not tied up together—pertain to the "psychological *Tatbestand* [fact]" and so are radically different from the objective states of affairs. Indeed, for him there was an egregious error to use psychological concepts in logic. From the very beginning, Lotze exercised a "logical critique over the psychological" (1843: 85). Later on he used to say: "Psychology cannot be a foundation of metaphysics, but the latter can be only a foundation of the former" (1879, § ix).

Significantly, what Barry Smith and Michael Dummett failed to see—that it was Lotze who introduced to the philosophical logic the notion of the objective content of judgment in logic—was a commonplace among German philosophers of the 1910s. For instance, Bruno Bauch—a professor in Jena at the beginning of the twentieth century, who also taught Rudolf Carnap there, insisted that it was Lotze who introduced the concept of objective (*sachliche*) "content" in logic (1918: 48).[7] Another philosopher from this period well acquainted with Lotze was Georg Misch. He too held the belief that Brentano followed Lotze in accepting that the judgment refers—through the objects (*Sachlichkeit*)—to reality (1912: xvii) (Milkov 2018).

5.2 The Consequence of Smith's Misunderstanding: His Theory of Truth-makers

Barry Smith mistakenly assumes that the term "state of affairs" was not introduced by Lotze, neither even by Julius Bergmann, but by the phenomenologists Stumpf, Meinong, Husserl who some hundred years ago tried to substantiate a specific ontology of judgments as different from that of the facts. One can trace Smith's error to the view of the phenomenologists who held that to different entities correspond different judgments upon one and the same fact; precisely and exclusively these entities are to be called states of affairs (Df.7). Some authors hold further that states of affairs thus understood are nothing but the verifiers—the "truth-makers"—of the judgments (Mulligan, Simons, Smith 1984; Armstrong 1997: 115 ff.). This conception found a clear formulation in some works of Husserl's student Adolf Reinach. Now, Smith is among those who revived and adopted Reinach's theory, and it is arguably this motive that sets him against Lotze's theory of judgment.

In contrast to Reinach and Smith, Lotze's actual conception of state of affairs does not require one to accept a special ontology of judgment as different in kind from the ontology of facts. Lotze concedes that the same factual material can be apprehended differently, so that different judgments can be made about one and the same fact. Thus, for example, the following three judgments are based on one and the same fact: "this rose is red," "redness inheres in this rose," and "this rose forms the substrate of this redness."[8] The ontology of these judgments is not different from the ontology of the fact about which they are made. This is so since (i) the possibility to compose different ensembles (complexes, states of affairs)[9] lies within the individuals of the factual material themselves, and (ii) in the judgments, on the one hand, and in the factual material, on the other hand, *one and the same* set of individuals (objects) are concatenated with one another but in different *arrangements* (relations, *Verhältnisse*).

The gist of our argument against the theory of Reinach and Smith is that the very possibility of different ontologies of the judgments are already contained in the factual material that grounds the judgments. This material can also be seen as a complex state of affairs, which contains in itself the ontology of the all possible atomic states of affairs (the ontology of judgments) that can be built on its bases. This means that it is theoretically otiose to accept two types of states of affairs—complex and simple—as different entities.

Since the elements of the judgment reciprocally relate to one another into the whole (the complex state of affairs), the whole is different in every particular case. The same factual material merely appears in different judgments differently. The underlying ontology is, however, unitary. It consists of the elements of the complex state of affairs—individuals and atomic states of affairs—which already possess in themselves the possibility to relate reciprocally this or that way: that is, to make up this or that complex state of affairs. The Lotzean provenance of this account is patent in his explicit claim that "the existence of everything [individual] presupposes the existence of some other [thing] to which [it] must be related"[10] (1856/64, iii: 471; 1885, ii: 584).

6 Lotze Abandons the Term *State of Affairs*: Inscrutability of Logical Forms

A difficulty in investigating Lotze's concept of state of affairs is that after its introduction in the *Logic* (1874) he used it only once—in his *Metaphysics* (1879). In *Logic*, he employed the term only twice: in § 138 and in § 327. In another two places of the book, § 36 and § 345, it is spoken about *"sachliches Verhalten"* (objects' relation) that is content of judgments. In *Metaphysics* he spoke of *"sachliches Verhalten"* in §§ 75, 181, and of *"Verhältnisse der Dinge"* (relations of things) in §§ 101, 131. Why this sparse use of the term?

The likely answer to this question is that Lotze productively used the method of eclecticism (Chapter 6: § 2). Following the methodology of eclecticism, he adopted a policy "to use the [old] terminology of different systems, after we gave to their foundations a common meaning" (1843: 25). New terms are rarely introduced in philosophy. The only justification for doing so could be the discovery of totally new concept. Now, for reasons indicated earlier, Lotze was convinced that he had lightened upon a concept which warranted a new name—"state of affairs"—only in his "greater" *Logic* and "greater" *Metaphysics*.

Soon, however, he realized that the "reciprocal relation" (*Verhältnis*) between the elements of the content of a judgment can be only defined negatively; we cannot articulate anything positive about what keeps the contents together: this species of relation is ineffable. The problem is that the composition of the whole has no multiplicity (1879: § 73). Consequently, this relation cannot be put into words; we can only grasp it via intuition. The "mutual reciprocity" of the elements in space, time, and in a causal relation is, in Lotze's view, inscrutable.

This account makes any attempt to express what is meant, for example, by "copula" doomed to failure. "Since, what in fact we want to say when we put together two content of presentation [*Vorstellungsinhalte*] S and P as subject and predicate . . . cannot be expressed or constructed [intuitively]" (§ 75). We can never express the *way* in which the *Verhältnisse* adhere (*"haften"*[11]) to individuals. At all events, the copula is not properly understood when one construes it as the "bald copula" of the logical schemata used widely in the textbooks on formal logic. In fact, the relation of copula is different every time.

Following these considerations, after briefly mentioning it in 1874 and in 1879, Lotze stopped using the term *state of affairs* altogether. In *Grundzüge der Logik* (1883: 115) he put the expression *"Verhältnis"* in quotation marks—indeed, it neither refers to things, nor to properties, nor to events.

It is well known that the problem of logical inscrutability has a central place in Wittgenstein's logic (Chapter 11). The latter assumed that "a proposition *shows* its sense" (1922: 4.022; italics added); but its sense cannot be expressed. It is also common knowledge among philosophers today that on this point Wittgenstein followed Frege. In the literature it was justly noticed that "the Frege–Wittgenstein notion of what comes on out but cannot be asserted is almost irresistible, in spite of its paradoxical nature, when we reflect upon logic" (Geach 1976: 56). What went unnoticed, however, is that it was Lotze who realized this principle much before them—and never abandoned it.[12]

7 How to Translate *Sachverhalte* in English?

Philosophers betray a lack of consistency when it comes to translating the German term *Sachverhalt* into English. Thus in *The Principles of Mathematics* (1903: § 429) Russell translates Lotze's *Sachverhalte* as "states of things." In Ogden's translation of Wittgenstein's *Tractatus logico-philosophicus* (1922)—approved by the author himself—*Sachverhalte* is rendered as "atomic facts" and *Sachlage* as "states of affairs." In the translation of the *Tractatus* of McGuinness and Pears (Wittgenstein 1961) *Sachverhalte* is rendered as "states of affairs" and *Sachlagen* as "situations." At the only place where Wittgenstein suggested a definition of states of affairs (2.01), McGuinness and Pears opt for a second translation "states of things." Conversely, in 1979 Elisabeth Anscombe translates Wittgenstein's *Sachverhalte* as "situations" and *Sachlage* as "states of affairs" (Wittgenstein 1979). Perhaps we can better understand how to translate Wittgenstein's, and also Husserl's *Sachverhalte*, into English if we review the context in which the term was introduced by Lotze.

Lotze understood the "things" (*Sachen*) as something alive,[13] as having sensitivity (as receptive), as subject of influence. This explains why George Santayana translated Lotze's *Verhältnisse*—an element of the states of affairs— with "behavior" (Santayana 1971: 182). These *Verhältnisse*—the way in which the things "hang together" with other things—are the result of "immediate inner interaction that the things ceaselessly interchange" (Lotze 1879: § 82). Indeed, as already seen in § 3.1 above, the things in a state of affairs mutually exercise a transient, minimal effect; they stay in *reciproca tantum* relation all the time. The concept *state of affairs* denotes precisely that "relation and behavior" (*Verhalten und Benehmen*) (1856/64, iii: 465; 1885, ii: 578) which things exhibit in certain situations in the whole that they constitute.

The literal translation of Lotze's "state of affairs" is a *minimal intercourse-of-things*, or, even better, a *minimal reciprocal relation of things*, or contents. Above all, it shows that this concept denotes an elementary judgment in which two simple contents are tied up together. Unfortunately, the phrase "a minimal reciprocal relation of things" is so convoluted and unwieldy to serve as a term of art in technical discourse.

Be this as it may, it is certain that *Sachverhalt* does not mean *status rerum*, as some authors have suggested (Smith 1992: 1002–4). Indeed, the term *status rerum* is translated in German as *Tatbestand* (fact) and, as already remarked, *Tatbestand* is a concept that has no place in Lotze's logic but figures rather in his psychology. That *Sachverhalt* does not mean *status rerum* is also clear from Lotze's insistence that things have content, state (*Zustand*), quality, and nature (1856/64, iii: 479; 1885, ii: 592). Thus *status* (state, *Zustand*) is not something pertaining to the whole (the substance, the *Sachverhalt*), but to the individual. This is plain when considering individuals such as institutions, persons, and other entities that characteristically have a *status*. By contrast, the substance has form, *Verhältnis*, and order (1856/64, iii: 493; 1885, ii: 606).[14]

Another fact substantiating that Lotze's *Sachverhalte* are neither *status rerum* nor situations is that he differentiates between *Relationen*, *Beziehungen*, and *Verhältnisse*. Whereas Lotzean *Relationen* are formally logical, *Beziehungen* are ontological and epistemological, while *Verhältnisse* are panpsychical.

The foregoing observations make evident at least three reasons why Ogden's translation of the Tractarian *Sachverhalte* as *atomic facts* is more appropriate than McGuinness's and Pears's translation *states of affairs* (Nelson 1999). First of all, atomic fact is exactly that minimal objective element that serves as the content of the elementary judgment. Secondly, there is no intrinsic difference, as we saw in Section 5.2, between facts (factual material) and contents of judgments. So there is no reason to introduce a new term for denoting the latter. And finally, the term "states of affairs" scarcely communicates, as does the German term *Sachverhalt*, the element of mutual interrelatedness of the objects of judgment's content.

Part Four

Edmund Husserl

Edmund Husserl and Bertrand Russell, 1905–1918

1 Introduction

1.1 Why Husserl and Russell

Historians of philosophy usually define phenomenology as a theory of intentionality and Husserl as a theorist of meaning. This explains why when students of phenomenology compare Husserl with analytic philosophers at all (indeed, for decades Husserl was considered antipodal to analytic philosophy) they usually turn to Frege. Typically, their comparative studies tend to concentrate on parallels between Frege's famed differentiation of "sense" from "meaning" and Husserl's distinction between *noema* from "object." One can trace an extended series of such studies beginning with Dagfinn Føllesdal and continuing through works of J. N. Mohanty, Michael Dummett, and others.

To be sure, this approach is not without its theoretical and historical value. However, we should not forget that "Husserl repeatedly states loud and clear that what he is trying to do is to find the basis of our conceptual world in *immediate experience*" (Hintikka 1995: 82), while Frege is anything but a philosopher of immediate experience. That was what the Cambridge philosophers G. E. Moore and especially Bertrand Russell were. It is this fact that motivates the venture here to examine the largely overlooked, yet historically and philosophically significant, relatedness of Husserl and Russell.

One reason why this topic has received little attention is that historians of phenomenology and of early analytic philosophy by and large still lack substantive knowledge of the theoretical stance of their counterparts. This is particularly true in the case of phenomenologists, who generally persist in the view that (i) Russell was nothing but a radical reductionist, and that (ii) his sense-data are nothing but Hume's impressions. Section 2.1, demonstrates (i) to be a fallacious judgment. As regards (ii), the reader may consult Milkov (2001b), which establishes that Russell's sense-data feature logical elements, something we cannot say about Hume's impressions.

On the other hand, while over the last few years analytic philosophers have undertaken a number of comparative studies of their philosophical tradition and phenomenology (Beaney 2008a; Overgaard 2011), many still tend to believe that even Husserl's *Logical Investigations* (1900/1) is a work of continental philosophy.

1.2 Why Husserl and Russell from 1905 to 1918?

Perhaps the most immediate challenge one faces in undertaking a philosophically substantive and historically consequential comparative analysis of Russell's and Husserl's philosophy is the protean character of their thinking as it evolved over the course of their respective careers. Hence one needs first to specify which Russell one intends to compare to which Husserl. As for Russell, one cannot at any rate look at the period of his *Principles of Mathematics* (1903). In that work he tentatively started to assimilate the logic of Peano and Frege, in particular, their technique of quantification. The important innovation of Russell's 1903 program was that it gave birth to a specific theory of logical forms as a part of exploring philosophy of language. To be more precise, this theory held that denoting phrases cannot be decomposed in the same way in which complexes are decomposed to their simples. The problem is that the meaning of the concepts in a denoting phrase depends on the way—the form—in which the denoting phrase is built up. In other words, the concepts in it do not have meaning in isolation. Russell concluded that there must be something beyond the concepts that unites them in the denoting phrase and this something is their logical form.

Only with the introduction of his Theory of Descriptions in 1905, however, did Russell clearly realize that the logical form of the propositions is quite different from their apparent form. It was along these lines that he elaborated a consistent program for the logical analysis of language, the task of which is to reveal the true logical form of its propositions.

Russell's joint work with Wittgenstein in 1912 (Milkov 2013) stimulated Russell further to spell out the role of logical forms in his philosophy.[1] Most notably, he introduced them also in the realm of epistemology (§ 3.1). What became his new philosophical program was most persuasively set forth in *Theory of Knowledge* (1913), *Our Knowledge of the External World* (1914) and in some papers written in 1913–14 but published only later, in *Mysticism and Logic* (1918).

Lamentably, Wittgenstein's criticism of Russell's *Theory of Knowledge* in May and June 1913 brought this important period of Russell's philosophical development to an end. In the lectures "The Philosophy of Logical Atomism" (spring of 1918) he simply summarized his philosophy of 1911–14 but failed to develop it further. Attempting a new start, in "On Propositions" (1919), Russell embraced the philosophy of neutral monism. This was the beginning of a new phase in his philosophical thinking, one more naturalistic and closely tied to the achievements of science.

By the same token, the years 1905–18 saw major developments in Husserl's phenomenology. To make a long story short, the period marks Husserl's turn to so-called "transcendental phenomenology." Starting with discussions with his pupils Johannes Daubert and Alexander Pfänder that produced Husserl's "Seefeld manuscripts" (1905) and through his lectures titled *The Idea of Phenomenology* (1907) Husserl advanced phenomenology as a "transcendental philosophy" whose task is to reveal the fundamental structure of consciousness. This project he initially presented in "Philosophy as Rigorous Science" (1911) and subsequently gave it its classic form in *Ideas I* (1913), where he formulated the conception of eidetic reduction and introduced the concepts of *noema* and *noesis*.

The new turn in Husserl's phenomenology meant that he systematically wrote out of his philosophy any form of naturalism, psychologism, or empiricism. Indeed, before the transcendental turn of 1905 Husserl simply attempted phenomenologically to explore the substantiation (the grounding) of logic and mathematics in consciousness. Transcendental phenomenology, in contrast, explores the structure of the pure Ego (*Ich*).

After 1918, however, Husserl's phenomenology developed along new lines. The leading concern shifted to elaborating the so-called "genetic transcendental phenomenology," which marked a break with the "static phenomenology" of 1905–1918.[2] To update the reader, the task of the genetic phenomenology is to investigate the development of the "Ego," analyzing its genealogy. The Ego thus proves to be something constructed over time, as a series of succeeding formed layers. In contrast, static phenomenology considers the unchanging "Ego" as given—as a pole from which the lines of intention start. So, whereas static phenomenology was descriptive (describing the structure of the "Ego"), genetic phenomenology was explanatory, in the sense that it undertook to make clear how the present structure of the "Ego" is constituted.

1.3 Summing Up the Tasks of This Chapter

It should be clear that this chapter pursues a path of inquiry that breaks with the trends of mainstream research in the area. Historians of philosophy currently tend to argue that if Husserl was in any sense an analytic philosopher, or did work related to analytic philosophy, one will find evidence of this in his *Logical Investigations* (1900/1). The generally accepted account is that Husserl strayed from the path that would have made him a player in the ascendancy of analytic philosophy, this by befriending the "wrong philosophers," among them Wilhelm Dilthey, under whose influence Husserl apparently took his "transcendental turn" in 1905. The result according to the received view was that with this turn Husserl became a kind of continental philosopher (Mulligan 1991; Sandmeyer 2008).

The story that follows in this chapter is different. We shall see that Husserl's turn of 1905 made him closer than he had previously been to Bertrand Russell's philosophy. The evidence that substantiates this conclusion emerges in the pages ahead as we explore some striking similarities between Husserl in his middle period and Russell in his. Specifically, we shall consider two orders of relatedness that obtained between Husserl and Russell in the years from 1905 to 1918: (i) One, which we take up in Section 2, has to do with the general striving of the two philosophers to fix the "fundamentals" of philosophy (Chapter 16: § 3). (ii) The other, our focus in Section 3, concerns similarities in their epistemology and philosophy of mind (see n. 18). Beyond making explicit these two lines of correlation, we shall see how the second kind of similarities, build upon the first sort. As we pursue this comparative analysis, however, we shall remain alert to some substantial differences between Husserl's and Russell's programs.

2 Husserl and Russell: Exploring Philosophical Fundamentals

Bertrand Russell saw as the defining characteristic of the new "analytic" philosophy its aim of discussing a "list of fundamentals" (1924: 328). He declared that, by contrast, the "speculative" philosopher—Henry Bergson, in particular—"never thinks about fundamentals" (1912c: 318). Husserl, for his part, spoke about "pre-given" phenomena as the fundamentals of both philosophy and science.

The first subsection that follows highlights similarities in the way Russell and Husserl explored the fundamentals. The second makes explicit the dissimilarities on this score. The third subsection critically examines the old story that Russell intended to write a review of Husserl's *Logical Investigations*.

2.1 Similarities between Husserl and Russell on This Point

The years from 1911 to 1918 found Russell championing the view that analytic philosophy investigates "logical forms." In this sense, he took analytic philosophy to be a kind of philosophical logic. Tellingly, Russell was unable to settle on a specific domain within which the investigation of logical forms ought properly to be pursued. In 1914, he often spoke of exploring the logical forms of propositions, while four years later he was mainly concerned with the logical forms of facts and of various fundamental ontological categories—of space, time, and number, for example (Milkov 2003: 71 ff.).[3] More generally, Russell maintained that our contemplation of forms is a "direct vision of [an] abstract truth upon which the possibility of philosophical knowledge depends" (Russell 1914: 243).[4]

During roughly the same period, Husserl argued in his own way to a similar conclusion, namely that the task of philosophy is to describe phenomena or essences. Husserl maintained that we can achieve such descriptions through a process of "analysis of essences" (*Wesensanalyse*), which is to say, of *eide*, or forms (the Greek "εἶδος" translates as "form"); and this by way of "eidetic intuition" (*Wesensschau*), or "intuition of forms."[5] The ultimate aim is the contemplation of *eide* made evident by nothing but the immediate (unmediated, *unmittelbar*) apprehension of their formal truth. Michael Beaney correctly holds that "what Husserl called 'essential intuition' Russell famously dubbed '[knowledge by] acquaintance'" (2008a: 208). Beaney means here surely Russell's acquaintance with logical forms (Russell 1913: 129–31) as different from his acquaintance with sense-data (see § 3.1).

Like his teacher Franz Brentano, Husserl employed the method of description. His philosophy, at least till 1918, discovers, probes, and describes phenomena. It is "phenomenology" in just this sense. Interestingly enough, Husserl saw phenomenological description as related to the "zoological or botanical descriptions" in that we learn phenomena "in direct intuition" (1939: 336). In ways similar to the theoretical thrust of Husserl's thinking, Russell during these years saw "philosophical logic . . . as an inventory, or if you like a more humble word, a 'zoo' containing all the different forms that facts may have" (1918a: 216). It is clear here that in respect of logical forms, Russell was not, as many phenomenologists assume, a reductionist. He was a descriptivist and eliminativist (Chapter 4: § 8.2).

Russell's theory of forms was married, moreover, with the conception that, properly speaking, the method of philosophy is nothing but philosophical-logical analysis, or analysis with the help of philosophical logic. Indeed, as he saw it, we discover logical forms only through a process of philosophical-logical analysis.[6] Evidently, it was the theory of forms that inspired Russell to conceive the program for a "piecemeal" approach to philosophical problems which he named *analytic*:

> By concentrating attention upon the investigation of logical forms it becomes possible at last for philosophy to deal with its problems piecemeal, and to obtain, as the sciences do, such partial and probably not wholly correct results as subsequent investigation can utilize even while it supplements and improves them. (1918: 85)

Paralleling Russell's conception of philosophical-logical analysis is Husserl's method of eidetic reduction, or reduction to forms that Husserl systematically introduced in *Ideas I* (1913). In "Philosophy as Rigorous Science" (1911), he had spoken in a key similar to that of Russell about the analysis of essences as pursued by the "eidetic analyst."[7]

It is of interest, both historically and philosophically, to compare Husserl's *eide* with Russell's forms in detail. Russell's logical forms inhabit not Euclidean but logical space, and hence they correspond only remotely to the objects of the real world. By the same token, Husserl's essences possess no real properties, no real parts, no causality, and undergo no change (1911: § 49). That explains why, in "Philosophy as Rigorous Science," Husserl explicitly rejected both naturalism and relativism generally, as he did the more specific doctrines of historicism and psychologism.

On these points, Husserl's views were yet again in accord with those of Russell in the years from 1905 through 1918. That Russell stood opposed to relativism is plain in view of the fact that his thinking chiefly reflected his abiding interest in the philosophical fundamentals. What's more, at least in 1913 and 1914, he explicitly inveighed against naturalism, asserting that while it presupposes a thorough grounding in scientific knowledge, philosophy is a discipline that transcends the natural sciences. It has its own clearly defined subject, namely the analysis and description of logical forms.[8] Husserl likewise distinguished philosophy from the sciences. He argued, for example, that the philosopher must not represent consciousness in terms of psychology, which as he saw it would be to "thingify" (*verdinglichen*) consciousness.[9] Rather, the philosopher must analyze essences as the very currency of consciousness.

We find further correspondence between Russell's notion of analysis and Husserl's of eidetic reduction when we take note that both proceeded in the same direction. Eidetic reduction, to start with it, moves from concrete (natural) phenomena to eidetic abstraction. The same applies to Russell's method of analysis, which takes as its point of departure data that are concrete, complex, and vague. Through the process of analysis, the data under consideration grow "at each stage more abstract, more refined, more difficult to apprehend" (Russell 1914: 245, 190) ultimately disclosing their purely logical form.[10]

Husserl also introduced thought experiments that in his system enable the analyst to apprehend phenomena through a process he characterized as *imaginative variation* (a notion originating with Bolzano). The process of imaginative variation leads one to find, for example, that thought without language is impossible.[11] It thus enables us to examine and correct our eidetic intuition by confronting its results with reality. In similar vein, Russell used thought experiments to assess the cogency of alternative philosophical theories. His modus operandi was to evaluate them in light of applicable philosophical puzzles and paradoxes (Ryle 1979: 16–17).

2.2 Grounds of the Shared Pursuit of Philosophical Fundamentals

Like the other similarities in the thinking of Husserl and Russell, that which had to do with their preoccupation with fundamentals of philosophy had its "deep grammar." This took the form of their exploration of, what Husserl had called, "pure logic" (Chapter 10). In short, both Husserl and Russell believed that the new achievements in mathematics open new perspectives in philosophy. This conviction explains why the programs of the two thinkers had both a formal (mathematical) and a philosophical side.

A salient difference, however, divided the two thinkers on this head. This concerned their divergent approaches to mathematics and mathematical logic— to which Russell's logicist program reduced mathematics. Whereas Russell's philosophy closely followed his exposition of mathematical logic, addressing its philosophical problems in the process, Husserl categorically rejected the move to approach philosophy through mathematics or mathematical logic. He was convinced that mathematical symbols achieve no more than a mechanistic "economy of thinking" (Mayer 2008: 49).[12] At the same time, however, the theory of manifolds (or of "super-mathematics") supplied Husserl's phenomenology with its mathematically formal inspiration.

Russell, on the other hand, was not a radical formalist in philosophy. He firmly believed that mathematical logic reveals its full theoretical significance only in conjunction with philosophy. In fact, such was the purport of his collaboration (as a philosopher) with A. N. Whitehead (as a professor of mathematics) in writing *Principia Mathematica* (1910/13).

2.3 Excursus on Did Russell Intend to Write a Review of Husserl's *Logical Investigations*?

An old story that originates with Herbert Spiegelberg's *The Phenomenological Movement: A Historical Introduction* (1960) and still circulates among the historians of analytic philosophy and phenomenology has it that while in Brixton Prison (May–November 1918), Russell had the idea of writing a review of the second edition of Husserl's *Logical Investigations* (1913–21) (*LI*).[13] Spiegelberg cited by way of evidence a letter from Russell to Husserl dated April 19, 1920, in which he tells Husserl that *LI* was one of the books he had with himself while in Brixton Prison.

In fact, the key document that confirms Russell's intention to prepare this review is his letter to his brother Frank from June, 1918, in which he wrote: "Please tell Professor Stout [Stout was at that time the editor of *Mind*] . . . that if he still wants review of Husserl's Logical Investigations, I will do it in time for the October 'Mind'" (Varga 2016: 28). Unfortunately, Russell never followed through this intent. Instructively, the main reason for this is set out in the same letter: "I have only 1st volume & half of 2nd. If the other half of 2nd has appeared & he [Stout] has it, will he please send it?" (ibid.). Unfortunately, part two of second volume only appeared in 1921.

The issue is even more puzzling since the list of the books and papers Russell read while in Brixton Prison (Russell 1986), which he himself prepared, tells us that he had on hand merely the first volume of *LI*, which contains only the Introduction (*Prolegomena*). One possible explanation is that in that list Russell was keeping track of what he had read. This means that he hadn't read volume two, part one, but merely had it in his cell.[14]

We may surmise that Russell showed an interest in Husserl's *LI*, first, in support of his own work on *Introduction to Mathematical Philosophy* (*IMP*) which he drafted while incarcerated at Brixton. Among other things, Russell intended in *IMP* finally to tackle the problem of the nature of "logical forms"; and he clearly remembered how much Germanic authors (Meinong, Frege) had in the past helped him to clarify his views. Russell was evidently already familiar with Husserl's work, especially the ideas presented in chapter 11 of the *Prolegomena* on the "pure theory of manifolds." Intending to write on logic as a science of forms—he explicitly addressed the question of the nature of logical forms in the concluding, eighteenth chapter of *IMP*—and having plenty of time on his hands during his confinement, he also planned to revisit the relevant sections (in particular, §§ 69 and 70) of the *Prolegomena*.

As it turned out, however, in the summer of 1918 Russell was preoccupied instead with the study of epistemological and psychological problems that related to his work on "On Propositions" (1919) and *The Analysis of Mind* (1921). Husserl's *LI* (vol. 1 and apparently also vol. 2, part one) was the only book on logic among forty-nine books and papers that Russell read in his cell. Almost all of them were on psychology.

In fact, in 1918 Russell applied himself to the task of writing of *IMP* simply in order to finish what was a long-planned project that for years he hadn't had the opportunity to complete.[15] His real interest now, however, lay in problems of philosophy of mind. This partly explains why the discussion of logical forms in *IMP* is rather sketchy. Russell maintained simply that the perfect logical language has only syntax, no vocabulary. We know the propositions of logic *a priori*. Further, logic is the study of logical forms. It investigates the arrangement of variables (1919: 201).

This brings us to the second probable reason why Russell did agree with Stout's suggestion to write a review of Husserl's *LI*. His intensive engagement with problems of philosophical psychology in 1918 made him eager to revisit those parts of Husserl's book (above all, Logical Investigations V and VI that were printed, respectively, in the last segment of part one and in part two of volume 2) that deal with this subject. This more so since, as we are going to see Section 3, Russell adopted elements of Husserl's philosophy of mind already in the years 1911–15.

3 Husserl and Russell Advanced Similar Philosophies of Mind and Epistemology

Firmly as we substantiated the conclusion of the preceding section, there remain points in Russell's development between 1911 and 1918 that supply still more unimpeachable grounds than we so far adduced for maintaining that in these years there was a clear kinship between his philosophy and Husserl's thinking. For those seven years Russell's thinking saw his way to the conviction that philosophical logic investigates the logical form not only of language and facts but also of the human mind and cognitive states (of perception, of judgment, etc.) as well (1918: 85; see n. 18).

Genealogically regarded, this can hardly come as a surprise. After all, Husserl's distinguished teacher, Franz Brentano, played a formative if indirect role in the education of Moore and Russell as well: one of their professors at Cambridge, G. F. Stout, was a Brentanist (van der Schaar 2013). Stout's *Analytic Psychology* (1886), in particular, "was the most accurate and detailed presentation in English of Brentano's contributions to psychology. The phrase 'Analytical Psychology' just is Stout's translation of Brentano's 'Descriptive Psychologie.'"[16] (Bell 1999: 201)

Russell, however, did not develop his philosophy under Brentano's influence alone. The years 1899–1907 saw him immersed in the works of Alexius Meinong, yet another former student of Brentano. It was under Meinong's influence that Russell developed his famed concept of "knowledge by acquaintance" (Milkov 2001b: § 2.1). The Meinong connection reveals still further indirect grounds of the theoretical consanguinity between Husserl and Russell from 1905 to 1918.

Building on the foregoing evidence, the three subsections that follow present a triad of themes in light of which one finds the salient relation, hitherto unrecognized in the literature, that obtains between Husserl's and Russell's philosophy of mind and epistemology through most of the second decade of the twentieth century.

3.1 The Structure of Human Mind and Knowledge

Relative to this theme, we first note an instance where Husserl exerted an indirect influence on Russell. Apparently, this occurred through August Messer's book *Empfindung und Denken* (1908), which is essentially a summary of Husserl's *Logical Investigations*. Moore reviewed it for *Mind* in 1910 (Chapter 12: § 2.3). Above all, Moore lauded Messer's "attempt to classify [to describe] all the kinds of elements which may occur as constituents of mental phenomena" (1910: 395). Actually, this was precisely Husserl's task not only in his *Logical Investigations* but also, and even more so, in *Ideas I*.

In fact, Moore reviewed Messer's book while he was composing his lectures *Some Main Problems of Philosophy*, initially delivered in 1910/11. It comes as no surprise, then, that in them Moore advanced a similar classification. To be more explicit, he adopted Husserl's conception that there is a variety of mental phenomena—supposing, judging, fearing, hoping, desiring, liking, disliking—which constitute subdivisions of three general classes of mental acts that he posits as categorically discrete from their objects: cognitive acts, emotional acts, and acts of will.

Moore's lectures significantly influenced Russell's epistemological scheme in *The Problems of Philosophy* (1912a),[17] a scheme that Russell continued to develop in *Theory of Knowledge* (1913), *Our Knowledge of the External World* (1914) and "The Philosophy of Logical Atomism" (1918a). Moore's Husserlian influence is particularly evident in *Theory of Knowledge*, where Russell argued that there are

- different *mental acts*: judging, feeling, willing, and desiring;
- different kinds of *propositional attitudes*: assertion, suggestion, volition, doubting, dis/believing, analyzing/synthesizing;
- different forms of *acquaintance*: (i) as regards *objects*, we are acquainted with logical forms, particulars or universals; (ii) as regards the *way we are acquainted* with objects, we are perceiving, dreaming, remembering, and imagining.

Moreover, Russell maintained that "the distinguishing mark of what is mental, or at any rate of what is cognitive,[18] is not to be found in the particulars involved, but only in the nature of the relations between them" (1913: 45). In other words, the difference between sensation, dreaming, remembering, and imagining is not a function of their object but of our cognitive attitude to the same object. The objects in a dream, for example, are different from the objects we perceive when we are awake only because the relation between the "I" and the object is different. There is no difference in their objects per se.

Mental states of different types have each their idiosyncratic "logical form." The important task, for philosophy, is to describe these logical forms (129 ff.). Russell adduces the following as an example of such a description: "The logical form of perception will be different from the logical form of believing. . . . Volition differs from desire logically, in a way strictly analogous to that in which perception differs from belief" (1918a: 228).

But Russell also held that the difference between the various kinds of acquaintance depends upon the nature of the objects to which it is directed: particulars, universals, and logical forms (1913: 97 ff.). These kinds of acquaintance he respectively terms apprehension, conceptualization, and "logical intuiting." The latter, in particular, exhibits a marked likeness to Husserl's concept of *noesis* as "experiencing [*erleben*] the truth" of *noemata*. The two are clear cases of intellectual intuition. Apparently, by introducing the conception of "logical forms" into his philosophy of mind (and *eo ipso* into his epistemology),

Russell came palpably close the Husserl of *Ideas I*. Both explored the forms/*eide* (the possible cognitive attitudes) of the mental events and phenomena.

3.2 The Structure of Perception

Even closer than their respective theory of mind and knowledge is the correlation between the theory of perception that Husserl advanced in his middle period and that of Russell at a similar point in his career.

Many general overviews of phenomenology (Sokolowski 2000: 17–21) elucidate Husserl's signature doctrine of eidetic analysis (or analysis of forms) of the immediate experience which he sought to articulate in 1913 by way of the example of the perception of a cube.[19] When we see a cube, what is given to us is an aspect of the cube in which its presently visible sides are "cointended" with a "halo" (*Hof*) of its potentially visible but actually absent sides: we apprehend the visible sides with the help of deliberative attention. The other sides are also given, but as absent. Perception, therefore, involves layers (*Schichten*) of presentation which can be both actual and potential.

To sketch this point of Husserl's phenomenology with schematic explicitness, when we see the cube we perceive:

(i) Some of the six *sides* of the cube.
(ii) Each of these sides can be given in different ways—these are the different *aspects* of the cube. The aspects are objective but we can perceive them only at specific points in time. Most of them are merely potentially perceivable.
(iii) One and the same aspect can be seen in different *profiles* (*Abschattungen*), or sketches. A profile is temporally individuated—a momentary presentation of the object; it is private and subjective.

Russell defended in *Our Knowledge of the External World* (1914) and in "The Relation of the Sense-data to Physics" (1914a) a theory of perception that is closely related to Husserl's in *Ideas I*.[20] Instead of speaking about a cube, however, Russell's example is our perception a penny. According to Russell:

(i) The world features infinitely many perspectives, or *aspects* of the penny. A commonsense object, such as a penny, is at any given moment a system (a series) of such *objective* aspects. Perspectives are objective and are mutually related (ordered). We may perceive them, or they may remain unperceived. (In Husserl's terms, the latter are merely potentially perceivable.)

(ii) The actually perceived perspectives are *private* (1914: 94 ff.).
(iii) The thing itself can be viewed as a *logical construction* (see § 3.3) composed of such aspects.

The three kinds of perception determine three kinds of space.

Another, related factor evidencing the close correlation obtaining between Husserl's and Russell's theories of perception is the prominent role that "attention" played in them. As just noted, Husserl held that we perceive objects as situated in a "halo" of potentially perceived objects. The latter are perceived too, but not clearly. Our attention entertains only one of them, at any particular point in time—but it changes focus continually. In fact, consciousness is marked by incessant changes in the focus of attention.

Russell, on his side, maintained that we perceive complex objects, such as "*a*-in-the-relation-*R*-to-*b*," as singularities, even as attention may reveal them to be complex. We then judge—in the example—that *a* and *b* stand in a relation *R* (Russell and Whitehead 1910, i: 43). In *Theory of Knowledge* Russell held that "attention is a selection among objects that are 'before the mind,' and therefore presupposes a larger field, constituted in some less exclusive manner, out of which attention chooses what it wants" (1913: 9).

At a deeper level, the shared features that one discerns in these two thinkers' accounts of perception reflect the formative influence that Leibniz exerted on their views in this connection. However, whereas Russell explicitly constructed his new epistemology/philosophy of mind on the model of the *Monadology* (1914: 94), Husserl merely alludes to the importance of Leibniz's as an influence on his thought, and this only in passing (see 1923/4: 199).

3.3 Constructivism

Russell and Husserl were both philosophical constructivists. Epistemologically, the middle Russell regarded material objects as entities constructed of sense-data. He conceived logical constructions to be classes of particulars logically collected together "on account of some property" (1915: 97).

Husserl's middle-period constructivism was even more pronounced, albeit he understood it in different sense. Following Kant, he maintained that the Ego actively constructs (constitutes, makes) the phenomena and hence the world, including the world's principal categories—space and time, numbers, tones, colors, and so on. The genetic phenomenology Husserl would champion in his later period went a step further, exploring the construction (the passive synthesis) of the Ego itself: its personal history as embedded in its environment.

Some commentators have tracked the complementarities in Russell's and Husserl's constructivism indirectly, and apparently unintendedly, from the angle of Husserl's supposed influence on the work of other, younger thinkers—the most notable being Rudolf Carnap in his constructivist *Aufbau* (Carnap 1928) (Roy 2004; Ryckman 2007; Rosado Haddock 2008). Mayer (1991), for example, has argued that Carnap, who attended Husserl's lectures in Freiburg in 1922, was directly influenced by him. In fact, however, all these authors could track down similarities between Husserl and Carnap not because Carnap was substantially influenced with Husserl but, above all, because he closely followed the constructivism of Russell's *Our Knowledge of the External World*. To be more explicit, Carnap's work can be easily interpreted as influenced by Husserl simply because of the clear relatedness between the middle Husserl and the middle Russell, in particular, between the forms of constructivism they followed. There was, however, a serious difference between Russell's (of 1912–18) constructivism and that of Husserl which consisted in that, whereas Husserl and the phenomenologists builds up (constructs) a unified world, Russell and Carnap assumed that scientifically oriented philosopher constructs many possible worlds (Chapter 15: § 3).

10

Husserl's Theory of Manifolds in Relation to Russell and Wittgenstein

1 Introduction

Husserl's theory of manifolds was developed for the first time, in a very short form, in the *Prolegomena* to his *Logical Investigations* (1900: 248–53; §§ 69–70), then repeatedly discussed in *Ideas I* (1913: 148–53; §§ 71–2), in *Formal and Transcendental Logic* (1929: 142–54; §§ 51–4), and finally in the *Crisis* (1936: 20–60; § 9). In fact, Husserl never lost sight of it: it was his idée fixe. He discussed this theme for over forty years, expressing the same, in principle, ideas on it in different terms and versions. His discussions of it, however, were always cut short and inconclusive, so that he never developed his theory of manifolds in detail. Apparently, the reason for this was that he had no clear idea about it—"it seems to serve [only] as a regulative ideal for future philosophical-mathematical work" (Smith 2002: 106).

Not only did Husserl himself fail to conclusively elaborate his theory of manifolds but it also remained a neglected theme in Husserl's studies. Only recently has it been discussed in a number of essays (Scanlon 1991, Hill 2000a, Smith 2002, Gauthier 2004, Hartimo 2007). This can be partially explained by the fact that Husserl's most instructive writings on this theme were published after Husserl's main works. Here we mean *Logik und allgemeine Wissenschaftstheorie*, chapter 2, first published in 1996, and *Einleitung in die Logik und Erkenntnistheorie*, §§ 18–19, available since 1984.

The main task in this chapter—we shall pursue it in Section 2—will be to fill this gap in Husserl studies. The importance of this task results from the fact that the theory of manifolds plays a central role in Husserl's philosophy. In fact, phenomenology and theory of manifolds are two alternative branches of a single discipline: the science of essences (*Wesenslehre*). The difference between them is that while phenomenology is the science of contents, the theory of manifolds is the formal one (Husserl 1913: 149 f.). A consequence of this divergence is that, whereas phenomenology is descriptive, the theory of manifolds is not. As we are going to see in the lines to come, the latter supplies primitive law-essences (*Wesensgesetze*) like axioms and is therefore deductive.

Furthermore, Husserl's theory of manifolds is twofold. It is (i) a theory of theories, advanced in the good German tradition of *Wissenschaftslehre*, launched first, in two different directions, by J. G. Fichte and Bernard Bolzano. The *Wissenschaftslehre*, in turn, is an offspring of the ancient tradition of *mathesis universalis*, explored in the modernity by Descartes and Leibniz. (ii) The theory of manifolds is also a formal theory of everything. Its objective is to provide a systematic account of how the indefinable things in the world hang together in wholes of quite different kind. It is to be noted that Husserl explicitly speaks about (i) and only implicitly about (ii). In this chapter we shall also show that the theory of everything is intrinsically connected with the theory of theories.

Finally, in Section 3 we are going to see that many points of Husserl's theory of manifolds were developed, independently from him, by Russell and Wittgenstein.

2 Husserl's Concept of Manifolds

Husserl's concept of manifolds is widely branched, ramification that starts on the level of his pure logic and theory of forms. We are going to discuss these two first (in §§ 2.1 and 2.2). Only then are we going to explore Husserl's theory of manifolds proper.

2.1 Sides, Levels and Layers of Husserl's Pure Logic

Husserl's logic has two *sides*: (i) It turns toward what is subjective; (ii) it turns toward the objective order of the ideal objects (concepts). (i) is developed by the *transcendental logic*, (ii) by what he called *pure logic*. Husserl insisted that (ii) has primacy over (i). What pertains to the purely logical is something ideal and has nothing to do with the subjects. Nevertheless, (ii) finds by him a necessary completion in (i).

Husserl also maintains that there are three *levels* (*Stufen*) of pure logic:

1) Traditional Aristotelian apophantic logic of truth.
2) The pure logic of second level deals with objects of indeterminate, general kind. We find here the theory of cardinal numbers, the theory of

ordinals, set theory, etc. This logic treats "forms of judgments, and forms of their constituents, forms of deduction, forms of demonstration, sets and relationships between sets, combinations, orders, quantities, objects in general, etc" (Hill 2000a: 168).

3) Abstracting further, we reach a third level of pure logic, the level of the *theory of possible theories*, or the science of theory-forms. "This is a science which tracks down and investigates the legitimate relations between the essential types of possible theories (or realms). All real theories are particularization of relevant theory-forms" (Husserl 1900: 251). Since they are the most general elements of our knowledge, the various disciplinary forms are similar to Kant's *a priori* ideas, laws and principles. What makes them different from Kant's *a priori* is that they are not invariant schemes. Indeed, we can construct ever new forms of this sort; you can even play with them.[1]

Husserl insists that the theory of theories is a completely new discipline. It is such in both the historical sense, in the sense that nobody spoke about it before Husserl, and in a theoretical sense, in the sense that it is a new level of logic. Indeed, whereas on the second level we deal with forms of propositions, forms of demonstrations, etc., this level logic deals with forms of systems of propositions.

This is the level of pure logic in which we can modify the shape of the real theoretical systems *ad libitum*. This means that we can construct an infinite number of forms of possible disciplines. "Any individual theory is a particular instance of the theory form corresponding to it" (Hill 2000a: 170).

But pure logic can be also considered as consisting of two *layers*. The lower level, the level of apophantic logic, investigates what can be said *a priori*. Its main categories are the proposition (predication) and the state of affairs. It is logic of truth that deals with forms of propositions and states of affairs.

The higher level of logic treats absolutely determined formal object-structures: sets, numbers, quantity, ordinals, multitudes, etc. (1906/7: 78). This layer of logic is also called *formal ontology*; it is *a priori* science of objects as such.

What is the relation between apophantic logic and formal ontology? On the one side, Husserl's formal logic depends on formal ontology. At the same time, however, formal ontology follows the laws of apophantic logic. The point is that formal ontology follows principles which are those of apophantic logic. Indeed, "we cannot think without thinking" (94). This is the case since the stem of the pure logic is the apophantic logic. It is true that formal ontology is its highest level; nevertheless it is based on the stem of pure logic—the apophantic logic (77).[2]

2.2 Husserl's Theory of Forms

Husserl also maintained that there are three kinds of forms:

1) *Disciplinal forms.* According to Husserl, different realms of investigation define different forms: physical form, mathematical form, logical form, ontological form, phenomenological form. "A rich ontology, then, will distinguish different types of form: in the domains of linguistic, conceptual, and mathematical, as well as physical and mental entities" (Smith 2002: 104). Husserl studied these different forms in his *Logical Investigations*. Indeed, the book examined rather different disciplines: pure logic, speech act theory (act, sense, reference), ontology (universals, parts/whole, ideal meanings), phenomenology (intentionality, structure of consciousness), epistemology (evidence, intuition).[3]
2) *Objectival forms.* Different objects of cognition have also different forms. In this sense Husserl discriminated between propositional form, forms of states of affairs, number forms (*Zahlenformen*), form of entailment (*Schlusselform*), categorical form, axiomatic form, theory form, disciplinal form, and manifold form.
3) *Pure forms.* Husserl, however, did not only study these disciplinal and objectival forms. He also investigated the pure form. In fact, Husserl's idea of a pure form was a product of his efforts to abstract the ideal forms in mathematics, logic, ontology, and phenomenology.[4] It is to be investigated by the discipline *mathesis universalis*. This is "a philosophical theory of the types of form that shape or situate entities of various types or categories" (105). As we are going to see in the next section, Husserl connected it with his theory of manifolds.

2.3 What Are Husserl's Manifolds?

Husserl started to examine the manifolds at the beginning of the 1890s. In his first works, "On the Concept of Number" (1887) and *Philosophy of Arithmetic* (1891), however, he rarely employed the term "manifold." Instead, he spoke about "quantity," "plurality," "totality," "aggregate," "collection," "set," and "multiplicity [*Menge*]."

In fact, multiplicity was the concept Georg Cantor used to denote what we today call "set." In this connection it can be instructive to remind the reader that between 1887 and 1901 Husserl taught at the same German University (at Halle a.d. Saale) in which Cantor also was a professor. More than this,

Cantor was a member of the committee that approved Husserl's habilitation dissertation "On the Concept of Number" in 1887. At the same time, we must point to the fact that except for their Platonism, Husserl's manifolds differ significantly from Cantor's multiplicity; the latter pertains to the second level of Husserl's pure logic (as described in § 2.1 (ii)) whereas the former to the third level.

But what exactly did the term *manifolds* mean? Husserl was explicit that he borrowed his concept of manifolds from contemporary geometry; in particular, from the n-dimensional manifolds as set up in the works of Hermann Grassmann, W. R. Hamilton, Sophus Lie and Georg Cantor (1900: 252). In this sense he called the theory of manifolds "a fine flower of modern mathematics" (250). This means that this new discipline, the theory of manifolds, was not just Husserl's vision. It became well outlined in the last years of the nineteenth-century mathematics. Husserl's dream was to apply this discipline to the whole categorial realm of human knowledge.

This claim of Husserl was interpreted in three different ways: (a) His manifolds were seen as being close to Riemann's theory of varieties. (b) Most often Husserl's concept of manifold was explained referring to the manifold of three dimensions in Euclidean geometry. Importantly enough, this interpretation can be straightforwardly supported with citations from Husserl (1917/18: 265). (c) Yvon Gauthier, by contrast, maintains that on this point Husserl followed the general theory of forms or "polynomials" of Leopold Kroneker's work *Foundations of an Arithmetical Theory of Algebraic Quantities* (2004: 122).

Despite this dissension in interpretation, we can easily outline unambiguous examples of the manifolds. One such example is that the conventional mathematician speaks of space. Instead, we can simply accept that space is the just-mentioned Euclidean manifold of three dimensions, so that every object in space is subject to the laws of this particular manifold (1917/18: 265). In this way we avoid to talk in terms of space altogether. We speak of axiomatic forms instead,[5] from which we can make inferences as to particular objects. Every object of such a manifold is subject to the laws of the manifold. At a next level of abstraction, we do not speak even of three dimensions but of n dimensions instead which have different particular manifolds. Not only do we not speak of space; we do not speak even of geometry (267).

In the light of the analysis made so far, it turns out that in the theory of manifolds the numbers are only number forms (*Zahlenformen*). Further, what is conventionally called arithmetic and algebra turns out to be nothing but hypothetical theories of particular manifolds (271). The signs 0, 1, etc., as well as +, x, =, were introduced in them only in order to make evident particular formal analogies.

It is time now to say something more about the pure manifolds. Husserl defines them as "endlessly opened sets of thought-of objectnesses [*Gegenständlichkeit*] which are defined through axiomatic forms" (274). This means that the objects in a pure manifold are absolutely undetermined. In contrast, Husserl calls mathematical manifolds "definite manifolds" (1913: 152) (Scanlon 1991). These are systems of axioms, defined in purely analytic way, and so are completely and unambiguously determined—there are no places for contingencies in them.

Let us now chart the scheme of different types of manifolds in Husserl's theory of manifolds: Euclidean manifolds; other particular manifolds; definite (mathematical) manifolds; pure manifolds.

2.4 Further Remarks on Husserl's Theory of Manifolds

In an earlier exposition of his logic (from 1906 to 1907), Husserl defined the theory of manifolds as the third, higher level of logic.[6] Later it was also called axiomatic mathematics. However—and we already have mentioned this—Husserl also called his theory of manifolds *mathesis universalis*.

Conventionally, the subject matter of mathematics is restricted to numbers and magnitudes. Instead, Husserl's *mathesis universalis* claims that "what is important in mathematics is to be found out not in its objects, but in the type of its method" (1906/07: 80). Pure mathematics produces "calculation truths," of any kind (Chapter 11: § 3.4). In geometry, for example, we calculate with constructions (*Gebilden*). But "we can [also] calculate with concepts and propositions, exactly as with lines, powers or surfaces" (81).

In other words, instead of numbers, powers, energies, light-beams, Husserl claims that it is better to think of letters and rules of calculating. Actually, we can consider the numbers, letters, etc. only as chips (*Spielmarken*) with the help of which we play the game of calculating.[7] If we adopt this position, then the problems in mathematics will be resolved in the higher possible completeness and generality. In this way we shall forget that we have to compute with numbers. What matters here is the "tissue of entailments" (*Gewebe von Schlüssen*).

This is the realm of pure logic which can be also called super-mathematics (*Übermathematik*), or mathematics of higher degree (Hartimo 2010). It can be seen as nothing but an interconnection (*Verkettung*) of entailments. As just mentioned, this is not mathematics of numbers or magnitudes. Rather, it is "mathematics" of an indefinitely general realm of thinking. The only thing that is determined in it is the form.⁸ Contemporary mathematics calls such undefined realms *manifolds*; the particular theoretical systems in mathematics are its consequences. We can construct (synthesize) manifolds through contingent definitions, after which we can mathematically deduce theoretical systems which follow from them. Such a construction is a product of the creative mathematical imagination (86–7).

A pure manifold is a class of objects; it is a construction of purely logical concept of possible objectnesses. The latter can be characterized through the forms of propositions which are valid for it. Actually, this is not a manifold of objects but of things which are thought of as objects. To put it in other words: a pure manifold consists of objects-senses, or of substrata-senses which are suitable to function in a system of judgments as substrata of predications (1929: 148). Or: in the theory of manifolds we operate with pure logical, principal concepts (*Grundbegriffe*).

These characteristics of the theory of manifolds allow some authors to call it "a formal theory of everything" and to see it as nothing but "a philosophical theory of the types of form that shape or situate entities of various types or categories" (Smith 2002: 105).

2.5 Husserl's Theory of Theories: Disciplinal Form

As already noted, Husserl also understood his theory of manifolds as a theory of theories. In the wake of this conception, some authors define his manifolds as "pure forms of possible theories which, like molds, remain totally undetermined as to their content, but to which the thought must necessarily conform in order to be thought and known in a theoretical manner" (Hill 2000a: 169).

Husserl's theory of theories is part of his more comprehensive philosophy of science. The latter distinguishes between normative and practical disciplines, on the one hand, and theoretical (explanatory) sciences, on the other. Theoretical sciences are nomological and analytical disciplines. They are formal *matheses*. As already noted in §§ 2.2 and 2.4, Husserl's declared aim is to advance "a new and higher form of formal *mathesis*—a science of the possible forms of theories— *mathesis universalis*" (1917/18: 257). Husserls's *mathesis universalis* addresses the "disciplinal form"—another name for theory form. Its aim is to gain a general concept of many formal, mutually independent axioms (272).⁹

We can analyze this way many existing theories, for example, we can look for the pure form of the Euclidean geometry, in particular, for the proofs in it. The result of such kind of analysis is a number of axioms from which the whole theory can be deduced.[10] This is an important task since in the real Euclidean geometry not all axioms are made explicit.

There are different possible relations between disciplinal forms. Usually, several theoretical disciplines have one group of axioms as a form. In other situations, a disciplinal form can be a part of another disciplinal form. Another case: the system of axioms of one disciplinal form can be a formal restriction of another one, etc. (262–3).

A disciplinal form can be widened up. One can explore different ways of its expansion, or can modify its axioms. In both cases we simply play with the forms of the possible theories (with the disciplinal forms). The only condition by these experiments is not to change the system of this particular discipline. At the end, we contemplate the infinity of possible disciplinal forms in one vision (268). We, more precisely, try to see the regularities which rule in the contexts and modifications (*Zusammenhänge und Abwandlungen*) of the system. The further our theoretical illumination reaches, the perfect our deductive work in this particular case is. Indeed, with the enlargement of the disciplinal form grows the power of the mathematical (aka. pure logical) thinking.

When an expert confronts such a possible theory, she assesses its applicability in her discipline. In other words, Husserl's new science constructs *a priori* forms of possible theories and possible sentences. Later these theory-forms can be used when actual theoretical contents are discussed (Husserl 1906/07: 89). Here are meant, however, only the deductive disciplines. We can thus define Husserl's *mathesis universalis* as a science about the possible forms of the deductive disciplines.

2.6 The Connection between the Theory of Manifolds and the Theory of Theories

The connection between the pure theory of manifolds and the theory of possible theories is that the first determines the second. The reason for this is that Husserl saw the manifold of a given deductive theory as the ontological form of the general complex state of affairs presented by it (Smith 2002: 110). As a matter of fact, the formal structure of any elementary state of affairs (*Rab*) can be seen as a simple type of manifold in Husserl's sense (115). On the other hand, any manifold can be seen as the form of a possible world.

In order to make this conception more convincing, Husserl posits complex forms of states of affairs which mirror the logical connectives and quantifiers.

Husserl further claims that there are conjunctive, disjunctive, negative and hypothetical states of affairs.[11] He, for example, recognizes connectional states of affairs like (*Rab* & *Qcd*). "This exceedingly complex state of affairs is, as it were, the 'world' of the theory *T*, or rather that part of the actual world characterized by *T*"[12] (Smith 2002: 118).

3 Theory of Manifolds by Russell and Wittgenstein

Different aspects of Husserl's theory of manifolds were developed by the early analytic philosophers Bertrand Russell and Ludwig Wittgenstein. We shall pass them in review here with the hope that this will help us to reveal new perspectives both in Husserl's project and in that of early analytic philosophy. We shall see that while Russell developed something like a Husserlian theory of theories, Wittgenstein advanced a theory of pure manifolds which prima facie was quite different from that of Husserl. In truth, it disclosed important new aspects of it (Chapter 11).

3.1 Russell

In his book *Our Knowledge of the External World* Russell developed, independently from Husserl, the idea of theory of theories in most clear form.[13] In particular, he connected the theory of theories with the new symbolic logic. The latter "suggest[s to science] fruitful hypotheses which otherwise could hardly be thought of" (1914: 51; 1924: 341). Ultimately, however, scientists must decide which theory fits the facts they now know and which do not fit them.

This makes out the difference between the new and the old logic. Whereas the old logic is canonic, the new (symbolic) logic is liberal: it holds that the problems under consideration have many possible solutions. Its task is not to criticize such solutions but, quite the reverse, to promote them. It has the effect of "providing an infinite number of possible hypotheses to be applied in the analysis of any complex fact" (68). Later, scientists can choose the hypothesis which is most appropriate to the empirical data now available.[14]

The difference between Husserl and Russell on this point was that while Russell believed that the theory of theories is suggested by the new symbolic (mathematical) logic, Husserl claimed that his theory of manifolds was a result ("a flower") of pure mathematics. That difference, however, is scarcely a big one since, to Russell, logic is the foundation of the pure mathematics.

As with the Husserl of the *Logical Investigations*, the early Russell likewise promulgated a lower-level theory of fundamentals. His express task in *The Principles of Mathematics* (1903: v), for example, is elucidating the "indefinables": space, time, numbers, beliefs, and so on. This is also the subject-matter of Russell's philosophical logic, as different from his symbolic logic.

3.2 Wittgenstein

The concept of manifold (multiplicity) played a central role also in Wittgenstein's *Tractatus*. At least prima facie, however, Wittgenstein used this concept in quite different sense from that of Husserl. In particular, he claimed that in a proposition there are exactly as many distinguishable parts as in the situation it represents. To Wittgenstein this means that they have the same logical (mathematical) manifold. The very picturing of reality is possible only because of this common manifold.

Wittgenstein was also convinced that this way of connecting matter and mind (language) is much more promising that the old idealistic conception of "spatial spectacles"—he termed so (in 1922, 4.0412) Kant's claim that we see the matter through the *a priori* forms of reason. Furthermore, Wittgenstein maintained that the two elements, fact and proposition, touch one another. To be more explicit, this touch is realized in the manifold which is common to these two—it is something of their intersection. It is the element on which the two quasi "hinge" (Milkov 2001: 408). Wittgenstein also saw the manifold—the common element between matter and mind (language)—as an *indefinable*.[15] Being such, it "of course, cannot itself be the subject of depiction. One cannot get away from it when depicting" (1922, 4.041). We can only show it.

In his works between 1929 and 1933 Wittgenstein continued to use the concept of manifold, with an important addendum, though. Now he connected it with the conception of copying actions. Similarly to pictures, the action we now make, following an exemplary action, has the same manifold as the action which we copy (1979: 112).

So far so good! The question, however, is what is the relatedness and what is the difference, between Wittgenstein's conception of manifolds and that of Husserl. We are going to discuss this in Chapter 11. In an effort to answer it right here, we can remind ourselves that Max Black has called the analogy between Husserl's theory of pure forms and Wittgenstein's conception of perfect, perspicuous language "striking" (Black 1964: 137). What is even more striking, however, is that the two conceptions were based on the idea of manifold. How is this?

This is the case because, according to Husserl's conception of manifolds, every state of affairs has its own manifold. The same with the complex states of affairs, including such macro-complexes as those presented in the theories of science. Further, states of affairs, of all kinds, can be seen as parts of possible worlds. This is exactly how the things were conceived in the formal ontology of Wittgenstein's *Tractatus*.

In another place (Milkov 2001: 405 f.) we have reconstructed Wittgenstein's Tractarian ontology as maintaining that states of affairs are combinative compositions out of many aspects (forms) of objects and of states of affairs. In the world of pure possibility, there are many such compositions: in Husserl's idiom, we can interpret the forms of states of affairs (the manifolds) as "compossible totalities" out of forms of objects. Further, exactly like in Husserl's formal ontology, the scientific theories in the Tractarian ontology posit possible worlds. The facts of the real world can make these possible worlds true or false.[16]

Finally, Husserl embraced a "robust *formal realism* holding that these types of form [the pure manifolds] are part of the world. Forms are abstract or ideal entities, along with numbers, universals, concepts, etc." (Smith 2002: 120). This means that forms do not reside in another world but are rather features of particulars in this world—they are something of *universalia in rebus*. The same with Wittgenstein—as David Pears has correctly noticed, in the Tractarian ontology "the forms revealed by logic are embedded in one and only one world of facts" (Pears 1987, i: 23).

11

Wittgenstein's Indefinables and His Phenomenology

1 Introduction

Philosophers from the analytic tradition are confronted with an embarrassing terminological problem. Many feel that the most appropriate characterization of the subject matter of their philosophy is "phenomenology." The problem is that this term has long been associated with the philosophy of Edmund Husserl alone, who around the year 1900 adopted the term to identify his signature doctrine. The following two examples illustrate this point: (i) Some thirty years ago, Hao Wang declared that his philosophy is nothing but *phenomenology*; and he deplored the circumstance that this term had been co-opted by a philosophical movement very different from his approach (1986: 37). To differentiate his doctrine from that of Husserl, Wang dubbed his philosophy *phenomenograpy*. (ii) Ten years later, Jaako Hintikka concluded that Bertrand Russell's philosophy is most accurately described as *phenomenology*. "Unfortunately," remarked Hintikka, "the term 'phenomenology' is in the current philosophical jargon associated with so many misconceptions that I hesitate to use it here" (1995a: 12).

It is something of an historical irony that at the same time the two leading phenomenologists of the twentieth century, Husserl and Heidegger, thought of their method, from the very outset, as that of *analysis*. Thus, in *Philosophy as Rigorous Science*, Husserl identified his distinctively new approach as eidetic analysis (*Wesensanalyse*) (1911: 26).[1] Later, in *Sein und Zeit*, Heidegger asserted that his "*fundamental ontology*, from which all others spring, must be sought in the *existential analysis of the being*" (1927: 13). Neither Heidegger nor Husserl could foresee that many of their disciples would repudiate the term "analysis."

Relative to the factors underlying this issue, the present chapter addresses the following questions: Why philosophers with quite different theoretical intuitions were inclined to call their philosophy by the same name? Why it was that some analytic philosophers, like Hao Wang, would eventually conclude that their philosophy is nothing but *phenomenology*, and why the early phenomenologists held their method to be nothing but *analysis*?

In order to resolve these historically significant questions, we once again (see Milkov 2013b) approach the issues from a bird's-eye perspective. From this standpoint it will become evident that if the thinking of Husserl and Wittgenstein—the exemplary representatives of the two most influential, albeit competing movements in twentieth-century philosophy (Chapter 9: § 1.1)—evolved at different rates and independently of one another, it nonetheless manifested throughout virtually one and the same end, namely advancing a scientifically *rigorous philosophy*.

A correlative point that this chapter brings to light is that in their pursuit of the same end, phenomenology and analytic philosophy effectively encapsulated the nature of academic Western philosophy: its subject matter is *phenomena* (a view developed in § 2), while its method is *analysis* (a thesis developed in § 3).

2 The Indefinables as the Data of Academic Philosophy

Academic Western philosophy starts its explorations with *indefinables* as givens. We apprehend the given *intuitively*. It is what *shows* itself because it *exists*, is *available*.

2.1 The Indefinables of Plato and Aristotle

The characteristics of the given were effectively sketched out as early as Plato and Aristotle. A central concept in Aristotelian metaphysics is that of substance (ὐροκείμενον) (Anscombe and Geach 1961: 5 f.). His teacher, Plato, gave an *ontological* definition of substances: they can be both forms and mathematical objects, yet also "the substances of sensible bodies" (*Met.*, 1028b19–20). Aristotle defined substance from a *logical* point of view as "that which is not predicated of a substratum, but of which all else is predicated" (*Met.*, 1029a7). For him ontological substances are essences, universals, genera, and substrata. Just like Plato, however, Aristotle held that "some of the sensible appearances are generally admitted to be substances" (*Met.*, 1029a34–35). For both Plato and Aristotle, substances are evidently not only universals but also phenomena. Despite the apophantic (propositional) theory of truth adopted by both philosophers, they also subscribed to the existence of phenomena which are given and are known intuitively. We cannot define them; moreover, we cannot articulate them: "*individuum est ineffabile*" (*Met.* 1039b27)—but we can contemplate them. They *show* themselves.[2]

2.2 Kant's Indefinables

Kant maintained that we can elucidate empirical concepts (i.e., indefinables) only through analysis. We can analyze them in one of the following two ways:

1) Through discussion (or exposition) which can help to make them "completely distinct" through "the connected (successive) representation of their marks" (1800: § 105). In this way we can make all marks of the indefinable distinct. Moreover, "if *all* the marks of a given concept are made clear, then the concept becomes *completely* distinct" (§ 104);[3]
2) Through description, which is to say, "[through] the exposition of a concept, insofar as it is not precise" (§ 105). Kant seems to have understood description as incomplete analysis—it is simply a subordinate concept of analysis.

In Section 2.6 we shall see how fruitful Kant's elucidation of given concepts is when one tries to make sense of Wittgenstein's understanding of indefinables and of his phenomenology.

2.3 Husserl's Phenomenology

Following Franz Brentano, Husserl maintained that his investigation of the phenomena of "pure" consciousness requires an "eidetic intuition" (*Wesensanschauung*). Its objects are essences, or phenomena. Grasped intuitively, phenomena are indefinable; they simply exist. Significantly enough, Husserl's phenomena are objects of one's intentionality. This explains why, according to Husserl, we contemplate the stream of phenomena, in which one phenomenon replaces another, in the same way in which we contemplate the stream of Hume's impressions; the only difference is that whereas Hume's impressions are falsifiable, Husserl's phenomena are appositive: they are distinguished by their possession of an indubitable (Cartesian) character. Since the most common of these essences, or phenomena, are sense-impressions, they serve, according to Husserl, as a paradigm case of phenomena.[4] It can be said "that the intuiting of essences is nothing but an 'experience' in the sense of perceiving, remembering, or some other act of the same type" (1911: 46).

Sense-impressions and other essences, or phenomena, are to be explicated in descriptions, or analyses. They cannot "be said" (indeed, they are ineffable) nor can they be explained or "whistled," as Wittgenstein's friend Frank Ramsey would put it. They are ineffable. That is why Husserl defined philosophy as descriptive science.[5] Incidentally, philosophy is understood as a descriptive discipline by all four of the philosophers under discussion in the next pages: Husserl, Moore, Russell, and Wittgenstein (see §§ 2.4 and 2.5).

According to Husserl, phenomena have no characteristics, no causal relations, are unchangeable, etc. They are both synthetic and necessary, and so have no alternatives. Tellingly, Husserl's phenomenology is concerned with mental phenomena only—as previously remarked, they are the indefinables of human mind. Saving his chosen phenomena as Cartesian objects given in mentation alone, Husserl defined them as "purely mental." He discriminated them this way from the empirical mental (psychic) phenomena. Husserl insisted that the realm of the empirically mental is totally different from the realm of the objective. The objective, or "natural," world, on the other hand, in contrast to the purely mental one, is contingent, not necessary.

Interestingly enough, the phenomenology of the "purely mental" associated with the name of Husserl, which today is taken to be phenomenology proper, was independently advanced by, among others, the Oxonian philosopher John Cook Wilson. We "try," taught Cook Wilson, "to find out what a given activity of thought presupposes as implicit or explicit in our consciousness, without allowing precious results to be interfered with by any preconceived opinion" (1927, i: 328).

2.4 The Indefinables of Moore and Russell

The fathers of analytic philosophy, Moore and Russell, maintained from its inception that there are different kinds of data, or givennesses. In contrast to Husserl, though, they dismissed the question of the metaphysical status of data—material or mental—as irrelevant: these are identical. At the beginning, in *Principia Ethica* (1903a), Moore introduced as general indefinables "good," "bad," "yellow," and other colors, as well as the mental acts and their objects. Later he included as indefinables numbers and the terms "true," "false," and "existence" (Milkov 2003: 23); moreover, in 1908 Moore identified "sense-data" as indefinables as well (Chapter 12). In *The Principles of Mathematics* (1903) Russell introduced five indefinables of logic. In 1913 Russell classified "logical forms" as among the basic indefinables. And he was later to refer to logical atoms in "The Philosophy of Logical Atomism," as "the smallest number of simple *undefined things*" (1918: 271; emphasis added).

From the outset, both Russell and Moore insisted that the business of the New Philosophy, later called "analytic," is the "discussion of indefinables" (Russell 1903: xv). After Russell's paper "On Denoting" appeared in 1905, they saw as their main task the working out of philosophical systems on the grounds of these indefinables. Moore made this clear in *Some Main Problems in Philosophy* (1909/10), while Russell's programmatic statement to this effect appeared in *Theory of Knowledge* (1913).

2.5 Wittgenstein's Indefinables and His Phenomena

Wittgenstein continued the trend of philosophers introducing new indefinables. In his *Tractatus* indefinables are "objects." That is why, as Wittgenstein sees it, "objects can only be *named*. Signs are their representations. I can only speak *about* them: I cannot *put them into words*. Propositions can only say *how* things are, not *what* they are" (3.221). This contention of Wittgenstein follows from the fact that in order to specify *what* objects are, one would need to know their history—but objects have no history.

The Tractarian objects are indefinables not just in the sense that we cannot give them a verbal definition. One cannot even define them ostensively: one cannot pick them out or point at them. Objects in Wittgenstein's view are thus radically indefinable. We can only *see* them since they merely *manifest*—show—themselves.

Indefinable objects are of special importance since they lay down the constitutive principles of all other things.[6] Moreover, since indefinables are the ultimate, the basic elements of all other things, they also provide grounds and resources for the analysis of all kinds of objects.

Among other consequences, this conception impelled Wittgenstein, as it did Husserl before him, to conceive of philosophy as "purely descriptive" (1979: 106). Wittgenstein maintained, in particular, that philosophy describes objects and logical forms. The latter are grasped in acts of intellectual intuition: "In a suitable notation we can in fact recognize the formal properties of propositions by mere inspection of the propositions themselves."[7] (1922: 6.122).

Besides objects and logical forms, the class of indefinables also includes the aesthetic and the mystical: in a word, all things seen as temporally unconditioned, *sub specie aeternitatis* (1979: 83). In the 1930s and the 1940s Wittgenstein introduced in his philosophy a number of new indefinables: mathematical proofs, language-games, and pragmatics (Milkov 1997, i: 395 ff.). What's more, he now came to regard the indefinables as synthesized and intuited dynamically, in a creative sense[8]—not statically, as in an act of passive contemplation. They either "come on the scene," as it were, or are invented in moments of creative insight.

In sum, the given that Wittgenstein was to discriminate is of two types: (i) static sense-data and logical forms and (ii) dynamic conceptual data. The latter are the data of our "mental eye," the grounding elements which "come to mind" when we are active mentally.

2.6 Indefinables of Different Order

Wittgenstein's conception of indefinables was first elaborated, we've noted, in the Tractarian theory of objects. In the early 1930s, he often developed it as "phenomenology." The most serious criticism Wittgenstein leveled at Husserl was that the latter considered phenomenology as a discipline niched between logic and science (1979b: 67 f.; 1977: II, 3). Rejecting this view, Wittgenstein argued that phenomenology pertains to logic only. His critical stance vis-à-vis Husserl makes sense in that, whereas the latter reduced the horizon of phenomenology to the objects of human intentionality, Wittgenstein's phenomenology amounted to what Husserl called "general theory of essences [*Wesenslehre*]." As we earlier remarked in Chapter 10: § 1, however, Husserl himself considered his "science of essences" as more fundamental than his phenomenology: it also includes the theory of manifolds.

Wittgenstein's chief contribution in all this is that his phenomenology features indefinables which fall into, at a minimum, four orders:

1) *First-order indefinables.* Wittgenstein's position in the early 1930s was that phenomena (objects) can be neither explained nor defined. Further, he asserted that they are not true or false, but merely possible. (In contrast, as we have seen in § 2.3, Husserl's phenomena are necessary.) Wittgenstein explained that these characteristics of phenomenological objects follow from the circumstance that when one introduces a phenomenon into ontology, one ipso facto introduces an entire logical system (1979b: 63). In other words, logic, being holistic, is a quasi-formal concomitant of every object (phenomenon, indefinable) by virtue of the object's very being what it is. To put it the language of Aquinas, every phenomenon introduces a new being (*esse commune*) with itself. Logical

systems, in their turn, such as those identified with space, time, and number, are not phenomena but "forms of representation" (214). The implication of this position is that logic depends on existing things. In this sense, one can say that logic is empirical.

2) *Second-order indefinables.* Wittgenstein argued, again in the early 1930s, that we calculate with objects (phenomena), and he contended that such calculi represent a different, dynamic order (beyond objects) of indefinables. Wittgenstein also maintained that there are different calculi, every one of which exhibits specific rules. The rules of calculi are contingent. It follows from this that, like phenomena, calculi are not the sort of thing that can be grounded (*begründet*), but only applied. What serves for the "ground" (*Grund*) of calculi, as their proof, is their application.

3) *Third-order indefinables.* A calculus, including the value of its elements, is determined through its rules. Significantly, the system of rules, or the "theory" of the calculus, is itself a calculus, albeit of another, third type. The "theory" *describes* something, whereas the calculus describes nothing: it, like all indefinables, simply *is*—it exists.

By the mid-1930s, however, Wittgenstein realized that rules, as well, cannot be defined with precision.[9] This, since in his view, the rules of calculi, like the moments of calculi and like phenomena, transcend definitions. The implication is that the "theory" of a calculus is itself a discrete species of calculus. In consequence, Wittgenstein downplayed the difference between calculus and theory.

4) *Fourth-order indefinables.* "Understanding," too, is nothing but a calculus: it is an application of the calculus called "language." In fact, this precept of Wittgenstein became no less than a leading idea in his *Philosophical Investigations*. We can think and speak, and also calculate in arithmetic and algebra, not because we possess some mental rules. Instead, we calculate mathematically because we are trained in certain practices and can employ them. Understanding is thus not an "occult process" (1953: § 38).

3 The Method of Analysis in Phenomenology

Given that the signature methodology of Western academic philosophy is analysis, it is requisite at this juncture to open a novel line of reflection on Wittgenstein's doctrine of indefinables.

3.1 Calculations as Discussion of Indefinables in Conceptual Analysis

Wittgenstein embraced a broad conception of analysis which he called alternatively "geometry," "logic," and "grammar." For example, in what one could characterize as Wittgenstein's "later phenomenology" (from his *Remarks on Colour*, 1950–1), he spoke about the "geometry of colours" (1977, III: § 86). He specified, further, that as a contemplation of possibilities,[10] or comparison and relating of indefinables, phenomenological analysis is actually a logical or grammatical investigation.[11] This goes with Wittgenstein's view that every phenomenon introduces a new logical system. The procedure of deliberating upon phenomena,[12] of contemplating their possibilities, is a mode of examination or *calculation*,[13] what both Plato and Aristotle called πειραστικός, or peirastic dialectic (Chapter 3: § 3.2; Milkov 2013b).

As he did in the early 1930s, the later Wittgenstein insisted that what he was doing was not phenomen*ology*, in the sense of a specific *theory* that lies somewhere between science and logic.[14] He claimed, rather, that he was addressing *phenomenological problems* (1977, III: § 248), such as clarifying "which are the simple [indefinable] colour concepts" (III, § 69). Relative to this latter problem, Wittgenstein points out that "the indefiniteness [the indefinability] of the concept of colour lies, above all, in the indefiniteness of the concept of the sameness of colours, i.e. of the method of comparing colours" (§ 78). In the process of comparing (analyzing) colors, Wittgenstein determines that "'internal properties' of a colour gradually occur to us which we hadn't thought of at the outset" (§ 63). He explains that this operation "can show us the course of a philosophical investigation. We must always be prepared to come across a new one [a new "internal property" of a color], one that has not occurred to us earlier" (ibid.). Here, *as if* following Kant's conception of analysis alluded to above (in § 2.2), Wittgenstein understood analysis as successively making the marks of the indefinable clear. In a manner, philosophers are *empirical discoverers* (§ 2.6, (i))—despite the fact that they discover something that always already is available for analysis, namely the indefinables that are given to us. In this sense, one can say that philosophy is *a priori*—this because such discoveries are of something which is given, before our eyes. The conclusion is that philosophy is synthetic *a priori* (Chapter 15: § 3).

Wittgenstein suggests that we describe phenomena by indicating "rules" according to which they behave (*sich verhalten*). The aim is to specify the possibilities of their occurring, which we can contemplate, or the calculations to which they can be subject. The task of phenomenological study is thus to identify the "rules" of the "games" of calculi; though, as we already have seen (in § 2.6 (iii)), the rules themselves are no more than another set of calculus. This means that they too are indefinables: dynamic indefinables. That is why one cannot unambiguously formulate them. If anything is clear after this analysis, it is that one cannot sharply discriminate Wittgenstein's discipline of "phenomenological remarks" from that of "pure calculation," that is, from calculation not merely with numbers but also with any kind of indefinables.[15]

3.2 Levels of Phenomenology

Wittgenstein also distinguishes four different types of calculi-involving phenomena.

1) *Pure Calculation.* Since the objects of phenomenology—phenomena—are *given*, phenomenology proceeds by way of pure calculation.[16] This concept is not to be confused with the calculus in arithmetic or algebra which operates with numbers and variables. Phenomenological calculi are of a higher order.
2) *Science.* Wittgenstein holds that science is a calculative enterprise, too. To be more explicit, he regards science as phenomenological as well, but of second order. It is a sort of "theory" of calculus with phenomena. If phenomenology investigates (contemplates, calculates) the possibilities of the given,[17] science formulates and tests hypotheses that are essentially schemes of connecting these possibilities (Milkov 2001: 410 f.).

    In order to make this conception clearer, we shall refer to Wittgenstein's discrimination between physics and phenomenology, which he spelled out in lectures delivered from late 1931 through early 1932. Wittgenstein declares that "the world we live in is the world of sense-data; but the world we talk about is the world of physical objects" (1980: 82). Phenomenology is preoccupied with static finding (in reality) of data, or with dynamic inventing of (logical) possibilities (with "contemplating possibilities") of data, that can be (but must not be) organized in scientific theories.[18]

    What we observe and describe in phenomenology are slices of the construct that the hypotheses of science suggest, or single out (1979b: 161). The particular kind of the construct in question is contingent: its "form is optional" (1922: 6.341). A necessary condition for such a speculative "game" to be judged successful is the construct that connects different moments be free of logical contradictions and errors of other sorts.

3) *Conceptual Analyses.* Wittgenstein also understood phenomenological analysis as conceptual analysis: as he put it, "phenomenological analysis is analysis of concepts" (1977, II: § 16). And we've already noted (in § 3.1) that conceptual analyses are synthetic and *a priori.* They are means of making discoveries, starting from the antecedently available conceptual resources.

4) *The Socratic Method* (Chapter 13: § 1.6), or peirastic dialectic, is phenomenology of highest order. To reiterate what we earlier observed (in § 3.1, again), this method is a dialectical means of deliberating upon phenomena that we approach as topics of inquiry. Following Plato, we can see it as the principal philosophical method.

3.3 Phenomenological Fusions

Wittgenstein's approach to investigating indefinables is also fundamental in that it justifies the fusion of a series of ontological and epistemological concepts conventionally regarded as contrastive or antithetical to each other. There follows three cardinal examples of such fusions:

1) *Fusion of mental and objective.* As the discussion thus far establishes, the dichotomy between mental ("pure mental") and objective phenomena adopted by Husserl is, Wittgenstein objects, a sham dichotomy. The more plausible "fusion or duality of the phenomenal and the objective" is widely identified as original with Wittgenstein (Hintikka 1986: 51). But as we have found (in § 2.3), Moore and Russell, prior to Wittgenstein, advanced precisely such a fusion when they asserted that data (i.e., sense-data) are objective parts of the real world.

2) *Fusion of calculation and contemplation of indefinables.* A false dichotomy retained, apparently, tongue-in-cheek by Wittgenstein is that between calculation and contemplation of indefinables.[19] It is a spurious dichotomy since, first, it is a "split" between two different types of data: between dynamic, conceptual data that are synthesized in an act of creation and passive data of phenomena that one merely contemplates. Both, however, are indefinables that are ineffable[20] and are known exclusively by intuition. Secondly, as previously remarked, when contemplating indefinables, we calculate with them as well.[21]

3) *Fusion of abstract and concrete philosophical study.* A third fusion is that between abstract and concrete philosophical study. We found it first in Husserl's phenomenology which claims that every object (every phenomenon) has its own logical structure[22] that calls for painstaking description. In this sense, Husserl's new, phenomenological philosophy explores the "things themselves." It is not abstract, as is the subject matter of traditional philosophy but rather intrinsically concrete. In the *Tractatus*, Wittgenstein expounded virtually the same thought: namely that objects themselves, and not just facts, have forms[23] that determine their behavior (*Verhalten*) in any state of affairs in which they occur.

What makes Wittgenstein's phenomenology clearly divergent from Husserl's—as in Wittgenstein's descriptions of different language-games, and in his conceptual analyses of color (§ 3.2, (iii))—is that it investigates the logical forms *in* phenomena. Not only has every indefinable, every phenomenon, its own logical structure but this logical structure is also an ingredient in the indefinable itself. Importantly enough, assuming that the logical forms are presented in objects, "Wittgenstein," observes Jaako Hintikka, "can so to speak have his logical forms and dispense with them too" (1994: 227). Hence, no εποχή (retention) is required in order to isolate logical form from objects for further analysis.

By contrast with Wittgenstein's, Husserl's phenomenology is essentially a philosophy of two worlds:[24] that of essences and that of naïve appearances from which essences are first educed (*herausgeschält*). The same is true of Russell's phenomenology (Chapter 7: § 2.4), a point David Pears made when he remarked (a remark we already referred to in Chapter 10: § 3.2) that unlike Russellian doctrine, the Tractarian ontology is "approximately Aristotelian" since in it "the forms revealed by logic are embedded in one and only one world of facts" (Pears 1987, i: 23). Russell's logical atomism adopts, on the other hand, a Platonic penetration of the autonomous world of logical forms into the autonomous world of facts.

3.4 Variety of Calculi

Wittgenstein specified different kinds of indefinables: colors, logical forms, mathematical proofs, physiognomies, works of art, forms of life, numbers, cultures, and others. They all are formal, synthetic, and *a priori*. Furthermore, Wittgenstein insisted that on the basis of these different types of indefinables we can introduce (invent) different types of calculi, such as those enumerated below:

- Philosophical accounts of states of affairs; sense-data; colors; particulars/universals; substance/accident discussion. These all can be considered different kinds of philosophical logics, which can be developed with different orders of rigor. In this sense Michael Beaney refers to a "toolbox" of "a common repertoire of analytic techniques ... that form the methodological basis of analytic philosophy" (2013: 26) (Chapter 3: §§ 3.1, 4).
- Mereology—calculi with "part" and "whole" as indefinables.
- Truth-functional logic—calculi with "truth" and "falsehood" as indefinables.
- Arithmetic—calculation with numbers.
- Algebra—calculation with variables.
- Euclidean geometry—calculation with figures.
- Theoretical physics—calculation with points of space and moments of time.
- Grammars informed by different theoretical intuitions.
- Games of various sorts, like chess.

Apparently, Wittgenstein thought in terms of "family resemblance" as obtaining among diverse calculi when he referred interchangeably and within a single context to mathematics, geometry, grammar, logic, and chess. He propounds, for example, a "logic of colour concepts" (1977, I: § 22), of "geometry of colour" (I: § 66; III: § 86), and of "mathematics of colour" (III: § 3).

Following Wittgenstein, one also finds in philosophical logic the calculus of particulars and universals championed by Moore (1900) and by Russell (1911), elements that F. P. Ramsey developed in his classic paper, "Universals" (1925). Some decades later, P. F. Strawson's *Individuals* (1959) introduced an entirely different species of philosophical calculus: that of monads, sounds, persons, as well as of the missing in this scheme but easy to point out items smells, tastes, and touches.

Being intuitive and thus immediate *per definitionem*, these alternative types of calculi are most economic (Chapter 4: § 5.1) in the sense that J. L. Austin had in mind when he spoke of "language economy." This "economy" is reflected in the fact that the apparatus of each type of calculus is orientationally concise, being at once most comprehensive and basic (fundamental). As a consequence, one can utilize the variety of calculi for "training in thinking" (Chapter 3: § 3.2) or for cultivating what Descartes called *bona mens* (Milkov 1992). This utility of calculi distinguishes philosophy as an inexhaustibly enriching, practical discipline of mind.

It is noteworthy, lastly, that each basic calculus features a specifically indexed "minimal conceptual scheme," a scheme that thus manifests itself differently in different calculi. Wittgenstein insisted that given the intrinsically variable character of the minimal conceptual scheme among calculi,[25] any attempt to limit philosophy to only one species of phenomenological analysis (for example, formal logic) amounts to a theoretically deficient, "one-sided diet" (Wittgenstein 1953: § 593).

Part Five

Two Neglected German Proto-analytic Philosophers

12

G. E. Moore and Johannes Rehmke

1 Introduction: Moore and German-speaking Philosophy

In recent years, several attempts have been made to show that Moore's "revolution in philosophy," which took place at the beginning of the twentieth century, was influenced by certain developments in the Germanophone philosophy of the time. Different avenues have been explored for this purpose. Some authors have claimed that in his formative years, Moore was under the decisive influence of Franz Brentano,[1] an influence that came via George Stout (Bell 1999); others turn their attention to similarities between Moore and Husserl (Künne 1991).[2] In Chapter 6: § 7, we have shown that the roots of German influence on Moore are even older—indeed, they can be traced back to Hermann Lotze.

In this chapter we shall demonstrate that the young Moore became acquainted with works of another group of German-speaking philosophers, that of the Greifswald objectivists, who date from the beginning of the twentieth century. Moreover, he showed considerable interest in them, and apparently was influenced by them. Unfortunately, today the school of the Greifswald objectivists—the most radical critics of psychologism in philosophy ever—has been consigned to oblivion. Not that the school was poor in ideas or arguments. The trouble is that in contrast to other Central European philosophical schools or philosophers, for example, to the school of the Austrian Brentanists, or to Frege, it failed to resurface after the Second World War.[3]

Fortunately, interest in the Greifswald objectivists has been recently revived by Martin Kusch (1995: 99, 118 ff.). The ideas developed in this chapter have been prompted by this newly awoken interest. To be more explicit, we shall trace Moore's connection with the Greifswald objectivists via one of his most obscure papers: his review of Dimitri Michaltschew, *Philosophische Studien: Beiträge zur Kritik des modernen Psychologismus* (1909), published in the January issue of *Mind*, 1911. Even such a careful investigation of his philosophy as Thomas

Baldwin's *G. E. Moore* (1990) is silent about it. Why did he write it? What is its place in Moore's philosophical development?

2 Moore and Michaltschew

2.1 Some Facts of Moore's Philosophical Biography

In order to find out why Moore wrote the Michaltschew review at all, we are first going to locate it on the map of his philosophical development.

After he graduated from Cambridge in 1896, Moore won a six-year fellowship at Cambridge's Trinity College (1898–1904). These years were most successful for his philosophical career. In 1903 he published the programmatic paper "The Refutation of Idealism." In the same year his magnum opus, *Principia Ethica*, was brought out. Despite the fact that the book won wide public recognition (among its admirers were such leading British intellectuals of the time as E. M. Forster, J. M. Keynes, and Virginia Woolf), Moore was not pleased with it. The reason for this is to be found in the fact that in the same year his closest philosophical friend—and rival—Bertrand Russell published *The Principles of Mathematics*. This book convinced Moore that Russell was speeding ahead of him in philosophy and logic, and that he must make up for lost time.

As soon as his fellowship came to end in 1904, Moore left Cambridge in order to live in comparative isolation in Edinburgh. Among other things, in these years he studied Russell's new logical-philosophical ideas with great intensity.[4] Around 1908, however, he started to feel that living in Edinburgh was harmful for his philosophical development. As a result, Moore moved to Richmond, Surrey, where he stayed until October 1911, when he was elected as university lecturer in moral science at Cambridge. His years of philosophical exile in the non-Cambridge world had finally come to an end.

The years 1908–11 are remembered by Moore's biographers for the fact that during this time he finally produced his new synthesis in philosophy. The synthesis itself came to light in a course of twenty lectures "On Metaphysics," delivered at Morley College, London, in the autumn 1910–winter 1911. The lectures were written out in a completely finished form and merely read to the audience (1942: 27), so that more than forty years later they were published almost without changes as *Some Main Problems of Philosophy* (1953). In short, Moore saw the task of these lectures as being to "metaphysically" assimilate the new logical results Russell had reached (Chapter 16: § 4.1). This was a first such attempt, later followed by Russell himself starting with *The Problems of Philosophy* (1912a) and finishing with the lectures "The Philosophy of Logical Atomism" (1918a). It is significant that Russell read the manuscript of Moore's lectures and that he used them extensively in his writings of the 1910s (Russell 1912: v). This fact highlights the prominence of Moore's lectures in the history of early analytic philosophy.

All these biographic facts about Moore and his philosophical development are of help in answering the question why he wrote the Michaltschew review at all. Our tentative answer is that he wrote it in preparation for his "On Metaphysics" lectures of 1910–11. The first reason for this guess (other reasons will be given below) is that the review, published in January 1911, was written in the summer of 1910, when the composition of the lectures was at full speed.

2.2 The Place of the Michaltschew's Review in Moore's Bibliography

This was—to focus on formal features—the last extensive review of the sixteen that Moore wrote in his lifetime.[5] It can be guessed that review-writing was a genre to which Moore addressed himself above all in the years of his philosophical apprenticeship. After he delivered the "On Metaphysics" lectures in 1910–11, and after he assumed the lectureship appointment in Cambridge in October 1911, Moore apparently felt that his philosophy had received its final shape. In consequence, he ceased to be interested in philosophy produced outside Cambridge and stopped writing reviews altogether.

A further formal observation: the majority of these sixteen reviews had books of ethics as their subject, while only three were on "first philosophy." Even more interesting is the fact that these last-mentioned three reviews were all of works by German-speaking philosophers. Of course, these figures are not important in themselves. The crux is that Moore wrote these three reviews when he was in serious philosophical trouble, confronted with the task of breaking new ground in philosophy. In other words, similarly to Russell, he used the works of certain Germanophone philosophers as both reference points and as a guide in his tentative efforts to advance new philosophical theory.

Moore wrote his first review of book by a German philosopher in the spring of 1905, when he discussed Hans Cornelius's *Einleitung in die Philosophie* (1903). Cornelius, to remind the reader, was a "critical realist" from Munich (later he taught in Frankfurt), an admirer, and follower of Ernst Mach. His book was interesting to Moore because it was occupied with one single (and to Moore's thinking, the central) problem of philosophy: How does mind relate to matter? Does matter exist independently of mind, or does it not? Cornelius claimed that when trying to answer such questions, he is a consistent objectivist.

Moore himself had been interested in the problem of objectivism/subjectivism since his revolt against idealism in 1898. In 1904–05, however, he faced a much more concrete—and difficult—task: that of reformulating his objectivism according to the new developments in logic introduced by Russell in *The Principles of Mathematics* and "Meinong's Theory of Complexes and Assumptions" (1904). In the latter paper, to remind the reader, Russell discriminates between knowledge by acquaintance and knowledge by description for the first time (Milkov 2001b). This was a clear move in direction of objectivism.

These developments explain why Moore found Cornelius's book disappointing: he soon became convinced that this author was not a true objectivist. Indeed, Cornelius identifies objective existence with the conception of "regular connexion between our perceptions"—not between objects themselves (1905a: 251). That solution, however, cannot rid us of solipsism. Cornelius holds furthermore "that the experience of other minds is wholly inaccessible to 'empirical' and 'scientific' proof" (ibid.). This prompted Moore's sharply critical reception of the book.

Moore made his next step toward objectivism in his first reaction to Russell's "On Denoting," which found expression in his paper "The Nature and Reality of Objects of Perception," read on December 18, 1905. In it he maintained that a "class of data" we perceive can be called "sense-contents": patches of color with dimension, for instance, as well as spatial relations and forms. Sense-contents are those things which are perceived not only by me but also by other minds too—in other words, they represent a way out of solipsism (1905b: 83). At the same time, Moore now rejected the notion that we perceive material objects directly. In other words, following the new ideas developed in "On Denoting," he claimed that there are two different types of existents: sense-contents and material objects. This was a cleat step toward elaborating his theory of sense-data.

2.3 On Husserl's Influence on Moore

In 1909–10 Moore was again pondering which philosophical road to take. Now, however, his task was a much more ambitious one: it was to write down the first full sketch of the New Philosophy, later called "analytic."

It was in this context that Moore wrote his second review of a German philosopher's book: August Messer's *Empfindung und Denken* (1908), published in the July issue of *Mind*, 1910 (1942: 27). This review can be seen as "a sort of companion piece to [the paper of Moore's] 'The Subject-Matter of Psychology'" (Künne, 1991: 105) which was read to the Aristotelian Society in London on December 6, 1909. In short, "The Subject-Matter of Psychology" systematically developed conceptions which Moore had distilled from Messer's book.

This fact is of utmost importance, since it provides evidence for the considerable, though indirect, influence of Husserl on the founding fathers of analytic philosophy: Moore and Russell.[6] We have come to this conclusion by following up a clue given by Wolfgang Künne, who has recently asserted that August Messer's book *Empfindung und Denken* "is nothing but a rather faithful summary of Husserl's *Logical Investigations*" (ibid.) and that Moore found Messer's work "an extraordinarily good book." How highly he appreciated its ideas is clear from the fact that he applied them in his "On Metaphysics" lectures on a large scale.

Exactly which ideas of Husserl and Messer's were it then that influenced Moore? Moore was particularly interested in Husserl's and Messer's "attempt to classify all the kinds of elements which may occur as constituents of mental phenomena" (1910: 395). On the basis of this classification, Messer went on to describe all the relations between the different parts of mind. In other words, Messer's book offered a good example of the development of a conceptual scheme of the ontology of mind based on objective (non-psychological) mind-elements.

As a matter of fact, Moore had already advanced such a scheme—an objective conceptual framework constructed from realistic elements—in *Principia Ethica*. Moreover, a rudimentary, realistic (Brentanesque) conceptual scheme was advanced by Moore and Russell as early in the years between 1898 and 1903, for example, in Moore's "The Nature of Judgment" (1899). Roughly, it consisted of subject, object, and the relation between them. The task of assimilating Russell's discoveries in philosophical logic of 1903–05, however, led Moore of necessity to introduce new, more refined elements into it, and it was exactly for this purpose that he borrowed some of Husserl's and Messer's ideas.

Where Moore followed them closest of all was in accepting that there is a variety of mental acts—supposing, judging, fearing, hoping, desiring, liking, disliking—which in turn are subdivisions of three great classes: cognitive acts, emotional acts, and acts of will. Moreover, he held "that every act of feeling or of will is always 'founded' upon a cognitive act directed to the same object" (1910: 400).

This idea was endorsed by Russell right away. In *Theory of Knowledge* (1913), for instance, he claimed that there are different mental acts—judging, feeling, willing, and desiring. Mental acts of diverse types are cases of different cognitive relations, every one of which has its own logical form (1913: 125 ff.). This conception was developed further in *Our Knowledge of the External World* (1914) and "The Philosophy of Logical Atomism" (1918a).

These pieces of evidence show how significant the impact of Husserl on the rising Cambridge analytic philosophy was. Clearly, this topic can only be mentioned in passing here, but suffice it to say that the phenomenologists pushed the two Cambridge men in the direction of a detailed philosophy (ontology) of mind. An echo of this influence can be traced in the philosophical psychology of Russell's *The Analysis of Mind* (1921) and especially in Wittgenstein's investigations in philosophical psychology of 1945–49.

This point helps us also to understand and articulate some similarities between the early analytic philosophers and the phenomenologists (see Part IV). Above all, both claim that there is an objective world, including our mental world, and that the task of philosophy is to describe it. In Section 3.1, (c), we shall see that this claim was *conditio sine qua non* for early analytic philosophy.

2.4 Michaltschew and the Greifswald Objectivists

Moore's paper "The Subject-Matter of Psychology" also introduced another major concept to early analytic philosophy, with most important consequences: the term sense-data. A year later he discussed this term in his "On Metaphysics" lectures.

Our claim is that it was with the precise intention of clarifying his concept of sense-data for himself that Moore wrote a review of a third Germanophone book on philosophy: Dimitri Michaltschew's *Philosophische Studien* (1909). It is even possible that Moore introduced the term under the influence of this book. Indeed, as already mentioned, the lecture "The Subject-Matter of Psychology" was read on December 6, 1909, while Michaltschew's book had been published some twelve months earlier.[7] In the second (April) issue of *Mind* for 1909 (vol. 18) we find it listed among the "New Books Received" (p. 309).[8] This shows that Moore would have had time enough to become acquainted with the book at least, before he started to write his paper "The Subject-Matter of Psychology," presumably in October–November 1909.

But who on earth was Dimitri Michaltschew? In addition to his relative obscurity elsewhere, this most eminent of Bulgarian philosophers (1880–1967) has been consigned to oblivion in his own country for the last seventy-five years. Here however is a man who, during his four years of postgraduate study in Greifswald with the German objectivist Johannes Rehmke (1848–1930), managed to write this voluminous work subtitled *Beiträge zur Kritik des modernen Psychologismus* (*Contributions to the Criticism of the Modern Psychologism*). The importance of the book arises from the fact that it appeared before his teacher's *manifesto*—Rehmke's *Philosophie als Grundwissenschaft* was published a year later (1910). In his preface to Michaltschew's book, Rehmke himself called it *filius ante patrem*, and at the same time, pronounced that it promulgated a wholly new strain of philosophy that elaborated a most radical form of anti-psychologism. Moore, who had fought against psychologism (and naturalism, in general) in philosophy for years, was, of course, intrigued.

The book was widely reviewed in the press of the time. Besides *Mind*, six other journals wrote about it. In *The Philosophical Review* for 1910, for example, we read: "[Michaltschew] is very successful in making his ideas clear, and his constructive results are interesting, if slow in coming to the surface" (Fite 1910: 323–24).

Some historical word about the Greifswald objectivists goes in order here. As their ancestors are considered the "immanents" Richard von Schubert-Soldern and Wilhelm Schuppe—the immanents, as one may recall, embraced the belief that there is no difference between subject and object in epistemology.[9] Between 1873 and 1910 Wilhelm Schuppe held a chair of philosophy at the University in Greifswald. In 1885 he organized the appointment of Rehmke as a professor of philosophy there, where Rehmke thought until 1921. The second generation of Greifswald objectivists includes the names Willi Moog and Johannes Erich Heyde.[10] Hans Driesch and Günther Jacoby, whom we shall refer to again in § 2.5, were also close to the Greifswald objectivists. In the 1920s and 1930s the philosophy of the Greifswald objectivists attracted many followers. Between 1919 and 1931 this group published the journal *Grundwissenschaft. Philosophische Zeitschrift der Johannes-Rehmke-Gesellschaft*.

2.5 Moore and Michaltschew: The Given, Sense-data, Conceptual Data

Where, however, is the evidence that Moore wrote this review in order to clear up the sense-data issue for himself, or even that he introduced the term under the influence of this book?

For one thing, in Michaltschew's book the concept of the "given"—*das Gegebene*, in German, or *datum*, in Latin—is central, and of "extreme importance" to him (Moore 1911: 114). Michaltschew fails to define it specifically, but it follows from what he says on many occasions that for him "given" means "directly known," or "immediately given." Further, he claims that everything that we find in our consciousness is given. This claim was the consequence of the Greifswald objectivists' acceptance of "epistemological monism": the subject is absolutely transparent; so much so that it disappears. The consequence is that it does not leave a trace on the objects and phenomena it knows.[11]

Let us now compare Michaltschew's conception of the given to Moore's conception of sense-data:

1) According to the Greifswald objectivist, "the givenness is still not determined" (1909: 110); it is "the undetermined [*unbestimmte*] multiplicity" (505). That is why we cannot ask anything about the given. We determine the given in judgments—it is in judgment that we start to discern the multiplicity and diversity of the given.

    Moore, for his part, maintained that there is a class of objects which we cannot define (1903a, 1903c and 1905b). Such "indefinables" are the colors, truth/falsehoods, sizes, shapes, existences, movements, relations, situations, etc. (Chapter 11: § 2.2). We know all of them immediately. The novelty in Moore's metaphysics in and right after December 1909 was that now he saw the indefinables that we know through senses as particular objects, with specific location. Importantly enough, these objects are different from material objects; the former are related to the latter, despite the fact that they cannot be reduced to them.

2) Michaltschew claims that what is given, and so objective, is "what is in the consciousness, no matter whether it is real or not, whether it is a fantasy or a dream, psychical or physical, a stone or a feeling, particular or general" (1909: 109). Similarly, Moore, and Russell after him, holds that perceptions when perceiving dreaming, daydreaming, and so on, are objective sense-data. Here is Moore's definition of sense-data, dating from December 6, 1909:

    > By sense-data I understand a class of entities of which we are very often directly conscious, and with many of which we are extremely familiar. They include the colours, of all sorts of different shades, which I actually see when I look about me; the sounds which I actually hear; the peculiar sort of entity of which I am directly conscious when I feel the pain of a toothache, and which I call "the pain"; and many others which I need not enumerate. But I wish also to include among them those entities called "images," of which I am directly conscious when I dream and often also when awake. (1909/10: 57)

What makes sense-data of material objects different from the sense-data of dreams is the character of their relation to one another (Chapter 9: § 3.1).

The only difference—albeit a very important one—between Michaltschew's epistemology, on the one hand, and Moore's and also Russell's on the other, was of how we know material objects, as well as concepts, such as numbers, abstract objects, etc. According to Moore and Russell of this period, both material objects and concepts are "incomplete symbols," signified by denoting phrases that are to be analyzed down to their constituents—the sense-data.[12] This view was based on the conviction that there is a radical divergence between sense-data and physical objects which can be inferred from them.

In contrast, according to Rehmke and Michaltschew, *everything* we know, or know about, is given to us—not only our perceptions but also all our knowledge of material objects, as well as of scientific and logical truths. In other words, what is in our consciousness and is not a sense-datum is a conceptual datum. Things signified by denoting phrases, Russellian style, are given as well. We can analyze them into particular data, but we need not do so; they are in order as they are.

Moore found this conception "extremely paradoxical." Certainly, there are many things that we do know, with which we are not directly acquainted—the multiplication table, for example, as well as other mathematical and logical truths, or the general truths of science. Moore of 1909–14 also assumed that the same is true of physical objects. It deserves notice that this signifies a radical change in his position from "The Nature and Reality of Objects of Perception" (1905b). As already mentioned in Section 2.2, at that time Moore called "sense-content"—the ancestor of his concept of sense-data—a "class of data" (83). Obviously, this mode of expression presupposes that there are other classes of data which we do not know immediately: the material objects, for example. Now, in 1911, Moore had arrived at the position that only the sense-data are "given." Besides, there is also an inductive and deductive knowledge that is not given.

2.6 On Carnap's Debt to the Greifswald Objectivists

Moore, however, was not the only early analytic philosopher who noticed how close was the objectivism of the Greifswald philosophers to the philosophical position of the early analytic philosophy. In the 1920s, another analytic philosopher who was even better acquainted with German philosophy than Moore, Rudolf Carnap, discovered the Greifswald objectivists for himself.

This Carnap did first in his 1924 paper "The Three-Dimensionality of Space and Causality," in which he postulated the *Aufbau* program of constructing the external world from the given for the first time. In particular, in this paper he introduced the distinction between the primary and the secondary world of experience. The first comprises the world of phenomena, the second the world of physical objects. Carnap similarly identified the primary world of experience with the given in the sense of Rehmke (1910) and tried further to build the secondary world on it (1924: 108). This means that his view of the primary experience contrasted the view of the given in both conventional empiricism and neo-Kantianism. Indeed, unlike the neo-Kantians, Carnap maintained that the *form* is already present in the world of phenomena or in the primary world of experience. It must not first be introduced into it—in the very process of cognizing. To put this in another perspective, contrary to empiricism, he claimed that the primary world of the *given* is already put into a form; it is not amorphous.

The same was in fact claimed by both Moore and Russell—and at this point the two philosophers are most often misunderstood. Their sense-data are not only simple but also complex items which combine empirical and formal elements into one (Milkov 2001b). Indeed, as already pointed out in Section 2.4, the sense-data of Moore and Russell are indefinables given in our senses and, at the same time, have such formal properties as size, shape, relations, movement, etc. Contrary to the mainstream belief, Moore's and Russell's concept of sense-data has characteristics that are clearly alien to the classical British empiricism (Chapter 9: § 1.1).

Later, in *Aufbau* Carnap used the concept of the given—with reference to Rehmke—in a similar sense (1928: §§ 64 f.). In this book Carnap also refers to two philosophers who, as already mentioned, are considered the ancestors of the Greifswald objectivists: the immanent philosophers Richard von Schubert-Soldern and Wilhelm Schuppe.

In this connection, we would like to briefly address another point. Some twenty years ago, two influential investigations of Carnap's *Aufbau* have been published, reassessing this important work of early analytic philosophy (Richardson 1998; Friedman 1999). Both claim that Quine's earlier interpretation of this work as empiricist, allegedly coming after "Russell's reductionism," is false. In fact, at that time Carnap was much more of a neo-Kantian than a Russellian. His task was to find out how objective science can be reconstructed out of private experience.

We have two objections to this interpretation: (i) *Pace* Quine and Sellars, Russell and still less Moore were not reductionists but "eliminativists" (Chapter 4: § 5.2). (ii) Carnap accomplished his task, above all, with the help of the German objectivists who, far from being neo-Kantians, were in fact anti-Kantians: namely, Rehmke together with Hans Driesch, Günther Jacoby (who received

Rehmke's philosophy professorship in Greifswald in 1928) and Hugo Dingler, as well as the immanents Schuppe and von Schubert-Soldern.[13] This, incidentally, can be seen from Carnap's *Aufbau* Index of Names alone, in which the references to neo-Kantians are far fewer in number than those to the German objectivists.

All of these six authors were objectivists in the sense that they were anti-psychologists. All of them, save Dingler, were either members of the Greifswald objectivist group or close to it. If we really wish to put the Greifswald objectivists into one of the philosophical pigeon-holes of the time, we would be justified in putting them next to the Brentanists, but most certainly not to the neo-Kantians. Incidentally, they were classified so in the numerous books aiming to delineate the main currents (*die Hauptströmungen*) in German-speaking philosophy of the time (Lehmann 1943: 113 f.; Moog 1922: 207; Müller-Freienfels 1923: 60).

We shall naturally not pursue this matter here in detail. We have mentioned it only in order to show that the Greifswald objectivist conception of *given* was undeniably close to the theoretical intuitions and tastes of the early analytic philosophers in general, and not just to those of G. E. Moore. But exactly how close was it?

3 Greifswald Objectivists and the Early Analytic Philosophy

In this part of the chapter we shall set out, on the basis of the historical analysis provided in Section 2, the nature of early analytic philosophy, in the sense of the philosophy of Moore and Russell of 1905–14, differentiating sharply between it and that which is not analytic philosophy in this sense. We shall refer at that to the definition of the early analytic philosophy we suggest in Chapter 16. Further, we shall try to set out what connects early analytic philosophy to the school of the Greifswald objectivists and also to phenomenology, and what makes them different. Our method will be to identify those philosophical practices that are *conditio sine qua non* to early analytic philosophy. If one of them was not exploited by a given philosophical school or group, this means that in all probability it was not truly analytic.

3.1 Further Ideas of Greifswald Objectivists

In order to clearly show the difference between the Greifswald objectivists and the early analytic philosophy we shall first present a short précis of Rehmke's and Michaltschew's objectivist philosophy. The latter made two primary claims and further tried to solve all philosophical problems in terms of these. Above all, Michaltschew adopted the Plato's and Aristotle's pair categories particular–universal as central to philosophy. Next, he set out that we find the universals in particulars; conversely, particulars are sums of universals. In this way, he maintained that universal and particular do not exist separately but are always "given" together.

In addition, Greifswald objectivists introduced the discrimination between real and objective: real (*wirklich*) is what acts upon (*wirkt*), whereas objective is what is merely given. Real is this airplane, this desk; objective is our dream of a golden mountain. Furthermore, Rehmke and Michaltschew discriminate between matter and soul using the same principle. The objects (*Dinge*) of the matter act upon other objects and so are real. In contrast, souls and consciousnesses do not act upon one another: they are only objective.

The same relation between real and objective can be found between universals and particulars: the universal is objective, the particular is real. Particulars change when the universals composing them come and go. Universals themselves, however, do not change. Particulars have such real characteristics as size, shape, and location. Objective items, such as universals and souls, have no such characteristics.

Similarly, persons are individuals; they are not merely particulars (i.e., bodies or minds). They are the interaction (*Wirkenszusammenhang*) between two particulars: the body and the mind. The secondary qualities, on their part, are effect of the interaction between the person and the object.

3.2 Why Greifswald Objectivists Were Not Analytic Philosophers?

A careful comparative analysis of the Greifswald objectivists and the Cambridge early analytic philosophers shows that the North Germans were not early analytic philosophers for at least three reasons:

1) *The Greifswald objectivists were not rigorous philosophers.* Moore's review of Michaltschew was a last example of a method that he followed at the time, a method that we have called "analytic hermeneutics" elsewhere (Milkov 1997 i: 162 ff.) (Chapter 16: n. 13). This was a technique of close inspection of the philosophical texts with the aim of pinpointing "the various meanings of a given ambiguous expression" (White 1958: 74–5), thus deconstructing it to the level of everyday language. Moore applied this method for the first time in (1897) and developed it further in (1903c; 1908; 1909). In all these papers, Moore's objective was to show that the philosopher under scrutiny uses ideas (concepts,

theories) in a sense that is significantly different from the sense in which this very philosopher *believes* that he uses them.

The early analytic philosophy is different. Its basic method is to avoid speculations and unclear ideas and to proceed slowly and circumspectly in its investigation, step by step, using only speculation-free, "aseptic" concepts.

Michaltschew's book, according to Moore, is confusing in this sense. Above all, it discusses too many notions and problems without first making them clear. Thus the meaning of the concept of *given* is not explained in it at all, in spite of the pronounced emphasis that the author puts on it. Further, Michaltschew criticizes many philosophical theories en bloc, without differentiating between them: Rickert's "teleological criticism," Mach's "empirio-criticism," Meinong's theory of objects, Husserl's phenomenology are often lumped together only in order to be collectively discarded away. In particular, for him all of them are guilty of psychologism: they maintain that what is given cannot subsist independently of consciousness.

Moreover, Michaltschew brings forward no argument in support of his conception of the *given* whatsoever; and this is a serious shortcoming which reveals him once more to be a pre-analytic, or proto-analytic, philosopher. Indeed, to Moore of 1909, philosophy consists first and foremost of advancing reasons and arguments. It is rigorous philosophy directed to achieving "solid results" (Chapter 16: § 3).

2) *The Greifswald objectivists were not linguistic philosophers.* The Greifswald objectivists were also pre-propositional. Indeed, they failed to join that form of anti-psychologism, or objectivism, which followed the so-called "propositional turn." Russell's philosophy took this turn already around 1900,[14] and intensified it after 1903 in direction traced by Frege. It was also embraced by Moore (in particular, in his "On Metaphysics" lectures), and later also by Wittgenstein. From this stance, the starting point in philosophy is the analysis of propositions, not simply the analysis of knowledge.

To be fair, similarly to Russell, Michaltschew and Rehmke were also against the influence of grammar on philosophy. They claimed that grammar misleads us to believe that judgment synthesizes elements of the given into one. In fact, what synthesizes is the language, whereas judgment discriminates—and so determines—the multiplicity of the given. Michaltschew and Rehmke did not, however, base this claim on conceptions introduced with the propositional turn.

3) *Greifswald objectivists were not descriptive philosophers.* The latter point brings us to the next "analytic deficiency" of the Greifswald objectivists. Their philosophy was not only inexact and pre-propositional but it was also non-descriptivist.[15] Indeed, in contrast to both Husserl and Messer and Moore and

Russell, Michaltschew's metaphysics does not aim at advancing a conceptual scheme which is articulated in descriptions. As we have already seen in Section 2.3, the conceptual scheme of Husserl and Messer's ontology of mind discriminates between a subject, a cognitive relation and an object. Further, it maintains that there are many kinds of cognitive relations or mental acts: sense-perception (seeing, hearing, feeling, smelling), remembering, dreaming, imagining, thinking, and observing. Besides mental acts, there are also other ways of knowing that things exist: memory, the already cited direct knowing of material objects, etc. All these mental acts and ways of knowing build up a well-ramified conceptual scheme that can be described in great detail.

There is no such a conceptual scheme in the philosophy of Rehmke and Michaltschew, however. The aim of the Greifswald objectivists—similarly to the aim of other "continental" philosophers of the time, Henry Bergson, for example—was, instead, to make a key philosophical discovery: to find out how mind and matter are connected, at one stroke, after which the whole of philosophy would be reformed.[16]

3.3 Closest Connections of the Greifswald Objectivist to the Early Analytic Philosophy

3.3.1 Radical Anti-psychologism

Despite the fact that they followed this old-fashioned one-stroke approach to philosophy, Rehmke and Michaltschew also joined the most progressive movement in the philosophy of the time—the objectivist anti-psychologism.[17] What is more, the anti-psychologism of the Greifswald objectivists was much more radical than that of their German-speaking contemporaries and, so, closer to Moore and Russell than any other philosophical school of the time.

Here we would remind the reader of a most important difference between Moore and Russell on the one hand, and the two heads of the German-speaking philosophy in about 1900, Frege and Husserl, on the other. Whereas the former adopted the conceptual scheme subject-act-object, the scheme of the latter was subject-act-*content*-object. The Cambridge realists rejected the content and so embraced the most straightforward and direct form of objectivism. Similarly, they denied that states of affairs have their own ontology (Chapter 8: § 5.2). In this respect they were closer to Rehmke and Michaltschew than to Frege or Husserl. This is also what constitutes the difference between Moore and Husserl-Messer. Whereas the latter believe that two acts having the same object can differ because of their "interpretative sense" (*Auffassungssinn*), "according to Moore the so-called difference in content of two acts with the same primary objects is 'in reality' the difference between their secondary objects. And this Husserl would not accept" (Künne 1991: 111).

3.3.2 Theory of Truth

In theory of truth, Michaltschew is again closer to Moore and Russell than to Frege or Husserl.[18] Michaltschew claims that "to say 'It is *true* that so and so is the case' is equivalent to saying, 'So and so is really (*in Wirklichkeit*) the case'" (Moore 1911: 115). By this, he apparently means that "every 'true' sentence must express something which 'exists,' in the sense in which particular things and persons exist at some times and not at others" (ibid.).

Here the closeness with which Michaltschew's position is related to that of Moore and Russell is obvious. As a matter of fact, in his discussion with Frege of 1904, Russell was eager to point out, as if in agreement with Greifswald objectivists, the following:

> I believe that in spite of all its snowfields Mont Blanc itself is a component part of what is actually asserted in the proposition "Mont Blanc is more than 4000 meters high." We do not assert the thought, for this is a private psychological matter: we assert the object of the thought. (Frege 1980: 169)

This position, called the "identity theory of truth" by some contemporary philosophers (Baldwin 1991), is very close to Michaltschew's theory of truth.

The only difference—very important one—is again that, in contrast to Michaltschew, Russell also assumed that true propositions refer to denoting phrases, such as "The author of Waverley," or "The infinite number." The words in such phrases have meaning by virtue of the logical form of the phrases, but not in isolation. Exactly this conception—the principle of contextual definition—introduced a new argument against psychologism in philosophy that was apparently unknown to Michaltschew and which can be called the "argument from philosophy of language" assumed with the propositional turn.

13
Leonard Nelson, Karl Popper, and Early Analytic Philosophy

Since Nelson's philosophy is little known today, the chapter commences with a brief account (in § 1) of how he developed elements of what was later dubbed analytic philosophy. Following that, we identify (in § 2) the main points of Nelson's impact on Popper, as well as some elements of divergence between them.

1 Leonard Nelson and Analytic Philosophy

1.1 Variants of Analytic Philosophy

Some scholars claim that analytic philosophy was introduced by G. E. Moore and Bertrand Russell. Others contend that it originated with Gottlob Frege. A third line of thought has it that in their "revolution in philosophy" Moore and Russell followed Franz Brentano. The present chapter argues that analytic philosophy traces back at least in part to another thinker, namely the German philosopher Leonard Nelson (1882–1927). Apparently, analytic philosophy evidently had various *naissances*. At the beginning of the twentieth century, the "world spirit" spontaneously produced elements of analytic (or proto-analytic) philosophy, albeit in different guises. Nelson's proto-analytic philosophy arose independently of Moore and Russell yet evinces remarkable parallels with their work. As one might expect, there were considerable differences in the approaches to analysis, and there are purists who find these sufficient grounds for denying that we can classify Nelson's thought as an originary ground of the same movement associated with the British thinkers (Glock 2011). The present section challenges this judgment by adducing a range of evidence that testifies to the fundamental relatedness of the analytic thinking that originated contemporaneously in Göttingen and Cambridge.

1.2 In What Sense Was Nelson an Analytic Philosopher?

Similarly to Russell, Nelson was a close student of science and mathematics. Also like Russell, he made precise, closely argued cases for his views, employing a lucid and unadorned discursive style that alienated him from his German colleagues of the time.

Nelson was openly hostile toward what was later called "continental" philosophy. His review of the book of the leading neo-Kantian Hermann Cohen, *System der Philosophie* (Nelson 1905), was so sharply critical that it made Nelson's life in German academia difficult. Nelson had discredited Cohen's discussions of mathematics for betraying fundamental deficits in his knowledge of the subject. As we are going to see later, the main characteristic of Nelson's philosophy was its radical openness toward mathematics and science. Nelson also wrote an article that attacked the philosophical coherence of Bergson's thinking (1910), something Russell later did two years later. Further, Nelson authored a pamphlet against Oswald Spengler (1921), a critique published the same year in which Otto Neurath's *Anti-Spengler* appeared.

Nelson's own philosophy closely followed the work of Jacob Friedrich Fries (1773–1843). In 1912, Nelson organized the Jacob Friedrich Fries Society, in many respects the forerunner of the Berlin Society for Empirical/Scientific Philosophy (Haller 1993: 79; Milkov 2008; 2013a). The aim of the Fries Society was to attract leading mathematicians, scientists and philosophers of the time by providing a forum whereby they could pursue interdisciplinary philosophical studies. On this count, the society achieved its end brilliantly. Its sessions drew many of the top mathematicians and scientists of the day—Max Born, Ernst Zermelo, Richard Courant and Paul Bernays, to name only a few of them (Peckhaus 1990: 153).

1.3 Jacob Friedrich Fries

Nelson's closest philosophical predecessor, Fries, was Hegel's contemporary and also his adversary and rival. Fries was sharply critical as well of Kant's "rationalistic prejudice" by means of which we may deduce all *a priori* concepts from a single principle belonging to one system. To this Fries opposed his own program for analyzing *a priori* forms of knowledge, a program that took as its modus operandi "self-observation," which he saw as an empirical ("anthropological") task. This is also a task of deducing *a priori* knowledge from our immediate knowledge. Importantly enough, while the subject of this investigation is the *a priori*, the way we reach it is a posteriori.[1] Kant mistakenly assumed that the process of transcendental deduction is logical. Denying this, Fries insisted that the general axioms and principles of the transcendental deduction cannot be logically proved. This is so, Fries maintained, since they are the last court of appeal—one cannot prove them by reference to something else. We can only abstract them from immediate knowledge, or the given.

In nineteenth-century Germany, critics often attacked Fries for his alleged "Locke-like empiricism." In fact, however, his "anthropological psychology was not empirical psychology" at all (Lehmann 1931: 119). Fries openly opposed experimental psychology, urging the development of philosophical psychology instead. Motivating Fries in this connection was his view that "immediate knowledge" also includes scientific and mathematical knowledge. Hence we are to look for *a priori* truths also in these disciplines. This explains the strong interdisciplinary thrust of his philosophy, which inspired some scientists in Germany at the time to undertake philosophical investigations. By the same token, Fries persuaded a number of philosophers to correlate their research with the latest discoveries in science and mathematics.

A related point that Fries argued for is that metaphysical knowledge, which consists of synthetic *a priori* judgments, grows, in particular, in the epistemological form of the advances in scientific and mathematical axiomatic.[2] Nelson held that the philosophy of mathematics (a sub-discipline that originated with Fries[3]) concerns itself with ongoing developments in mathematical axiomatic. The potentially pivotal significance of this new sub-discipline was historically borne out when, after Fries's death, the non-Euclidean geometry appeared, bringing with it novel mathematical axioms. Philosophy of mathematics set itself the task of reducing to a minimum the number of the new mathematical axioms that came with each new innovation in the field, retaining only those necessary for its logical substantiation (Nelson 1928: 110).

1.4 Nelson's Method of Regress

One of the difficulties in seeing Nelson as an analytic philosopher is that he employed terminology incomprehensible to contemporary philosophers. A paradigmatic example is his identifying as "regressive method" what most philosophers of the present day think of as analysis. It is worth noting in this connection, however, that Bertrand Russell himself, prior to 1911 (when he adopted the concepts "analytic philosophy" and "analytic method"), also made regular use of the term "regressive method," and in virtually the same sense as Nelson (Russell 1907; Peckhaus 2002).

What exactly was Nelson's regressive method? He claimed that the transition from factual consequences to factual premises occurs in accord with the laws of *induction*; the transition from consequence to "epistemological premises," however, involves the *deductive* method of abstraction. What we abstract is the structure of "our mind"—in search of "fundamentals" of mathematics and science—from the vague matter of knowledge, including scientific knowledge (n. 2). This is the "method" that Nelson understood as "regressive." It does not supply new knowledge but simply clears up points in our reasoning which were already available in it, although in a vague form (1922: 33).

Russell's argument in support of the regressive method was that in philosophy "a comparatively obscure and difficult proposition can be a premise for a comparatively obvious proposition" (1907: 272). From vague premises we can deduce simpler propositions. In *Our Knowledge* Russell expressed this idea thus: while in mathematics we move from simpler to more complex knowledge, in philosophy we move from complex (and vague) to more simple (1914: 189–90); while mathematics is synthetic, philosophy is analytic—"regressive," both as he used the word in his older terminology and as Nelson utilized it.

In the same wake, Wittgenstein would later define philosophy as a synthetic *a priori* discipline. It is synthetic since it investigates items well known to us all, simply casting them in a new perspective, and it is *a priori* since its truths are generally valid. Regarded from this standpoint, the task of philosophy could be construed as rearranging common (immediate) knowledge (Milkov 1997, i: 387). Nelson understood this as a way that we study our mind. Wittgenstein, on his side, investigated the concepts of philosophical psychology in a kind of conceptual analyses (Chapter 11: § 3.2).

1.5 Vagueness

We can read these points of relatedness between Nelson, on the one hand, and Russell and Wittgenstein, on the other, as the first signs that these three thinkers explored elements of what we already have called "early analytic philosophy." Nelson's discussions of human knowledge also thematize particular ideas that substantiate this observation: for example, the concept of "vagueness."

Both Fries and Nelson claimed that, similar to judgment, immediate knowledge, or the given (Chapter 12), is initially vague or "dark" (*dunkel*), indefinable (Chapter 11), and takes two different forms: perceptual and conceptual. As we have noted, the movement from data of sense (immediate knowledge) to their premises (from the singular to the general) is inductive; the movement from conceptual data (immediate knowledge) to their premises, on the other hand, is a movement of deductive abstraction. What about metaphysical judgments which deduce the structure of experience from the immediately given conceptual data of our mind? They cannot be proven because they set up the first principles of human knowledge (see § 2.4) nor can they be demonstrated by induction. They can only be abstracted; not through intuition, however, but through reflection, or critique (see Chapter 11: § 2.2).

Such a deduction reveals the *a priori* valid structure of our mind—despite the fact that we investigate it empirically. Since it brings to light the structure of human mind, this is a task of a philosophical anthropology. Fries and Nelson spoke about it more specifically as psychological knowledge. Of course, it is not psychological in the sense in which Lotze, Husserl, Frege, and Russell criticized the psychologism in philosophy. Indeed, the objects of this study are valid *a priori*. It is more like Wittgenstein's philosophical psychology, but with a clear scientific orientation. It is relative *a priori*.

In sum, both Fries and Nelson understood that the unique concerns of philosophy have to do with immediate non-intuitive knowledge and conceptual data. It approaches these matters by investigating facts—facts of our "inner sense" to which pertain also facts of science and mathematics. This kind of knowledge is synthetic *a priori*. It is a product of human reason (*Vernunft*) and is capable of progress and growth.

1.6 Socratic Method

Nelson believed that truth in philosophy is singular, that it is wrong to regard philosophy as mosaic of standpoints. In fact, it was Leibniz who was the first to defend this view; he fought against a plurality of philosophical schools, claiming that in philosophy, just as in science and mathematics, the cliquishness of competing philosophical schools is inimical to the search for truth (1679: 223; A VI, 4: 265). In a similar manner, Nelson insisted that philosophy is not the search for ever-new standpoints that ought to guide philosophers in their work. Rather, like the other sciences, philosophy must orient itself to searching for truth in the context of other, previously established truths (1908: 201).

In this sense, Nelson claimed that "the greatest philosophical discoveries are a common achievement of all distinguished philosophers" (1922: 25). He especially praised two great figures in the history of philosophy: Plato and Kant. Between them there were long periods of philosophical regression. What is more, philosophers of these periods also paved the way for reactionary ideas in politics.

Like the sciences and mathematics, philosophy, according to Nelson, develops successfully only when it follows an appropriate method—a method that guarantees continuity in philosophical studies, and so progress in the discipline. Nelson understood Socrates and the early Plato to be champions of such a method, namely peirastic dialectic (see Milkov 2013b: § 2), which is led by a "sense of truth" (*Wahrheitsgefühl*) (1922: 27). It entails critically examining every posited argument, theory, or fact.[4] Historically, Kant's critical method was nothing but a revival of the method of Socrates and Plato.[5]

The principal advantage of this method is that it eliminates dogmatism in teaching; in fact, it eliminates any doctrinal (*belehrende*) judgment. Instead, by it, the mind learns to find the premise of the philosophical truths in itself: "The philosophical lesson fulfils its task if it gradually eliminates the influences in the student which handicap the illumination of the student's philosophical knowledge" (1922: 45). The instructor works at teaching the lesson "from outside." In other words, the objective of pedagogic philosophical dialogue is not (as Frege believed) to establish solid *results*; rather (as also the later Wittgenstein believed), it must help to disclose a *method* for achieving solid results.

Detailed investigation in the history of the early analytic philosophy (Milkov 1997, 2003) reveals that until at least 1960 practically all of the movement's leading representatives practiced the peirastic method. That this held for Nelson, as well, further establishes that he qualifies as an (proto-) analytic philosopher. A fact that additionally bears out this historical contention is that Nelson seminally influenced one of the central figures of the Oxford Ordinary Language Philosophy—R. M. Hare (Franke 1991: 49). In particular, the latter's works on ethics employ Nelson's method of "weighing up of interests" (Hare 1963: 90 ff.; Alexy 1979). In contemporary political theory this notion has evolved into the concept of *reflective equilibrium*.[6]

Nelson's influence was also pronounced in Richard Hare's philosophy of education. Indeed, the declared objective of the latter is "to teach his students to think" (Hare 1959: 3). To this end, Hare embraced the Socratic dialogue as the central method of teaching (ibid.: 5). And as we have just seen, the revival of the Socratic dialogue in philosophy was one of Nelson's central objectives.

2 Nelson's Influence on Popper

2.1 Opening

It was M. H. Hacohen who first underscored the "formidable" impact that Nelson's philosophy exerted upon Popper, who "probably borrowed from [Nelson] the 'Socratic Method.' Both Nelson and Popper," asserts Hacohen, "identified the method with critical dialogue and awareness of the limits of cognition" (2000: 125–26). This assessment has become standard in the literature (Morgenstern and Zimmer 2002: 32–3).

Besides the critical method, Popper also adopted Nelson's rational attitude to the problems of philosophy in general, something Nelson often referred to as "intellectual responsibility." The theoretical orientation of both Nelson and Popper falls under the rubric of the "critical attitude [which] is the attitude of reasonableness, or rationality" (Popper 1963: 51).[7] Popper identified his approach as "critical philosophy"—the same term that both Fries and Nelson applied to their own.

Hacohen has also observed that Nelson's philosophy "was a departure point to which he [Popper] continuously returned [in order] to check his own developing views" (2000: 126). In general, asserts Hacohen, one can say that "'critical philosophy' set the problem situation that enabled Popper to make his radical theoretical move, reformulate the question of the validity of knowledge, and achieve his great breakthrough in the philosophy of science" (ibid.: 127).

2.2 Cryptic Influence

In a letter from 1992, Popper recalled that he "wrote, between 1925 or 26 and 1933, very intensively on a book, essentially about Kant–Fries–Nelson. . . . I tried hard to understand them." On the other hand, Popper also made statements that disguise Nelson's influence on him. In his "Intellectual Autobiography," for instance, he claimed that "from Tarski [he] learned more . . . than from anybody else" (1974: 70). Popper further remembered that he changed his orientation from psychology to logic under the influence of Oswald Külpe's logic.

It will become clear presently, however, that Tarski, Külpe, and others did not decisively influence Popper. Leonard Nelson was the prime influence, and behind him Fries. Nelson impelled Popper to adopt the Platonic method of peirastic dialectics, and to develop it into his famous method of conjectures and refutations, of trials and errors. At the time Popper himself called this method "dialectical" (1930/3: 316 ff.). Ironically enough, today Popper is best known as the arch enemy of dialectic. In truth, however, his main work on this theme, the paper "What is Dialectic?" (1940) had a clear ideological (anti-Marxist) message and reduced dialectics to an impoverished Hegelian variant, making of it a caricature.

Nelson's influence on Popper is well documented. In the early 1930s, Popper took on the Vienna Circle's idea of demarcation (*Abgrenzung*) between meaningful and meaningless propositions, with the aim of isolating the propositions of metaphysics from those of science. Popper defended this position at length (1930/3). But just as he began publishing his findings, Julius Kraft induced him to change his account (Gattei 2009: 18 ff.). This change is clearly evident in the first volume's subsequently published eleventh section and the work's second volume. While retaining his notion of the demarcation of metaphysics, Popper now argued that falsification, rather than verification, is the means by which to distinguish meaningful propositions in science.

Nelson also influenced Popper with his radical scientific orientation. On this point he was close to Hans Reichenbach, who in the summer of 1914 became intensively involved with Nelson's group in Göttingen.[8]

One of the reasons why Nelson's influence on Popper is difficult to recognize was articulated by Popper himself, who explained that one cannot identify any genuine students of Nelson.[9] Indeed, his teaching does not consist of theses,[10] but is rather merely an "attitude which put stress on the use of reason and intellectual responsibility" (1962: 4).

Another reason why Popper was not explicit about the decisive impact Nelson's philosophy had on his development is that Popper neither connected Nelson with his (Popper's) method of conjectures and refutations nor with his philosophy of science. He mainly related Nelson's philosophy to his epistemology. Important as it was for Popper, however, Nelson's views on epistemology did not play the formative role in his philosophical development that Nelson's peirastic and philosophy of science did.

2.3 How This Influence Came About: The Role of Julius Kraft

It was Julius Kraft (1898–1960) who introduced Popper to Nelson's philosophy.[11] Kraft was a distant relative of Popper's from Hanover and wrote his PhD dissertation under Nelson. In 1924, he came to Vienna to write his *Habilitation* (a post-doctoral dissertation) under Hans Kelsen, who, by the way, stood opposed to Nelson's thinking. Kraft remained in Vienna until 1926, after which—having failed to win his *Habilitation*—he moved to Frankfurt to become an assistant of Nelson's friend Franz Oppenheimer.[12]

Popper and Kraft carried on a lively correspondence till the beginning of the Second World War. Their in-person discussions from 1924 to 1926 "were endless . . . often lasting into the small hours of the morning" (Popper 1974: 59). This was of great importance for Popper's philosophical ego—Kraft was the first person with a doctorate in philosophy who showed a genuine interest in engaging in sustained philosophical dialogue with the young undergraduate student. Popper later recalled that about half of his discussions with Julius Kraft "were centered on criticism of Marx. The other half were about the theory of knowledge: mainly Kant's so-called 'transcendental deduction' (which I regarded as question-begging), his solution of the antinomies, and Nelson's 'Impossibility of the Theory of Knowledge'" (ibid.). This reminiscence of Popper's substantiates the contention at the end of the last section that Popper himself did not connect Nelson's influence on himself with the method of peirastic dialectic.

Interestingly, Popper was to work with Kraft three decades later, in the 1950s, a collaboration interrupted only by Kraft's death in 1960. The most important product of this cooperation was the founding of the journal *Ratio* in 1957, a successor of *Abhandlungen der Fries'sche Schule*, second series, which Nelson had inaugurated over half a century earlier, in 1904.[13]

2.4 Popper and Nelson's Epistemology and the Philosophy of Science

Today Nelson's most widely known thesis is that the theory of knowledge, which has held a central place in philosophy since Descartes, is impossible. Such is the case, according to Nelson, because there is no valid criterion for the truth of knowledge. Indeed, if every kind of knowledge needs to be justified, it follows that there is a kind of knowledge (that of knowledge itself) which is not justified, which is a contradiction. Nelson concluded that we cannot posit a theory of knowledge without making presuppositions.[14] Like his own philosophical predecessor Fries, Nelson fought the demand to justify scientifically everything that is to be accepted as knowledge, rejecting what he called this "predilection for proofs" (Popper 1930/3: 106). Both Fries and Nelson held the possibility of knowledge to be not a problem but simply a fact. They argued that the criterion for the truth lies in the immediate knowledge (perceptual and conceptual) which is solid and secure. Indeed, human understanding proceeds from the conviction that immediate knowledge harmonizes with reality.[15]

We earlier remarked (in §§ 1.2–4) that while it accepted that knowledge brings with it unproven presuppositions, critical philosophy also called for their examination. What Nelson argued was that instead of trying to deduce the *a priori* principles from "pure reason," we must bring to light the "anthropological facts" that justify us in taking these principles as true. Nelson in this way abandoned the theory of knowledge for a "psychology of knowledge." Particularly worthy of note in this connection are two distinguishing aspects of this doctrine of "fact" as it figures in Nelson's psychology of knowledge: (i) "Facts," in Nelson's view, include the data of science and the truths of mathematics, and here Nelson proved himself to be an accomplished philosopher of mathematics and science. Further, (ii) Nelson regarded facts as neither intuitive nor self-evident but, instead as "vague" (*dunkel*). In order to deduce the *a priori* truths from such data, we must discern their multiplicity in an act of Socratic reflection (§ 1.5).[16]

Until the end, Popper remained critical of Fries and Nelson's views on ultimate immediate knowledge—the given (1992). Against them, he followed the British pragmatist Ferdinand Schiller, who argued that this position overlooks the option of commencing the effort to acquire knowledge by postulating insecure presuppositions that we can confirm over the course of an investigation. At the same time, however, Popper concurred with Fries's and Nelson's call for closely linking philosophical research with science and mathematics.

As it turns out, Popper's interpretation of Fries's and Nelson's epistemology on this point was inaccurate. According to Popper, Fries claimed that since the requirement for logical justification of scientific hypotheses leads to regress ad infinitum, we must justify scientific theories through "perceptual experience" (1934: 60). Actually, however, Fries and Nelson never referred in this connection to perceptual experience but rather to immediate knowledge in general, which also includes immediate conceptual, or scientific, knowledge.

Popper rightly noted that, whereas to Fries and Nelson the basic statements (axioms) of science have the character of dogmas, "this kind of dogmatism [is] ... innocuous since, should the need arise [through new scientific discoveries], these statements can easily be [revised]" (ibid., 70). A typical example in this respect (one cited in § 1.3, above) is the new set of axioms that proved necessary for the non-Euclidean geometry which Riemann formulated after Fries's death. This, in fact, was the *critical* stance of Fries's and Nelson's epistemology that Popper adopted. Our knowledge, Popper famously declared, proceeds by way of *conjectures*, followed by their *refutations*, which in their turn are followed by new conjectures, and so on.

But Popper went beyond Fries and Nelson when he claimed that scientific progress consists in moving toward theories that manifest ever greater deductive power. From this standpoint "scientific progress turned out not to consist in the accumulation of observations but in the overthrow of less good theories and their replacement by better ones, in particular by theories of greater content" (1974: 62–3).[17]

Popper felt that most philosophers of science were misguided in believing that their work makes use of induction in an operation of *justifying* theories by making observations or experiments. Especially zealous in this respect were the Logical Positivists of the Vienna Circle who used induction in the form of the principle of verification. Similarly to Nelson, Popper claimed that induction is a myth "which had been [already] exploded by Hume" (1974: 63). Popper championed, instead, a doctrine of deduction based on falsifiability or testability. He maintained that "the falsification or refutation of theories through the falsification or refutation of their deductive consequences [is], clearly, a deductive inference (*modus tollens*)" (62).

Popper regarded himself as indebted to Fries and Nelson for this conception, but only for the sharp distinction that both Fries and Nelson had drawn between induction and deduction (1934: 70 n. 3). In fact, however, the influence was much more profound. The two philosophers contended that deduction must be applied in metaphysics, that is, in the foundations of mathematics and science, and in ethics as well. This is metaphysics of changeable (or relative) *a priori* truths that are deductively discovered through Socratic examination of the phenomena science investigate. Despite the fact that Popper rejected metaphysics, he adopted Nelson's thesis of changeability of scientific truths in the form of falsificationism, which defended the "deductive method of testing" scientific theories (30, 32, 47).

2.5 Critique of Positivism and Empiricism

Nelson's critique of induction informed the challenge he mounted against two other positivist positions. It was evident in the doubts he raised about the positivists' insistence that science is descriptive and so has no properly theoretical charge; that its task is merely to lay down the "bare facts." It was evident, as well, in Nelson's questioning the existence of such things as sense-data and "simple" ideas or impressions, which he took to be inventions based on mistaken attempts to adapt the atomism of physics to psychology.

Popper followed Nelson on both of these points.[18] He also concurred with Nelson's criticism (see § 2.4) of the verification principle, which invoked the authority of David Hume. This positivist principle sponsored a naïve, pre-Humean form of empiricism.[19] Its revival, by philosophers like Hans Kelsen, is unwarranted and constitutes a clear case of regression in philosophy (see § 1.6). Hume himself had unequivocally shown that empiricism fails to explain not only science but also ordinary human experience. Starting from this point, Nelson concluded that science without metaphysics is impossible. Popper closely followed him in this too, although Popper's form of "metaphysics" differed from that of Nelson.

To Nelson, metaphysics has its own signature task, namely deducing the presuppositions of our ethical, mathematical, and scientific knowledge. Popper accepted a related but manifestly different position: instead exploring metaphysics, he pursued philosophy of science that investigates the methods of special sciences—which is to say, it investigates scientific problems and their tentative solutions, as well as the issue of scientific progress. From a strict Nelsonian point of view, Popper's position itself was positivistic. Indeed, Nelson was convinced that philosophy has nothing to do with the *methods* of special science and must instead simply lay out their first principles. In short, philosophy is not to be replaced with methodology of science.

2.6 Epilogue: Why Popper Was Not an Analytic Philosopher?

In addition to the other influences, Nelson's thought aided Popper formulating his criticism of one of the Vienna Circle's lead doctrines, namely that we primarily philosophize over language and concepts. Members of the circle derived this position from the *Tractatus* of Wittgenstein, who himself was drawing upon Frege (Chapter 14). Early on, Popper categorically rejected it and never back-pedaled on his initial judgment. He also criticized the claim of Frege and (the early) Wittgenstein that concepts must have explicit boundaries (1974: 21).[20]

Among other things, this stance brought Popper close to Susan Stebbing in the mid-1930s.[21] As early as in 1932, Stebbing had criticized both Wittgenstein and the Vienna Circle along the same lines (Chapter 14: § 3)[22] pairing their views and comparing them as opposed to the "good philosophy" of Moore and Russell which proceeds not from language but from reality. Besides the shared aversion to the conception that philosophy is primarily philosophy of language, Stebbing was sympathetic to Popper because of the latter's conviction that discussions in theoretical philosophy can help to orient us in practical matters; that "our often unconscious views on the theory of knowledge and its central problems are decisive for our attitude towards ourselves and towards politics" (Popper 1974: 91). In this sense, *The Poverty of Historicism* and *The Open Society* might be said to have grown out of the theory of knowledge of *The Logic of Scientific Discovery* (see § 2.3). The following declaration of Stebbing's reveals an orientation that parallels Popper's:

> Anyone who has been able to learn something of Moore's way of thinking, . . . could not, I think, succumb to the muddle-headed creed of Fascism or National Socialism. For, to be imbued with his critical yet positive spirit is to be forearmed against the forces of irrationalism. (1942: 532)

But Popper consequently opposed not only the linguistic analysis of Frege and Wittgenstein; he also rejected elements of the analytic philosophy of Moore and Russell who were widely esteemed "philosopher's philosophers." He failed to grasp the importance of the exploration of fundamentals. Popper's judgment that early analytic philosophers produced doctrines that are unacceptably "minute" in character coincides with the charges that many Bergsonians and Heideggerians leveled against it.

However, early analytic philosophy is "minute in character" because it discusses, what Russell called, the "fundamentals" (Chapter 16: § 3). As we already have seen it (Chapter 9: § 2), on this point it shook hands with the early and middle phenomenology. Russell, incidentally, knew quite well that his new philosophy is "dry." He, however, did not feel that he "owe[d] any apology for any sort of [inborn] dryness or dullness in the world [itself]" (1918a: 281).

Hence, it is no accident that the epigraph of *The Logic of Scientific Discovery*, "Hypotheses are nets: only he who casts will catch," comes from the arch romanticist Novalis, nor that *Two Fundamental Problems of Theory of Knowledge*, the title Popper gave his first work, was a paraphrase of Arthur Schopenhauer's *Two Fundamental Problems of Ethics*. After all, Schopenhauer, together with Eduard von Hartmann, was among the writers who considerably influenced Popper in his youth. Moreover, Popper did not hesitate to borrow ideas from Henry Bergson—a philosopher whom both Russell and Nelson unconditionally repudiated. For example, Popper states that his "view can be expressed by saying that every discovery contains an 'irrational element,' or 'a creative intuition,' in Bergson's sense" (1934: 7).

This last fact about Popper's thought makes it patent that he was no mere epigone of Nelson's. That said, however, a close review of Popper's work reveals that in his most successful thinking he followed Nelson. And conversely, on those issues that found him opposed to Nelson, Popper typically produced his least distinguished ideas. A paradigmatic example of the latter is Popper's attack on Nelson's concept of the given under the banner of anti-foundationalism, a position that opened Popper to severe and warranted criticism for relativism (Stove 1982).

Part Six

Different Conceptions of Analytic Philosophy

14

Wittgenstein and the Vienna Circle versus G. E. Moore and Russell

1 Introduction: Two Concepts of Analytic Philosophy

In the first decade after the First World War it was common to speak of early Cambridge analytic philosophy as the philosophy of the English realists. While the old metaphysics, for example, that of McTaggart, was a systematic study of the ultimate nature of the world, the new realistic metaphysics studied the phenomena of the world. It was pluralistic, piecemeal, developed step by step, and recognized one authority only: the reality with which we are acquainted directly. It was the philosophy of the concrete (Chapter 16: § 4 (a)).

By contrast, in Susan Stebbing's paper "Logical Positivism and Analysis" (1933), which was read to the British Academy at a Henriette Hertz lecture on March 22, 1933, and shortly thereafter published separately, a new enemy of Moore's realism was found. She was anxious to distinguish not only between Cambridge Realists and British idealists but also between the former and the Logical Positivists of the Vienna Circle. Stebbing was adamant that the analysis practiced by the English Realists is not to be confused with the "logical analysis" of the "Viennese Circle."

Not only this, this keen woman philosopher was the first author to see considerable differences in the philosophy of Moore, on the one hand, and Wittgenstein's *Tractatus*, on the other. The latter was seen by her as the product of a non-British tradition in philosophy that has its roots in the continent. This explains why the ideas of the *Tractatus* were not only embraced faithfully by the Vienna Circle but also developed further in their true spirit—so much so that Stebbing tried to reconstruct Wittgenstein's philosophy post-1929 from the newly published works of the philosophers of the Vienna Circle (ibid.: 53 ff.).

The decision to explicate Wittgenstein's philosophical views of 1929–1932 by analyzing the papers of the Vienna Circle was a judicious one indeed. The published views of the philosophers of the Logical Positivists of the time were, at least at some points, so close to those of Wittgenstein that in the summer of 1932 the latter was afraid that when he published his long-prepared "new book," he would be found guilty of plagiarism. This is well documented in a letter to Carnap of August 20, 1932 (Nedo and Ranchetti 1983: 381), in which Wittgenstein accuses Carnap of publishing some of his (Wittgenstein's) own ideas without acknowledgment in a paper of his.[1] As a matter of fact, this article of Carnap's was the one discussed at greatest length (on nine pages, out of thirty-five) in Stebbing's "Logical Positivism and Analysis."

2 Differences between Moore and Wittgenstein and the Vienna Circle

Susan Stebbing underlines that Moore and Wittgenstein start from one and the same idea: they are both convinced that the clarification of thoughts has priority in philosophy. From this point on, however, they go in different directions.

First and foremost, Wittgenstein maintains that we can clarify thinking when we rightly understand the logic of language. This means that he, like the Logical Positivists, is interested above all in language, not in facts. In contrast, Moore is interested above all in facts, which, however, he indeed investigated by analyzing philosopher's propositions.

One implication of Wittgenstein's stress on clarifying language and thinking through the resources of the "new logic" (see on this term § 3) was his adopted policy of making everything clear at once. In contrast, Stebbing is adamant that the process of clarification is to proceed step by step. This point is supported by Moore's insistence that there are degrees of understanding: "It is a grave mistake to suppose that the alternatives are understanding, on the one hand, and simply not understanding, on the other. We understand more or less clearly" and then reflect on what we had so understood in a process of analysis (ibid.: p. 81).

This conception of piecemeal, step-by-step analysis plays a central role in Stebbing's attack on Wittgenstein—it, more precisely, takes the form of criticism of the flawless (*lückenlose*), exhaustive analysis from the perspective of Moore's philosophy of common sense. Stebbing namely insisted that "we can understand a sentence (i.e., know how to use it correctly) without knowing what its correct analysis is" (1938/9: 77).

In what follows, we shall see that these ideas were connected with Moore's project of "directional analysis." Before we proceed to discuss the directional analysis, however, we shall try to answer the question: Why did Stebbing consider Moore, on the one hand, and Wittgenstein and his friends in Vienna, on the other hand, so different one from another?

3 Where Did the Difference between Moore and Wittgenstein and the Vienna Circle Come From?

There are good reasons to suppose that they were a result of Frege's influence on the Vienna analysts. Indeed, both Wittgenstein and the Logical Positivists maintained that we communicate thoughts to other persons through language, so we can analyze thought by analyzing language only. As Stebbing put it: "[For them,] to communicate is to use language. Hence, . . . for Logical Positivists, the problem of knowledge resolves itself into the problem how language can be used to communicate" (1933: 67–8). These were all ideas of Frege's.

Of course, somebody can rightly notice that the philosophers of the Vienna Circle scarcely ever referred to Frege. This point, however, only suggests that Frege's influence on them came through some indirect channel. Clearly, this channel was Wittgenstein's *Tractatus*—so that following the *Tractatus*, Logical Positivists adopted two leading ideas of Frege's, which they occasionally refer to as the "new logic." First, a main tenet of Wittgenstein's book was that the task of philosophy is to make our thinking clear by finding out what true symbolism—impeccable language—is (Milkov 2017). Second, Logical Positivists accept a thorough deductivism.[2]

That the leading ideas of the *Tractatus* were essentially Fregean was explicitly shown for the first time by another woman philosopher, Elisabeth Anscombe, as early as in (1959). Later this point was also developed by Michael Dummett in his celebrated piece "Frege and Wittgenstein," in which he maintains that when he follows Frege, "Wittgenstein is at his happiest"; when he criticized Frege, "he was almost at his worst" (1991a: 237, 239).

Here one is reminded of the fact that when speaking of a German influence on the Vienna Circle at all, philosophers usually maintain either that the representatives of the Vienna Circle were Kantian or that they were massively influenced by the Marburg neo-Kantians (Richardson 1998; Friedman 1999), and perhaps also by Husserl. All this is true. However, the influence of the neo-Kantians, does not exclude Frege's—the former merely supplemented, and augmented, the latter. This is best revealed by the example of the philosophical impacts exerted on Rudolf Carnap. On the one hand, he was directly influenced by Frege; indeed, Carnap attended no fewer than three courses of Frege's lectures in Jena, and was, as he later remembered, immediately impressed by Frege's logic. On the other hand, he was a student of one of the philosophers of the Southwest (not of the Marburg!) School of neo-Kantians, Bruno Bauch. Characteristically enough, Bauch was, in turn, influenced by Frege. This only indicates how closely related the neo-Kantians and Frege were (Gabriel 1986).

4 What Is Directional Analysis?

Stebbing first specifies that the point of her study is the "intellectual analysis," as opposed to chemical or physical analysis, or to psychoanalysis: "[It] consists in discerning relations and characteristics which are in no way altered by the process of analyzing" (1932/3: 77). In contrast, the task of the "material analysis" is the resolving of the analysandum to its ingredients.

There are three types of intellectual analysis: metaphysical, grammatical, and symbolic. Grammatical analysis is done by the linguists; it aims at revealing the syntactical form. Symbolic analysis is the analysis practiced by the formal logicians, for example, by the Theory of Descriptions; it starts from postulates,[3] is hypothetical, and deductive.

While the grammatical and symbolic analyses remain at one and the same level, "the aim of metaphysical analysis is to determine the elements and the mode of combination of those elements to which reference is made when any given true assertion is made" (79). The elements of the resultant are most often on some different, more basic level. In this sense, metaphysical analysis is directional analysis: it is directed from facts of less basic to facts of more basic level, as for example, "If we analyze a statement about a Committee into a statement about individuals, then the analysis is directional, and the levels are different. If we again analyze the statement about individuals into statements about bodily and mental states, then the analysis is directional [too]" (1934: 35–6).

The aim of directional analysis is to reveal, in the resultant, more clearly the multiplicity of the analyzed fact. When successfully done, the analyzed fact and the resultant, including the final resultant, have the same multiplicity as the initial fact. The resultant, however, shows the multiplicity in a more conspicuous way (1933: 81). That is also why it is called *metaphysical*: it *elucidates* the structure of the facts.

Stebbing further maintains that we can in principle reach the level of basic facts. The basic facts are "the set of simple facts terminating a directional analysis" (ibid.: 82). They are absolutely specific. As if following Russell, she also holds these to be the ultimate constituents of the world. Stebbing even specifies what a simple, involved in such facts, can be: "An absolutely specific shade of colour, or taste, or sound" (1932/3: 91). Referring to such statements, some of her contemporaries treated Stebbing as a follower of Russell (Bronstein 1934).

She was not, however, and this for four reasons:

1) It is true that, according to Stebbing, the sentence "This is a table" entails the set of basic facts upon which it is grounded. The opposite, however, is not the case. The basic facts do not entail the macroscopic object. Apparently, this means that from the basic facts we can construct different material objects. Consequently, the final resultant does not yield a complete analysis of the initial fact, as Russell believed to be the case. For this purpose, says Stebbing vaguely, we must know how the symbols are used (1933: 82). Unfortunately, Stebbing did not explore this idea further.
2) In contrast to Russell's theory of the external world, Stebbing maintained that her directional analysis did not mean reduction of material bodies to their constituting elements;[4] the reason for this: she did not believe that we can prove that material bodies are built up of basic elements.
3) That directional analysis aims at basic facts does not mean that it requires that we *must come* to the basic facts. "A philosopher might employ directional analysis without being successful in carrying the analysis to completion" (1934: 36).
4) It was never part of Stebbing's intention either to prove that basic facts exist (ibid.: 34).

Following Moore, Stebbing was instead concerned with the analysis of our knowledge of some complex material things which we know, with certainty, to exist—such as this table, the books on it, the chairs in the seminar room, etc. to perceptual situations, perspectives, etc. In other words, she adopted the materialist position that "the external world is the world of macroscopic objects, in their spatial and temporal relations" (1933/4: 10). So we need not construct the external world: it is given to us (Chapter 15: § 1, (a)).

All these assumptions show that Stebbing conceived of the problem of the external world as "a problem of *analyzing* what it is we know when we do know a [table, say]" (1934: 27). It is true that we do not know the whole table directly.

Nevertheless, the table is given to us—though indirectly. We must abandon the belief that all that is given to us is given directly (1933: 78). That the macroscopic objects are given to us indirectly poses the following task to the philosopher: she should make their structure clearer by revealing those aspects of them which are given directly to us.

Stebbing was convinced that the philosophical problem is not that we are to construct the world from simple elements, sense-data, for example. As already noted, she specifically criticizes Russell's obsession with finding the individual data upon which to erect our knowledge of the external world (1933/4: 20). Even worse, the Logical Positivists, Rudolf Carnap, in particular, transformed it into the linguistic principle that every sentence I understand can be translated into a sentence, every element of which could be used demonstratively (Chapter 15: § 1). Both approaches—of Russell and of the Logical Positivists—lead to solipsism which, according to Stebbing, is a philosophical dead-end. She put it in the following Moorean way: "I have the best grounds for denying solipsism, namely, I know it to be false" (1933: 77).

5 Criticism of Logical Constructions

Stebbing agrees that the objects of the external world can be called "logical constructions" in the sense that macroscopic objects—tables, chairs, etc.—can be seen as made (composed) of low-level elements through logically definable connections. True to her idea of directional analysis, however, she is reluctant to use this expression—she does not believe that something is really "constructed" here. This explains why the sentence "'Tables are logical constructions' is a sensible remark and is also true. . . . But 'Logical constructions exist' is a nonsensical statement" (1933/4: 19). She concludes, "It would have been better to avoid the use of the word 'construction' altogether" (ibid.: 20). In fact, the external world is not constructed, neither are the macroscopic material objects. We have constructions in physical theories, not in the world.

This explains why when speaking of constructions, philosophers often make mistakes. So Russell was in a muddle when he stated that "perspectives" are basic for logical constructions (Russell 1914: 94 ff.). The point is that whereas a perspective is partial, a construction is abstract. "Hence, constructions cannot be fitted together" (Stebbing 1933/4: 24–5) whereas perspectives can.

Another point of difference between true analytism and construction-making is that whereas constructed systems cannot be exhaustive, analysis can.

The reason for this is that "analysis is not abstract *relatively to the analysandum* of which it is an analysis" (ibid.: 25–6), while constructed systems are. What is more, exhaustive analysis is the aim of directional analysis. "The base is provided (in the case of propositions about the external world) by *perceptual situations*" (ibid.: 26; italics added).

When speaking of logical constructions, we must constantly bear in mind that a system is always constructed relative to a certain base. More importantly, "whatever base be chosen, other bases would be possible. . . . [Hence,] no constructed system could be exhaustive with reference to the external world" (ibid.: 25). In other words, construction is something like a hypothesis. There are always alternative systems of constructions, based on the same facts. This is exactly what is assumed by the Logical Positivists and their master—Wittgenstein. Above all, for Wittgenstein in the *Tractatus*, the facts are hypothetical facts, which can verify the propositions. In contrast, "in Russell's view a fact is what *makes* a proposition *true*, or *false*" (1933: 85; italics added).[5] This is also what Stebbing accepts.

Stebbing's analysis in these lines is question-begging, though. As we are going to see in Chapter 15, her criticism of the concept of logical constructions is to be directed toward the middle Russell (of 1913–15) and the early Carnap (1928), but not toward Wittgenstein and Frege.

6 The History of Moore's Idea of Directional Analysis

From the critical remarks addressed to Russell's kind of analysis cited at the end of Section 4, it follows that besides differences between Moore, on the one hand, and Wittgenstein and the Vienna Circle, on the other, there were considerable differences between Moore and Russell as well (see Ewing 1934). These became especially conspicuous after 1925. According to Moore of this period, "the belief follows is . . . not to be taken to mean that it follows 'according to the rules of inference accepted by Formal Logic'" (Stebbing 1942: 525). There are quite different types of following that are not to be confused with one another. In contrast, Russell maintained that following is of one type only—that of formal logic. In connection with this, he sought in epistemology "a basis for certain knowledge," from which he hoped to be in a position to infer any other knowledge with necessity.

As Moore had noted in his "Autobiography," it was Russell's *Principles of Mathematics* as well as the Theory of Descriptions that persuaded him to reformulate his method of examining "what on earth this-and-this philosopher means by *p*?"—that he so successfully applied in the *fin de siècle*—into the terms of philosophical logic. This Moore did in his lectures *Some Main Problems of Philosophy* (1953), delivered in 1910–11, in which he adopted the propositional approach to philosophy (Chapter 12: § 3.2). For example, he divided the "contents of the Universe" into two classes: propositions and non-propositions (1953: 56).

Gradually, however, Moore felt more and more uncertain in respect to the philosophical logic of Russell type and eventually returned to his old philosophical realism in an attempt to reformulate and refine it. One can only guess that this change was supported by his discussions with Wittgenstein in April 1914, written down in "Notes Dictated to Moore in Norway" (1979: 108–19) and eventually by the publication of the *Tractatus* in 1922. A real breakthrough in this direction was marked by his inaugural lecture as professor of philosophy at Cambridge, "A Defense of Common Sense" (1925), which for many years was considered the starting point of analytical philosophy (Duncan-Jones 1937). This development gathered momentum in his first course of lectures as a professor at Cambridge in 1925–26, later published in *Lectures on Philosophy* (Moore 1966), where the directional analysis was discussed for the first time. It reached its pinnacle in Moore's open criticism of Russell in (Moore 1940/44) and (Moore 1944).

7 Its Logic

The point in which Moore opposed Russell's philosophical logic was the treatment of "incomplete symbols." The term was introduced in Russell/Whitehead's *Principia Mathematica* (1910) in the sense of a symbol which is not used in isolation, but in a context only. The prime example of an incomplete symbol is "definite description"; another example is "logical construction," a term Russell introduced in 1912 (Chapter 15: § 1, (a)). These are all logical fictions.

In 1925–26, in *Lectures on Philosophy*, Moore insisted, contrary to Russell, that "incomplete symbols," as well as "logical constructions," and "definite descriptions," are not fictitious. Russell's failure to grasp their true nature is easily seen in that it is not possible to perceive a fictitious entity; while we clearly perceive what is supposed to be an entity named by definite descriptions—this table, for example. The same is true of logical constructions (Stebbing 1933/4: 19), as well as of incomplete symbols.

The most important outcome of the difference made by Moore and Stebbing between incomplete symbols and logical fictions is that the two concepts give rise to two different types of logical consequence: imply, and entail. Imply is a strict logical consequence, whereas entail is metaphysical one, and is not exclusive. Here is one example of this distinction. The proposition "unicorns are fictitious," where "unicorns" are incomplete symbols, implies (metaphysically) that there are no unicorns in the real world. In contrast, "lions are logical fictions" logically entails that "there are no lions," in a sense in which this is a *proposition* about words (Moore 1966: 122). The first proposition presupposes a directional analysis, the second one logical analysis. As we are going to see in the next chapter, in the mind-1920s Moore moved (back) to the type of analysis also followed by Frege and Wittgenstein, opposing it to Russell's one.

8 The Fate of Moore's Directional Analysis

Some historians of analytic philosophy consider Quine's criticism voiced in his seminal paper "Two Dogmas of Empiricism" (1951) on Carnap's strict distinction between *a priori* and empirical knowledge a harbinger of the end of analytic philosophy (Romanos 1983; Koppelberg 1987). In fact, however, there were early analytic philosophers, above all Moore, Stebbing, and John Wisdom, who refused to accept such a distinction as long ago as the late 1920s and the early 1930s. For them, analytical (directional) knowledge is not *a priori*, and also not necessary. Apparently, Quine's conception of analytic philosophy (and that of his followers) was, to say the least, one-sided.

Unfortunately, nobody developed this kind of analytic philosophy—the analytic philosophy based on directional analysis—systematically, and to its full extent. In truth, already while teaching at St. Andrews in the early 1930s, John Wisdom embraced the understanding that the task of philosophy is to seek for illumination of facts already known, thus reaching beyond their first-level structure. He developed this insight even before Stebbing, in his early book *Interpretation and Analysis* (1931), and in his five papers on "Logical Constructions" published in 1931-3 (1969). However, in 1934 Wisdom came to teach philosophy at Cambridge and came to attend Wittgenstein's lectures. As a result, he experienced a "propositional turn," which can be very well seen in his celebrated paper "Philosophical Perplexity", which reads: "It's not the stuff, it's the style that stupefies" (1936:38). This development irritated his old ally Stebbing, who openly criticized Wisdom's new "mnemonic slogan" (1938/9: 80 n., 84). Of course, Wisdom never turned pure linguistic philosopher in the sense of Frege or Wittgenstein. Under the guise of his linguisticism, he continued to do directional analysis, which is clearly discernible in his mature works (1965). In these, Wisdom tried to reveal some deeper aspects of the common-level structure of the facts which are well known to all. Among other things, they can address such typically metaphysical problems as the meaning of life (see Milkov 2019a).

Even deeper were the traces of Moore's type of analytic philosophy, so eloquently articulated by Stebbing, Ryle, and especially by J. L. Austin, who used to say in the 1950s: "Some like Witters,[6] but Moore is *my* man" (Grice 1989: 381). Indeed, some twenty years after Stebbing, Austin fought against the pursuit of the flawless justification of human knowledge which brings to life the fetishism of truth and precision; he was also against concepts like sense-data and knowledge by acquaintance in philosophy. Exactly like Moore and Stebbing (see Stebbing 1932/3: 72) (see § 5, para. 3), Austin was convinced that in epistemology we must start from the perceptual situations, not from sense-data (1962a). Exactly like Moore and Stebbing, again, he was interested in the meaning of words, not in their grammar.

Despite these clear cases of sympathy with the kind of analysis practiced by Moore and Stebbing, the latter remained a "road less traveled." The reason for this was mainly that after the Second World War it was completely ousted by the powerful voice of American analysts, above all Quine. This development was hastened by Stebbing's early death in 1943, as well as by Moore's personality, which was less than suitable for defending the true line of a school of philosophy he cofounded. As a result, the project of philosophy done in terms of directional analysis was consigned to oblivion.

9 The Effects of Stebbing's Paper

The main idea of Stebbing's Henriette Hertz Lecture—the opposing of two kinds of analytism, that of Moore and that of the Vienna Circle Wittgenstein's—did not go without notice. In the years before the Second World War it was often discussed in Britain. Thus on May 31, 1934, John Wisdom read a paper at the Moral Science Club in Cambridge on "Moore and Wittgenstein" in which he summed up the difference between the two as follows: "Moore recommends 'What is the meaning of the word so and so?' . . . In contrast Wittgenstein recommends: 'What is the grammar of the word so-and-so?'" (Nedo and Ranchetti 1983: 266). Wittgenstein attended this lecture and it may be well the case that it motivated him to further distance himself from the Vienna Circle type of analysis (see § 10).

We shall discuss the effects of Stebbing's paper on Wittgenstein in the next section. All that is to be noted here is that five years later, this difference found its clearest expression in a paper of Max Black's which reads: "It is . . . the different direction given to the practice of philosophical analysis in England by Moore's example, to which the current difference between English analysts and Logical Positivists can be traced" (Black 1939/40: 26). What Black could not know in 1939 was that this was also to constitute the rift between American analytical philosophy and British analytical philosophy which became fairly obvious in the 1950s (see Ryle 1949). In hindsight, this is not surprising. Indeed, the beginning of American analytic philosophy was deeply influenced by some European émigrés, such as Carnap and Tarski, who were either members of the Vienna Circle or close to it. There were only a handful of followers of Moore's kind of analytic philosophy in America, who could not match in strength the alternative, Quinesque kind, formed in critical discussion with Logical Positivists.

10 The Significance of Stebbing's Criticism for the Philosophical Development of Wittgenstein

Stebbings's "Logical Positivism and Analysis" was exceptionally critical of Wittgenstein's *Tractatus*. In this connection it is to be noted that at the time, Wittgenstein was facing considerable resistance in Cambridge. Charles Broad did not accept his philosophy nor did Frank Ramsey, who called it "scholastic." Finally, it was also criticized in a paper on Cambridge philosophy of the time by Richard Braithwaite, a close friend and follower of Ramsey, which was published in March 1933 (Braithwaite 1933).

Nobody was as specific, nor as forceful, in her or his criticism of Wittgenstein as Susan Stebbing in her paper "Logical Positivism and Analysis" though, which can be comfortably seen as nothing but a list of Wittgenstein's "muddles." As a matter of fact, Stebbing's paper made a considerable use of Braithwaite's piece, which she read when it was still unpublished. Her paper, however, was much more disapproving than that of Braithwaite.

At this point it is to be noted that after Stebbing published her *A Modern Introduction to Logic* in 1931, she enjoyed considerable authority among British philosophers. In 1931–32 she was a visiting professor at Columbia University. Early in 1933 Stebbing was elected professor at Bedford College, London, and president of the Aristotelian Society. In the summer of 1933 she cofounded the journal *Analysis*.

Accordingly, it is not difficult to imagine how disquieting her criticism was for Wittgenstein. To be sure, there is no evidence that Wittgenstein read Stebbing's paper; it is most reasonable, however, to assume that part of its contents leaked out to him through his friends and students. Wittgenstein's immediate reaction was his notorious letter to the editor of *Mind*, written in May 27, 1933, in which he "disclaim[ed] all responsibility for the views and thoughts which Mr. Braithwaite [and so also Stebbing] attributes to [him]" (1933).

Wittgenstein escaped philosophical defeat thanks, for one thing, to Moore's support. Indeed, in the paper Stebbing opposed Wittgenstein's "bad" to Moore's "good" philosophy. Moore, however, openly declared that he learned much from Wittgenstein and in 1930–33 regularly attended his lectures. In this way, he tacitly acknowledged that Wittgenstein's kind of analysis goes in the same direction as his.

Secondly, after March 1933, that is, immediately after Braithwaite's and Stebbing's criticism, Wittgenstein made a turn in his philosophy almost as drastic as his turn of 1929—a turn which invalidated this criticism. The turn can be easily tracked down in his Cambridge lectures, delivered in 1932–33, and found expression mainly in two changes:

1) After the 26th lecture (1979a: 31), Wittgenstein stopped speaking of "verification," "visual field," "private language" altogether. Instead, Wittgenstein started to maintain that the meaning of the word is nothing but its use. Here it should be remembered that the main accusation of both Braithwaite and Stebbing against Wittgenstein was "his solipsism"— his "insisting that the verification of a proposition which I assert must be in my own experience" (Braithwaite 1933: 27).
2) In addition, immediately after March 1933 he made the criticism of the private language argument a central theme in his writings.

These theoretical changes in Wittgenstein's philosophy led to changes in his writing project too. To be more specific, in the summer of 1933, he started revisions of TS 213, on which part of *Philosophical Grammar* and the *Blue Book* was based. In these he began to prepare to write his "new book"—*Philosophical Investigations*. Susan Stebbing can be well seen as the midwife of this philosophical rebirth of Wittgenstein.

Two Concepts of Early Analytic Philosophy

1 Two Concepts of Philosophy

Recent years have seen an increasing range of publications on the history of analytic philosophy. Among other things, these works outline different concepts of *analysis* associated with this philosophical movement—logical analysis, conceptual analysis, connective analysis, deconstructive analysis, directional analysis, eliminative analysis, and analysis as explication (Beaney 2008a, 2009, 2016, 2017). Another leading direction of history of analytic philosophy concerns the concept of *analyticity* (Soames 2003, 2014/17, 2017).

This chapter introduces a different approach, concentrating instead on two concepts of early analytic philosophy: one that involved the construction of many possible worlds (or many models of the world) by means of logic, and a second that explored the forms of a single logical world. The two leading originators of the first type were Bertrand Russell and Rudolf Carnap. The second type was pursued by Gottlob Frege and Ludwig Wittgenstein. We can refer to these two conceptions of analytic philosophy as (i) that of the *logical construction* of the world, and (ii) that of *carving out* the conceptual structure of the logical world,[1] respectively.

1.1 Exploring the Logical World

In epistemology, the technique of "logical construction" was introduced by Bertrand Russell in the paper "On Matter"[2] (1912) (Milkov 2013) and was extensively applied in *Our Knowledge of the External World* (1914), and in some papers published in *Mysticism and Logic* (1918). According to Russell, we do not know what material objects really are. However, we have good reasons to assume that they are formed in determinate ways. Logical constructions show, in experimental terms, how things could be. In other words, they are models for epistemologically sound understanding of the external world. One example of this approach is the conception that Russell introduced in the paper "On Matter" (1912). It maintains that the world can be presented as consisting of independent (autonomous) units—sense-data—that are ordered in different logical series. Out of them, we can construct the physical objects, as well as the objects of common sense. Russell, however, did not claim that physical objects exist in that form.

Russell introduced a second example of logical constructivism in his book-project *Theory of Knowledge* (1913), where he maintained that there is one primitive epistemological relation: the relation of acquaintance. Judgments, emotions, wishes, and volitions all presuppose an act of acquaintance to which they bring additional elements. In terms of acquaintance, and with the help of the new logic, in particular, of the theory of relations, we can construct the whole body of human knowledge.

The flipside of Russell's logical constructivism is the central place that supporting arguments play in it. Specifically, Russell believed that arguments (i) serve as pillars that underpin logical constructions; (ii) promote formulation of novel logico-philosophical conceptions. As we shall see in § 4 below, supporting arguments played a lesser role in the thinking of Frege and Wittgenstein.

In *Der logische Aufbau der Welt* Rudolf Carnap embraced a constructivism similar to Russell's. Carnap's objective was "the analysis of reality"—physical reality, along with social and cultural reality—carried out "with the aid of the theory of relations" (1928: the title of § 3). To this purpose, Carnap advanced a "constitutional system," a family tree (*Stammbaum*) of concepts that ultimately refers to the given. All other concepts can be reduced to that system. Invoking his tree of concepts, Carnap argued that we can "rationally reconstruct" the conceptual systems of all sciences. Significantly, Carnap did not claim that the genealogical tree of concepts suggested in the *Aufbau* is unique. We can develop alternative family trees, such as one based upon physicalist terms. Furthermore, Carnap held that we can interpret every constitutional system in different ways. For example, the system of concepts that he championed in the *Aufbau* features four different interpretations, or languages.

Carnap called his magnum opus *The Logical Construction of the World*.[3] That title will refer, in what follows, to the general project of analytic philosophy typified by the work of the middle Russell and early Carnap.

1.2 Delineating the Boundaries of the Logical World

After 1912, Russell championed his new method of logical construction as the core of the "scientific method of philosophy." He saw it as instrumental to resolving an entire spectrum of philosophical *aporiai* in logically sound terms. Russell thus became convinced that his method of logical construction could effect "solid results" in philosophy. This is what makes analytic philosophy different from both traditional and contemporary continental philosophy (Chapter 16: § 3): its claims are at once immune to straightforward critique yet open to falsification by logically conclusive counterarguments. This was something guaranteed by the sound logic that grounds its arguments, as well as by the "neat logical properties" of their building blocks, such as the sense-data. By contrast, speculative philosophy, Bergson's for example, produces results that are not solid in this sense, for they cannot survive in the face of conclusive counterarguments.

The principal focus of the present chapter is not, however, on Russell's and Carnap's program, but rather on the project advanced by Frege and Wittgenstein, which was dedicated to exploring the logical world by drawing its boundaries. Importantly enough, what was at stake for Frege and Wittgenstein was not only the "outer" boundary of the logical world, a theme widely explored in the literature, but also its "inner" contours and limits: the lines between its different areas and layers. In other words, the task was not simply to distinguish what pertains to the logical world from what lies beyond it, determining what can from what cannot be said. Additionally, the aim was to also make fine-grained discriminations in the logical world itself. To use the felicitous expression coined later by Gilbert Ryle (1949a: 9f.), Frege and Wittgenstein sought to draw the "logical geography" of the concepts in logic and philosophy, an end they realized in series of logical-philosophical "discoveries."

2 More on Frege's and Wittgenstein's Approach

Although Frege and Wittgenstein developed what constitutes a determinate means of achieving significant results in philosophy, their projects were marked by considerable differences that it is essential to spell out.

Frege instituted sharp boundaries in the world of logic as early as his *Conceptual Notation* (1879), in which he originated his new logic. Among other things, he there insisted (i) that his Conceptual Notation is categorically discrete from ordinary language; (ii) that confirmation and content of judgment are radically different from each other; and (iii) that one must not confuse the course of impressions (*Vorstellungsverlaufe*) with judgment.

Five years later, in *The Foundations of Arithmetic* (1884), Frege introduced a second set of precise distinctions in philosophy, most notably (i) between concept and object; (ii) between ideas (*Vorstellungen*), on the one side, and concepts and objects, on the other; (iii) between propositions that can be true or false and concepts that cannot (a distinction Michael Dummett later termed the "context principle").

After 1890, Frege discriminated between (i) the sense (the thought) and the meaning (the truth-value) of a proposition; (ii) function and object; (iii) private idea (*Vorstellung*) and thought, understood as typically intersubjective (Frege 1891: 145).

Frege's practice of making conceptual discriminations was a function of his belief in an ontologically discrete logical world that he ultimately denominated the "third world." This Fregean third world featured sharp distinctions between, for example, seeing a thing, having an idea, and grasping a thought—three epistemological relations that Frege insisted we must not confuse (1918/19: 44) since they lie on different planes and are divided by clear-cut boundaries.[4] Frege settled on these third-world distinctions, being convinced that they are all that was necessary for building up his "logical house."[5]

The early Wittgenstein pursued his logical-philosophical project in a manner similar to Frege. In fact, his *Notebooks 1914–1916* are nothing but a register of the discoveries he made during these years in fits of deep concentration, such as the Picture Theory, the Doctrine of Showing, and the Doctrine of the Tautological Character of the Logical and Mathematical Propositions (Milkov 2018b).[6]

3 The Role of Language and of the Analyticity

Another way to put the difference in the two concepts of early analytic philosophy is in terms of the role they assigned to language. While Frege and Wittgenstein embraced the view that there is but one world and one language, Russell and Carnap contended that there are many languages and many worlds.[7] That is why Frege and Wittgenstein were not exclusively interested in translating one natural or formal language into another (see § 9). Translation was, however, a principal concern of Russell and Carnap, who interested themselves in the construction of many languages and models of the world. Their goal was to develop a sound procedure for translating one language into another *salva veritate* (see § 7).

Furthermore, the inner boundaries drawn by Frege and the early Wittgenstein between the different realms and segments of the third world have the character of conceptual necessities and are *a priori* true. However, since Frege and Wittgenstein themselves discovered these conceptual necessities, they took them to be synthetic. This is the case not only with Frege's investigations in general philosophical logic but it also extended to the way he thought about the logical dependencies of the arithmetic propositions. Frege thus claimed that

> the conclusions we draw from them [from the general laws of arithmetic] extend our knowledge, and ought therefore, on Kant's view, to be regarded as synthetic. The fruitful conceptual definitions draw boundary lines that were not previously given at all. What we shall be able to infer from them, cannot be inspected in advance.[8] (1884: § 88)

In *Remarks on the Foundations of Mathematics* Wittgenstein developed this position further. Mathematicians, he contended, create (synthesize) mathematical proofs. At the same time they are *a priori*. That is why the propositions of mathematics are synthetic *a priori*. But many mathematical objects, like prime numbers, are synthetic too. Indeed, Wittgenstein understood them to be given, which is to say, they are to be discovered and not merely deduced from basic, primitive ideas (1956, III: §§ 30, 42).

Apparently, Frege and Wittgenstein believed that the logical, third world is an ontologically discrete realm. The task of the logician is simply to discover (to carve out) its inner and outer boundaries,[9] to outline its features in a kind of logical geography. These features do not, however, come to us on a silver platter. The new logical domain can be determined only through a kind of "intellectual action," the very possibility of which is guaranteed by the implicit availability and intelligibility of the "third world." In this sense, Frege and Wittgenstein saw their task as rendering explicit and formally delineating the boundaries of the logical world. (The logical world[s] of Russell and Carnap was quite different, since it [they] had to be constructed *de novo*.[10]) This sort of "intellectual action" would come to be construed as "conceptual analysis" by both the later Wittgenstein (see § 5) and the Oxford ordinary language philosophers (see § 8; see Chapter 16: § 6).

4 Chiseling Out the Truths of Philosophical Logic

Michael Dummett has convincingly explained why Frege never returned to the context principle after once having launched it in the *Grundlagen*: Frege was sure that the context principle was so well-defined that any new venture to explore it would be a waste of time (1991: 3 ff.). One finds in Wittgenstein a similarity on just this methodological score, namely in connection with his reference to different modes of contemplating *sub specie aeternitatis*. On October 7, 1916, he wrote: "The work of art is the object seen *sub specie aeternitatis* and the good life is the world seen *sub specie aeternitatis*" (1979: 83e). Typically, Wittgenstein provided no argument to substantiate any part of this observation. It was just another sententious perception of his. Hence it comes as no surprise that he subsequently never took occasion to elaborate on it, although without so much as a reference to it, he supplemented the concept fourteen years later, observing that

> there is a way of capturing the world *sub specie aeterni[tatis]* other than through the work of the artist. Thought has such a way—so I believe—it is as though it flies above the world and leaves it as it is—observing it from above, in flight. (1980a: 5e)

Wittgenstein apparently considered his position from 1916 perfectly true, so that in 1930 he felt justified simply to build upon it. Another instance of this modus operandi is the aspect-change issue that Wittgenstein introduced in the *Tractatus* 5.5423 and further discussed more than twenty years later in *Zettel*, § 249.

The foregoing observations suggest that when exploring conceptual problems, Wittgenstein often took for granted that he could baldly promulgate ideas that were so solid he could simply build on them without comment years later. Similarly, when in 1891 Frege replaced his concept of "judgeable content" (1879) with "sense and meaning," he just built a new discovery over the earlier one.

Apparently, the method of carving out the boundaries of the logical world that both Frege and (the early) Wittgenstein followed was that of a step-by-step "chiseling" out of logical-philosophical truths out of the quasi Platonic block of the potential third world. In a sense, it was a construction of the *logical world*. This type of work sets up a new conceptual geography in a monolithic form. Interestingly enough, Bertrand Russell contended that the "statuesque" method of doing philosophy was typical of "the great continental systems of the seventeenth century" (1945: 589). He was convinced this approach had been entirely superseded by the advent of the new, "analytic philosophy." But what Russell failed to recognize was that his friends Frege and Wittgenstein championed precisely this putatively superannuated method.

By contrast, the assembly structures of Russell and Carnap can be easily dismantled; their logically well-ordered claims and their chains of arguments, as well, can be left aside. However, rather than theoretical dead ends, such "deconstructions" are taken as signals that we are to abandon the old construction and to advance a new one instead.

5 The Case of the Later Wittgenstein

So as to provide a better basis for coming to grips with the character of Wittgenstein's logico-philosophical discoveries, it will be well, next, briefly to sketch the main idea of his *Tractatus*.[11] Wittgenstein's objective in the *Tractatus* was similar to that of Frege in the *Conceptual Notation*, namely, to set out a new, "perfect" symbolism in order to make our language and thinking clearer. Wittgenstein's position is that we learn about how our language and thinking proceeds by way of mastering this symbolism. Consequently, once we've completed the process of mastering the symbolism we no longer need it and can dispense with it. What this boils down to is that the conceptual distinctions that Wittgenstein introduced in the *Tractatus* are necessary only as a means of bringing order to our language and thinking. With this objective achieved, we can discard them.[12] The logical and conceptual distinctions of the *Tractatus* are thus purely instrumental in nature.

It will be helpful to restate the foregoing from a genetic standpoint. In the final months of composing the *Tractatus*, Wittgenstein realized that what he had recorded in his book were not a series of logico-philosophical discoveries (Milkov 2018b). This led him to conclude that the philosophically sound findings he outlined so far could remain in the shadows, without giving the impression that one could dismiss them as in any sense erroneous. For, to reiterate, Wittgenstein viewed them as "solid," notwithstanding the fact that they might be invisible from this newly acquired perspective.[13] A typical example is the fate of Wittgenstein's "picture theory" in the 1930s and 1940s. As a distinguished commentator has long since remarked (and he was not alone), "If the picture theory disappears from the picture in Wittgenstein's later philosophy, it ... is not because it was not thrown by the board but because it faded away" (Hintikka 1976: 110).

This tendency in Wittgenstein's philosophy reached new stage after 1929 when his attention shifted from the relation between language and reality to the relation between mind and reality and, especially, to the role human action plays in it (Milkov 2012). As a result, and in apparent opposition to Frege, Wittgenstein now understood himself not to be making discoveries, but rather making grammatical or conceptual "remarks." Importantly enough, now he held that we do not need sharp boundaries between them. But while we certainly do not need to delineate sharp boundaries between the two activities, "you can *draw* one," he declared, even if "none has so far been drawn" (1953: § 68).

Among the most significant implications of these developments in Wittgenstein's thinking was that instead of carving out the logical geography of the logical world, Wittgenstein became convinced that he only advanced conceptual remarks: these were the successors of his "logical discoveries" of 1912–16. Correspondingly, instead of the "logical world," he now spoke of the "conceptual world" (1980b: § 398). The essential point is that the conceptual analyses he undertook were not logically necessary, and were not the only correct ones. In general, what was new in the later Wittgenstein was that he no longer held to the notion of a "third world." This shift in theoretical orientation meant that he saw himself as preoccupied with charting the "grammatical geography" of concepts, not the "logical geography" of the world.

6 Differences between Russell and Carnap

Similarly to the differences between Frege's and Wittgenstein's concepts of construction of the logical world distilled in Section 5, those between Russell's and Carnap's concepts of the logical construction of the world were also considerable.

Starting with his statement, "the discussion of indefinables ... forms the chief part of philosophical logic" (1903: xv), Russell was also engaged in conceptual analyses. Conceptual analyses, however, were neither Russell's particular strength nor his chief research interest. His principal theoretical concern lay in logical constructivism and in advancing long, rigorously cogent chains of arguments which support one another. This fact sheds light on the remark that Wittgenstein made in a letter to Russell dated December 15, 1912: "Neither you nor I knew ... , I think, a year and a half ago ... what a huge and infinitely strange science logic is" (1974: 45)—this to the coauthor of *Principia Mathematica* published only two years earlier. Apparently, Wittgenstein was referring here not to mathematical but to philosophical logic, whose task is to describe logical forms discovered in the Fregean third world—a view shared, tellingly enough, by Russell at that period. In "The Philosophy of Logical Atomism" (1918a: 216) he defined philosophy as exploring "logical forms,"[14] describing them as the zoologist describes different forms of life—or, one could say, as the geographer of the "third world" discovers new logical land and draws on his "3-D map" (in non-Euklidean space) new formal lines (see the blurb of the present book).

That said, Russell and Wittgenstein were also quite differently gifted philosophers. Wittgenstein was simply not good at analytic reasoning. On this head, Russell reported that "when there are no clear arguments, but . . . only inconclusive considerations to be balanced, and unsatisfactory points of view to be set against each other, he [Wittgenstein] is no good" (Monk 1996: 293). In other words, Wittgenstein lacked the aptitude for constructing series of logically cogent monotonic chains of supporting arguments, something that was Russell's forte. By the same token, however, Russell noted that "when everything has been done that can be done by method [by logical arguments], a stage is reached where only direct philosophical vision can carry matters further. Here only genius will avail" (1914: 245). In such cases, Russell felt that even when he "put out all [his own] force," he himself could "only just equal" Wittgenstein, no more (Monk 1996: 252).

As for Carnap, he had apparently limited power to directly contemplate "the facts" of the logical world (Russell 1921: 212). We see this in the way he construed Wittgenstein's practice of discovering philosophical truths in dramatic episodes of deep concentration (see § 2), something well documented in Carnap's "Autobiography":

> When [Wittgenstein] started to formulate his view on some specific philosophical problem, we often felt the internal struggle that occurred in him at that very moment, a struggle by which he tried to penetrate from darkness to light under an intense and painful strain, which was even visible on his most expressive face. When finally, sometimes after prolonged arduous effort, his answer came forth, his statement stood before us like a newly created piece of art or a divine revelation. (1963: 25–6)

Carnap surely miscast Wittgenstein when he compared him to "a religious prophet or seer."[15] Wittgenstein's objective was not to deliver divinely imparted truths but to discover solid answers to logical-philosophical problems. His truths were rigorous and threw light on fundamental problems of philosophical logic.

7 Historical Roots of the Two Methods

Historically, we can see the method that Frege and Wittgenstein championed relative to Franz Brentano's philosophical method, and that of his school, which opposed Kant's "predilection for constructions." Arguably, what the Brentanists targeted for criticism in Kant was his construction of formal schemes and the systematic implication that different realms of human knowledge and mind function according to them. In contrast, Brentano and his acolytes aimed logically to explore the "things themselves." More precisely, their discipline of descriptive psychology was introduced as a "Cartesian science" that produces logically and epistemologically "neat results," which in turn can provide sound foundations for the both philosophy and science. It deserves noting that for adopting this position, Brentano was considerably indebted to Hermann Lotze (Milkov 2015, 2018).[16]

Among Brentano's followers, Edmund Husserl originated the most radical form of logical geography. Husserl's program involved searching for ever new layers of the basic structures of our consciousness by way of "phenomenological reflection." His dramatic philosophical development can be seen as an epic journey in which Husserl discovered and eventually "colonized" ever new philosophical-logical territory. His method demanded strenuous emotional effort to escape familiar and exhaustively explored domains of phenomenology and transcendental psychology.

It deserves notice that also the project which preoccupied both Russell and Carnap had its roots in the German philosophical tradition—specifically the one originating in Leibniz, according to whose doctrine of the identity of indiscernibles "two terms are the same [*eadem*] if one can be substituted for the other without altering the truth of any statement [*salva veritate*]"[17] (A IV, 4: 846). At the same time, however, Leibniz also maintained that there is a quasi "third world" (*regio idearum*) of "God's thought" (*Discours de métaphysique*: § 14; see Chapter 3: § 2.1) that can be explored only by true philosophers. *This* idea of Leibniz was followed by Frege and Wittgenstein.

8 Connective versus Reductive Analyses

While the record suggests that the two methodological programs of analytic philosophy have not previously been considered along the lines of the foregoing discussion, the critical approach advanced in these pages has not gone totally unnoticed in the history of analytic philosophy. Perhaps the most salient precedents were studies, dating from the 1950s, of the difference between connective and reductive analysis and between decompositional and progressive analysis (Chapter 16: § 4 (a)). More than sixty years ago, the Oxford ordinary language philosopher Peter Strawson made the case that there are two concepts of analytic philosophy. According to Strawson, Carnap and W. V. Quine, both working in America, were the chief exponents of the view that "logic provides a skeleton language in which the meaning of every element is absolutely precise. ... By using this framework ... other systems of concepts can be constructed" (1956: 32–3). Strawson identified as the competing orientation the "English School" of ordinary language philosophers which was charting by way of conceptual analysis the logical geography of received language and concepts.[18] Thirty years later, in his book *Analysis and Metaphysics* (1992), Strawson would recast the method of the English School as "connective analysis," its program being to chart the complex map of our everyday and the concepts of scientific discourse (1992: 30) (see Chapter 2: §§ 3 and 4). Strawson sharply contrasted the connective analysis with the "reductive analysis" practiced by Russell and Carnap (see Chapter 14: n. 4).

It remains to address the question as to why it was Peter Strawson, a member of the ordinary language philosophy group in Oxford, who was the first to call attention to the alternative methodological orientations in the early analytic philosophy. The answer is that in the 1950s the ordinary language philosophers progressively assimilated elements of Fregean conceptual analysis (Milkov 2003: 8 f., 2003b). This fact also explains why Gilbert Ryle's concept of "logical geography" correlates so closely with what we've discussed as the Fregean practice of "carving out the boundaries of the logical world" (see § 1, (b)).

9 Hybrid Methodologies

We have just seen that there are cases in which the early analytic philosophers do not precisely qualify as either simple logical constructivists or as explorers mapping out (carving out) the logical world. In practice, these two research methodologies scarcely ever appeared in their pure form. As we've remarked, Russell in particular was no slavish adherent to either of the camps. While he championed a constructivist approach as a method of achieving substantive results in philosophy research, he also retained faith in the epistemological authority of the classical direct contemplation of facts of the logical world (§ 6).

On the other side, Frege, too, held that we are free to translate ideal languages *salva veritate*. For example, he defined cardinal numbers as "the class of all those classes which are 'similar' to a given class" (Russell 1924: 327). By contrast with both Russell and Carnap, however, Frege adopted Leibniz's concept of identity of indiscernibles (in the case above, of class) only as a regulative principle, not as a definition (Künne 2010: 111). This immediately made his language translation different from that of Russell and Carnap. In particular, despite the fact that it can be done *salva veritate*, Frege's translations also bring out changes in the target language. This conception went hand in hand with Frege's claim that the propositions of arithmetic are also synthetic (§ 3).

Definitions play an important role also in the early Wittgenstein. He conceived them as "rules for translating from one language into another. [And he declared that] Any correct sign-language must be translatable into any other in accordance with such rules" (3.343). One explanation of this side of Wittgenstein's *Tractatus* is that it was based on ideas Wittgenstein introduced in order to present his logical-philosophical discoveries, dating from 1913 to 1916, as correlative with *Russell's* logical philosophy at that period (Milkov 2013). In other words, they were formulated under Russell's influence.

Of no little historical interest here is that two giants of modern philosophy—Hume and Kant—proceeded in a manner similar to that which distinguishes the thinking of Frege and the early Wittgenstein. Hume's famed "fork," for example, radically discriminates between empirical and *a priori* truths, while Kant, adopting this dichotomy, developed it in original and historically influential ways in his teaching about *a priori* and a posteriori truths. Hence, one can suitably say that Hume and Kant undertook to carve out the boundaries of the "epistemological world." Be this as it may, Frege sharply diverges from both Hume and Kant in that (i) his logical ontology did not achieve its final form after merely a single discovery, but rather underwent several transformations over the years; (ii) while Hume and Kant used their dichotomies to clarify and construct the whole of "human understanding," Frege utilized his variegated dichotomies simply to better orient his logic in the widely ramified world of "eternal truths."

In fact, Kant was mainly a constructivist philosopher. According to him, the objects of human knowledge, including those of science and mathematics, are constructed (constituted) with the help of a single, and unifying, table of categories. But in contrast to the full-fledged logical constructivism that Russell and Carnap practiced, Kant was convinced that the "transcendental scheme" that he deduced from "pure reason" is a singularity that admits of no alternatives.

Another preeminent explorer of the logical world (taken as the *sole* such world), Edmund Husserl, also employed a constructivist method of logically "constituting" that world. Oddly enough, some commentators found in this modus operandi sufficient grounds for arguing that Carnap's *Aufbau* program not only bore the impress of Husserl's thought but was also actually a continuation of his phenomenology (Chapter 1: § 1). As we have seen, however, with its doctrine of many possible worlds, Carnap's *Aufbau* was orientationally at odds with phenomenology as a categorically one-world philosophy.

10 Analytic Dogmatism

The method of constructing a logical world rendered the philosophy of Frege and the early Wittgenstein to a certain degree dogmatic. This is clearly evident in Wittgenstein's *Tractatus*, which simply promulgates theses without any supporting arguments. Russell was quick to point out the problematic character of this idiosyncratic method and sought to persuade his student and friend to modify his method—without success:

> I told him he ought not simply to state what he thinks true, but to give arguments for it, but he said arguments spoil its beauty, and that he would feel as if he was dirtying a flower with muddy hands. (Monk 1996: 264)

This method of pursuing philosophical truth manifests a kind of "interpretative dogmatism," something further evidenced in the way that both Frege and Wittgenstein sharply resisted any and all moves to interpret their positions. What they opposed in particular were attempts to abstract the salient characteristics of their teaching and the pretentions of anyone else who designed further to develop their logical philosophy.

Peter Simons has recently observed that there are two cultures of philosophy that differ in the degree of "tolerance that a philosopher has towards differences of doctrinal opinion with his students, pupils, acolytes, followers" (2004: 12). Simons has found that this was particularly evident in Austrian philosophy, where Schlick and Carnap promoted an open theoretical culture, while Brentano, Husserl, and Wittgenstein fostered a closed one. More generally, Simons has noted that "analytic philosophy tends to have an open culture, and continental philosophy tends to have a closed culture" (11–12). Furthermore, "open-cultured philosophers," according to Simons, "tended to be empiricists or have a higher respect for empiricism than the closed cultured" (p. 30).

The picture that emerges in the present discussion is different. Frege and Wittgenstein, two leading early analytic philosophers, embraced a closed philosophical culture and were not empiricists but preponderantly rationalist thinkers. At the same time, two other leading early analytic philosophers, Russell and Carnap, were open to revisions of their teachings and were also empiricists.

Frege and Wittgenstein expressly sought to identify—to "discover"—logico-philosophical truths. Since they understood such truths to be necessary, they regarded them as formally self-contained and eternal. Hence, in their view nobody, their acolytes included, could make changes in such discoveries. In other words, the "closed" nature of their research enterprise was neither a matter of intolerance nor what William James denominated "philosophical temperament." Rather, it was mainly theoretical in character and purport.

At the other pole were the logical constructivists, Russell and Carnap. They followed an "open door policy" and hence were receptive to criticism that could sponsor substantial changes and transformations in their doctrine. The models of philosophical logic that they fielded were subject to amendments and improvements in principle. Ironically enough, this feature of their philosophy eventuated in their removal from the pantheon of analytic philosophy as a consequence of the unanswerable criticisms leveled at them by Wittgenstein and Quine, respectively.

11 Criticism of Quine and Soames

This investigation commenced by calling attention to the fact that the study of history of analytic philosophy today, which explores the types of analysis that analytic philosophy developed, is marked by a critical one-sidedness. This concluding section calls into question, in particular, the credibility of Quine's claim that analytic philosophy ultimately proceeds by way of categorically discriminating between analytic and synthetic truths—with the implication that as its name suggests analytic philosophy pursues exclusively analytic truths. And having held himself to have established that the analytic/synthetic distinction is theoretically unsound, Quine argued that the entire project for analytic philosophy must be rethought.

This proved to be a massively influential claim, one that informs as settled fact the thinking of many currently active historians of analytic philosophy. A typical example in this respect is Scott Soames (2003, 2014/17), who reads the history of analytic philosophy, from Russell to Kripke, as a successive step-by-step dismantling of the idea of analyticity. Soames offers not a word, however, about the analytic-synthetic necessities pursued by Frege and Wittgenstein.

The argument advanced here, by contrast, establishes that from the outset there were two different conceptions of analytic philosophy. From this standpoint Quine's account holds, in the main, for the logical constructivists, Russell and Carnap, these champions of analytic definitions and logical translations. Of course, this can come as no surprise given that Quine knew analytic philosophy mainly in its Carnap variant. Frege and Wittgenstein, on the other hand, eluded Quine's critique on two counts:

1) They were interested not only in analytic truths but also, as we've noted, in synthetic necessary truths. They did not deduce the latter; instead they discovered them in the third world, of which they carved out their own conceptual map. In other words, Frege and Wittgenstein did not hold that necessary truths are only analytic. Hence, even if, as Quine claimed, no analytic propositions are immune to empirical verification, it does not follow that there are no other solid philosophical results, for necessary synthetic propositions have nothing to do with experience and empirical science. Moreover, as distinct as they are from empirical science, such synthetic propositions are a legitimate concern of analytic philosophy.

2) Frege and Wittgenstein were not interested in empiricism, reductionism, or directly in empirical science. This is patently evident in Frege's claim that natural laws are eternal truths (1897: 135). As for Wittgenstein, he declared his position clearly and unequivocally in the *Tractatus*, 4.1122: "The Darwinian theory has no more to do with philosophy than has any other hypothesis of natural science." Empiricists and philosophers of science were, in his view, logical constructivists, paradigmatically Russell and Carnap.

16

What Is Analytic Philosophy?

1 Introduction

This concluding chapter endeavors to articulate a clear definition of the analytic philosophy, applying the findings of the preceding chapters. The purpose is to help foster a more historically informed and theoretically nuanced understanding of analytic philosophy in general. Of course, this is a challenging task, something attested by the dozens of papers and scattered monographs that have been dedicated to it. The present chapter offers, however, something original, namely the bid to define analytic philosophy on the basis of an idea originating with Bertrand Russell (§ 3), arguably, the founding father of this movement (§ 6). The point of this venture is to address a pressing need in the philosophical community today, namely for more knowledge on this movement in order to gain a clear and more adequate understanding of both its methodologies and its defining themes. The historical study that comes to conclusion with this chapter can prove helpful on this head.

In taking up the question as to the nature of early analytic philosophy, we follow two methodological principles: (i) "Any characterization of 'analytic philosophy' which excludes Moore, Russell, and the later Wittgenstein, as well as the leading figures of post–Second World War analytic philosophy must surely be rejected" (Hacker 1996a: 247). The correct definition of analytic philosophy will be consistent with the philosophy of its generally recognized founding fathers. (ii) Any definition of "analytic philosophy" that was clearly presented in both earlier and more recent histories of philosophy must be rejected too. To be sure, Moore, Russell, and Wittgenstein, and later also Ryle, Austin and their colleagues, were doing a type of philosophy they consciously understood to be radically innovative—it was intrinsically a New Philosophy. This means that anyone with detailed knowledge of the full historical context of the analytic movement, with the context of both its emergence and development, would be firmly pressed to identify and define the truly novel character of this philosophy.

2 Incomplete Definitions

The literature is replete with definitions of analytic philosophy that fail to meet the two methodological requirements suggested above. Despite the fact that they put into focus important sides of analytic philosophy, they are all but adequate definitions. Here are some of them:

1) *Analytic philosophy as theory of logical forms.* Some authors maintain that despite all the complexity of the subject, analytic philosophy typically pursues a unified "theory of logical form as a regulating ideal relative to which all philosophical analyses are ultimately to be given" (Cocchiarella 1987: 2). Apparently, in this definition logical form was understood as forms of symbolic logic.[1] The approach envisaged by Cocchiarella was originally introduced by Frege who persistently discriminated between true and apparent logical form. Russell's theory of descriptions applies that same distinction in a most persuasive way—for this reason it was called by Frank Ramsey a "paradigm for philosophy" (1931: 261n.),—leading many scholars to regard it as essential to the New Philosophy. Perhaps the most celebrated example of its application is Carnap's article "Elimination of Metaphysics through Logical Analysis of Language" (1931). Carnap sought in that essay to demonstrate that Heidegger's conception of metaphysics fails the "logical form" (in this sense) test. However, there were analytic thinkers who do not operate with axioms of symbolic logic. One may count to them Moore, Ryle, J. L. Austin, John Wisdom, the late Friedrich Waismann and, most significantly, the late Wittgenstein. It is evident, then, that this definition of analytic philosophy is too narrow.

2) *Philosophy of language as prima philosophia.* Michael Dummett formulated the identifying characteristics of analytic philosophy in this way:

> What distinguishes analytical philosophy, in its diverse manifestations, from other schools is the belief, first, that a philosophical account of thought can be attained through a philosophical account of language, and, secondly, that a comprehensive account can be only so attained. (1993: 4)

The pre-analytical philosophers, in contrast, were interested in investigating thinking as such. Dummett goes on to remark that analytic philosophy is post-Fregean philosophy:

> Important as Russell and Moore both were, [their philosophy] neither was the, or even *a*, source of analytical philosophy. . . . The sources of analytical philosophy were the writings of philosophers, who wrote, principally or exclusively, in the German language. (ix)

Against Dummett, however, the evidence supports the conventional view that it was Russell alone who was the founding father of analytic philosophy (see §§ 3, 6). Gordon Baker and Peter Hacker convincingly substantiate this position:

> It is curious to find Dummett and Sluga joining hands in contending that Frege was the founder of analytic philosophy, *the characteristic tenet of which is that philosophy of language is the foundation of the rest of philosophy.* If "analytic philosophy" includes the later Wittgenstein, Ryle, and Austin among its luminaries, if analytic philosophy of law includes Hart or Kelsen, if analytic philosophy of history includes Berlin or Dray, if analytic philosophy of politics includes Nozick or Rawls, then it is *not* a characteristic tenet of the "school." On the contrary, it would be denied, both in theory and in practice, by all these philosophers. (1984: 7 n.)

What's more, it is a historical fact that a variant of what we've called "proto-analytic" philosophy was expressly not a philosophy of language. Recall, for example, that the philosophy associated with the major proto-analytic figure, Franz Brentano, is a species of descriptive psychology. In the literature there has been a strong tendency to follow this view. Today more and more philosophers are beginning to realize that analytic philosophers are anything but only philosophers of language.

3) *Analytic philosophy is anti-speculative philosophy.* Analytic philosophy is also not simply antithetical to speculative philosophy. In fact, during its early years, it was pursued in conjunction with traditional speculative philosophy, if with a clear division sense of their divergent competencies (Broad 1924; Wisdom 1931: 8f., 1934).

In truth, the categorically dismissive attitude of analytic philosophy toward speculative metaphysics emerged only after the Vienna Circle's consuming engagement with Wittgenstein's *Tractatus*. Bertrand Russell, for example, had nothing against inductive speculation in philosophy. When asked later in his life what philosophy is, he answered: "Philosophy consists of speculations about matters where exact knowledge is not yet possible" (1960: 11). The early analytic philosophers evidently did not employ "speculative" as an explanatory term.

4) *Analytic philosophy clarifies thoughts.* In a famous paper, published more than seventy years ago, Henry Price used the terms "clarification" and "analysis" as synonyms (1945: 3)—to him, analytic philosophers are "clarificatory philosophers." This, however, does not pass muster as a comprehensive definition of analytic philosophy either. Indeed, while the latter was introduced as the name of something radically new—as a revolution in philosophy—in the history of philosophy, the criterion of "clarity" as a distinguishing factor of a philosophical school or current stretches back to antiquity. Sextus Epicurus, for example, "was so lucid a writer that in the work *On Rhetoric* he makes clearness the sole requisite" (Diog. Laert., *Vitae philosophorum*, X,13). Moreover, philosophy was later often seen as clarification, by Descartes, for instance, by Rousseau, and in the early twentieth century by the Germanophone critical realist Hans Cornelius.

5) *Analytic philosophy proceeds in analyses.* Some authors (Hacker 1996a; Monk 1996; Beaney 2013, 2017) maintain that analytic philosophy is characterized, *nomen est omen*, by producing analysis. Unfortunately, this, like the foregoing definitions, is also incomplete.

First of all, while analysis is an important element of the methodology of the New Philosophy, there were also salient exceptions. Gilbert Ryle, for example, made it clear that "analytic philosophy" is not preoccupied simply with analysis (1949a: 203), as did John Wisdom (1965: 60ff.).

What's more, neither Moore nor Russell was by any stretch the first thinker to introduce the method of analysis in philosophy, something already highly developed by Plato (Sayre 1969) and the later philosophers who frequently followed it. For example, the "eighteenth-century European philosophy, in general, and the German Enlightenment, prior to Kant's *Critique of Pure Reason*, in particular, largely conceived of themselves as analytic philosophers" (Engfer 1982: 10). This was as true of the leading rationalists (Spinoza and Leibniz), as it was of the most influential empiricists (Berkeley and Hume). Finally, the method of analysis plays a central role in the principal works of the towering figures of continental philosophy, the later Edmund Husserl and Martin Heidegger (Chapter 11: § 1).

6) *Analytic philosophy is exact philosophy.* Some authors maintain that analytic philosophy can be defined as "exact philosophy" (Mulligan 1993: 133). In fact, the chief methodological innovation of the proto-analytic Brentano school was simply "the introduction of a new level of

exactness into philosophy" (Mulligan 1986: 86). According to Brentano, "philosophy must be rigorous, scientific, exact, and clear," including possible counterexamples and counterfactuals (ibid.). Censuring Kant's "philosophems" as "monstrous, in their arrogance," Brentano objected (1975: 8) above all, and in a way that looked forward to G. E. Moore, to the lack of clarity in thinking and language. Methodologically, Brentano was but part of a tradition of "criticism of every sort of antiscientific and obscure philosophizing" (Mulligan 1986: 89). At the same time, he did not believe that scientific exactness could be introduced via the analysis of language.

But this is to assign the term "exact" a rather narrow meaning, as in the phrase "exact sciences." When applied to philosophy, "exact" in this sense indicates that philosophic theories are expressed in formally precise terms and figures. In this way, the term "exact philosophy" is used "to signify *mathematical philosophy*, i.e. philosophy done with the explicit help of mathematical logic and mathematics" (Bunge 1973: v). Clearly, this is not an explanatory definition of analytic philosophy.

A second reason for rejecting any move to define analytic philosophy as "exact" philosophy is evidenced in the work of J. L. Austin. One of the prominent figures of the Oxford school of language philosophy, Austin expressly opposed exactness in philosophy, as did the later Wittgenstein.

3 Bertrand Russell's Definition

We have already mentioned that analytic philosophy first presented itself as a revolution in philosophy. In this connection, some authors speak of it as "philosophy's second Revolution" that was a late development of the European Enlightenment, the philosophy of Descartes being the start of its first revolution (Clarke 1997). From this perspective, the most concise description of the impact of Russell's philosophy is that it "unmasked the great nineteenth-century metaphysicians as authors of a monstrous hoax played upon generations eager to be deceived" (Berlin 1997: 604). In this respect, Moore's and Russell's innovations were sometimes conceived of as, that we already called, New Philosophy, a term that was soon associated with English analytic philosophy in general, and understood to refer to both the Cambridge and the Oxford schools.

It is true that nowadays that "the movement has lost its former revolutionary ethos. It is no longer a philosophy fighting prejudices and superstitions. . . . It has, to some extent, itself become an idol, enthroned in self-satisfaction and thus inviting new iconoclasts" (von Wright 1993: 41–2). This reflects, however, nothing but the present-day problem of "analytic scholasticism" that many decry as a evidencing the sterility and ever-multiplying complications of analytic philosophy, a fault identified many decades ago by Frank Ramsey (1931: 269). Analytic scholasticism is typical for the late analytic philosophy (see §§ 4.1, 6, below).

In more concrete terms, the New Philosophy, which Russell would term "analytic" only faute de mieux,[2] became fully and concretely explicit during the first months of Russell's acquaintance with Wittgenstein, from October 1911 to November 1912 (Milkov 2007, 2013). In the first months of this period, Russell also met Henri Bergson, with whom he engaged in critical discussion. Russell's attitude to Bergson was rather dismissive. Be this as it may, it was his debates with Bergson that impelled Russell more clearly to formulate the idea for a New Philosophy, one radically different from traditional philosophy.

Above all, according to Russell, and in contrast to Bergson's doctrine, the analytic philosophy produces "solid results"[3] (1918: 38)—results that do not disintegrate when subjected to the "test of reason." Russell believed that the New Philosophy achieves this by being an "examined philosophy"—which is to say, a philosophy examined by reason. More specifically, Russell conceived of analytic philosophy as an approach that uses "the harmonizing mediation of reason, which tests our beliefs by their mutual compatibility, and examines, in doubtful cases, the possible sources of error on the one side and on the other" (ibid.: 17).[4] This is a philosophy of "scientific restraint and balance" (ibid.: 20).[5] Its findings and formulations are submitted to the test of reason. Conversely, the philosophy Russell sought to overthrow produces theories and ideas that are not examined this way and as a result are persuasive only to unsympathetic minds. Seen critically from another, alternative perspective, the traditional metaphysical systems one and all disintegrate.

In fact, already Kant advanced philosophy that puts the philosophical speculations at the "tribunal of reason" (A669/B697). Russell's approach was different, thought. He directly connected it to his (and Moore's) realism and to the concrete common sense and scientific observations. In contrast, Kant's "tribunal of reason" was guided by abstract examination of the "sources of knowledge."

Analytic philosophy also meant for Russell "rigorous philosophy." However, this term was first used by Edmund Husserl in the title of his book *Philosophy as Rigorous Science* (1911) (Chapter 9). What was different from Husserl's approach was considering the philosophical rigor as an end in itself. In this connection, it is helpful to remind ourselves of a famous saying of J. L. Austin: "Importance is not important; truth is."

This side of analytic philosophy explains its penchant for taxonomies, for example, for producing lists of "grammatical" categories, or of ontological "nomenclatures."[6] As one of its critics once put it, "an 'analytic' philosopher . . . earn[s] this title by grinding away at the consequences of this or that particular proposition as if filing a legal brief" (Barrett 1978: 66). If nothing else, such practices yield solid results.

Main characteristic of the philosophical solid results is that they have no alternatives and so cannot be disproved. In this connection, however, it can be recalled that producing theses which have no alternatives is an old philosophical practice used, among others, by Kant again, for example, when he maintained that no system of propositions contains in itself its own truth. This is an apodictic metaphysical axiom about the necessary relation of the unconditioned to the conditioned can't be refuted in principle (Brandt 2007: 203). This example reveals a problem in Russell's definition since, apparently, his approach was already in use by philosophy's past masters.

Furthermore, Russell also maintained that main characteristic of the rigorous philosophy is the discussion of the fundamentals. In a letter to Lucy Donnelly of October 28, 1911, Russell wrote: "Bergson's philosophy, though it shows constructive imagination, seems to me wholly devoid of argument and quite gratuitous: he never thinks about fundamentals, but just invents pretty fairly-tales" (1912c: 318). In contrast, the New Philosophy is highly theoretical.

Unfortunately, also this definition of analytic philosophy is too broad. Husserl's phenomenology discussed the fundamentals exactly in the same sense as Russell did (see Chapter 9: § 2). What is more, the main subject of the leading figure of continental philosophy, Martin Heidegger, was the "fundamental ontology" of human being.

The last two points demonstrate that, despite being the most accurate one, also Russell's definition of analytic philosophy was incomplete.[7]

4 Factions of the Early Analytic Philosophy

In the preceding chapter we discussed two concepts of analytic philosophy. In fact, however, analytic philosophy was essentially dualistic from the very beginning. Philosophy must be strict, rigorous, its results to be proved by arguments—despite sharing this modus operandi, the founding fathers of analytic philosophy, Moore and Russell, embraced different methodological strategies. While Russell outlined a "scientific method in philosophy," Moore was more of, what can be called, an interpretive analyst.

4.1 Interpretive Analysis

This philosophical method is marked by Moore's question: "What on Earth means this philosophical proposition?" Consistent with this, Moore repeatedly tried "to translate the propositions [of philosophers] into the concrete" (1917: 209).[8] Importantly enough, Moore was not a pure interpretive analyst but mainly so.[9] Shortly before 1900, Russell urged Moore to continue exploring philosophical logic, which Moore went ahead and did (Chapter 12: § 2). On the other hand, Russell always believed that the New Philosophy has its own—called by him "analytic"—method, which he understood to be related to Moore's "interpretive analysis."[10] In other words, in contrast to the late analytic philosophers Quine and Sellars, Russell always was somewhat of an interpretative analyst. This helped him to underpin the belief that he had established a revolutionary new philosophical method by means of which he could defeat not only the old, non-concrete ("scholastic") philosophy but also resolve problems of politics and society (Russell 1968).

Despite some shared fundamental in Moore's and Russell's philosophical outlook, the divide between their different types of analytical methodology widened, when Russell's Germanophone student, Wittgenstein, came to Cambridge. This development produced the two influentially articulated forms of early analytic philosophy we previously reviewed in Chapter 15: that of Russell, later adopted by Carnap (and criticized by Quine who knew analytic philosophy only in this form), and that of Wittgenstein, which was substantiated by insights of Gottlob Frege and associated in Cambridge in the 1930s and 1940s with the likes of Moore, Stebbing and John Wisdom, as well as with the Oxford ordinary language philosophers after the Second World War. Consequentially enough, in the hands of the ordinary language philosophers this approach developed into "connective analysis." To be more explicit, connective analysis consists of interpretative conceptual analyses that are logically connected, without forming, however, a closed (finite) system. This methodological characteristic distinguishes this method from that of Hegel who, arguably, also pursued conceptual analyses (Chapter 5: § 4); the latter, however, were jammed into the Procrustean bed of his speculative logic. At the same time, the intrinsic logical connectedness of its results differentiated it from Russell's method with its single-minded aim of yielding "solid results" in philosophy (see § 7, below).

The principal disadvantage of interpretive analysis is that it *can* easily, albeit not necessarily, turn into what was dubbed at the time, a "philosophy without tears": a general discussion of general topics. Lacking any particular subject matter, this method proved difficult to teach at the overcrowded larger universities of the post–Second World War world. This explains why after 1955, Austin and Strawson mainly abandoned connective analyses. The period of "analytic anarchy," reigning in Britain during and immediately after the "trouble times" of the Second World War, pursuing philosophy without specific subject matter, associated with the names of Wittgenstein, Ryle, and John Wisdom,[11] thereby came to an end. In North America, in particular, some philosophers read this development this way.[12] Be this as it may, it is a matter of fact that this turn took clear shape only after Quine and his acolytes attacked the *a priori*.

4.2 Analytic Philosophy Producing Chains of Arguments

The main drawback of interpretive analysis makes it easy to understand why analytic philosophers felt strongly impelled to adopt other forms that would build consistent systems of propositions, every one of which would be unimpeachably grounded. This is not surprising since it would appear to be the most straightforward way to arrive at solid results in philosophy. One of its upshots was the program of Russell and Carnap for "logical construction of the world," which we discussed in Chapter 15. This program was informed by Russell's 1912 definition of analytic philosophy we referred to in § 3. It was completed by, what can be called, the reasons-giving analysis.

By the mid-1960s, the triumph of the method of reasons-giving analysis was irreversible. In 1963 Michael Dummett, in his paper on (anti-) "Realism," and Donald Davidson, in "Actions, Reasons, and Causes," fielded decisive arguments that discredited connective analysis. To this the connective analysts Ryle, Strawson, and David Pears reacted by changing gears and pursuing analytic-historical investigations in Plato (Ryle 1966), Kant (Strawson 1966), and Russell (Pears 1967), respectively. This wholesale realignment of the enterprise culminated in Michael Dummett's radical historicizing of analytic philosophy in his studies on Frege (Dummett 1973; see Chapter 1: § 5).[13]

The disadvantages of this kind of analytic philosophy are even more considerable than those of interpretive analysis. Most problematically, since the aim is now, first and foremost, to build strictly consistent systems of statements, analytic philosophy readily degenerates into little more than a mere mind game. What is a typical of the philosophical mind games is that they create in players the illusion that they are not really games but something perfectly "serious." Unfortunately, they are not!

In fact, this side of analytic philosophy was discernible even prior to the Second World War. Already at that time it became clear that one of the reasons for the captivating allure of analytic philosophy was that it suggests "intellectual games with chess-like indifference.... It is the sheer intellectual virtuosity of the performance which in large measure captivates student interest" (Nagel 1936: 197).

Be this as it may, this method has prevailed as the modus operandi (if not the modus vivendi!), above all, of late analytic philosophy. Disappointingly, what philosophy has to show for itself on this score is rather discouraging. For example, the shift from theory of thinking to theory of reference led many to believe that a new age in philosophy had begun. This proved not, however, to be the case: the anticipated reign of a newly revelatory perspicuity proved little more than a pipe dream. Some forty years ago, Arthur Danto confirmed as much, balefully observing that "current theories of reference are as dense and varied as reflections on the Trinity of Byzantine philology" (1980: 634).

In short, in the latest forms of analytic philosophy proliferate often pointless studies. Today, more and more often we hear claims that contemporary, late analytic philosophy is "empty of import for, or as regards to, concrete reality" (Unger 2014: 6). The problem is that

> practitioners [of analytic philosophy today often] do not, by the large, believe that philosophy is or can be a science, i.e. they do not believe that it can add to the stock of positive human knowledge.... In positive science results are expected. In analytic philosophy everyone waits for the next new puzzle. Like the brain twisters holidaymakers take onto the beach, philosophical puzzles divert from the life's hardship. (Mulligan, Simons, Smith 2006: 63 f.)

5 Analytic Philosophy versus Continental Philosophy

Today, the antipode of analytic philosophy is held to be the so-called "continental philosophy." As various authors noted long ago, the latter is ill-named, since analytic philosophy, too, has its roots in the continent of Europe. Be this as it may, what counts here is to determine (i) what continental philosophy is and how it differs from analytic philosophy; (ii) whether a reunification of these two currents of philosophy is possible, and also desirable. The latter question was repeatedly mooted in recent years. This is understandable since the two movements share the same roots. Immanuel Kant, for example, is a thinker who can be seen as both analytic and continental philosopher. In this section we shall discuss the above questions in order.

5.1 Disparities between Analytic and Continental Philosophy

5.1.1 As Regards Method

Returning to Russell's criticism of Bergson, we find that according to Russell, the main problem with the Old Philosophy, and with Bergson in particular, is that it

> does not depend upon argument and cannot be upset by argument. His [Bergson's] imaginative picture of the world, regarded as poetic effort, is in the main not capable of either proof or disproof. Shakespeare says life's but a walking shadow, Shelly says it is like a dome of many-colored glass, Bergson says it is a shell which bursts into parts that are again shells. If you like Bergson's image better, it is just as legitimate. (1912c: 336)

In other words, the insufficiency of continental philosophy is connected with the fact that its results are not solid. You can agree with a philosopher under scrutiny—if you are sympathetic to his or her style of thinking—but you can also as readily demur. Hence, while analytic philosophy, from its beginnings, has endeavored to emulate the method of science, continental philosophy followed a method close to that of myth and poetry.

The contrasting characteristics of the two movements were set in high relief in the debate between Carnap and Heidegger in Davos in March 1929 (Friedman 2000). In the aftermath of this debate, Carnap formulated the difference more clearly than ever between the philosophy delivering solid results and the other more poetic philosophy, maintaining that he sometimes reads Nietzsche because what the latter writes is a kind of literature, but he refuses to read Hegel and Heidegger since they present their throughout mystical, poetically inspired writings as academic products. After his clash with Carnap in Davos, Heidegger, apparently swayed by Carnap's arguments, was even more convinced that poetry and not science best demonstrates the superiority of human mind that philosophy tries to explicate (Heidegger 1935: 28).

This interpretation can be supported with reference to the so-called "Oldest System Program of German Idealism" (1796) which is rightly considered to be the manifesto of what later was called "continental philosophy":

> The philosopher must possess just as much aesthetic power as the poet. People without aesthetic sense are our pedantic philosophers [*Buchstabenphilosophen*]. The philosophy of spirit is aesthetic philosophy. One cannot be spiritual about anything, one cannot even reason spiritually about history—without aesthetic sense. (Critchley 2001: 130)

On can conclude from the above that, while continental philosophy is in a way close to poetry, analytic philosophy is interested in the truth only.[14] In fact, there cannot be a surprise that continental philosophy fails to produce truths. Already Kant realized that poetry cannot do that since it expresses thoughts that are not immediately based on experience. It merely produces "regulative ideas." In consequence, it brings "us to think without definite thoughts (concepts)" (Kant 1791: § 49). This explains why continental philosophy is convincing only to readers predisposed to share its specific outlooks.

Further, since regulative ideas guide continental philosophy, its practitioners offer insights that either are connected in closed (finite) systems, as with the German idealism (Chapter 4), or are autonomous ideas with no logical connection to other of the same philosopher's insights.[15] Analytic philosophers, in contrast, endeavor to articulate their ideas in webs of logical connections, albeit not within closed systems.

5.1.2 As Regards the Subject Matter

In this respect the so-called continental philosophy is a product of introducing a new subject matter in the center of philosophy—the *conditio humana*, either in its personal or in its social dimension.[16] Its basic questions concern the meaning and value of person's life and about person's relation to God, freedom, and immortality. This explains why its representatives often, in the words of Anthony Quinton, "rely on dramatic, even melodramatic, utterance rather than sustained rational argument" (1995: 161). That is also why "so much continental philosophy is concerned," as Simon Critchley notes, "with relations to non-philosophy, whether art, poetry, psychoanalysis, politics or economics" (2001: 87).

In addition to existential issues continental philosophy also concerns itself with contemporary problems of social praxis, specifically with how we can change and better organize society—with problems of emancipation. "In other words, the touchstone of philosophy in the continental tradition might be said to be the practice; that is to say, our historically and culturally embodied life in the world as finite selves" (Critchley 1997: 357).

Besides, since it discusses regulative ideas, in contrast to what we've determined to be the nature of analytic philosophy, continental philosophy "is problem free, [and this cannot be a surprise:] positions that are systematically undetermined can never achieve the sort of focus that comes from pursuing a particular problem throughout the twist and turns of the different argument for and against different solutions" (Mulligan 1993: 135).

Our next claim is that continental philosophy is a derivate of traditional philosophy which, as we've seen, puts *at the center* of philosophy a new subject matter: *conditio humana*. This thesis is supported by the fact that "what gets called 'analytic' philosophy is the philosophical movement most continuous with the 'grand' tradition in philosophy, the tradition of Aristotle and Descartes and Hume" (Leiter 2011).

An argument in support of this thesis is that the results of continental philosophy can be in principle probed and assessed by methods of analytic philosophy. This explains why we have analytic Marxism, analytic feminism, and also analytic readings of Kant—but not vice versa: there is no continental philosophy of rigid designators, or of possible-world semantics.

5.2 Can, *Must*, the Two Philosophies Come Together?

Continental philosophy is thus in a way subordinated to analytic philosophy. This fact helps to answer the second question posed at the outset of this section, namely is a reunification of the two types of philosophy possible? The answer to this question must clearly be negative. In truth, the rise of the continental philosophy, both with and after Kant, brought a new philosophical sub-discipline. It was not a "mistake" that the systematic analytic thinker should regret. The advent of continental philosophy enriched the discipline, it did not degrade it. Historically, the most open-minded way to view this development is to see it within the context of the fact that from the very beginning philosophy gave birth to ever new disciplines, the most recent ones being political economy, psychology, and sociology. Continental philosophy is a product of just such a break with its classical base. Analytic philosophy, in contrast, is a further development of mainstream Western philosophy as it has evolved in over 2,500 years.

We close this section with the prophetic words of Michael Dummett: "We have reached a point at which it is as if we're working in different subjects" (1993:

193). They help us to positively answer the question: Is a dialogue between analytic and continental philosophy possible?[17] Of course, it is possible, in fact, highly desirable—but as an interdisciplinary exercise, no more.

6 The Possibility for Substantive Renovations of Analytic Philosophy

The foregoing discussion largely traced the thinking of the conventional, received view that G. E. Moore and Russell were the founding fathers of analytic philosophy, adding to this picture also Ludwig Wittgenstein. In fact, however, analytic philosophy had only one founding father—Bertrand Russell. As was made clear earlier (Chapter 8: § 9), we do best to think of G. E. Moore as its "midwife": analytic philosophy in its full-fledged form was Russell's creation. It was he who encouraged the young Moore to collaborate with him. Furthermore, it was Russell who discovered Frege and that at a time the latter was largely ignored as a philosophical non-entity: after Russell's *Principles of Mathematics* was published in 1903, with "Appendix A" on "The logical and arithmetical doctrines of Frege," Hermann Cohen, Ernst Cassirer and Leonard Nelson, among others, were moved to debate Frege thinking and innovations. Finally, Russell discovered in his student Wittgenstein a philosophical genius, taught him the theoretical problems which preoccupied him (Russell) (Landini 2007), worked with him in 1912 on a joint project (Milkov 2013) and was also instrumental in helping Wittgenstein publish the *Tractatus*. Wittgenstein, in his turn, discovered in Frege a number of philosophically pregnant ideas and combined them with Moore's interpretative method. This fussion marked a pivotal advance in the New Philosophy, leading to the methodological innovation termed "connective analysis" (§ 4 (a)).[18]

The account above makes it clear that Russell must count as the great visionaries of twentieth-century philosophy. He was the first to catch sight of the progressive developments in both German and British philosophy (he was excellently acquainted with both of them) and clearly articulated them in a new philosophical program. Regrettably, at the same time Russell often saw the task of the New Philosophy in a rather simplistic way. To start with, his initial project to ground mathematics on logic, which he first undertook in 1898, was based on mereology. Importantly enough, this conception was married with the method of decompositional analysis. It was in August of 1900 when he learned from Peano that this program is a nonstarter (Milkov 2017). (Peano himself learned the technique of quantification and its implications for logic from Frege.) But when in years from 1911 through 1913 Russell started to work out the New Philosophy, he turned back, at least partly, to the decompositional analysis. Soon, however, he received a second check—this time from Wittgenstein, with reference to critical remark of Frege (Milkov 2013). Russell finally came to feel that philosophy cannot be successfully pursued by means of decompositional analysis alone, based on theory of complexes. When Russell found himself sinking with the New Philosophy into ever-more involved technical complications,[19] his interest in philosophy faded. This explains why, as David Pears remarked more than fifty years ago, "by the end of 1919 Russell already had most of his more important ideas on his work-bench" (1967: 12).

In Section 3, we have already seen that Russell's definition of analytic philosophy as philosophy of "scientific restraint and balance," is incomplete. This explains why it often devolved into the sort of mind games typical of late analytic philosophy, which is to say it led to philosophy out of touch with positive human knowledge.[20] As a matter of fact, the textbooks of late analytic philosophers on philosophy of mind (e.g., Ravenscroft 2005) or on analytical metaphysics (e.g., Carroll and Markosian 2010) do little more than catalogue the competing intuitions[21] of different philosophers or groups of philosophers.

Given this state of affairs, one can hardly be blamed for looking for a way out. Back in Chapter 1 we saw that analytic philosophy, at least in its early phase, held out more promising directions for philosophical inquiry than those predominating in the analytic movement at present. Above all, early analytic thought was inextricably connected with logic—with philosophical logic. The philosophical logic, in turn, was connected with the external world: with the third world. This fact was saliently foregrounded in this book's explication of Germanic proto-analytic and analytic philosophy of the "big nineteenth century". The present work thereby offers contemporary analytic philosophers an alternative line of academic exploration, one rich with the promise of positive human knowledge.

As a matter of fact, this direction is already being taken by philosophers currently undertaking to revive the method of conceptual analysis (Jackson 1998), a method that underwrites the *a priori* character of philosophy. This approach is in a way close to Oxford connective analysis, the most important difference between them being that practitioners of conceptual analysis as such do not need to subscribe to the dubious position that analytic "philosophy is not continuous with but altogether distinct from science" (Hacker 2007: 127). In reality, this is also a historical truth. Despite the fact that all early analytic philosophers, including Russell, were explicit that philosophy is different from science, they were not against working with it. Perhaps the most telling example was Wittgenstein who often collaborated with leading mathematicians in Cambridge, including Allan Turing (Floyd 2016). Furthermore, Wittgenstein took a serious interest in both Gödel's theorem and Wolfgang Köhler's Gestalt psychology; he also discussed for years with the eminent political economist Pierro Sraffa. J. L. Austin, for his part, significantly contributed to the debates among linguists of the time, while Peter Strawson was deeply influenced by Noam Chomsky's transformative grammar. Also today, the Oxford acolyte John Searle tries to keep in step with the advances of science. For more than thirty-five years now he has sought to attune his philosophy of mind to the developing insights and discoveries of the cognitive sciences (1984). Searle has also developed an inspiring conception of social reality (2010).

The above examples of scientifically interdisciplinary lines of development offer, we can see, a way out of the crisis and provide a whole spectrum of theoretical bases for renewing the project for analytic philosophy. One can thus appreciate how an informed view of the history of this movement can bring to bear more clarity, one consequence of which is that it can inspire with a deep sense of purpose those thinkers who feel called to take on this historic task.

Notes

Preface

1 Some outcomes of this seminar have been published in Mark Wilson (2007).

Chapter 1

1 Of course, there were also other influences. Thus, Russell's philosophy was stimulated by the works of the American William James, by the French Louis Couturat and Henri Poincare, and Wittgenstein's philosophy by the Russian L. N. Tolstoy (Milkov 2003a). Most importantly, Moore's and Russell's analytic philosophy was profoundly influenced the British tradition in philosophy (Pears 1967).
2 Otto Neurath was the first to articulate this attitude in full-fledged form (1936). Today, this position is called the Neurath-Haller thesis (Smith 1996).
3 That stance is usually supported by the authority of the Pittsburgh philosophers Wilfred Sellars and Robert Brandom. Griffin (1991) and Hylton (1990) also explore the influence of Hegel's theories on the early Moore and Russell.
4 On analytic philosophy as philosophy that produces "solid results," see Chapter 16: § 3.
5 For criticism of this thesis, see Beaney (2002: 93).
6 It's worth noting here that, decades before Glock, Gilbert Ryle made a similar point, observing that British philosophers traditionally considered philosophy a "science of mind," related to other sciences like physics, chemistry, and zoology. At the same time, being in tune with the philosophical-political mood of his period, Ryle criticized German philosophy for considering philosophy a "sublime science" (1951: 3). In fact, however, this sublime science was nothing but philosophical logic supplemented by substantive work in the philosophy of mathematics, a field virtually beyond the pale for French and British philosophers of the eighteenth and substantial parts of the nineteenth centuries. Long before Glock, Hans Sluga, too, brought this fact about German influence to light (1980: 11). Also prior to Glock, Gottfried Gabriel persuasively argued that German logical philosophy was the principal inspiration of early analytic philosophy (1984, 1986).
7 Russell was explicit that "philosophy is a study apart from other sciences" (1914: 240). This was also the position of Edmund Husserl (Chapter 9).
8 In fact, it remained more interested in philosophy of language.

9   The divergence between these two wings of analytic philosophy is discussed in Milkov (2013a: 26 ff.).
10 In contrast, when Hannah Arendt prepared her lectures on political theory in 1954 she was convinced that philosophy and political studies have nothing in common (1990).
11 See on it issue 1, vol. 6 of the online journal *philosophical inquiries* dedicated to the *History of Late Analytic Philosophy*: https://www.philinq.it/index.php/philinq/issue/view/15
12 Hacker (1996) fixed the end of analytic philosophy to the 1970s. See also Robert Hanna (2001).
13 Similar approach follows also Schwartz (2012).
14 For criticism of this approach, in defense of the "coarse-grained study" in history of analytic philosophy, see Preston (2007).
15 We agree with Kevin Mulligan that analytic philosophy is "the culture ... of the distinction, of description, examples and counter-examples" (1993: 134 f.). The author of the present book applied the descriptive method in history of philosophy, in somewhat different form (we are going to explore it in more detail in Chapter 2), in two earlier books on the history of analytic philosophy (Milkov 1997, 2003). Regrettably, certain reviewers misconstrued and eventually mispresented it. See, in particular, Pincock (2004).
16 That early analytic philosophy used a method close to Socrates's and Plato's peirastic dialectics (Milkov 2013b: § 3.2; Chapter 13: §1.6) is anything but an idiosyncratic claim. One can readily confirm it by consulting *Plato's Progress* (1966) by Gilbert Ryle.
17 Elements of this history were tracked down in Ryle 1957 (Chapter 2: § 6, (i)).

Chapter 2

1 Beaney (2005), among others, sees German philosophy between 1870 and 1914 as dominating the discipline worldwide.
2 In fact, this final product would synthesize the historical map with the actual map of concepts into an integral map of concepts and problems (Chapter 15: § 8).
3 That explains why the latter easily became a target of justified attacks on the side of Collingwood referred to in § 2.
4 Daniel Garber called this approach "disinterested history of philosophy" (1988: 33).
5 Ryle's *The Concept of Mind* was, of course, not a study in the history of philosophy. Its power to guide us in such matters comes from the fact that it laid out the achievements of the analytic movement in philosophy as it was developed in England between 1900 and 1950.

6 In the English-speaking world, Hartmann's idea for a history of concepts was echoed in A. O. Lovejoy's project for a "history of ideas," which concentrates on the history of the *unit–ideas* by which theories in philosophy can be analyzed (Mandelbaum 1965: 35 ff.).
7 For an example of their confusion, see Sellars (1963: 140), where this author claims that Russell's sense-data are "inner episodes."
8 This also includes discoveries made in philosophers' biographies. On this subject, see Monk (2002).
9 The very fact that, as Martin Kusch himself tells us, it is modeled on the *sociology* of scientific knowledge (1995: 15) suggests that it is not intrinsically philosophical.
10 On the false Analytic Ideal in history of philosophy, see the last paragraph of § 2.

Chapter 3

1 Leibniz's analysis is not to be confused with what Russell understood under this name. It is more of what Kant, but also Russell, called "regressive analysis" (Peckhaus 2001, 2002; see Chapter 13: § 1.4).
2 Apparently, this turn was occasioned by Leibniz's encounter in 1679 in Herford with Francis Mercury van Helmont, a leading Christian Cabbalist (Coudert 1995: 36).
3 Frege's knowledge of Leibniz has as a source mainly Trendelenburg (1867).
4 Similar criticism was also advanced by Husserl (1979).
5 The term is borrowed from Smith (1992: 49). However, this author uses it in a different sense—as a characteristic which is a mirror of reality.
6 Many authors of today are also conscious that "how a finally acceptable directly depicting language will look, will clearly depend on what the world is like" (ibid.: 58).
7 Among the philosophers who tried to do that, but whose efforts we would not discuss here, were Franz Brentano and Edmund Husserl (see Chapter 10).
8 In the *Tractatus* (6.5), Wittgenstein brought up this point so: "If a question can be framed at all, it is also *possible* to answer it."
9 Husserl's phenomenology, too, can be seen as theory of forms (Chapter 9: § 2.1).
10 In some later writings, Russell even defined philosophy as "the art of rational conjecturing" (1974).
11 Cf. with Wittgenstein's *Tractatus*: 4.112: "Philosophy is not a body of doctrine but an activity."
12 In ordinary usage, too, conjecturing is conceived as a kind of "calculation without numbers" (cf. Chapter 11: § 3.1).

13 It is not accidental that Gilbert Ryle, the leading figure of the Oxford ordinary language philosophy, showed great interest in Plato's peirastic dialectics. Unfortunately, Ryle's *Plato's Progress* remained less explored by the historians of analytic philosophy.
14 In fact, it was introduced in Plato (*Parm.* 132b).
15 In this sense we used Wittgenstein's theory (model) of subject as divided into empirical, metaphysical, and willing, for elucidating the problem of the meaning of life (Milkov 2005a).
16 On this point, we are paraphrasing Leibniz (see n. 6).
17 Leibniz defined *characteristica universalis* as program for calculating individuals much later (see § 2.3).

Chapter 4

1 Hegel was influential above all among the German historians of philosophy.
2 Despite the fact that Wittgenstein himself spoke about the mystical, he himself was not a mystic (Milkov 2004).
3 This stance was also a commonplace of scholastic philosophy. According to Bonaventura, for example, God possesses a particular way of knowing also called *ars aeterna*. "It has all that human reason cognizes as different but it has it in a complete unity; at that not only as what is actually given but also all the truth that is expressed and brought to light and also everything that *can* be thought" (Speer 2010: 38–9).
4 There will be more to say about the relatedness between Frege and the German idealism in Chapter 5.
5 In (1992: ch. 2) we called it "analectical method," presenting it as a hybrid between the analytic and dialectical method.
6 As we are going to see in Section 5.2, this stance brought Frege to reductionism, and Russell to eliminativism. These differences give us reason enough to exclude Frege from the narrowest circle of early analytic philosophers consisting of Moore, Russell, and Wittgenstein.
7 On problems with late analytic philosophy, see Chapter 16: § 4.2.
8 We must not forget at that that Hegel's "science of logic," like all classical logic before Frege, was built "within the bounds of a mereological idea of logic" (Stekeler-Weithofer 1992: 100).
9 This concept, by the way, indicates the common roots of early analytic philosophy and phenomenology that are to be found in Hermann Lotze (Chapter 8).
10 Wittgenstein himself speaks about "*the process of analysis*" (1979: 46), and a process takes time.
11 According to Kant, explications "make clear the predicate that lay undeveloped (*implicite*) in the concept of the subject through *development* (*explicatio*)" (1800: § 37).

12 The later Wittgenstein would say, "without intermediary [*Mittelwegen*]" (*PI*, § 94) (see Milkov 2001).
13 This understanding was also criticized by Marx, Husserl, and Heidegger (see Chapter 9, n. 9).

Chapter 5

1 Dummett's explanation "Frege barely troubled to attack Idealism at all; he simply passed it by" (1967: 225) is not convincing.
2 This claim is clearly opposed to the message of the manifesto of the Vienna Circle, one of the most important documents of the early analytic philosophy: "There are no depths in science" (Hahn et al. 1929: 15).
3 In Germany, this connection was well known. Bruno Bauch, for example, discussed it in his book *Wahrheit, Wert und Wirklichkeit* (1923: 62; see also Goedeke 1927: 116). Scholz (1941) too connected Frege's ideas with those of Leibniz and Kant.
4 Russell was one among them, especially before August 1900 (Milkov 2003: 50). Beaney (2008: 203) also underlines that Frege's function-argument analysis is quite different from the "decompositional conception of analysis embraced by Moore and Russell." See also Hylton (2010). In *The Principle of Mathematics* (1903), however, Russell started to follow the principle of "unity of propositions."
5 Apparently for "analytic" reasons, Frege's "*Keim*" was often translated as "kernel," instead of as "germ."
6 "Saturation": http://en.wikipedia.org/wiki/Saturation_(chemistry) (retrieved on February 12, 2019).
7 It is interesting to compare Frege's solution of this problem with that of Wittgenstein who was much more pronounced defender of analysis$_2$. According to Wittgenstein, the elements of the state of affairs hold together because of their topology alone: no concrescence, no fusion, as well as no mortar that connects them together is needed (Milkov 2001) (see Chapter 4: § 6.4).
8 In his *Philosophical Investigations* Wittgenstein developed this idea to the fullest.
9 Cf. Friedrich Schiller's famous saying "Life is serious, art is cheerful" from the prologue to *Wallenstein's Lager*. That Frege was well acquainted with Schiller's works is clear from his reference to *Don Carlos* (1897a: 130). Frege also often opposed "poetry" to "truth" (1893: xxi) with a hint to the subtitle of Goethe's autobiography *From my Life: Poetry and Truth* [*Dichtung und Wahrheit*] (1811–1833). On Goethe's influence on Frege's logic, via Trendelenburg, see Gabriel (2008: 121).
10 This anthropocentric stance of logic was also adopted by Wittgenstein. For Wittgenstein's anthropocentricity, see Pears (1971: 30).

11 This point supports Paul Linke's statement that "Frege actually brought psychology into, meaning right inside, his new foundations for logic" (1946: 67). His severe criticism of "psychologism" can be explained away with the fact that "he confused the bad psychology which was prospering at the time with psychology in general" (69).
12 Arguably, this conception was developed further by J. L. Austin, the first translator of Frege's *Grundlagen* into English, in the concept of "illocutionary force."
13 In fact, the act of judgment was connected with the free will already by Descartes (Steinvorth 2007: 136).
14 Many worlds are typical for Russell of the mid-1910s and for Carnap, not for Frege (Chapter 15: § 3).
15 Our translation from German; this term was often used by Wittgenstein later (see, e.g., 1953: § 122).
16 Already R. M. Martin (1967: 8) saw Frege's logic as following the "German traditions," opposing the English tradition in logic as presented by J. S. Mill and his friends.
17 This point found expression in the fact that while Kant investigated the "pure reason," Frege's logic explored "pure thinking."
18 Russell first learned Frege's logic of quantification via Peano in August 1900.
19 To this we would add that Russell was sensitive to the problem of infinity because of his Hegelian past: infinity was, according to Hegel, a prime paradox (Chapter 7: § 1 (iii)).
20 See Leśniewski (1927/31: 17); Gödel (1944: 135); and Weir (2010: 8).

Chapter 6

1 Today the word "eclecticism" is only used and understood in a pejorative sense. It is astonishing how successfully Lotze used this method. It is interesting to note that Lotze showed admiration toward eclecticism already in his pre-theoretical period: in 1840 he wrote the poem "Eclecticism" (Kroneberg 1899: 218).
2 This is especially true of Ward, who studied with Lotze in Göttingen in 1870. Note that in comparison to his two other teachers at Cambridge, Sidgwick and Stout, Ward exercised the strongest influence on Russell (Griffin 1991: 35).
3 Green said once to Bosanquet: "The time which one spent on such a book as that (the ['greater'] *Metaphysics* [of Lotze]) could not be wasted as regards one's own work" (Lotze 1888).
4 We are going to show why Lotze's logic was philosophical in Section 4.
5 On the history of the context principle, see Milkov (2003: 126 f.).
6 This point explains Bosanquet's claim: "These two distinguished men [Lotze and Green], however different in method and style of thought, had some fundamental tendencies in common" (Lotze 1888: v).

7 Georg Misch had once noted (1912: xxix) that in adopting relationism, Lotze followed Kant. To be more exact, he subjugated the general concepts of philosophy to scientific ones. Furthermore, Lotze's relationism followed the tendency in Kant to consider scientific concepts relational, which he apparently borrowed from d'Alambert and Lagrange.
8 Sluga sees in this position an ancestor of Frege's logicism: "Among the many things that Frege owes to Lotze, the most important is perhaps the idea of logicism" (1980: 57).
9 In support of non-formal exposition of logic, Lotze explicitly refers to Trendelenburg. Similar argument was later used by Husserl (Chapter 9: § 2.2).
10 For Lotze's concrete influence on Russell, see Chapter 7.
11 Today it is widely accepted that "Bradley's attack on psychologism was . . . by far and away [his] most important contribution to modern logic" (Griffin 1996: 216).
12 Up to the end of the nineteenth century, Bolzano's anti-psychologism remained largely unknown.
13 Manser is, of course, wrong when he claims that Lotze did not accept the context principle since the latter allegedly contradicted his atomism (1984: 310).
14 Lotze expressly acknowledges Hegel as its source.
15 See Section 8 for basic similarities between Lotze and Wittgenstein.
16 David Bell (1999) suggested that Moore's theory of judgment was decisively influenced by Brentano's analytical psychology, which G. F. Stout made popular at Cambridge. Bell, however, overlooks the fact that prior to Brentano, Lotze had developed the elements of analytical psychology and that Brentano was a student of Lotze's elder fellow objectivist-revolutionary in philosophy, Adolf Trendelenburg. On Brentano's debt to Lotze, see Milkov (2018).
17 This conception was developed in Frege (1891) in his theory of judgment as a fusion of the function with the argument.
18 This point shows the inaccuracy of Russell's interpretation of Lotze's logic as implying "that all propositions consist in the ascription of a predicate to subject, and that this ascription is not a relation" (1903: § 426) (§ 6.3).
19 Already P. G. Kuntz has noted that Lotze's "theory of truth . . . was later developed conspicuously by Bertrand Russell" (1971: 29).
20 On September 8, 1879, William James wrote in a letter: "This summer I've read about a half of Lotze's *Metaphysik*. He is the most delectable, certainly, of all German writers—a pure genius" (Perry 1935: 16).
21 Our translation from the German; similar translation is suggested in Garver (1994: 134).
22 That the problem of compositionality found by Wittgenstein and Lotze the same solution is also obvious from the common use of the term of "[logical] scaffolding" by the two (Lotze 1874: § ix; Wittgenstein 1922: 3.42, 4.023). On Wittgenstein's concept of scaffolding (logical and of the world), see Milkov (2001).

23 On Lotze's panpsychism, see Kuntz (1971: 34). On this point Lotze was also followed by William James and A. N. Whitehead.
24 Wittgenstein was only critical of the word "infer" here: we infer only in logic, not in natural science, and of course not in general discourse. He insisted that it would be better to say, "as I can see my spirit in my physiognomy."

Chapter 7

1 Understandably, Russell dedicated his *Essay on the Foundations of Geometry* (1897a) to McTaggart.
2 Lotze's impact on the neo-Kantians is not surprising if one bears in mind that Otto Liebmann, the architect of this movement and the author of the groundbreaking *Kant und die Epigonen* (1865), was a student of Lotze. It deserves noting that the two leading branches of the neo-Kantianism, the Southwest School and the Marburg School, were inspired by different aspects of Lotze's philosophy.
3 "The proposition, 'things exist,' has no intelligible meaning except that they [the things] stand in relations to each other" (1887: 186).
4 In the early 1840s Lotze was closely befriended with Fries's acolyte Ernst Friedrich Apelt (Woodward 2015: 45–9). On Fries, see Chapter 13: § 1.3.
5 In 1844 Lotze succeeded Herbart as a professor of philosophy at the University of Göttingen.
6 Later similar ideas were promulgated by Russell and Carnap.
7 It deserves notice—despite the fact that we are not going to discuss this point here—that this practice was also followed by Russell in his project for scientific method in philosophy which "deal[s] with its problems piecemeal" (1918: 85) (Chapter 9: § 2.1).
8 The very term "truth-value" was introduced by Lotze's pupil, Wilhelm Windelband, in (1882) (Gabriel 1984).
9 The idea was introduced by Plato, was also addressed by Kant, but after Hegel it remained in shadow (Ryle 1971a, 1971b).
10 It was to become a central idea in Frege's logic (1891).
11 The last two concepts were embraced by Lotze's student Frege (1884, 1891) and today are mainly associated with Frege's name.
12 In Russell's terms, we should pursue metaphysical enquiries only when our investigation reaches *indefinables*, such as numbers, space, time, and colors. Russell called the discipline which discusses them "philosophical logic" (1903: v) (see Chapter 11).
13 The book was finished in October 1896 and published in May 1897.
14 Cf. Lotze's thought (discussed in § 2) that in order to say something reasonable, we must think of objects and terms in relation to each other.

15 Typically, Russell himself believed that this is an idea of Bradley and Bosanquet (1897a: §§ 187 f.). In fact, it was Lotze's idea adopted by Bradley and Bosanquet.
16 Here is an example Russell set out that shows the uniqueness of the moments of time as compared to events: two time points can be different only when they are mutually external; in contrast, two events can happen together in time.
17 There was no such distinction in Kant.
18 Lotze's position here was a part of a criticism of the subjectivity of space and time in Kant, which started with the publishing of the above-mentioned *Logical Investigations* by Adolf Trendelenburg in 1840 and continued until the end of the nineteenth century (Adair-Toteff 1994).
19 In support of this argument, Russell refers to Lotze (1879: § 106).
20 We learned first about them from Passmore's remark: "Russell's notes on a lecture McTaggart gave on Lotze still survive" (1995: 195).
21 In fact, Russell changed the term "judgment" to "proposition" only in "The Classification of Relations" (Russell 1899). The paper was read in January 1899; in it the full conclusions from his March–April 1898 turn were made.
22 The first signs of the change of Russell's mind are to be seen in Russell (1912) (Chapter 15: § 1 (a)).
23 Two years later Russell was explicit on this point (1900b: 225).
24 "Intensive magnitudes" are aesthetic perceptions (qualities) like pleasure (1903: § 171).
25 Ray Monk notes that Russell's acquaintance with Dedekind's *Nature and Meaning of Numbers*, teaching him "to regard the notion of order, rather than that of quantity, as the central notion in the definition of number," played a crucial role in Russell's turn of 1898 (1996: 116). However, this was only the first part of this turn. What Russell still needed was a new conception of logic, which is wholly absent from Dedekind's pamphlet.
26 Lotze called the requirement that we cannot justify series if we do not assume individuals "law of juxtaposition" (1856/64: 491).
27 We see here again a most important characteristic of Russell's philosophy of mathematics and of his logic in general: he connected it inextricably with the real world.
28 This is clearly evident in the example of the history of the concept of state of affairs. In was introduced by Lotze in 1874, only to be embraced by Carl Stumpf in 1888, and a couple of years later by the early Husserl (Chapter 8).

Chapter 8

1 Barry Smith mistakenly claimed (1996: 326–7) that, under the influence of Bergmann, "in the second edition of *Logic* of 1880" Lotze allegedly made some changes in his understanding of states of affairs. In fact, where he spoke of states of affairs (57 n.) the two editions are identical.

2. Following Lotze, Ernst Cassirer (1910) embraced a theory of concepts keyed to the model of the mathematical notion of function, specifically the seriality of members ("particulars") as a function of a serial principle ("universal"). Importantly enough, Cassirer explicitly credited Hermann Lotze as the father of this new theory of concepts.
3. This concept of being in *reciproca tantum* relation is often used in constructivist ontologies (Smith 1998: 524, 533, 539), but never explicitly and theoretically developed in full. This is a realm of ontology which still waits appropriate elaboration.
4. Cf. with the discussion of the most economic type of connection between the entities of mereological unities in Chapter 4: § 8.
5. This position cannot be a surprise since Lotze was convinced that what *exist* are elements that stay in relations (Chapter 7: § 2).
6. Cf. with Fries's "sense of truth" (Chapter 13: § 1.6).
7. It is of interest to mention here that despite Bauch's sympathy with Frege, and in spite of his good knowledge of Frege's logic, he was convinced that "in the realm of logic since Hegel, nothing has surpassed in value Lotze's contributions" (1918: 45).
8. This example is suggested in Smith (1987: 201), from which he, indeed, made the contrary conclusion.
9. Simons (1985) advanced arguments for the claim that the complexes and states of affairs are not different in type were advanced in.
10. Cf. with Wittgenstein from the *Tractatus*: "Objects contain the possibility of all situations" that they make up (2.014). In this argument Lotze also makes use of the "ontology of ways" that would later play a central role in Wittgenstein's *Tractatus* (Milkov 2019).
11. An expression often used by Frege (see e.g., 1971: 83).
12. The task to find out to what extent Frege followed Lotze on this point exceeds the scope of the present chapter.
13. There are clear elements of Panpsychism here (Chapter 6: § 8.2).
14. Incidentally, Wittgenstein himself considered the introduction of *status rerum* in the translation of the *Tractatus* in English (1973: 21). However, he deliberated to translate *Sachlage*, not *Sachverhalt* (state of affairs).

Chapter 9

1. Later Russell remembered: "At the time when I wrote *The Principles of Mathematics*, I had not yet seen the necessity of logical types [or forms]" (1924: 333).
2. For an alternative interpretation, see Lohmar (2011).

3 In Section 1.2 we have already noted that, genealogically, the investigation of logical forms in language preceded that of logical form in epistemology.
4 Later, in *Analysis of Mind*, he spoke of a "direct contemplation of facts [forms]" which discards language (Russell 1921: 212).
5 In *Formale und Transzendentale Logik* (1929) § 87, Husserl holds that essences can be both formal and material. In other words, there are essences that are not formal. Phenomena are only the material essences. The middle Husserl, however, refused to speak about "formal *eide*" (see Chapter 10).
6 The other type of analysis Russell practiced was the well-known decompositional analysis. It was connected with the mereological period of his philosophical development that Russell embraced in 1898 (Griffin 2008). Despite the fact that with the introduction of his Theory of Denoting (1903) Russell realized that the decompositional analysis has its limitations, he tried to restore it in *PM* and in the early 1910s (Milkov 2003, 2013).
7 Beaney (2008a: 208) maintains that Husserl's "reduction" (which, incidentally, includes not only the eidetic but also the phenomenological reduction) is virtually synonymous with "what Russell calls 'analysis.'"
8 "Philosophy does not become scientific by making use of other sciences.... Philosophy is a study apart from the other sciences" (Russell 1914: 240) (Milkov 2013: § 5.2).
9 This was also the main thesis of Wittgenstein's *Philosophical Investigations* (Milkov 2003: 71). Similar claims were also made by Hegel, Marx, and Heidegger (see Chapter 4: n. 13).
10 The relatedness between Husserl and Russell on this point is to be explained with reference to the fact that the two philosophers worked in the context of the German post-Kantian philosophy. Kant was the first to maintain that in philosophy we start with the concrete and the vague ideas only to end with the clear and abstract ones. In mathematics, in contrast, we start with the clear and abstract ideas and end with the complex and vague. Russell virtually repeated this position. He only called the second kind of analysis "regressive method," the first one "progressive" (1907; see Chapter 13: § 1.4).
11 Wittgenstein, too, used this technique, asking questions of the kind: "Can one play chess without the queen?" or "Are zebras without stripes zebras?" One of his acolytes in Cambridge, John Wisdom, deemed such questions to be "Wittgenstein's biggest contribution to philosophy" (1965: 88).
12 In this connection, Husserl severely criticized Andreas Voigt, a former student of Ernst Schröder, who defended the logical formalism in philosophy (Hamacher-Hermes 1994).
13 Gilbert Ryle also supported the rumor (1970: 9).
14 This explanation was suggested by Kenneth Blackwell.

15 Russell first mentioned the project to expose the ideas developed in *Principia Mathematica* in short form, which will be also read by open-minded philosophers, as early as 1911–13. In these years he projected a book on "Advanced Logic" (1984: xxiii, 183).
16 Small wonder, then, that later Russell remembered: "I had originally accepted Brentano's view that in sensation there are three elements: act, content and object" (1959: 100).
17 Russell explicitly underlined this in (1912a: v).
18 We see here that to Russell of that time epistemology is only a part of the philosophy of mind. It deserves notice that Russell was one of the founding fathers of the discipline "philosophy of mind" as we know it today. His discussions of this subject were later explored by Wittgenstein under the title of "philosophical psychology" only to be summarized in Ryle's *The Concept of Mind* (1949a) which today is considered the pioneering work of this philosophical discipline.
19 The example with the die was introduced in Husserl's *Encyclopaedia Britannica* article (1929a: 79).
20 In *The Analysis of Mind* (1921) and in *Human Knowledge* (1948) Russell embraced a similar theory.

Chapter 10

1 This conception is supported by David Hilbert's meta-mathematics. Hilbert's former student and philosopher of science and mathematics, Walter Dubislav (1933), developed this idea in detail. It is worth noting that Hilbert was Husserl's colleague at the University of Göttingen for some fourteen years—from 1901 to 1915.
2 Similarly, David Hilbert maintained that mathematics is a leading academic discipline, but it needs the logic in order to secure that its calculi are free from contradictions (Dubislav 1925/26, 1930).
3 Interestingly enough, Husserl's philosophy teacher, Carl Stumpf, clearly differentiates the discipline of phenomenology from that of "eidology," or theory of forms (1906: 26 ff.).
4 In the same way in which Cantor claimed that we can obtain the concept of set by abstracting the elements both from properties and from the order in which they are given. On the similarities between Husserl's philosophy and Cantor's mathematics, see Hill (2000).
5 On axiomatic method, see n. 9.
6 We have already seen, however, that Husserl's third level of logic is preserved for the theory of theories. This is not a contradiction since we have previously declared (at the beginning of § 2.3) that Husserl used to call his theory of theories theory

of manifolds. On the connection between the theory of theories and the theory of manifolds, see Section 2.6.

7 Cf. Wittgenstein's position from 1932–3 (Milkov 2003: 116 ff.) (Chapter 11: § 3.4).
8 See Russell (1919: 201) (Chapter 9: § 2.3).
9 Cf. with David Hilbert's axiomatic method which claims that "anything at all that can be the object of scientific thought becomes dependent on the axiomatic method. ... By pushing ahead to ever deeper layers of axioms in the sense explained above we also win ever-deeper infight into the essence of scientific thought itself, and we become ever more conscious of the unity of our knowledge" (1918: 1115).
10 Here a similarity between Husserl's theory of manifolds and Frege's logicism becomes prominent. The difference between them is that whereas Frege analyses arithmetic to logic, Husserl analyses all deductive science to pure logic.
11 Which, here it is to be remembered, Wittgenstein rejects in the *Tractatus*.
12 We developed a similar conception in our paper "Tractarian Scaffoldings": in science a formation (a theory) represents another formation (a part of the world) (Milkov 2001: 407).
13 In fact, its first elements were already set up in *The Problems of Philosophy* (1912a).
14 Clearly, this conception was connected with Russell's program for logical constructions of possible worlds he defended after 1912 (Chapter 15).
15 "Indefinables" are intuitively knowable simples (Milkov 2003: 95) (Chapter 11). Some authors maintain that the discovery of the indefinable by Moore and Russell signaled the beginning of analytic philosophy (Quinn 1977: 209 ff.).
16 Here we concern the problem of truth-making. On its history, see Milkov (2001a, 2018b).

Chapter 11

1 On similarities between Russell's logical analysis and Husserl's eidetic analysis, see Chapter 9: § 2.1.
2 Hence the prime importance of the concept of *showing* in Wittgenstein and Heidegger.
3 On "complete analysis" see Chapter 14: § 4.
4 That in the development of his new study of phenomenology Husserl started from Hume is well known to historians of philosophy (Murphy 1991).
5 Interestingly, philosophy is defined as descriptive also by Wilhelm Dilthey (1894) who, usually, is considered to be a continental philosopher.
6 Leibniz called them "genuine units," "primary forces," or "metaphysical points," which are to be discriminated from the mathematical points (Leibniz 1695: 139, 142).
7 Similarly, in *Theory of Knowledge*, Russell famously spoke of "knowledge by acquaintance" vis-á-vis logical forms (1913: 99 ff., 129–31).

8 For logical static and dynamic, see Ryle (1954: 125).
9 We know this position from Wittgenstein's *Philosophical Investigations*, § 201.
10 The concept of *contemplation of possibilities* was treated at length by John Wisdom (1952: 6, 33), Wittgenstein's acolyte and his successor as the chair of philosophy at Cambridge (following the tenure of G. H. von Wright from 1948 to 1951).
11 That logical and grammatical studies coincide was also realized by the Oxford ordinary language philosophers.
12 The concept of "rational deliberation" is used today when discussing "indefinables" in political theory and practice.
13 In most European languages the term "calculates" applies not only to numbers but also to different cognitive situations and strategies of acting.
14 Philosophers are misled to believe in the theoretical authority of phenomenology since "sentences are often used on the borderline between logic and the empirical, so that their meaning shifts back and forth and they are now expressions of norms, now treated as expressions of experience" (III: § 19).
15 Cf. Leibniz's *characteristica universalis* (Chapter 3). This point evidences the relatedness of Wittgenstein's phenomenology to Allan Turing's philosophy of calculation (Floyd 2016).
16 On "pure calculi," cf. the last two paragraphs of § 3.4; cf. Husserl's "pure logic" and "pure forms" (Chapter 10).
17 "The possibility of its occurring in a state of affairs is the form of an object" (1922: 2.0141).
18 On static and dynamic phenomena, see § 2.5 and n. 8.
19 In contrast, in his transcendental aesthetics (A 19–49), Kant adopts the real dichotomy between elements and forms, between analysis and matter.
20 We *can* formulate a "theory" of calculation, but we must not do that. The relevant point in this connection is that we can *work* with calculation, that we can *apply* it.
21 Among other things, this fusion shows Wittgenstein as a forerunner of Quine's famous criticism of the dichotomy between analytic and synthetic judgments. The dichotomy between calculation and contemplation was criticized in Schneider (1992).
22 "Every material thing has its idiosyncratic type of essence" (Husserl 1913: 9).
23 How the Tractarian logical forms are forms of objects is demonstrated in Hintikka (1996: 25).
24 We previously criticized (in § 2.3) Husserl's phenomenology as theory of two worlds, but in another sense, as a theory of "pure consciousness" which is discrete from the theory of the empirical consciousness.
25 In a first attempt to describe it, the early Wittgenstein called the minimal conceptual scheme (misleadingly, as it later turned out) a "general logical form" (1922, 4.5). Husserl simply referred to it as the "theory of everything" or "science of essence" (see Chapter 10).

Chapter 12

1. In support of this claim, Moore (1903b) is often cited.
2. We shall discuss this strain of influence on Moore in Section 2.3.
3. Here we agree with Martin Kush and Peter Simons that "the way philosophical disputes get decided and the way subsequent history is written depend little on the dialectical strength, adequacy or sophistication of the position posed" (Simons 1997: 442).
4. Cf. this note of Moore's: "I worked very hard indeed for a very long time in trying to understand his [Russell's] *Principles of Mathematics*; and I actually wrote a very long review of this work, which was however never published" (1942: 15; 2018).
5. The only exception were three short reviews of his—of one page each—of new books of philosophers he became acquainted and made friends with in Cambridge: of Johnson (1921), Russell (1921) and of Whitehead (1927).
6. "Moore admired the *Logische Untersuchungen* [of Husserl]." W. R. Boyce Gibson (Spiegelberg 1979: 15)
7. The book was actually published in December 1908 (see Michaltschew 1996: 83 f.). In fact, the term "sense-data" was also in use in philosophy before December 6, 1909. As we have shown in Milkov (2001b), it was introduced in 1882 by Josiah Royce. In the early 1890s the term was widely used by William James. In 1896–98 Russell incidentally spoke of sense-data too. In the next thirteen years, however, he apparently discarded them—indeed, between 1898 and 1911 he did not use the term at all. This explains why Russell was thus impressed by Moore's innovation of December 1909.
8. Messer's book *Empfindung und Denken* was listed in the same issue of *Mind* on p. 308. It may well be that Moore had gone through this list of newly received book and picked them out for reviewing.
9. Despite the fact that this kind of epistemology sounds related to the neutral monism of Mach and James, it was justified in quite different way.
10. Heyde wrote the article "Rehmke" in Paul Edwards's *Encyclopaedia of Philosophy* (1967).
11. This conception is conspicuously close to the view on the subject as exposed in Wittgenstein's *Tractatus*, 5.631–3.
12. Only by Russell was this doctrine laid out in such a clear form (e.g., in 1912a). Moore, in contrast, "is symptomatically unclear about this matter" (Baldwin 1990: 155). Be this as it may, Russell's theory of incomplete symbols clearly underlies Moore's conception of material objects of the time. On the different concepts of incomplete symbols by Moore and Russell (see Chapter 14: § 7).
13. In his "Autobiography" Carnap remembered: "The choice of a phenomenalistic basis was influenced by some radical empiricist or positivist German philosophers

of the end of the last century whom I had studied with interest, in the first place Ernst Mach, and further Richard Avenarius, Richard von Schubert-Soldern, and Wilhelm Schuppe" (Carnap 1963: 18).
14 "All sound philosophy should begin with an analysis of propositions" (Russell 1900a: 6).
15 Typically descriptivist analytic philosophers were Moore, Wittgenstein, and the Oxford connective analysts (Chapter 15).
16 Gerhard Lehmann expressed this point as follows: Rehmke's works "are poor in material, but consistent in following the path once chosen" (1943: 117).
17 The anti-psychologism in philosophy was launched by Lotze (Gabriel 1989b: xi), and followed by Christoph Sigwart and Wilhelm Wundt, among others. However, anti-psychologist ideas were already in work by Kant and Hegel (Chapter 4: § 4).
18 The distinction in question was introduced by Lotze again (see Chapter 7: § 3).

Chapter 13

1 Kuno Fischer claimed that this task cannot be fulfilled in principle (1862: 99).
2 This thesis was called by Michael Friedman (2001) "relative a priori"; Friedman himself distillated it from Hans Reichenbach's works. Reichenbach himself adopted it from Nelson via Kurt Grelling (Milkov 2015a) (see § 2.2, below).
3 This was Nelson's claim. Michael Dummett, in contrast, held that philosophy of mathematics was introduced by Frege.
4 See the discussion of peirastic dialectic in Section 2.
5 That Kant's *CPR* is above all a "Treatise on Method" is unmistakably declared in (A838/B866).
6 Only recently philosophers turn attention to the place of the method of reflective equilibrium in early analytic philosophy (Olson and Griffin 2019: 300–2).
7 According to Graciela de Maliandi, "a 'critical attitude' as understood by Popper is synonymous which 'rational attitude'. . . . It means respect for the principle of rational argumentation and unlimited possibility for the review of all arguments" (1991: 27).
8 Having in mind the life-long rhetoric of Popper and Reichenbach against each other, the claim for relatedness between their philosophies of science is rather surprising. To a great extent, however, this animosity can be explained psychologically (Milkov 2013a; see also n. 18).
9 Nelson, surely, has pupils in the conventional sense which, by the way, were strongly loyal to their master. Among them were Gerhard Hessenberg, Otto Meyerhof, Heinrich Goesch, Alexander Rüstow, and Kurt Grelling (Peckhaus 1990: 132).
10 On this point Nelson was similar to Wittgenstein. On the relatedness between Nelson and Wittgenstein, see Birnbacher (2002).
11 On Julius Kraft, see Popper (1962). Besides Kraft, Popper also knew three other "excellent pupils" of Nelson's (ibid.: 3).

12 Among Oppenheimer's students in Frankfurt there were the young Theodor Adorno and also the father of the West Germany's *Wirtschaftswunder* Ludwig Erhard, minister of finance in the 1950s and federal chancellor of that country in the 1960s.
13 The latter journal ceased being issued in 1937, ten years after Nelson's death and four years after Hitler came to power. In it, Paul Bernays published four papers and Kurt Grelling his famous paradox. The first series of the journal was published in 1847–49, edited by E. F. Apelt, Oscar Schmidt, and Oskar Schlömilch.
14 Cf. Moore's, Russell's and Wittgenstein's indefinables (Chapter 11).
15 This claim of Fries and Nelson is clearly related to G. E. Moore's defense of common sense.
16 To remind the reader, Russell often used the terms "analysis" and "reflection" interchangeably (see 1918a: 180). Sometimes he also spoke about "the method of analysis and reflection" (ibid.).
17 This conception of Popper is often criticized as irrational and is clearly aside from the position of the early analytic philosophers.
18 In his criticism of sense-data and simple impression, Popper was also influenced by Karl Bühler and Otto Selz.
19 Interestingly enough, a similar position was also taken by Hans Reichenbach— and this is a second similarity between him and Popper (see n. 7). Reichenbach repeatedly referred to Hume's demonstration of the inconsistency of empiricism— he replaced it with a kind of probabilistic empiricism. Furthermore, similarly to Popper, Reichenbach was critical of the principle of verification of his Vienna friends, accusing them of neglecting the problems of real (actual) science.
20 Of course, the later Wittgenstein didn't claim that (Chapter 15: § 2).
21 Susan Stebbing was instrumental in Popper's starting a career in the English-speaking world. In 1935 she invited him to England for nine months, after which Popper, supported by other friends of his (above all by Karl Polanyi), received an appointment at the University of Canterbury, New Zeeland.
22 This fact disproves Popper's claim, made in 1933 in *The Two Fundamental Problems*, that this work is "the first harsh criticism of Wittgenstein's *Tractatus*" (Popper 1930/3: xxxv).

Chapter 14

1 Here Wittgenstein means Carnap (1931a).
2 Stebbing herself identifies the "new logic" with these two ideas (1933: 65f.).
3 Whereas in (1932/3: *passim*) Stebbing spoke of "symbolic analysis," in (1933: 80f.) she spoke of "postulational analysis."
4 In fact, however, Russell was not a reductionist but an eliminativist (Chapter 4: § 5.2).

5. In fact, the concept of truth-making was introduced by the early Wittgenstein (1979: 95) and was later adopted by Russell (1918: 182). On the history of the term, see Milkov (2001a).
6. The insinuation here was of Wittgenstein.

Chapter 15

1. Cf. Plato's phrase "carving nature at its joints" (*Phaedrus* 265e).
2. Linsky (2008) contends that Russell spoke about logical constructing as early as *Principia Mathematica* (1910). On logical constructions, see Chapter 14: § 5.
3. That is the way the leading expositors of Carnap, A. W. Carus, Michael Friedman, Alan Richardson, and Thomas Uebel, translate *Der logische Aufbau der Welt* instead of *The Logical Structure of the World*, translated so by R. A. George (Carnap 1967).
4. Under the philosophers that insisted on strict discrimination between different realms in epistemology was Frege's professor in Göttingen, Hermann Lotze. Among other things, Lotze radically opposed existence, becoming, and value (Milkov 2010: § 3, (b)).
5. Recently, the conception of "logical house," built up with the help of logically impermeable walls, was sharply criticized by Mark Wilson. The problem with it is that it looks like "a very fine mansion, but it remains an empty shell at present, for we've not attempt[ed] to put any furniture in its rooms. When we begin this process—that is, assign concrete allotments of predicative content to specific words,—unhappy tensions begin to emerge" (Wilson 2007: 99). Unfortunately, Wilson mistakenly attributed the project for building up logical house exclusively to Russell, instead to Frege who was its true architect (cf. Milkov 2010a).
6. That was why Wittgenstein needed the silence of his cabin in Norway: he sought to master an absolute absorption that would intensify and sharpen his powers of penetration in order to make his logical-historical findings. As Brian McGuinness reports, Wittgenstein's "notebooks were distillate of long periods of concentration" (1988: 181). Wittgenstein realized that he was not making discoveries only at the end of composing the *Tractatus* (Milkov 2018b).
7. In contrast, van Heijenoort saw Russell as advocate of the "one world—one language" conception (1967: 327). In fact, this is true about Russell from *Principia Mathematica* but not about Russell after 1912 (see § 1 (a)). We shall discuss Russell's ambiguity on this point in § 9.
8. Our translation from German—N. M.
9. Correspondingly, "the work of science [on its side] does not consist in creation, but in the discovery of true thoughts" (Frege 1918/19: 368).
10. As Saul Kripke, who was significantly influenced with Carnap's modal logic, noted, "'possible worlds' are *stipulated*, not *discovered*" (1980: 44).
11. This review follows the account in Milkov (2017a).

12 In this sense, Wittgenstein wrote in the final remark of the book: "Anyone who understands me eventually recognizes [the propositions of the *Tractatus*] as nonsensical" (6.54). Some interpreters, Cora Diamond and James Conant among them, falsely interpreted this statement claiming that (almost) all propositions of the *Tractatus* are nonsense. For criticism, see Milkov (2017a, 2018b).
13 As put by H.-J. Glock, "conceptual claims can be abandoned . . . , yet without being falsified" (2016: 94).
14 Already in *Mysticism and Logic* Russell defined philosophy as "concerned with the analysis and enumeration of logical *forms*" (1918: 85) that can be seen as nothing but denizens of the third world.
15 In recent years, the profound misunderstanding of this type of analytic philosophy was perpetuated in the claim that Wittgenstein was not an analytic philosopher at all. The later Wittgenstein, in particular, "might be seen," announces one contemporary commentator, "as more like continental than analytic philosopher" (Morris 2007: 68).
16 The first to notice the relatedness between the Brentano School and Frege which, apparently, was realized through the mediation of Lotze, was Paul Linke (1946). The relatedness between Brentano and Wittgenstein was carefully explored in Sebestik (1990).
17 Among other things, this point explains why Carnap's apprentice, Quine, connected analytic philosophy with the concept of analyticity exclusively. In his history of analytic philosophy, Soames follows exactly his lead (see § 11).
18 As we have seen, Frege and the early Wittgenstein were not only interested in concepts. They also believed that they really were carving out the form of the logical world.

Chapter 16

1 As we have seen in Chapter 9: § 2.1, however, in the 1910s Russell had a different understanding of the term "logical form". There are not only logical forms of the symbolic logic but also of the philosophical logic.
2 In the period of 1912/13 Russell often referred to it as philosophy following "scientific method."
3 Frege (1882: 94) spoke about the "rigidity" (*Starrheit*) of his conceptual notation as a necessary condition for achieving truth in logic.
4 Cf. this definition of analytic philosophy with that suggested by J. L. Cohen: "The unifying force in analytical philosophy is its engagement with the reasoned investigation of reasons" (1986: 57).
5 Russell's definition is clearly related to the method of "checks and balances" that serves as a main principle of liberal system of government.
6 This characteristic of "analytic philosophy" was best expressed, as regards Austrian proto-analytic philosophy, by Kevin Mulligan: "Description of a domain must have

priority over every type of explanation that refers to how a phenomenon comes into being" (1986: 87).

7   We are going to say more about the problems in Russell's understanding of analytic philosophy in Section 6.

8   For this reason, Moore can also be called an "analytic hermeneutist." The term "analytical hermeneutic" was introduced, concerning G. E. Moore, by G. H. von Wright (1971: 181 n. 86). Roy Howard labels as analytic hermeneutists von Wright and Peter Winch (1982: 33 f.).

9   In Chapter 15: § 9, we have seen that the two concepts of analytic philosophy that took shape after 1912 (we are going to discuss them in the next paragraph)—as logical construction of the world, practiced by the middle Russell and the early Carnap, and as a construction of the logical world practiced by Frege and Wittgenstein—had also hybrid character.

10 For Moore's role by elaborating Russell's theory of descriptions, see Milkov (1997, i: 278–81).

11 On John Wisdom, see Milkov (2019a).

12 The friction between the British "analytic philosophy" and American "scientific philosophy" in the late 1940s and in the 1950s (at that time few American philosophers *called* themselves "analytic") found clear expression in Ryle (1949).

13 P. M. S. Hacker falsely took the reasons-supplying turn in the English analytic philosophy as the end of analytic philosophy as such (1996, 1996a). In fact, this was the end of the *early* analytic philosophy only. Besides, he states incorrectly that this took place in the mid-1970s.

14 To put this in *other words*, analytic philosophy is interested in what Hegel and Heidegger called "correctness."

15 Typical example is the "discovery" of Jean Paul Sartre that "Hell is other people."

16 Problems of religion and meaning of life were also discussed by Russell and Wittgenstein (Milkov 2005a, 2018a). These, however, did not lie at the center of their attention.

17 This question is, apparently, the main concern of Zahavi (2016: 83 f.).

18 Frege's solid logico-philosophy also was not enough since it failed to follow the method of analytic imediacy (see Chapter 4: § 5.1).

19 Famous are Russell's word said to Wittgenstein in discussions in 1913: "Logic is hell" (McGuinness 1988: 154).

20 Some philosophers today realize that the later Russell, who maintained that logic, including philosophical logic, "is not part of philosophy" (1948: 5) (see Chapter 1: § 5), "anticipates the analytic philosophy of the last quarter of the twentieth century and the beginning of the twenty-first" (Wahl 2019: 2).

21 J. Ladyman and D. Ross correctly specify that "unjustified appeals to *intuition* play a central role in the methodology of analytic metaphysics" (Dorr 2010).

References

Adair-Toteff, C. (1994), "The Neo-Kantian Raum Controversy," *British Journal for the History of Philosophy*, 2: 131–48.
Akerhurst, T. (2010), *The Cultural Politics of Analytic Philosophy: Britishness and the Specter of Europe*, London: Continuum.
Alexy, R. (1979), "R. N. Hares Regeln des moralischen Argumentierens und L. Nelsons Abwägungsgesetze," in: P. Schröder (ed.), *Vernunft, Erkenntnis, Sittlichkeit*, 95–122, Hamburg: Meiner.
Ammerman, R., ed. (1965), *Classics of Analytic Philosophy*, New York: McGraw-Hill.
Anellis, I. (2004), "The Genesis of the Truth-Table Device," *Russell*, 24: 55–70.
Anscombe, E. (1959), *An Introduction to Wittgenstein's Tractatus*, London: Hutchinson.
Anscombe, E., and P. T. Geach (1961), *Three Philosophers*, Oxford: Blackwell.
Arendt, H. (1990), "Philosophy and Politics," *Social Research*, 57: 71–103.
Armstrong, D. (1978), *Universals and Scientific Realism*, 2 vols., Cambridge: Cambridge University Press.
Armstrong, D. (1997), *A World of States of Affairs*, Cambridge: Cambridge University Press.
Arndt, A. (2004), *Unmittelbarkeit*, Bielefeld: transcript Verlag.
Austin, J. L. (1952), "Critical Notice: *Aristotle's Syllogistic* by Jan Łukasiewicz," *Mind*, 61(243): 395–404.
Austin, J. L. ([1961] 1970), *Philosophical Papers*, 2nd ed., Oxford: Oxford University Press.
Austin, J. L. (1962), *How To Do Things With Words*, Oxford: Oxford University Press.
Austin, J. L. (1962a), *Sense and Sensibilia*, ed. G. Warnock, Oxford: Oxford University Press.
Ayer, A. J. ([1936] 1971), *Language, Truth, and Logic*, Harmondsworth: Penguin.
Ayer, A. J. (1971), *Russell and Moore: The Analytical Heritage*, London: Macmillan.
Ayers, M. (1978), "Analytical Philosophy and the History of Philosophy," in: J. Ree et al., *Philosophy and Its Post*, 41–66, Hassocks: Harvester.
Baker, G., and P. M. S. Hacker (1984), *Frege: Logical Excavations*, New York: Oxford University Press.
Baldwin, T. (1990), *G. E. Moore*, London: Routledge.
Baldwin, T. (1991), "Identity Theory of Truth," *Mind*, 100: 35–52.
Barrett, W. (1978), *The Illusion of Technique*, Norwell: Anchor.
Bauch, B. (1918), "Lotzes Logik und ihre Bedeutung im Deutschen Idealismus," *Beiträge zur Philosophie des Deutschen Idealismus*, 1: 45–58.
Bauch, B. (1923), *Wahrheit, Wert und Wirklichkeit*, Leipzig: Felix Meiner.

Beaney, M. (2002), "Decompositions and Transformations: Conceptions of Analysis in the Early Analytic and Phenomenological Traditions," *The Southern Journal of Philosophy*, 40 (Supplementary Volume): 53–99.

Beaney, M. (2005), "The Rise and Fall of German Philosophy," *British Journal for the History of Philosophy*, 13: 543–62.

Beaney, M. (2008), "Function-Argument Analysis in Early Analytic Philosophy," in: P. Bernhard and V. Peckhaus (eds.), *Methodisches Denken im Kontext*, 203–15, Paderborn: mentis.

Beaney, M. (2008a), "Conceptions of Analysis in the Early Analytical and Phenomenological Traditions. Some Comparisons and Relationships," in: M. Beaney (ed.), 196–216.

Beaney, M., ed. (2008b), *The Analytical Turn: Analysis in Earl Analytic Philosophy and Phenomenology*, London: Routledge.

Beaney, M. (2009), "Analysis," in: Edward N. Zalta (ed.), *The Stanford Encyclopedia of Philosophy*. http://plato.stanford.edu/entries/analysis/

Beaney, M. (2013), "What Is Analytic Philosophy," in: *idem* (ed.), *The Oxford Handbook of History of Analytic Philosophy*, 3–29, Oxford: Oxford University Press.

Beaney, M. (2016), "The Analytic Revolution," *Royal Institute of Philosophy Supplement*, 78: 227–49.

Beaney, M. (2017), *Analytic Philosophy: A Very Short Introduction*, Oxford: Oxford University Press.

Becher, E. (1929), "Hermann Lotze," in *idem*, *Deutsche Philosophen*, 47–72, München: Duncker & Humblot.

Bell, D. (1999), "The Revolution of Moore and Russell: A Very British Coup?" in: A. O'Hear (ed.), 193–208.

Bennett, J. (1988), "Response to Garber and Ree," in: P. Hare (ed.), 62–69.

Bergmann, J. (1879), *Allgemeine Logik. Erster Teil: Reine Logik*, Berlin: Mittler.

Berlin, I. (1997), *The Proper Study of Mankind: An Anthology of Essays*, ed. H. Hardy, London: Chatto & Windus.

Berto, F. (2007), "Hegel's Dialectics as a Semantic Theory: An Analytic Reading," *European Journal of Philosophy*, 15: 19–39.

Birnbacher, D. (2002), "Philosophie als sokratische Praxis: Sokrates, Nelson, Wittgenstein," in: D. Birnbacher and D. Krohn (eds.), 166–97.

Birnbacher, D., and D. Krohn, eds. (2002), *Das sokratische Gespräch*, Stuttgart: Reclam.

Black, M. (1939–40), "Relation between Logical Positivism and the Cambridge School of Analysis," *Erkenntnis*, 8: 24–35.

Black, M. ([1964] 1971), *A Companion to Wittgenstein's Tractatus*, Cambridge: Cambridge University Press.

Bradley, F. H. ([1883] 1922), *Principles of Logic*, 2 vols., Oxford: Oxford University Press.

Bradley, F. H. (1893), *Appearance and Reality*, London: George Allen & Unwin.

Bradley, F. H. (1914), *Essays in Truth and Reality*, Oxford: Clarendon Press.

Bradley, F. H. (1999), *Selected Correspondence, January 1905–June 1924*, ed. C. A. Keene, Bristol: Thoemmes Press.
Braithwaite, R. (1933), "Philosophy," in: H. Wright (ed.), *University Studies, Cambridge. 1933*, 1–32, London: Nicholson & Watson.
Brand, R. (2007), "Kant: Freiheit, Recht und Moral," in: U. an der Heiden und H. Scheider (eds.), *Hat der Mensch einen freien Willen?* 199–212, Stuttgart: Reclam.
Brandom, R. (2013), "From German Idealism to American Pragmatism—and Back," in: S. Bacin et al. (eds.), *Akten des XI. Internationalen Kant-Congress*, 5 vols., i: 107–25, Berlin: de Gruyter.
Braun, L. (1973), *Histoire de l'histoire de la philosophie*, Paris: Ophrys.
Brentano, F. ([1895] 1998), "The Four Phases of Philosophy and Its Current State," in: B. Mezei and B. Smith (eds.), *The Four Phases of Philosophy*, 81–112, Amsterdam: Rodopi.
Brentano, F. (1975), "Was ist an Reid zu loben?" *Grazer philosophische Studien*, 1: 1–18.
Broad, C. (1924), "Critical and Speculative Philosophy," in: J. H. Muirhead (ed.), *Contemporary British Philosophy*, 1st ser., 75–100, London: Allen and Unwin.
Bronstein, E. (1934), "Miss Stebbing's Directional Analysis and Basic Facts," *Analysis*, 2 (1/2): 10–14.
Bunge, M., ed. (1973), *Exact Philosophy*, Dordrecht: Reidel.
Butler, C. (2011), *The Dialectical Method: A Treatise Hegel Never Wrote*, New York: Humanity Books.
Carnap, R. (1924), "Dreidimensionalität des Raumes und Kausalität," *Annalen der Philosophie und philosophischen Kritik*, 4: 105–30.
Carnap, R. (1928), *Der logische Aufbau der Welt*, Berlin: Weltkreis Verlag.
Carnap, R. ([1931] 1959), "The Elimination of Metaphysics through Logical Analysis of Language," in: A. J. Ayer (ed.), *Logical Positivism*, 71–93, Glencoe: The Free Press.
Carnap, R. (1931a), "Die physikalische Sprache als Universalsprache der Wissenschaft," *Erkenntnis*, 2: 432–65.
Carnap, R. (1931b), "Überwindung der Metaphysik durch logische Analyse der Sprache," *Erkenntnis*, 2: 220–41.
Carnap, R. (1947), *Meaning and Necessity*, Chicago: Chicago University Press.
Carnap, R. (1950), "Empiricism, Semantic and Ontology," *Revue Internationale de Philosophie*, 4: 20–40.
Carnap, R. (1963), "Autobiography," in: P. A. Schilpp (ed.), *The Philosophy of Rudolf Carnap*, 3–84, La Salle: Open Court.
Carnap, R. (1967), *The Logical Structure of the World*, trans. R. A. George, Berkeley: University of California Press.
Carroll, J., and N. Markosian (2010), *An Introduction to Metaphysics*, Cambridge: Cambridge University Press.
Cassirer, E. (1910), *Substanzbegriff und Funktionsbegriff*, Berlin: Bruno Cassirer.
Clarke, D. (1997), *Philosophy's Second Revolution: Early and Recent Analytic Philosophy*, Chicago: Open Court.

Cocchiarella, N. (1987), *Logical Studies in Early Analytic Philosophy*, Columbus: Ohio State University.
Coffa, A. (1991), *The Semantic Tradition from Kant to Carnap*, Cambridge: Cambridge University Press.
Cohen, J. L. (1986), *The Dialogue of Reason: An Analysis of Analytical Philosophy*, Oxford: Clarendon.
Collingwood, R. G. ([1939] 1944), *An Autobiography*, 2nd ed., Harmondsworth: Penguin.
Collins, R. (1998), *The Sociology of Philosophies*, Cambridge: Belknap.
Cornelius, H. (1903), *Einleitung in die Philosophie*, Leipzig: Teubner.
Coudert, A. (1995), *Leibniz and the Kabbalah*, Dordrecht: Kluwer.
Critchley, S. (1997), "What is Continental Philosophy?" *International Journal of Philosophical Studies*, 5: 347–65.
Critchley, S. (2001), *Continental Philosophy: A Very Short Introduction*, Oxford: Oxford University Press.
Cuming, A. (1917), "Lotze, Bradley, and Bosanquet," *Mind*, 26: 162–70.
Damböck, C. (2012), "Rudolf Carnap and Wilhelm Dilthey: 'German' Empiricism in the Aufbau," in: R. Greath (ed.), *Rudolf Carnap and the Legacy of the Logical Empiricism*, Dordrecht: Springer.
Damböck, C. (2016), *Deutscher Empirismus: Studien zur Philosophie im deutschsprachigen Raum 1830–1930*, Berlin: Springer.
Danto, A. (1980), "Analytic Philosophy," *Social Research*, 57: 612–34.
de Maliandi, G. (1991), "Popper, Nelson and Kant," *Manuscrito*, 14: 19–40.
Descartes, R. (1977), *The Philosophical Writings of Descartes*, trans. J. Cottingham et al., Cambridge: Cambridge University Press.
Dilthey, W. (1894), "Ideen über eine beschreibende und zergliedernde Psychologie," *Sitzungs-berichte der Königlich Preußischen Akademie der Wissenschaften zu Berlin*, Berlin: Springer.
Dorr, C. (2010), "James Ladyman and Don Ross, *Every Thing Must Go: Metaphysics Naturalized*," Notre Dame Philosophical Reviews, June 6. https://ndpr.nd.edu/news/every-thing-must-go-metaphysics-naturalized/
Dubislav, W. (1925/6), "Über das Verhältnis der Logik zur Mathematik," *Annalen der Philosophie und philosophischen Kritik*, 5: 193–208.
Dubislav, W. (1930), "Über den sogenannten Gegenstand der Mathematik," *Erkenntnis*, 1: 27–48.
Dubislav, W. (1933), *Naturphilosophie*, Berlin: Junker und Dünnhaupt.
Dummett, M. (1956), "Nominalism," in: *idem*, 1978, 38–49.
Dummett, M. (1967), "Gottlob Frege," in: P. Edwards (ed.), *Encyclopaedia of Philosophy*, 8 vols., iii: 225–37, New York: Macmillan.
Dummett, M. (1973), *Frege. Philosophy of Language*, London: Duckworth.
Dummett, M. ([1975] 1978), "Can Analytical Philosophy Be Systematic, an Ought It to Be?" in: *idem*, 437–58.

Dummett, M. (1978), *Truth and Other Enigmas*, London: Duckworth.
Dummett, M. (1981), *The Interpretation of Frege's Philosophy*, London: Duckworth.
Dummett, M. (1991), *Frege: Philosophy of Mathematics*, London: Duckworth.
Dummett, M. (1991a), *Frege and Other Philosophers*, 65–78, Oxford: Oxford University Press.
Dummett, M. (1993), *Origins of Analytical Philosophy*, London: Duckworth.
Duncan-Jones, A. (1937), "Does Philosophy Analyze Common Sense?" *Proceedings of the Aristotelian Society*, 16 (Supplementary Volume): 139–61.
Einstein, A. (1944), "Remarks on Bertrand Russell's Theory of Knowledge," in: P. A. Schilpp (ed.), *The Philosophy of Bertrand Russell*, 277–92, La Salle: Open Court.
Engfer, H. J. (1982), *Philosophie als Analyse*, Stuttgart-Bad Cannstatt: Frommann-Holzboog.
Erdmann, B. (1917), *Die Idee von Kants Kritik der reinen Vernunft*, Berlin: Reimer.
Eucken, R. ([1886] 1906), "Zur Erinnerung an Adolf Trendelenburg," in: *idem, Beiträge zur Einleitung in die Geschichte der Philosophie*, 2nd ed., 112–25, Leipzig: Dürr.
Ewing, A. (1934), "Two Kinds of Analysis," *Analysis* 2 (3): 60–64.
Fischer, K. (1862), *Akademische Reden*, Stuttgart: Cotta.
Fite, W. (1910), "[Review of] *Philosophische Studien*, by D. Michaltschew," *The Philosophical Review*, 19: 323–27.
Flach, W. (2007), "Kants Begriff der Kultur und das Selbstverständnis des Neukantianismus als Kulturphilosophie," in: M. Heinz and C. Krijnen (eds.), *Kant in Neukantionismus: Fortschritt oder Rückschritt?* 9–24, Würzburg: Königshausen & Neumann.
Floyd, J. (2016), "Chains of Life, Turing, *Lebensform*, and the Emergence of Wittgenstein's Later Style," *Nordic Wittgenstein Review*, 5: 7–89.
Franke, H. (1991), *Leonard Nelson*, Ammersbek: Verlag an der Lottbek.
Frede, M. (1988), "The History of Philosophy as a Discipline," *The Journal of Philosophy*, 85: 666–72.
Frege, G. (1879), *Begriffsschrift*, Halle a.d.S.: Nebert.
Frege, G. ([1880] 1979), "Logic," in: *idem*, 1–8.
Frege, G. ([1880/81] 1979), "Boole's Logical Calculus and the Concept-Script," in: *idem*, 9–46.
Frege, G. ([1881] 1972), "On the Scientific Justification of a Conceptual Notation," in: *idem*, 83–89.
Frege, G. (1882), "Über die wissenschaftliche Berechtigung einer Begriffsschrift," in: *idem*, Funktion, Begriff, Bedeutung, ed. G. Patzig, 91–97, Göttingen: Vandenhoeck & Ruprecht, 1986.
Frege, G. ([1882/3] 1972), "On the Aim of the 'Conceptual Notation'," in: *idem*, 90–100.
Frege, G. ([1883] 1979), "17 Key Sentences on Logic," in: *idem, Posthumous Writings*, ed. B. McGuinness, 174–75, Oxford: Blackwell.
Frege, G. ([1884] 1980), *The Foundations of Arithmetic*, trans. J. L. Austin, 2nd ed., Oxford: Blackwell.

Frege, G. ([1891] 1981), "Function and Concept," in: *idem*, 137–56.
Frege, G. ([1892] 1981), "On Sense and Meaning," in: *idem*, 157–67.
Frege, G. (1893), *Grundgesetze der Arithmetik*, 2 vols., i, Jena: Pohle.
Frege, G. ([1897] 1981), "On Mr. Peano's Conceptual Notation and My Own," in: *idem*, 234–48.
Frege, G. ([1897a] 1979), "Logic," in: *idem*, 126–51.
Frege, G. ([1906] 1979), "Review of Arthur Schoenflies' book *The Logical Paradoxes of Set-theory*," in: *idem*, 176–83.
Frege, G. ([1906a] 1979), "Introduction to Logic," in: *idem*, 184–96.
Frege, G. ([1914] 1979), "Logic in Mathematics," in: *idem*, 203–50.
Frege, G. ([1918/9] 1981), "Thoughts," in: *idem*, 351–72.
Frege, G. (1971), *Schriften zur Logik und Sprachphilosophie*, ed. G. Gabriel, Hamburg: Felix Meiner.
Frege, G. (1972), *Conceptual Notation and Related Articles*, ed. and trans. T. Bynum, Oxford: Clarendon.
Frege, G. (1976), *Wissenschaftlicher Briefwechsel*, ed. G. Gabriel et al., Habmurg: Felix Meiner.
Frege, G. (1979), *Posthumous Writings*, Oxford: Blackwell.
Frege, G. (1980), *Philosophical and Mathematical Correspondence*, ed. B. F. McGuinness, trans. H. Kall, Oxford: Blackwell.
Frege, G. (1981), *Collected Papers on Mathematics, Logic and Philosophy*, ed. B. F. McGuinness, trans. M. Black et al., Oxford: Blackwell.
Frege, G. (2011), "Frege–Wittgenstein Correspondence," in: E. De Pellegrin (ed.), *Interactive Wittgenstein*, 15–74, Dordrecht: Springer.
Friedman, M. (1999), *Reconsidering Logical Positivism*, Cambridge: Cambridge University Press.
Friedman, M. (2000), *A Parting of the Ways: Carnap, Cassirer, and Heidegger*, Chicago: Open Court.
Friedman, M. (2001), *Dynamics of Reason*, Stanford: CSLI Publications.
Fries, J. F. ([1811] 1837), *Logik*, 2nd ed., Heidelberg: Winter.
Gabriel, G. (1984), "Fregean Connection: *Bedeutung*, Value and Truth-Value," in: C. Wright (ed.), *Frege: Tradition & Influence*, 186–94, Oxford: Blackwell.
Gabriel, G. (1986), "Frege als Neukantianer," *Kantstudien*, 77: 84–01.
Gabriel, G. (1989a), "Einleitung des Herausgebers: Lotze und die Entstehung der modernen Logik bei Frege," in: H. R. Lotze, *Logik, Erstes Buch. Vom Denken*, xi–xliii, Hamburg: Meiner.
Gabriel, G. (1989b), "Einleitung des Herausgebers: Objektivität: Logik und Erkenntnistheorie bei Lotze und Frege," in: H. R. Lotze, xi–xxxiv.
Gabriel, G. (2002), "Frege, Lotze, and the Continental Roots of Early Analytic Philosophy," in: E. Reck (ed.), *From Frege to Wittgenstein: Perspectives on Early Analytic Philosophy*, 39–51, Oxford: Oxford University Press.

Gabriel, G. (2007), "Windelband und die Diskussion um die Kantischen Urteilsformen," in: M. Heinz and C. Krijnen (eds.), *Kant im Neukantianismus. Fortschritt oder Rückschritt*, 91–108, Würzburg: Königshausen & Neumann.

Gabriel, G. (2008), "Wie formal ist die formale Logik?" in: P. Bernhard and V. Peckhaus (eds.), *Methodisches Denken im Kontext*, 115–31, Paderborn: mentis.

Garber, D. (1988), "Does History Have a Future?" in: P. Hare (ed.), 27–43.

Garver, N. (1994), *This Complicated Form of Life: Essays on Wittgenstein*, Chicago: Open Court.

Gattei, S. (2009), *Karl Popper's Philosophy of Science: Rationality without Foundations*, London: Routledge.

Gauthier, Y. (2004), "Husserl and the Theory of Multiplicities 'Mannigfaltigkeitslehre,'" in: R. Feist (ed.), *Husserl and the Sciences: Selected Perspectives*, 121–28, Ottawa: University of Ottawa Press.

Geach, P. T. (1976), "Saying and Showing in Frege and Wittgenstein," *Acta Philosophica Fennica*, 28: 54–71.

Geach, P. T., and Anscombe, G. E. M. (1973), *Three Philosophers*, Oxford: Blackwell.

Glock, H.-J. (1999), "*Vorsprung durch Logik*: The German Analytic Tradition," in: A. O'Hear (ed.), 137–66.

Glock, H-J. (2008), *What Is Analytic Philosophy?* Cambridge: Cambridge University Press.

Glock, H-J. (2011), "Nelson und die analytische Philosophie," in: A. Berger et al. (eds.), *Leonard Nelson: ein früher Denker der Analytischen Philosophie?* 39–70, Münster: Lit-Verlag.

Glock, H.-J. (2016), "Impure Conceptual Analysis," *The Oxford Handbook of Philosophical Methodology*, 77–100, Oxford: Oxford University Press.

Goedeke, P. (1927), *Wahrheit und Wert*, Hildburghausen: Erben.

Goodstein, R. L. (1972), "Wittgenstein's Philosophy of Mathematics," in: A. Ambrose and M. Lazerowitz (eds.), *Ludwig Wittgenstein: Philosophy of Language*, 271–86, London: Allen & Unwin.

Gracia, J. (1992), *Philosophy and Its History*, Albany: SUNY Press.

Grattan-Guinness, I. (1977), *Dear Russell–Dear Jourdain*, New York: Columbia University Press.

Grattan-Guinness, I. (1985/6), "Russell's Logicism Versus Oxbridge logic, 1890–1925," *Russell*, 6: 101–31.

Grice, P. (1989), *Studies in the Way of Words*, Cambridge: Harvard University Press.

Grice, P., D. Pears and P. Strawson (1957), "Metaphysics," in: D. Pears (ed.), *The Nature of Metaphysics*, 1–22, London: Macmillan.

Griffin, N. (1991), *Russell's Idealistic Apprenticeship*, Oxford: Clarendon Press.

Griffin, N. (1996), "F. H. Bradley's Contribution to the Development of Logic," in: J. Bradley (ed.), *Philosophy After F. H. Bradley*, 195–230, Bristol: Thoemmes Press.

Griffin, N. (2008), "Some Remarks on Russell's Early Decompositional Style of Analysis," in: J. Beaney (ed.), 75–90.

Griffin, N., and A. C. Lewis (1990), "[Comments to] An Analysis of Mathematical Reasoning," in: *idem* (eds.), *Collected Papers of Bertrand Russell*, vol. 2, 155–61, London: Routledge.

Hacker, P. (1996), *Wittgenstein's Place in the Twentieth-Century Analytic Philosophy*, Oxford: Blackwell.

Hacker, P. (1996a), "The Rise of Twentieth Century Analytic Philosophy," Ratio, n.s., 9: 243–68.

Hacker, P. (2007), "Analytic Philosophy: Beyond the Linguistic Turn and Back Again," in: M. Beaney (ed.), *The Analytic Turn: Analysis in Early Analytic Philosophy and Phenomenology*, 125–41, London: Routledge.

Hacking, I. (2002), "Wittgenstein as Philosophical Psychologist," in: *idem*, *Historical Ontology*, 214–26, Harvard: Harvard University Press.

Hacohen, M. H. (2000), *Karl Popper—the Formative Years*, 1902–1945, Cambridge: Cambridge University Press.

Hager, P. (1987), "Russell's and Zeno's Arrow Paradox," *Russell*, 7: 3–10.

Hager, P. (1994), *Continuity and Change in the Development of Russell's Philosophy*, Dordrecht: Kluwer.

Hahn, H., O. Neurath, and R. Carnap (1929), *Wissenschaftliche Weltauffassung der Wiener Kreis*, Wien: Wolf.

Haller, R. (1993), *Neopositivismus*, Darmstadt: Wissenschaftliche Buchgesellschaft.

Hamacher-Hermes, A. (1994), *Inhalts- oder Umfangslogik? Die Kontroverse zwischen E. Husserl und A. H. Voigt*, Freiburg: Alber.

Hanna, R. (2001), *Kant and the Foundations of Analytic Philosophy*, Oxford: Oxford University Press.

Hannequin, A. (1896), *Essai critique sur l'hypothèse des atomes dans la science contemporaine*, Paris: Alcan.

Hare, P., ed. (1988), *Doing Philosophy Historically*, Buffalo: Prometheus Books.

Hare, R. M. (1959), "Das Philosophiestudium in Oxford," *Ratio*, 2: 1–12.

Hare, R. M. (1963), *Freedom and Reason*, Oxford: Clarendon Press.

Hare, R. (2005), "Hinges and Frames: Wittgenstein's Surrogates for Necessity," in M. E. Reich and J. C. Marek (eds.), *Experience and Analysis*, 39–48, Vienna: öbv&hpt.

Hare, W. (2001), "Bertrand Russell on Critical Thinking," *Journal of Thought*, 36: 1–16.

Hartimo, M. H. (2007), "Towards Completeness: Husserl on Theories of Manifolds 1890–1901," *Synthese*, 156: 281–310.

Hartimo, M. H., ed. (2010), *Phenomenology and Mathematics*, Berlin: Springer.

Hartmann, E. v. (1888), *Lotzes Philosophie*, Leipzig: Friedrich.

Hartmann, N. (1910), "Zur Methode der Philosophiegeschichte," *Kant-Studien*, 15: 459–85.

Hauser, K. (2003), "Lotze and Husserl," *Archiv für Geschichte der Philosophie*, 85: 152–78.

Hegel, G. W. F. ([1806] 1977), *Phenomenology of Spirit*, trans. A. V. Miller, Oxford: Clarendon Press.

Hegel, G. W. F. ([1818] 2010), *The Science of Logic*, trans. and ed. G. di Giovanni, Cambridge: Cambridge University Press.

Hegel, G. W. F. ([1830] 2010), *Logic*, vol. 1 of Encyclopaedia of the Philosophical Sciences, trans. and ed. K. Brinkmann and D. Dahlstrom, Cambridge: Cambridge University Press.

Hegel, G. W. F. (1836), *Vorlesungen über die Geschichte der Philosophie*, ed. K. L. Michelet, vol. 3, Berlin: Duncker & Humblot.

Heidegger, M. (1927), *Sein und Zeit*, Tübingen: Niemeyer.

Heidegger, M. (1935), *Einführung in die Metaphysik (Vorlesungen)*, in: *idem*, Gesamtausgabe, vol. 40, Frankfurt: Klostermann, 1983.

Heidegger, M. (1960), "Hegel und die Griechen," in: D. Heinrich (ed.), *Die Gegenwart der Griechen im neueren Denken*, 43–57, Tübingen: Mohr.

Heidegger, M. (1978), *Frühe Schriften*, Frankfurt: Klostermann.

Heijenoort, J. v. (1967), "Logic as a Calculus and Logic as Language," *Synthese*, 17: 324–30.

Hempel, C., and P. Oppenheim (1948), "Studies in the Logic of Explanation," *Philosophy of Science*, 15 (2): 135–75.

Henrich, D. (1976), *Identität und Objektivität. Eine Untersuchung über Kants transzendentale Deduktion*, Heidelberg: Winter.

Heyde, E. (1967), "Rehmke," in: P. Edwards (ed.), *Encyclopedia of Philosophy*, 8 vols., vii: 102–4, London: Macmillan.

Hilbert, D. (1918), "Axiomatic Thought," in: W. Ewald (ed.), *From Kant to Hilbert*, 2 vols., i: 1105–14, Oxford: Oxford University Press.

Hill, C. O. (2000), "Did Georg Cantor Influence Edmund Husserl?" in: C. Hill and G. E. Rosado Haddock, 137–59.

Hill, C. O. (2000a), "Husserl's Mannigfaltigkeitslehre," in: C. Hill and G. E. Rosado Haddock, 161–79.

Hill, C. O., and G. E. Rosado Haddock (2000), *Husserl or Frege?: Meaning, Objectivity, and Mathematics*, Chicago and La Salle: Open Court.

Hintikka, J. (1976), *Essays on Wittgenstein in Honor of G. H. Von Wright*, Amsterdam: North-Holland Publishing Company.

Hintikka, J. (1990), "Wittgenstein and the Problem of Phenomenology," in: I. Niiniluoto et al. (eds.), *Language, Knowledge, and Intentionality*, 15–46, Helsinki: The Academic Bookstore.

Hintikka, J. (1994), "An Anatomy of Wittgenstein's Picture Theory," in: C. C. Gould and R. S. Cohen (eds.), *Artifacts, Representations and Social Practice*, 222–56, Dordrecht: Kluwer.

Hintikka, J. (1995), "The Phenomenological Dimension," in: B. Smith and D. Smith (eds.), *The Cambridge Companion to Husserl*, 78–105, Cambridge: Cambridge University Press.

Hintikka, J. (1995a), "The Longest Philosophical Journey," in: J. Hintikka and K. Puhl (eds.), *The British Tradition in 20th Century Philosophy*, 11–26, Vienna: Hölder-Pichler-Tempsky.

Hintikka, J. (1996), *Ludwig Wittgenstein: Half-Truths and One-and-a-Half-Truths*, vol. 1 of *idem*, *Selected Papers*, 2 vols., Dordrecht: Kluwer.

Hintikka, J., and M. Hintikka (1986), *Investigating Wittgenstein*, Oxford: Basil Blackwell.

Holz, H. H. (1990), "Spekulation," in: H.-J. Sandkühler (ed.), *Europäische Enzyklopädie zu Philosophie und Wissenschaft*, 4 vols., iv: 397–402, Hamburg: Felix Meiner.

Howard, R. (1982), *Three Faces of Hermeneutics: An Introduction to Current Theories of Understanding*, Los Angelis: University of California Press.

Höffding, H. (1896), *Geschichte der neueren Philosophie*, vol. 2, Leipzig: Reisland.

Husserl, E. ([1887] 1970), "On the Concept of Number," in: P. Mc Cormick and F. Elliston (eds.), *Husserl: Shorter Works*, 92–120, Notre Dame: University of Notre Dame Press.

Husserl, E. (1891), *Philosophy of Arithmetic*, Halle: Pfeffer.

Husserl, E. ([1900] 1992), *Logische Untersuchungen*, vol. 1, *Prolegomena zur reinen Logik*, Hamburg: Meiner.

Husserl, E. ([1905] 1966), "Seefelder Manuskripte über Individuation," in: *Husserliana*, vol. 10, 237–68, Den Haag: Martinus Nijhoff.

Husserl, E. ([1906/7] 1984), *Einleitung in die Logik und Erkenntnistheorie. Vorlesungen 1906/1907*, in: *Husserliana*, vol. 24, Dordrecht: Kluwer.

Husserl, E. ([1907] 1958), *Die Idee der Phänomenologie. Fünf Vorlesungen*, in: *Husserliana*, vol. 2, Den Haag: Nijhoff.

Husserl, E. ([1911] 1965), *Philosophie als strenge Wissenschaft*, Frankfurt: Klostermann.

Husserl, E. ([1913] 1992), *Ideen zu einer reinen Phänomenologie und phänomenologischen Philosophie*, Hamburg: Meiner.

Husserl, E. ([1917/18] 1996), *Logik und allgemeine Wissenschaftstheorie. Vorlesungen 1917/1918*, in: *Husserliana*, vol. 30, 217, Dordrecht: Kluwer.

Husserl, E. ([1923/4] 1956), *Erste Philosophie I*, in: *Husserliana*, vol. 7, Den Haag: Nijhoff.

Husserl, E. (1929), *Formale und transzendentale Logik*, Halle a.d. Salle: Mohr.

Husserl, E. ([1929a] 1971), "Phenomenology," ed. R. E. Palmer, *The Journal of the British Society for Phenomenology*, 2: 77–90.

Husserl, E. ([1936] 1970), *The Crisis of European Sciences and Transcendental Philosophy*, Evanston: North-Western University Press.

Husserl, E. (1939), *Erfahrung und Urteil. Untersuchungen zur Genealogie der Logik*, Prag: Akademia.

Husserl, E. (1979), "Der Folgerungskalkül und die Inhaltslogik," in: *Husserliana*, vol. 22, 44–66, Dordrecht: Kluwer.

Hylton, P. (1990), *Russell, Idealism and the Emergence of Analytic Philosophy*, Oxford: Clarendon Press.

Hylton, P. (2010), "Frege and Russell," in: M. Potter and T. Ricketts (eds.), 509–49.

Imaguire, G. (2001), *Russells Frühphilosophie: Propositionen, Realismus und die sprachontologische Wende*, Hildesheim: Olms.
Inwood, M. (1992), *Hegel's Dictionary*, Oxford: Blackwell.
Irwin, T. (1988), *Aristotle's First Principles*, Oxford: Clarendon Press.
Jackson, F. (1998), *From Metaphysics to Ethics: A Defense of Conceptual Analysis*, Oxford: Oxford University Press.
Johnson, W. E. (1921), *Logic*, 3 Parts, Cambridge: Cambridge University Press.
Joseph, H. W. B. (1949), *Lectures on the Philosophy of Leibniz*, ed. J. L. Austin, Oxford: Clarendon Press.
Jourdain, P. E. B. (1910/1912), "The Development of the Theories of Mathematical Logic and the Principles of Mathematics," *The Quarterly Journal of Pure and Applied Mathematics*, 41: 324–52/43: 219–314.
Kant, I. (1791), *Critique of the Power of Judgement*, Riga: Hartknoch.
Kant, I. (1800), *Logik. Ein Handbuch zu Vorlesungen*, ed. G. B. Jäsche, Königsberg: Nicolavius & Benjamin.
Käufer, S. (2005), "Hegel to Frege: Concepts and Conceptual Content in Nineteenth-century Logic," *History of Philosophy Quarterly*, 22: 259–80.
Kneale, W., and M. Kneale (1962), *The Development of Logic*, Oxford: Clarendon Press.
Köhnke, K. (1986), *Entstehung und Aufstieg des Neukantianismus*, Frankfurt: Suhrkamp.
Koppelberg, D. (1987), *Die Aufhebung der Analytische Philosophie*, Frankfurt: Suhrkamp.
Kraushaar, O. (1938/1939), "Lotze as a Factor in the Development of James's Radical Empiricism and Pluralism," *The Philosophical Review*, 47: 517–26/49: 455–71.
Kreiser, L. (2000), "Gottlob Frege: ein Leben in Jena," in: G. Gabriel and U. Dathe (eds.), *Gottlob Frege. Werk und Wirkung*, 9–24, Paderborn: mentis.
Kripke, S. (1980), *Naming and Necessity*, Oxford: Blackwell.
Kronenberg, M. (1899), *Moderne Philosophen. Porträts und Charakteristiken*, München: Beck.
Künne, W. (1991), "The Nature of Acts: Moore on Husserl," in: B. Hale (ed.), *The Analytical Tradition*, 104–16, Oxford: Blackwell.
Künne, W. (2010), "'Eadem sunt, quae sibi mutuo substitui possunt, salva veritate'. Leibniz über Identität und Austauschbarkeit," *Jahrbuch der Akademie der Wissenschaften zu Göttingen*, 2009: 110–19.
Kuntz, P. G. (1971), "Rudolf Hermann Lotze, Philosopher and Critic," in: G. Santayana (ed.), *Lotze's System of Philosophy*, 3–94, Bloomington: Indiana University Press.
Kusch, M. (1995), *Psychologism: A Case Study in the Sociology of Philosophical Knowledge*, London: Routledge.
Landini, G. (2004), "Wittgenstein's Tractarian Apprenticeship," *Russell*, 23: 101–30.
Landini, G. (2007), *Wittgenstein's Apprenticeship with Russell*, Cambridge: Cambridge University Press.
Lehmann, G. (1931), *Geschichte der nachkantischen Philosophie*, Berlin: Junker.
Lehmann, G. (1943), *Die deutsche Philosophie der Gegenwart*, Stuttgart: Kröner.

Leibniz, G. W. ([1678] 1969), "What Is an Idea?" in: *Philosophical Papers and Letters*, 207–8.

Leibniz, G. W. ([1678/9] 1989), "Preface to a Universal Characteristic," in: R. Ariew and D. Garber (eds.), *Philosophical Essays*, 5–10, Indianapolis: Hackett.

Leibniz, G. W. ([1679] 1969), "On Universal Synthesis and Analysis, or the Art of Discovery and Judgment," in: *Philosophical Papers and Letters*, 229–34.

Leibniz, G. W. ([1686] 1988), "Discourse on Metaphysics," in: *idem, Discourse on Metaphysics and Related Writings*, ed. and trans. R. N. D. Martin and S. Brown, Manchester: Manchester University Press.

Leibniz, G. W. ([1695] 1989), "A New System of the Nature and Communication of Substances, and the Union of the Soul and Body," in: *idem*, 138–45.

Leibniz, G. W. ([1956] 1969), *Philosophical Papers and Letters*, ed. and trans. L. E. Loemker, 2nd ed., Dordrecht: Reidel.

Leibniz, G. W. (1989), *Philosophical Essays*, ed. R. Ariew and D. Garber, Indianapolis: Hackett.

Leiter, B. (2011), "'Analytic' and 'Continental' Philosophy," The Philosophical Gourmet Report, https://www.philosophicalgourmet.com/analytic-and-continental-philosophy/ (retrieved on September 25, 2018).

Leśniewski, S. (1927/31), "On the Foundations of Mathematics," trans. V. F. Sinisi, *Topoi*, 2: 3–52.

Levy, P. (1979), *G. E. Moore and the Cambridge Apostles*, London: Weidenfeld and Nicolson.

Linke, P. ([1946] 1998), "Gottlob Frege as Philosopher," trans. C. O. Hill, in: R. Poli (ed.), *The Brentano Puzzle*, 49–72, Aldershot: Ashgate.

Linsky, B. (2008), "Logical Analysis and Logical Construction," in: M. Beaney (ed.), 107–22.

Locke, J. ([1688] 1894), *Essay Concerning Human Understanding*, 42nd ed., ed. A. C. Fraser, Oxford: Clarendon Press.

Lohmar, D. (2011), "Genetic Phenomenology," in: S. Luft and S. Overgaard (eds.), 266–75.

Lotze, R. H. (1841), *Metaphysik*, Leipzig: Weidmann.

Lotze, R. H. (1843), *Logik*, Leipzig: Weidmann.

Lotze, R. H. (1847), *Über Bedingungen der Kunstschönheit*, Göttingen: Vandenhoeck und Ruprecht.

Lotze, R. H. (1856/64), *Mikrokosmus*, vol. 3, Leipzig: Hirzel.

Lotze, R. H. (1857), *Streitschriften*, Heft 1, Leipzig: Hirzel.

Lotze, R. H. (1874), *Logik*, Leipzig: Hirzel.

Lotze, R. H. (1879), *Metaphysik*, Leipzig: Hirzel.

Lotze, R. H. (1880), *Logik*, 2nd ed., Leipzig: Hirzel.

Lotze, R. H. ([1883] 1912), *Grundzüge der Logik und Encyclopädie der Philosophie*, 4th ed., Leipzig: Hirzel.

Lotze, R. H. (1885), *Microcosmus: An Essay Concerning Man and his Relation to the World*, trans. E. Hamilton and E. E. Constance Jones, Edinburgh: T&T Clark.

Lotze, R. H. (1886), *Kleine Schriften*, ed. D. Peipers, Leipzig: Hirzel.
Lotze, R. H. (1887), *Logic*, trans. B. Bosanquet et al., 2nd ed., Oxford: Clarendon Press.
Lotze, R. H. (1888), *Metaphysics*, trans. B. Bosanquet et al., 2nd ed., Oxford: Clarendon Press.
Lotze, R. H. (1989), *Logik. Drittes Buch. Vom Erkennen*, ed. G. Gabriel, Hamburg: Meiner.
Lotze, R. H. (2003), *Briefe und Dokumente*, ed. R. Pester, Würzburg: Königshausen & Neumann.
Luft, S. (2015), *The Space of Culture: Towards a Neo-Kantian Philosophy of Culture (Cohen, Natorp, and Cassirer)*, Oxford: Oxford University Press.
Luft, S., and S. Overgaard, eds. (2011), *The Routledge Companion to Phenomenology*, London: Routledge.
Lugg, A. (2006), "Russell as Precursor of Quine," *Bertrand Russell Society Quarterly*, 128/9: 9–21.
Mandelbaum, M. (1965), "The History of Ideas, Intellectual History, and the History of Philosophy," *History and Theory*, supp. vol. 5: 33–66.
Manser, A. (1983), *Bradley's Logic*, Oxford: Blackwell.
Manser, A. (1984), "Bradley and Frege," in: A. Manser and G. Stock (eds.), *The Philosophy of F. H. Bradley*, 303–17, Oxford: Clarendon Press.
Martin, R. M. (1967), "On Proper Names and Frege's *Darstellungsweise*," *The Monist*, 51: 1–8.
Martin, R. (1993), "Having the Experience: The Next Best Thing to Being There," *Philosophical Studies*, 70: 305–21.
Mayer, V. (1991), "Die Konstruktion der Erfahrungswelt: Carnap und Husserl," *Erkenntnis* 35, 287–303.
Mayer, V., ed. (2008), *Edmund Husserls Logische Untersuchungen*, Berlin: Akademie-Verlag.
Mayer, V. (2016), "Der *logische Aufbau* als Plagiat," in: G. E. Rosado Haddock (ed.), *Husserl and Analytic Philosophy*, 175–260, Berlin: de Gruyter.
McGuinness, B. F. (1988), *Wittgenstein, A Life*, vol. 1, *Young Ludwig*, 1889–1921, London: Penguin Books.
McGuinness, B. F. (2002), *Approaches to Wittgenstein: Collected Papers*, London: Routledge.
McCulloch, G. (1993), "The Very Idea of the Phenomenological," *Proceedings of Aristotelian Society*, 93: 39–57.
McIntosh, C. A. (2016), "Graham Priest, *One: Being an Investigation into the Unity of Reality and Its Parts, Including the Singular Object which is Nothingness*," *Philosophy in Review*, 36 (3): 130–2
McTaggart, G. M. E. (1896), *Studies in Hegelian Dialectic*, Cambridge: Cambridge University Press.
Messer, A. (1908), *Empfindung und Denken*, Leipzig: Quelle & Meyer.
Michaltschew, D. (1909), *Philosophische Studien. Beiträge zur Kritik des modernen Psychologismus*, Leipzig: Engelmann.

Michaltschew, D. (1996), *Iz korespondencijata na Akademik Dimitar Michalcev* [*Selected Letters*], ed. A. Stojnev, Sofia: Drinov (in Bulgarian).
Milkov, N. (1987), "On the Reconstruction of the Early Wittgenstein's Philosophy," *Darshana International*, 27 (1): 47–53.
Milkov, N. (1992), *Kaleidoscopic Mind*, Amsterdam: Rodopi.
Milkov, N. (1997), *The Varieties of Understanding: English Philosophy Since 1898*, 2 vols., Frankfurt: Peter Lang.
Milkov, N. (1999), "The Latest Frege," *Prima philosophia*, 12: 41–8.
Milkov, N. (2001), "Tractarian Scaffoldings," *Prima philosophia*, 14: 399–414.
Milkov, N. (2001a), "Verifikation II," in: J. Ritter, K. Gründer and G. Gabriel (eds.), *Historisches Wörterbuch der Philosophie*, vol. 11, 702–3, Basel: Schwabe & Co.
Milkov, N. (2001b), "The History of Russell's Concepts 'Sense-data' and 'Knowledge by Acquaintance,'" *Archiv für Begriffsgeschichte*, 43: 221–31.
Milkov, N. (2002), "The Logical Form of Biological Objects," *Analecta Husserliana* 77: 13–28.
Milkov, N. (2003), *A Hundred Years of English Philosophy*, Dordrecht: Kluwer.
Milkov, N. (2003a), "Tolstoi und Wittgenstein: Einfluss und Ähnlichkeiten," *Prima philosophia* 16: 187–206.
Milkov, N. (2003b), "What is Analytic Philosophy," Paper read at the 21st World Congress of Philosophy, Istanbul, Turkey, August 10–17.
Milkov, N. (2004), "Ist Wittgensteins *Tractatus* in irgendeinem Sinne mystisch?" *Theologie und Philosophie*, 79: 511–26.
Milkov, N. (2004a), "Phenomenology and Analytic Philosophy: Common Sources, Related Results," in S. Kaneva (ed.), *Challenges Facing Philosophy in United Europe*, 119–26, Sofia: IFR.
Milkov, N. (2005), "Bertrand Russell Early Philosophy of Time (1899–1913)," *Contributions of the Austrian Ludwig Wittgenstein Society* 13: 188–90.
Milkov, N. (2005a), "The Meaning of Life: A Topological Approach," *Analecta Husserliana*, 84: 217–34.
Milkov, N. (2006), "Hermann Lotze's *Microcosm*," in: A.-T. Tymieniecka (ed.), *Islamic Philosophy and Occidental Phenomenology on the Perennial Issue of Microcosm and Macrocosm*, 41–65, Berlin: Springer.
Milkov, N. (2007), "Russell, Wittgenstein, and the Project for 'Analytic Philosophy,'" *Contributions of the Austrian Ludwig Wittgenstein Society* 15: 188–90.
Milkov, N. (2008), "Russell's Debt to Lotze," *Studies in History and Philosophy of Science*, Part A, 39: 186–93.
Milkov, N. (2008a), "Die Berliner Gruppe und der Wiener Kreis: Gemeinsamkeiten und Unterschiede," in: *Ausgewählte Beiträge zum 8. Kongress der Österreichischen Gesellschaft für Philosophie*, 157–65, Frankfurt: Ontos.
Milkov, N. (2010), "Rudolf Hermann Lotze," *Internet Encyclopedia of Philosophy*. http://www.iep.utm.edu/lotze/
Milkov, N. (2010a), "Mark Wilson, *Wandering Significance: An Essay on Conceptual Behaviour*. Oxford: Clarendon Press," *Pragmatics & Cognition*, 20: 188–95.

Mikov, N. (2011), "Hans Reichenbachs wissenschaftliche Philosophie", in: Hans Reichenbach, *Ziele und Wege der heutigen Naturphilosophie*, ed. by N. Milkov, vii–xliv, Hamburg: Felix Meiner.

Milkov, N. (2012), "Wittgenstein's Method: The Third Phase of Its Development (1933–36)," in: A. Marques and V. Nuno (eds.), *Knowledge, Language and Mind: Wittgenstein's Early Investigations*, 65–79, Berlin: de Gruyter.

Milkov, N. (2013), "The Joint Philosophical Program of Russell and Wittgenstein and Its Demise," *Nordic Wittgenstein Review*, 2: 81–105.

Milkov, N. (2013a), "The Berlin Group and the Vienna Circle: Affinities and Divergences," in: N. Milkov and V. Peckhaus (eds.), *The Berlin Group and the Philosophy of Logical Empiricism*, 3–32, Dordrecht: Springer Verlag.

Milkov, N. (2013b), "Kant's Transcendental Turn as a Second Step in the Logicalization of Philosophy," in: Stefano Bacin et al. (eds.), *Kant and Philosophy in a Cosmopolitan Sense: Proceedings of the XI. International Kant Congress*, vol. 1, 655–67, Berlin: de Gruyter.

Milkov, N. (2015), "Carl Stumpf's Debt to Hermann Lotze," in: D. Fisette and R. Martinelli (eds.), *Philosophy from an Empirical Standpoint: Essays on Carl Stumpf*, 101–22, Leiden: Brill, 2015.

Milkov, N. (2015a), "Die Berliner Gruppe des logischen Empirismus," in: *idem* (ed.), *Die Berliner Gruppe: Texte zum Logischen Empirismus. Eine Anthologie*, ix–lxi, Hamburg: Felix Meiner.

Milkov, N. (2017), "The 1900 Turn in Bertrand Russell's Logic, the Emergence of his Paradox, and the Way Out," *Siegener Beiträge zur Geschichte und Philosophie der Mathematik*, 7: 29–50.

Milkov, N. (2017a), "The Method of Wittgenstein's *Tractatus*: Toward a New Interpretation," *Southwest Philosophy Review*, 33 (2): 197–212.

Milkov, N. (2017b), "Hermann Lotzes philosophische Synthese," in: N. Milkov (ed.), *Hermann Lotze, Mikrokosmos*, 3 vols., i: xi–lxxv, Hamburg: Felix Meiner Verlag.

Milkov, N. (2018), "Hermann Lotze and Franz Brentano," *Philosophical Readings*, 10 (2): 115–22.

Milkov, N. (2018a), "Bertrand Russell's Religion without God and Dogma," in: R. Nicholls and H. Salazar (eds.), *The Philosophy of Spirituality*, 250–72, Leiden: Brill Publishing.

Milkov, N. (2018b), "Wittgenstein's *Notebooks* and the Composition of the *Tractatus*," paper presented at the 24th World Congress of Philosophy, Peking, China, August 18, 2018.

Milkov, N. (2019), "Wittgenstein's Ways," in: S. Wuppuluri and N. da Costa (eds.), *Wittgensteinian (adj.): Looking at Things from the Viewpoint of Wittgenstein's Philosophy*, Berlin: Springer (forthcoming).

Milkov, N. (2019a), "John Wisdom," *Internet Encyclopedia of Philosophy*. https://www.iep.utm.edu/wisdom/

Milkov, N. (2020), "From Kant's Encyclopedic Approach in Philosophy to Hegel's Philosophical Encyclopedia," in *Proceedings of the 13th International Kant Congress*, Berlin: de Gruyter (forthcoming).

Misch, G. (1912), "Einleitung," in: H. Lotze, *Logik*, 2nd ed., v–cxxiii, Leipzig: Meiner.
Monk, R. (1996), *Bertrand Russell: The Spirit of Solitude*, vol. 1, New York: Free Press.
Monk, R. (1996a). "Was Russell Analytic Philosopher?" *Ratio*, 9: 227–42.
Monk, R. (2002), "Philosophical Biography: The Very Idea," in: J. Klagge (ed.), *Wittgenstein: Bibliography and Philosophy*, 3–15, Cambridge: Cambridge University Press.
Moog, W. (1922), *Die Deutsche Philosophie des 20. Jahrhunderts*, Stuttgart: Enke.
Moore, G. E. ([1897] 1986), "In What Sense, If Any, Do Past and Future Time Exist?" in: *idem*, 17–24.
Moore, G. E. ([1898] 1986), "On the Nature of Judgement," in: *idem*, 59–80.
Moore, G. E. (1899), "The Nature of Judgement," *Mind*, 8: 176–93.
Moore, G. E. ([1900] 1986), "Necessity," in: *idem*, 81–100.
Moore, G. E. (1903a), *Principia Ethica*, Cambridge: Cambridge University Press.
Moore, G. E. (1903b), "Review of F. Brentano, *The Origin of the Knowledge of Right and Wrong*," *International Journal of Ethics*, 14: 115–23.
Moore, G. E. ([1903c] 1922), "The Refutation of Idealism," in: *idem*, 1–30.
Moore, G. E. (1905a), "Review of H. Cornelius, *Einleitung in die Philosophie*," *Mind*, 14: 244–53.
Moore, G. E. ([1905b] 1922), "The Nature and Reality of Objects of Perception," in: *idem*, 31–96.
Moore, G. E. ([1908] 1922), "William James' 'Pragmatism,'" in: *idem*, 97–146.
Moore, G. E. ([1909] 1922), "Hume's Philosophy," in: *idem*, 147–67.
Moore, G. E. (1909/10), "The Subject-Matter of Psychology," *Proceedings of the Aristotelian Society*, 10: 36–62.
Moore, G. E. (1910), "Review of Messer, *Empfindung und Denken*," *Mind*, 19: 395–409.
Moore, G. E. (1911), "Review of D. Michaltschew, *Philosophische Studien*," *Mind*, 20: 113–16.
Moore, G. E. ([1917] 1922), "The Conception of Reality," in: *idem*, 197–219.
Moore, G. E. (1922), *Philosophical Studies*, London: Allen & Unwin.
Moore, G. E. ([1925] 1959), "A Defence of Common Sense," in: *idem*, 32–59.
Moore, G. E. ([1940/4] 1959), "Four Forms of Skepticism," in: *idem*, 196–226.
Moore, G. E. (1942), "An Autobiography," in: P. A. Schilpp (ed.), *The Philosophy of G. E. Moore*, 1–39, Evanston: North-Western University Press.
Moore, G. E. ([1944] 1959), "Russell's 'Theory of Descriptions,'" in: *idem*, 151–95.
Moore, G. E. (1953), *Some Main Problems of Philosophy*, London: Allen & Unwin.
Moore, G. E. (1959), *Philosophical Papers*, London: Allen & Unwin.
Moore, G. E. (1966), *Lectures on Philosophy*, London: Allen & Unwin.
Moore, G. E. (1986), *The Early Essays*, ed. T. Regan, Philadelphia: Temple University Press.
Moore, G. E. (2018), "'Unpublished Review of B. Russell,' *The Principles of Mathematics*," *Russell*, 38: 138–63.
Morgenstern, M., and R. Zimmer (2002), *Karl Popper*, München: dtv.
Mormann, T. (2006a), "Between Heidelberg and Marburg: The Aufbau's Neo-Kantian Origins and the AP/CP-Divide," *Sapere aude*, 1: 22–50.

Mormann, T. (2006b), "Werte bei Carnap," *Zeitschrift für philosophische Forschung*, 60: 169–89.
Morris, K. (2007), "Wittgenstein's Method: Ridding People of Philosophical Prejudices," in: G. Kahane et al. (eds.), *Wittgenstein and His Interpreters: Essays in Memory of Gordon Baker*, 66–87, Oxford: Blackwell.
Müller-Freienfeld, R. (1923), *Die Philosophie des zwanzigsten Jahrhunderts in ihren Hauptströmungen*, Berlin: Mittler.
Mulligan, K. (1985), "'Wie die Sachen sich zueinander verhalten.' Inside and Outside the Tractatus," *Teoria*, 2: 145–74.
Mulligan, K. (1986), "Exactness, Description and variation: How Austrian Analytic Philosophy Was Done," in: J. C. Nyíri (ed.), *Von Bolzano zu Wittgenstein—Zur Tradition der österreichische Philosophie*, 86–97, Wien: Hölder–Pichler–Temsky.
Mulligan, K., ed. (1987), *Speech Act and Sachverhalt: Reinach and the Foundations of Realist Phenomenology*, Dordrecht: Reidel.
Mulligan, K. (1989), "Husserl on States of Affairs in the Logical Investigations," *Epistemologia*, 12 (fascicolo speciale): 207–34.
Mulligan, K. (1991), "Introduction: On the History of Continental Philosophy," *Topoi*, 10: 115–20.
Mulligan, K. (1993), "Post-Continental Philosophy: Nosological Notes," *Stanford French Review*, 17: 133–50.
Mulligan, K., P. Simons, and B. Smith (1984), "Truth-Makers," *Philosophy and Phenomenological Research*, 44: 287–321.
Mulligan, K., P. Simons, and B. Smith (2006), "What is Wrong with Contemporary Philosophy?" *Topoi*, 25: 63–67.
Murphy, R. (1991), "Husserl and Hume: Overcoming Skepticism?" *Journal of the British Society for Phenomenology*, 22: 30–44.
Nagel, E. ([1936] 1956), "Impressions and Appraisals of Analytic Philosophy in Europe," in: *idem*, *Logic without Metaphysics*, 191–246, Glencoe: The Free Press.
Nagel, T. (1979), "What It is Like to be a Bat?" in: *idem*, *Mortal Questions*, 165–80, Cambridge: Cambridge University Press.
Nedo, M., and M. Ranchetti (1983), *Ludwig Wittgenstein*, Frankfurt: Suhrkamp.
Nelson, J. (1999), "Is the Pears–McGuinness Translation of the *Tractatus* Really Superior to Ogden's and Ramsey's?" *Philosophical Investigations*, 22: 166–75.
Nelson, L. (1905), "Rezension von Hermann Cohen: *System der Philosophie*, 1. Teil. *Logik der reinen Erkenntnis*," *GS*, ii: 1–28.
Nelson, L. (1908), "Über die Unhaltbarkeit des wissenschaftlichen Positivismus in der Philosophie," *GS*, i: 200–6.
Nelson, L. (1910), "Henri Bergson, Einführung in die Metaphysik," *GS*, iii: 345–7.
Nelson, L. (1911a), "Die Unmöglichkeit der Erkenntnistheorie," *GS*, ii: 459–83.
Nelson, L. (1911b), "Thesen und Schlusswort: Zur Diskussion des Vortrags," *GS*, ii: 485–501.
Nelson, L. ([1917] 1922), *Die Reformation der Gesinnung durch Erziehung zum Selbstvertrauen*, 2nd ed., Leipzig: Der Neue Geist.

Nelson, L. (1918), *Die Reformation der Philosophie durch die Kritik der Vernunft*, Leipzig: Der Neue Geist.
Nelson, L. (1921), *Spuk: Einweihung in das Geheimnis der Wahrsagekunst Oswald Spenglers*, Leipzig: Reinhold.
Nelson, L. (1922), "Die sokratische Methode," *GS*, i: 269–316; new edition in: D. Birnbacher and D. Krohn (eds.), 2002, 21–72.
Nelson, L. (1928), "Kritische Philosophie und mathematische Axiomatik," *Unterrichtsblätter für Mathematik und Naturwissenschaften*, 34: 108–15; 136–42.
Nelson, L. (1962), *Fortschritte und Rückschritte der Philosophie von Hume und Kant bis Hegel und Fries*, ed. J. Kraft, Frankfurt: Öffentliches Leben.
Nelson, L. (1962a), "Was ist Geschichte der Philosophie?" *Ratio* 4: 119–31.
Nelson, L. (1971/3), *Gesammelte Schriften [GS]*, 9 vols., Hamburg: Meiner.
Neurath, O. (1921), *Anti-Spengler*, München: Callwey.
Neurath, O. (1929), "The Vienna Circle of the Scientific Conception of the World," in: *idem, Empiricism and Sociology*, ed. M. Neurath and R. S. Cohen, 301–18, Dordrecht: Reidel.
Neurath, O. ([1936] 1981), "Die Entwicklung des Wiener Kreises und die Zukunft des logischen Empirismus," in: *idem, Gesammelte philosophische Schriften*, ed. R. Haller et al., vol. 2, ii: 673–702, Wien: Hölder–Pichler–Tempsky.
Nicholson, P. (1990), *The Political Philosophy of the British Idealists*, Cambridge: Cambridge University Press.
Normore, C. (1990), "Doxography and the History of Philosophy," *Canadian Journal of Philosophy*, 16 (Supplementary Volume): 203–26.
Nuzzo, A., ed. (2009), *Hegel and the Analytic Tradition*, London: Continuum.
O'Hear, A., ed. (1999), *German Philosophy Since Kant*, Cambridge: Cambridge University Press.
Olsen, D., and N. Griffin, (2019), "Russell's Bridge," in: R. Wahl (ed.), 286–311.
Orth, E. W. (1997), "Brentanos und Diltheys Konzeption einer beschreibenden Psychologie in ihrer Beziehung auf Lotze," *Brentano Studien*, 6: 13–29.
Orth, E. W. (1997a), "Metaphysische Implikationen der Intentionalität. Trendelenburg, Lotze, Brentano," *Brentano Studien* 7: 15–30.
Orth, E. W. (1984), "Dilthey und Lotze. Zur Wandlung des Philosophiebegriffs in 19. Jahrhundret," *Dilthey-Jahrbuch*, 2: 140–58.
Orth, E. W. (1994), "Die Einheit des Neukantianismus," in: E. W. Orth und H. Holzhey (eds.), *Neukantianismus: Perspektiven und Probleme*, 13–30, Würzburg: Königshausen & Neumann.
Overgaard, S. (2011), "Analytic Philosophy," in: S. Luft and S. Overgaard (eds.), 563–73.
Passmore, J. ([1957] 1966), *A Hundred Years of Philosophy*, 2nd ed., Harmondsworth: Penguin.
Passmore, J. (1967), "Historiography of Philosophy," in: P. Edwards (ed.), *The Encyclopaedia of Philosophy*, vol. 6, 226–30, London: Macmillan.

Passmore, J. (1995), "Editing Russell's Papers: A Fragment of Institutional History," *Grazer Philosophische Studien*, 49: 189–205.
Pears, D. (1967), *Bertrand Russell and the British Tradition in Philosophy*, London: Collins.
Pears, D. (1971), *Ludwig Wittgenstein*, London: Collins.
Pears, D. (1987), *The False Prison*, Oxford: Clarendon Press.
Peckhaus, V. (1990), *Hilbertprogramm und Kritische Philosophie: das Göttinger Modell interdisziplinärer Zusammenarbeit zwischen Mathematik und Philosophie*, Göttingen: Vandenhoeck u. Ruprecht.
Peckhaus, V. (1997), *Logik, mathesis universalis und allgemeine Wissenschaft*, Berlin: Akademie Verlag.
Peckhaus, V. (2001), "Die regressive Methode," in: W. Stelzner and M. Stöckler (eds.), *Zwischen traditioneller und moderner Logik*, 65–80, Paderborn: mentis.
Peckhaus, V. (2002), "Regressive Analysis," *Logical Analysis and History of Philosophy*, 5: 97–110.
Peckhaus, V. (2009), "Language and Logic in German Post-Hegelian Philosophy," *The Baltic International Yearbook of Cognition, Logic and Communication*, 4: 1–17.
Perry, R. B. (1935), *The Thought and Character of William James*, Boston: Little, Brown, and Co.
Pester, R. (1997), *Hermann Lotze*, Würzburg: Königshausen & Neumann.
Pincock, C. (2004), "Nikolay Milkov, *A Hundred Years of English Philosophy*," *Notre Dame Philosophical Reviews*, October 6, 2004.
Pincock, C. (2013), "On Hans-Johann Glock, *What is Analytic Philosophy?*" *Journal for the History of Analytic Philosophy*, 2 (2): 6–10.
Popper, K. (1930/3), *Die beiden Grundprobleme der Erkenntnistheorie*, Tübingen: J. C. B. Mohr, 1979.
Popper, K. ([1934] 1969), *Logik der Forschung*, 3rd ed., Tübingen: J. C. B. Mohr.
Popper, K. (1940), "What Is Dialectic?" *Mind*, 49: 403–26.
Popper, K. (1962), "Julius Kraft," *Ratio*, 4: 2–10.
Popper, K. (1963), *Conjectures and Refutations*, London: Routledge.
Popper, K. (1974), "Intellectual Autobiography," in: P. A. Schilpp (ed.), *The Philosophy of Karl Popper*, 2 vols., i: 3–181, La Salle: Open Court.
Popper, K. (1992), "Letter to Kelly L. Ross, Dec. 12". www//friesian.com/ross/popper.htm.
Potter, M. (2010), "Introduction," in: M. Potter and T. Ricketts (eds.), 1–31.
Potter, M., and T. Ricketts (eds.) (2010), *The Cambridge Companion to Frege*, Cambridge: Cambridge University Press.
Preston, A. (2007), *Analytic Philosophy: The History of an Illusion*, London: Continuum.
Price, H. H. (1940), *Hume's Theory of the External World*, Oxford: Clarendon.
Price, H. H. (1945), "Clarity is Not Enough," *Proceedings of the Aristotelian Society*, 19 (Supplementary Volume): 1–31.

Priest, G. (2014), *One*, Oxford: Oxford University Press.
Quine, W. (1951), "Two Dogmas of Empiricism," in: *idem, From a Logical Point of View*, 20–46, Harvard: Harvard University Press.
Quine, W. (1960), *Word and Object*, Boston: MIT Press.
Quinn, A. (1977), *The Confidence of British Philosophers*, Leiden: Brill.
Quinton, A. (1995), "Continental Philosophy," in: Ted Honderich (ed.), *Oxford Companion to Philosophy*, 161–63, Oxford: Oxford University Press.
Ramsey, F. ([1925] 1931), "Universals," in: R. B. Braithwaite (ed.), *The Foundations of Mathematics*, 112–34, London: Routledge.
Ramsey, F. (1931), *The Foundations of Mathematics and other Logical Essays*, London: Kegan Paul.
Ravenscroft, I. (2005), *Philosophy of Mind*, Oxford: Oxford University Press.
Redding, P. (2007), *Analytic Philosophy and the Return of Hegelian Thought*, Cambridge: Cambridge University Press.
Rehmke, J. (1910), *Philosophie als Grundwissenschaft*, Frankfurt: Kesselring.
Reichenbach, H. (1938), *Experience and Prediction*, Chicago: University of Chicago Press, 1938.
Reichenbach, H. (1953), *Der Aufstieg der wissenschaftlichen Philosophie*, trans. M. Reichenbach, Berlin: Herbig.
Richardson, A. (1998), *Carnap's Reconstruction of the World: The Aufbau and the Emergence of Logical Positivism*, Cambridge: Cambridge University Press.
Romanos, G. (1983), *Quine and Analytic Philosophy*, Cambridge: MIT Press.
Rosado Haddock, G. (1991), "On Husserl's Distinction Between State of Affairs (*Sachverhalt*) and Situation of Affairs (*Sachlage*)," in: T. M. Seebohm et al. (eds.), *Phenomenology and The Formal Sciences*, 35–48, Dordrecht: Kluwer.
Rosado Haddock, G. (2008), *The Young Carnap's Unknown Master: Husserl's Influence on 'Der Raum' and 'Der logische Aufbau der Welt'*, Farnham (Surrey): Ashgate.
Ross, W. D. (1939), "The Discovery of Syllogism," *The Philosophical Review*, 48: 251–71.
Roy, J.-M. (2004), "Carnap Husserlian Reading of the Aufbau," in: S. Awodey and C. Klein (eds.), *Carnap Brought Home: The View from Jena*, 41–62, Chicago: Open Court.
Russell, B. ([1895] 1990), "Review of Heymans, *Die Gesetze und Elemente des wissenschaftlichen Denkens*," in: *idem*, 35–43.
Russell, B. ([1896a] 1990), "On Some Difficulties of Continuous Quantity," in: *idem*, 44–58; textual notes 563–6.
Russell, B. ([1896b] 1990), "Review of Hannequin, *Essai critique sur l'hypothèse des atomes dans la science contemporaine*," in: *idem*, 35–43.
Russell, B. ([1896/8] 1990), "Various Notes on Mathematical Philosophy," in: *idem*, 6–28.
Russell, B. (1897a), *An Essay on the Foundations of Geometry*, Cambridge: Cambridge University Press.

Russell, B. ([1897b] 1990), "Why Do We Regard Time, But Not Space, as Necessarily a Plenum?" in: *idem*, 91-97.
Russell, B. ([1897c] 1990), "Can We Make a Dialectical Transition from Punctual Matter to the Plenum?" in: *idem*, 22-23.
Russell, B. ([1898] 1990), "An Analysis of Mathematical Reasoning," in: *idem*, 163-222.
Russell, B. ([1899] 1990), "The Classification of Relations," in: *idem*, 136-46.
Russell, B. ([1900a] 1937), *A Critical Exposition of the Philosophy of Leibniz*, 2nd ed., Cambridge: Cambridge University Press.
Russell, B. ([1900b] 1993), "Is Position in Time Absolute or Relative?" in: *idem*, 219-33.
Russell, B. (1903), *The Principles of Mathematics*, London: Allen & Unwin.
Russell, B. ([1903a] 1994), "Points about Denoting," in: *idem*, *The Collected Papers of Bertrand Russell*, ed. Alasdair Urquhart, vol. 4, 305-13, London: Routledge.
Russell, B. ([1904] 1973), "Meinong's Theory of Complexes and Assumptions," in: D. Lackey (ed.), 21-76.
Russell, B. ([1905] 1956), "On Denoting" in: *idem*, 39-56.
Russell, B. ([1907] 1973), "The Regressive Method of Discovering the Premises of Mathematics," in: D. Lackey (ed.), 273-83.
Russell, B. ([1911] 1956), "On the Relations of Universals and Particulars," in: *idem*, 103-24.
Russell, B. ([1911a] 1992), "Knowledge by Acquaintance and Knowledge by Description," in: *idem*, 147-61.
Russell, B. ([1911b] 1992), "Analytic Realism," in: *idem*, 132-46.
Russell, B. ([1912] 1992), "On Matter," in: *idem*, 77-95.
Russell, B. ([1912a] 1932), *The Problems of Philosophy*, London: Butterworth.
Russell, B. ([1912b] 1992), "What Is Logic?" in: *idem*, *The Collected Papers of Bertrand Russell*, ed. J. G. Slater, vol. 6, 54-56, London: Routledge.
Russell, B. ([1912c] 1993), "The Philosophy of Bergson," in: *idem*, *Collected Papers Papers of Bertrand Russell*, ed. J. G. Slater, vol. 6, 313-37, London: Routledge.
Russell, B. ([1913] 1984), *Theory of Knowledge*, in: *idem*, *The Collected Papers of Bertrand Russell*, ed. E. R Eames, vol. 7, London: Routledge.
Russell, B. ([1914] 1926), *Our Knowledge of the External World*, 2nd ed., London: Allen & Unwin.
Russell, B. ([1914a] 1918), "The Relation of Sense-data to Physics," in: *idem*, 108-31.
Russell, B. ([1915] 1918), "The Ultimate Constituents of Matter," in: *idem*, 94-107.
Russell, B. ([1918] 1963), *Mysticism and Logic*, London: Allen & Unwin.
Russell, B. ([1918a] 1956), "The Philosophy of Logical Atomism," in: *idem*, 175-281.
Russell, B. ([1919] 1956), "On Propositions," in: *idem*, 285-320.
Russell, B. (1921), *The Analysis of Mind*, London: Allen & Unwin.
Russell, B. ([1924] 1956), "Logical Atomism," in: *idem*, 321-45.
Russell, B. (1945), *A History of Western Philosophy*, New York: Simon & Schuster.
Russell, B. (1948), *Human Knowledge: Its Scope and Limits*, London: Allen & Unwin.
Russell, B. (1956), *Logic and Knowledge*, ed. R. C. Marsh, London: Allen & Unwin.

Russell, B. (1959), *My Philosophical Development*, London: Allen & Unwin.
Russell, B. (1960), *Bertrand Russell Speaks His Mind*, ed. W. Wyatt, Cleveland: The World Publishing Company.
Russell, B. (1967), *The Autobiography of Bertrand Russell*, 3 vols., i, London: Allen & Unwin.
Russell, B. (1968), *The Art of Philosophizing, and Other Essays*, Savage: Littlefield Adams.
Russell, B. (1973), *Essays in Analysis*, ed. D. Lackey, New York: Braziller.
Russell, B. (1974), "The Art of Rational Conjecture," in: *idem, The Art of Philosophizing*, 1–36, Lanham: Littlefield.
Russell, B. (1986), "Philosophical Books Read in Prison", in: J. G. Slater (ed.), *The Collected Papers of Bertrand Russell*, vol. 8, 315–28, London: Routledge.
Russell, B. (1990), *The Collected Papers of Bertrand Russell*, ed. N. Griffin and A. C. Lewis, vol. 2, London: Routldege.
Russell, B. (1992), *The Collected Papers of Bertrand Russell*, ed. J. G. Slater, vol. 6, London: Routledge.
Russell, B. (1993), *The Collected Papers of Bertrand Russell*, ed. G. H. Moore, vol. 3, London: Routledge.
Russell, B., and A. N. Whitehead ([1910/13] 1925), *Principia Mathematica*, 2nd ed., Cambridge: Cambridge University Press.
Rutherford, D. (1995), "Philosophy and Language in Leibniz," in: N. Jolley (ed.), *The Cambridge Companion to Leibniz*, 224–69, Cambridge: Cambridge University Press.
Ryckman, T. (2007), "Carnap and Husserl," in: M. Friedman and R. Greath (eds.), *Cambridge Companion to Carnap*, 81–105, Cambridge: Cambridge University Press.
Ryle, G. (1932), "Locke on the Human Understanding," in: *idem*, vol. 1, 126–46.
Ryle, G. (1939), "Plato's *Parmenides*," in: *idem*, vol. 1, 1–44.
Ryle, G. ([1946] 1971), "Review of Marvin Farber: *The Foundations of Phenomenology*," in: *idem*, 215–24.
Ryle, G. ([1949] 1971), "Discussion of Rudolf Carnap: 'Meaning and Necessity,'" in: *idem*, vol. 1, 225–35.
Ryle, G. (1949a), *The Concept of Mind*, London: Hutchinson.
Ryle, G. (1951), "Ludwig Wittgenstein," *Analysis*, 12:1.
Ryle, G. (1954), *Dilemmas*, Cambridge: Cambridge University Press.
Ryle, G. (1966), *Plato's Progress*, Cambridge: Cambridge University Press.
Ryle, G. (1970), "Autobiographical," in: O. P. Wood and G. Pitcher (eds.), *Ryle*, 1–15, London: Macmillan.
Ryle, G. (1971), *Collected Papers*, 2 vols., London: Hutchinson.
Ryle, G. ([1951] 1971a), "The Verification Principle," in: *idem*, vol. 2, 287–93.
Ryle, G. ([1957] 1971b), "The Theory of Meaning," in: *idem*, vol. 2, 350–72.
Ryle, G. (1979), "Bertrand Russell: 1872–1970," in: G. Roberts (ed.), *Bertrand Russell Memorial Volume*, 15–21, London: Allen & Unwin.
Sandmeyer, B. (2008), *Husserl's Constitutive Phenomenology: Its Problems and Promise*, London: Routledge.

Santayana, G. ([1889] 1971), *Lotze's System of Philosophy*, ed. P. G. Kuntz, Bloomington: Indiana University Press.
Sayre, K. (1969), *Plato's Analytic Method*, Chicago: Chicago University Press.
Scanlon, J. (1991), "'Tertium non datur': Husserl's Conception of a Definite Multiplicity," in: T. M. Seebohm et al. (eds.), *Phenomenology and the Formal Sciences*, Dordrecht: Kluwer.
Schmitz, H. (1989), *Was wollte Kant?* Bonn: Bouvier.
Schneider, H.-J. (1992), *Phantasie und Kalkül*, Frankfurt: Suhrkamp.
Scholz, H. (1941), *Metaphysik als strenge Wissenschaft*, Köln: Staufen.
Schwartz, S. (2012), *A Brief History of Analytic Philosophy*, Oxford: Blackwell.
Searle, J. (1984), *Minds, Brains and Science*, London: BBC.
Searle, J. (2010), *Making the Social World*, Oxford: Oxford University Press.
Sebestik, J. (1990), "The Archeology of the Tractatus: Bolzano and Wittgenstein," in: R. Haller and J. Brandl (eds.), *Wittgenstein—Towards a Re-Evaluation*, 3 vols., i: 112–18, Munich: Bergmann Verlag.
Sellars, W. (1963), "Empiricism and the Philosophy of Mind," in: *idem, Science, Perception and Reality*, 127–96, London: Routledge.
Shosky, J. (1997), "Russell's Use of Truth Tables," in: *Russell*, 17: 11–24.
Simons, P. (1985), "The Old Problem of Complex and Fact," *Teoria*, 5: 205–26.
Simons, P. (1997), "Review of Kush, *Psychologism*," *British Journal for the Philosophy of Science*, 48: 439–43.
Simons, P. (2004), "Open and Closed Culture: A New Way to Divide Austrians," in: A. Chrudzimski and W. Huemer (eds.), *Phenomenology and Analysis: Essays in Central European Philosophy*, 11–32, Frankfurt: Ontos.
Sluga, H. (1975), "Frege and the Rise of Analytic Philosophy," *Inquiry*, 18: 471–98.
Sluga, H. (1980), *Gottlob Frege*, London: Routledge & Kegan Paul.
Sluga, H. (1984), "Frege: The Early Years," in: R. Rorty et al. (eds.), *Philosophy in History*, 329–56, Cambridge: Cambridge University Press.
Sluga, H. (1987), "Frege against the Booleans," *Notre Dame Journal of Formal Logic*, 28: 80–98.
Smith, B. (1978), "Wittgenstein and the Background of Austrian Philosophy," in: E. Leinfellner et al. (eds.), *Wittgenstein and his Impact on Contemporary Thought*, 31–35, Vienna: Hölder-Pichler-Tempsky.
Smith, B. (1987), "On the Cognition of States of Affairs," in: K. Mulligan (ed.), *Speech Act and Sachverhalt. Reinach and the Foundation of Realist Phenomenology*, 189–225, Dordrecht: Nijhoff.
Smith, B. (1990), "Towards a History of Speech Act Theory," in: A. Burkhardt (ed.), *Speech Acts, Meanings and Intentions: Critical Approaches to the Philosophy of John R. Searle*, 29–61, Berlin/New York: de Gruyter.
Smith, B. (1990a), "*Logica Kirchbergensis*," in: P. Klein (ed.), *Praktische Logik*, 123–45, Göttingen: Vandenhoeck & Ruprecht.

Smith, B. (1992), "Characteristica Universalis," in: K. Mulligan (ed.), *Language, Truth, and Ontology*, 48–77, Dordrecht: Kluwer.
Smith, B. (1992a), "Sachverhalt," in: *Historisches Wörterbuch der Philosophie*, vol. 8, 1102–13, Basel: Schwabe.
Smith, B. (1994), *Austrian Philosophy: The Legacy of Franz Brentano*, Chicago: Open Court.
Smith, B. (1996), "Logic and the State of Affairs," in: L. Albertazzi et al. (eds.), *The School of Franz Brentano*, 323–41, Dordrecht: Kluwer.
Smith, B. (1996a), "The Neurath-Haller Thesis," in: K. Lehrer and J. C. Marek (eds.), *Austrian Philosophy: Past and Present*, 1–20, Dordrecht: Kluwer.
Smith, B. (1997), "Realistic Phenomenology," in: L. Embree et al. (eds.), *Encyclopaedia of Phenomenology*, 586–90, Dordrecht: Kluwer.
Smith, B. (1998), "Ontologie des Mesokosmos," *Zeitschrift für philosophische Forschung*, 52: 522–41.
Smith, B. (2005), "Against Fantology," in: M. Reicher and J. Marek (eds.), *Experience and Analysis*, 153–70, Vienna: ÖBV & HPT.
Smith, B. (2008), "The Benefits of Realism: A Realist Logic with Applications," in: K. Munn and B. Smith (eds.), *Applied Ontology*, 109–24, Frankfurt: Ontos.
Smith, B. (1996), "In Defense of Extreme (Fallibilistic) Apriorism," *Journal of Libertarian Studies*, 12: 179–91.
Smith, D. W. (2002), "Mathematical Form in the World," *Philosophia Mathematica*, 3rd series, 10: 102–29.
Soames, S. (2003), *Philosophical Analysis in the Twentieth Century*, 2 vols., Princeton: Princeton University Press.
Soames, S. (2014/17), *Analytic Tradition in Philosophy*, 2 vols., Princeton: Princeton University Press.
Soames, S. (2017), *Analytic Philosophy in America: And Other Historical and Contemporary Essays*, Princeton: Princeton University Press.
Sokolowski, R. (2000), *Introduction to Phenomenology*, Cambridge: Cambridge University Press.
Sorell, T. (2005), "On Saying No to History of Philosophy," in: T. Sorrel and G. A. J. Rogers (eds.), *Analytic Philosophy and History of Philosophy*, 43–59, Oxford: Oxford University Press.
Speer, A. (2010), *Fragile Konvergenz. 3 Essays zu Fragen metaphysischen Denkens*, Bonn: Salon Verlag.
Spiegelberg, H. (1960), *The Phenomenological Movement: A Historical Introduction*, Den Haag: Nijhoff.
Spiegelberg, H. (1979), "Husserl in England: Facts and Lessons," *The Journal of the British Society for Phenomenology*, 1: 4–15.
Stalnaker, R. (1973), "Presuppositions," *Journal of Philosophical Logic*, 2: 447–57.
Stebbing, S. (1932/3), "The Method of Analysis in Metaphysics," *Proceedings of the Aristotelian Society*, 33: 65–94.

Stebbing, S. (1933), "Logical Positivism and Analysis," *Proceedings of the British Academy*, 19: 53–87.
Stebbing, S. (1933/4), "Constructions," *Proceedings of the Aristotelian Society*, 34: 1–30.
Stebbing, S. (1934), "Directional Analysis and Basic Facts," *Analysis*, 2 (3): 33–6.
Stebbing, S. (1938/9), "Some Puzzles About Analysis," *Proceedings of the Aristotelian Society*, 39: 69–77.
Stebbing, S. (1942), "Moore's Influence," in: P. Schilpp (ed.), *The Philosophy of G. E. Moore*, 515–32, La Salle: Open Court.
Steinvorth, U. (2007), "Descartes. Willensfreiheit als Verneinungsfreiheit," in: U. an der Heiden und H. Schneider (eds.), *Hat der Mensch einen freien Willen?* 128–41, Stuttgart: Reclam.
Stekeler-Weithofer, P. (1992), *Hegels analytische Philosophie*, Paderborn: Schöningh.
Stenius, E. (1964), *Wittgenstein's Tractatus*, Oxford: Blackwell.
Stevens, G. (2005), *The Russellian Origins of Analytic Philosophy: Bertrand Russell and the Unity of the Proposition*, London: Routledge.
Stout, G. F. (1886), *Analytic Psychology*, London: Swan Sonnenschein.
Stove, D. C. (1982), *Popper and After: Four Modern Irrationalists*, Oxford: Pergamon.
Strawson, P. (1952), *Introduction to Logical Theory*, London: Methuen.
Strawson, P. (1956), "Construction and Analysis," in: A. J. Ayer et al., *The Revolution in Philosophy*, 97–110, London: Macmillan.
Strawson, P. (1959), *Individuals: An Essay in Descriptive Metaphysics*, London: Methuen.
Strawson, P. (1966), *The Bound of Sense*, London: Methuen.
Strawson, P. (1971), *Logico-Linguistic Papers*, London: Methuen.
Strawson, P. (1992), *Analysis and Metaphysics*, Oxford: Oxford University Press.
Stumpf, C. ([1870] 2008), *Über die Grundsätze der Mathematik*, ed. W. Ewen, Würzburg: Königshausen & Neumann.
Stumpf, C. (1906), "Zur Einteilung der Wissenschaften," *Abhandlungen der Königlich-Preußischen Akademie der Wissenschaften, Philosophisch-historische Klasse*, Berlin: Verlag der Königliche Akademie der Wissenschaften, 1–94.
Stumpf, C. (1910), *Philosophische Reden und Vorträge*, Leipzig: Barth.
Stumpf, C. (1924), "Carl Stumpf," in: R. Schmidt (ed.), *Die Philosophie der Gegenwart in Selbstdarstellungen*, vol. 5, 205–65, Leipzig: Felix Meiner.
Sweet, W. (1995), "Was Bosanquet a Hegelian?" *Bulletin of the Hegel Society of Great Britain*, 31: 39–60.
Taylor, A. E. (1925), "F. H. Bradley," *Mind*, 34: 1–12.
Thomas, G. (1987), *The Moral Philosophy of T. H. Green*, Oxford: Clarendon Press.
Trendelenburg, A. ([1840] 1862), *Logische Untersuchungen*, Leipzig: Hirzel.
Trendelenburg, A. (1867), "Über Leibnizens Entwurf einer allgemeinen Charakteristik," *Historische Beiträge zur Philosophie*, vol. 3, 1–47, Berlin: Bethge.
Unger, P. (2014), *Empty Ideas: A Critique of Analytic Philosophy*, Oxford: Oxford University Press.
Urmson, J. O. (1956), *Philosophical Analysis*, Oxford: Oxford University Press.

Urmson, J. O. (1990), *The Greek Philosophical Vocabulary*, London: Duckworth.
Vallicella, W. (2000), "Three Conceptions of States of Affairs," *Noûs*, 34: 237–59.
van der Schaar, M. (2013), *G. F. Stout and the Psychological Origins of Analytic Philosophy*, Basingstoke: Palgrave.
Varga, P. A. (2016), "The Non-Existing Object Revisited: Meinong as the Link Between Husserl and Russell?" in: M. Antonelli and M. David (eds.), Existence, *Fiction, Assumption: Meinongian Themes and the History of Austrian Philosophy*, 27–57, Berlin: de Gruyter.
von Wright, G. H. (1971), *Explanation and Understanding*, London: Routledge & Kegan Paul.
von Wright, G. H. (1993), "Analytic Philosophy," in *idem, The Tree of Knowledge and Other Essays*, 1–34, Leiden: Brill.
Wahl, R., ed. (2019), *The Bloomsbury Companion to Bertrand Russell*, London: Bloomsbury Academic.
Waismann, F. (1956), "How I See Philosophy," in: H. D. Lewis (ed.), *Contemporary British Philosophy*, vol. 3, 447–501, London: Allen & Unwin.
Wang, H. (1986), *Beyond Analytic Philosophy*, Cambridge: MIT Press.
Warnock, G. J. (1958), *English Philosophy since 1900*, Oxford: Oxford University Press.
Weiner, J. (2004), *Frege Explained: From Arithmetic to Analytic Philosophy*, Chicago: Open Court.
Weir, A. (2010), *Truth through Proof: A Formalist Foundation for Mathematics*, Oxford: Oxford University Press.
White, A. ([1958] 1969), *G. E. Moore: A Critical Exposition*, Oxford: Blackwell.
White, M. (1957), "The Decline and Fall of the Absolute," in: *idem*, (ed.), *The Age of Analysis*, 13–20, New York: New American Library.
Whitehead, A. N. (1927), *Religion in the Making*, New York: Macmillan.
Wilson, J. C. (1927), *Statement and Inference*, 2 vols., Oxford: Clarendon Press.
Wilson, M. (2007), "Scott Soames, Philosophical Analysis in the Twentieth Century," *The Philosophical Review*, 115: 517–23.
Windelband, W. ([1882] 1884), "Was ist Philosophie?" in: *idem*, 1–54.
Windelband, W. ([1883] 1884), "*Sub specie aeternitatis*," in: *idem*, 333–45.
Windelband, W. ([1884] 1922), *Präludien*, 9th ed., Tübingen: Mohr.
Windelband, W. (1892), *Geschichte der Philosophie*, Freiburg: J. C. B. Mohr.
Wisdom, J. (1931), *Interpretation and Analysis*, London: Kegan Paul.
Wisdom, J. (1934), *The Problems of Mind and Matter*, Cambridge: Cambridge University Press.
Wisdom, J. (1936), "Philosophical Perplexity," in: *idem*, (1965), 36–50.
Wisdom, J. (1952), *Other Minds*, Oxford: Blackwell.
Wisdom, J. (1953), "The Logic of God," in: *idem*, (1965a), 22–51.
Wisdom, J. ([1953] 1965), *Philosophy and Psychoanalysis*, 2nd ed., Oxford: Blackwell.
Wisdom, J. (1965a), *Paradox and Discovery*, Oxford: Blackwell.
Wisdom, J. (1969), *Logical Constructions*, New York: Random House.

Wittgenstein, L. ([1913] 1979), "Notes on Logic," in: *idem*, 93–107.
Wittgenstein, L. (1922), *Tractatus Logico-Philosophicus*, trans. C. Ogden and F. Ramsey, London: Allen & Unwin.
Wittgenstein, L. (1933), "[Letter] To the Editor of Mind," *Mind*, 42: 415.
Wittgenstein, L. (1953), *Philosophical Investigations*, ed. and trans. G. E. M. Anscombe, Oxford: Blackwell.
Wittgenstein, L. (1956), *Remarks on the Foundations of Mathematics*, ed. and trans. G. E. M. Anscombe, R. Rhees and G. H. von Wright, Oxford: Blackwell.
Wittgenstein, L. (1961), *Tractatus Logico-Philosophicus*, trans. D. Pears and B. McGuinness, London: Allen & Unwin.
Wittgenstein, L. (1969), *On Certainty*, ed. G. E. M. Anscombe and G. H. v. Wright, Oxford: Blackwell.
Wittgenstein, L. (1973), *Letters to C. K. Ogden*, Oxford: Blackwell.
Wittgenstein, L. (1974), *Philosophical Grammar*, ed. R. Rhees, trans. A. Kenny, Oxford: Blackwell.
Wittgenstein, L. (1977), *Remarks on Colour*, ed. G. E. M. Anscombe, Oxford: Blackwell.
Wittgenstein, L. (1979), *Notebooks 1914–1916*, 2nd end., ed. G. E. M. Anscombe and G. H. v. Wright, Oxford: Blackwell.
Wittgenstein, L. (1979a), *Wittgenstein's Lectures. Cambridge, 1932–1935*, ed. A. Ambrose, Oxford: Blackwell.
Wittgenstein, L. (1979b), *Wittgenstein and the Vienna Circle*, ed. B. F. McGuinness, Oxford: Blackwell.
Wittgenstein, L. (1980), *Cambridge Lectures. 1930–1932*, ed. D. Lee, Oxford: Blackwell.
Wittgenstein, L. (1980a), *Culture and Value*, ed. G. H. von Wright, Oxford: Blackwell.
Wittgenstein, L. (1980b), *Bemerkungen über der Philosophie der Psychologie*, G. E. M. Anscombe et al. (eds.), vol. 2, Oxford: Blackwell.
Wittgenstein, L. (1993/8), *Wiener Ausgabe*, ed. M. Nedo, Vienna: Springer.
Wittgenstein, L. (1995), *Cambridge Letters*, eds. B. F. McGuinness and G. H. von Wright, Oxford: Blackwell.
Wolff, M. (1995), *Die Vollständigkeit der Kantischen Urteilstafel*, Frankfurt: Klostermann.
Woodward. (2015), *Hermann Lotze. An Intellectual Biography*, Cambridge: Cambridge University Press.
Wundt, W. (1877), "Philosophy in Germany," *Mind*, o.s., 2: 493–513.
Zahavi, D. (2016), "Analytic and Continental Philosophy: From Duality through Plurality to (Some Kind of) Unity," in: S. Rinofner-Kreidl and H. Wiltsche (eds.), *Analytic and Continental Philosophy: Methods and Perspectives*, 79–93, Berlin: de Gruyter.

Index

Abbe, Ernst   54
absolute   42, 62–3, 89, 91
acquaintance, knowledge by   22, 115, 120–1, 194, 213, 237
action   98–9, 134, 197, 199
acts   60, 128, 140–1, 145, 155, 164–5, 175, 194
  cognitive   121, 155
  emotional   121, 155
  mental   121, 139, 155–6, 164
  speech   39, 128
  of will (*see* will)
aesthetic   79–80, 86, 140, 219
aggregate   50, 55, 59, 87, 128
Alexander, Samuel   78
algebra   32, 129, 142, 144, 147
Ammerman, Robert   3
analysis   11, 32–3, 48, 56–7, 115, 117, 136–8, 142–3, 163, 182–7, 190, 193–4, 211, 216, 237
  conceptual   44–6, 143, 145, 169, 193, 197, 203, 215, 222
  connective   45, 193, 203, 215–16, 221–2, 240
  decompositional   57, 202, 222, 229, 235
  directional   183–90
  interpretative   215–16
  logical   16, 49, 112, 116, 181, 189, 193, 237
  metaphysical   184
  reductive   32–3, 38, 193, 202–3
  two concepts of   56–7, 214–16, 244
analytic (-al)   6, 17, 24, 39, 49, 51, 56, 116, 130–1, 140, 147, 154, 161, 163, 166, 168, 201, 206–7, 216, 220
  hermeneutic   162, 244
  ideal   18, 27
  ideas   17, 27
  immediacy   48–51 (*see also* mediacy, mediation)

  metaphysics   244
  scholasticism   191, 213
  school   11, 46
analyticity   8, 193, 196, 206, 243
Anscombe, Elisabeth   106, 183
anthropological   83–4, 86, 90, 92, 167–8, 175
anti-
  foundationalism   178
  holistic   12
  mechanicism   55
  narturalistic   9
  psychologism   44, 63, 73, 157, 161, 163–4, 231, 240
a posteriori   168, 204
a priori   9, 39, 87, 119, 127, 132, 134, 143, 145–6, 167–70, 174, 176, 189, 197, 204, 216, 222
  relative   176, 240
  synthetic   39, 143, 145–6, 168–70, 197, 204
Aquinas, Thomas   15, 141
Archimedes   33
Aristotle, Aristotelian   8, 12, 15, 17, 19, 32, 34, 42, 50, 54–5, 100, 126, 137, 143, 146, 155, 162, 191, 220
arithmetic   32, 44, 53, 56, 63, 129, 142, 144, 147, 197, 204
ars characteristica   35
art   35, 198, 201
aspects   48, 50, 84, 122–3, 135
  -changing   198
atomism, atomists   71, 74–5, 88, 90, 176
  logical   51, 113, 121, 140, 146, 153, 156, 200
atoms, -ic   22, 74, 87–8
  facts   107
  logical   140
attention   122–3
Aufbau (Carnap)   4, 124, 159–61, 194, 205

Austin, John Langshaw 11, 17, 39, 46, 90, 147, 190, 208–10, 212, 214, 216, 223

Bacon, Francis 33
Baker, Gordon 210
Baldwin, Thomas 81, 152
Bauch, Bruno 70, 103, 184
Beaney, Michael 115, 147
being 90
Bell, David 8, 24
Bergmann, Julius 96, 100, 103,
Bergson, Henry 114, 164, 167, 178, 195, 213–14, 218
Berlin, Isaiah 167, 210
Bernays, Paul 167
Berto, Francesco 45
biographic(al), biography 25, 152–3
biology 45, 58
Black, Max 134, 191
Blue Book (Wittgenstein) 192
Böhme, Jacob 33–4
Bolzano, Bernard 4, 7, 13, 83, 117, 126
bona mens 36, 147
Boole, George 35, 55–6, 59, 61
Born, Max 167
boundary 195–7, 199
Bradley, Francis Herbert 67, 69–71, 73–4, 82
Braithwaite, Richard 191–2
Brandom, Robert 5, 46
Brentano, Franz 4, 8, 12, 16, 24, 39, 42, 71, 94, 96, 102–3, 115, 120, 138, 151, 166, 201–2, 205, 210–2
British
  empiricism 3, 160, 202
  philosophy 9, 67–70, 191, 221
Broad, Charles 69, 181, 191

Cabbala 33
calculation 31–3, 37–8, 52, 143–5, 147
  with concepts/propositions 130
  without numbers 227
  pure 55, 144
calculus 35, 40, 52, 57, 61–2, 92, 142, 144, 147–8
  calculus ratiotinator 35, 61
Cantor, Georg 82, 128–9, 236
Carnap, Rudolf 3–4, 16, 22, 50, 103, 124, 159–61, 182, 184, 186–7, 189, 191, 193–8, 200–7, 209, 215–16, 218
Cassirer, Ernst 4, 221
Cauchy, Augustin–Louis 63
characteristica universalis 31–6, 38–40, 228, 238
chemistry 34, 57–8
chess 38, 147, 217, 235
Chisholm, Roderick 16
Chomsky, Noam 223
clarification 182, 211
Cocchiarella, Nino 209
Coffa, Alberto 4, 6
Cohen, Hermann 167, 172, 221, 243
Collingwood, Robin George 16
Collins, Randall 26
colour(s) 14, 143, 147, 158, 185
combinatorics 33, 38
common sense 3, 18, 76, 182, 194, 213, 241
complex(es) 55, 59, 61, 104, 112, 135, 222, 234
compositionality 78, 231
Concept of Mind (Ryle) 21, 226
concepts 6, 12–13, 20–5, 34, 44, 49, 50, 55–6, 58–9, 62–4, 71–2, 78, 80, 83, 85–6, 92, 96–7, 100–1, 103–7, 120–1, 126, 128–9, 131, 134, 137–8, 143–4, 156–7, 160, 163, 165, 171, 187, 193, 196, 203–4, 234, 243
conceptual 7, 20, 37, 46, 87–8, 128, 175, 197–9
  analysis (*see* analysis)
  data 141, 145, 157, 170
  geography 45, 198
  necessities 197
  notions 34, 36, 40, 51, 60–1, 195
  scheme 148, 155, 164
  world 111, 200
Conceptual Notation (*Begriffsschrift*) (Frege) 34–6, 40, 51, 56, 57, 60–3, 195, 199
conditio humana 52, 219–20
conjecture 32, 36, 172–3, 175, 227
consciousness 6, 34, 43, 45, 98, 100, 102, 113, 116, 123, 128, 138–9, 158–9, 162–3, 202
constructivism 123–4, 194, 200, 204, 234, *see also* logical constructions

content
  judgment of 23, 71, 77, 85, 97–8, 100–1, 103, 105, 107, 195
  objective 7, 23–4, 71, 85, 90, 97, 101–3, 155
  perception of 23, 85, 101
  science of 125
  sense of 154
context principle 12, 22–3, 44, 70–1, 85, 100, 196–7, 231
Cornelius, Hans 153–4, 211
cosmology 43
counting 92–3
Courant, Richard 167
Critchley, S. 219–20
culture, cultural 4–6, 43, 52, 85, 146, 194, 205, 220, *see also* philosophical, culture
Cuming, Agnes 69

Danto, Arthur 217
data 11, 46, 51, 76, 117, 137, 139, 141, 144–5, 159, 186
  class of 154
  conceptual (*see* conceptual, data)
  empirical 133
  of science 175
Daubert, Johannes 113
Davidson, Donald 216
deconstructions 199
Dedekind, Richard 91
deduction 38, 56, 127, 132, 168–70, 174, 176
  deductive sciences 237
deliberate (-ing) 31–2, 143, 145, *see also* reflective equilibrium
denoting phrase(s) 63, 112, 159, 165
Descartes, René 16, 31, 33, 35–6, 42, 55, 126, 147, 174, 211–12, 220
dialectic(s) (-al) 38, 46–51, 55, 75–6, 81, 100, 145, 173, *see also* peirastic
  immediacy 48
Dilthey, Wilhelm 237
Dingler, Hugo 161
discovery (-ies) 145, 196–9, 206, 242
dogma, dogmatism 61, 171, 175, 205
  interpretative 205
Dray, William 210
Driesch, Hans 157, 160
dualism 83, *see also* monism

Dummett, Michael 3, 6, 8, 12, 15–16, 23, 40, 53, 60, 72, 102–3, 111, 183, 196–7, 209–10, 216, 220, 229, 240

eclecticism 68, 71, 75, 105, 230
Ego 113, 123
eide 115–16, 122, 235
  eidology 236
eidetic 116, 122, 136, 232, 237
  reduction 113, 116–17, *see also* intuition
eliminativism 48–9, 51, 228, *see also* reductionism
elucidation 45, 76, 98, 184, *see also* explanation
empiricism 53, 102, 113, 160, 168, 176–7, 205–7, 211
  British (*see* British empiricism)
  inconsistency of 241
  logical 4, 9
encyclopedia 20, 36–9, 46, 81
Epicurus, Sextus 211
epistemology (-ical) 23, 47–9, 51, 63, 74, 76, 98, 107, 112, 114, 119–21, 123, 128, 145, 157–9, 168–9, 173–5, 187, 190, 193–4, 196, 203–4
  and philosophy of mind 236
Erdmann, Benno 73
Essay on the Foundations of Geometry (Russell) 82
essences 116
ethic (-al) 16, 37, 76, 80, 84–6, 153, 171, 176–7
Eucken, Rudolf 15
exactness 33, 48, 55, 63, 69, 73, 89, 212
existence, existent 47, 59, 72, 75, 80–1, 83, 90, 104, 137, 139, 142, 154, 157–8, 176, 234, 242
explanation 9, 11, 86, 118, *see also* elucidation
externality 87, 90

falsification 173, 176, 195
family
  resemblance 147
  tree 194
Fechner, Gustav Theodor 7, 84
Fischer, Kuno 67
force 45, 60, 86, 100, 201
  illocutionary 230

form(s)   11–12, 34, 37–40, 42–3, 50–1,
    78, 87–8, 90, 98–100, 113, 115–16,
    122, 126–32, 134–5, 144, 146,
    160, 167–8, 176, 184, 198
  disciplinal   128, 131–2
  general logical   79
  in language/epistemology   235
  of life   80, 99, 200
  logical   7, 39, 43–4, 51, 61, 77–9, 104,
    112, 115–21, 128, 139–41, 146,
    156, 165, 200, 209, 237, 243
  metaphysical   34, 40
  objectival   128
  ontological   98, 132
  particular   38–9
  pure   128, 131, 203
  substantial   34, 42
formalism, formalist   61, 118, 235
Forster, Edward Morgan   152
Fortlage, Karl   54
foundation(s)   56, 73, 86, 91, 97, 103,
    134, 176, 202, 210
Frege, Gottlob, Fregean   3, 6, 8–9, 12–13,
    16–17, 22–3, 26, 34–5, 40–1, 44,
    48–9, 53–64, 70, 72, 78, 101–3,
    105, 111–12, 118, 151, 163–6,
    170–1, 177–8, 183–4, 187, 189,
    193–207, 209–10, 215–16, 221–2
Friedman, Michael   4, 6, 8, 218, 240, 242
Fries, Jakob Friedrich   7, 12, 84, 88,
    167–70, 172, 174, 175–6
function   4, 13, 47, 58–9, 62–3, 74, 85,
    92, 121, 131, 147, 196, 231, 234
fundamentals   114, 116–17, 134, 169,
    178, 214

Gabriel, Gottfried   54
Galileo, Galilei   33
game   130, 144–5, 147, 217, 222, *see also*
    play
  language (*see* language-games)
Gauthier, Yvon   129
geography
  grammatical   200
  logical   11, 21, 45, 195, 197, 200, 202–3
geometry   129–32, 143, 147, 168, 175
  Euclidean   129, 131–2, 147
  non-Euclidean   168, *see also* space,
    logical
German   3–5, 23, 34, 41, 58, 68, 83,
    98, 100, 103, 106–7, 118, 126,
    128, 151, 153, 161, 164, 167–8,
    210–11
idealism   7, 26, 53–7, 60–2, 64, 84,
    219
philosophy (-ers)   3–5, 7–9, 11,
    13–16, 18, 41–2, 54–5, 61,
    67–70, 74, 84, 103, 153–4, 159,
    166, 202, 221
Romantics   26, 54
Germanophone philosophy(ers)   4, 7,
    13–14, 151, 153, 156, 211, 215
given, the   139, 141, 143–4, 157–9, 162,
    168–9, 175, 185
God   81, 202, 219
Gödel, Kurt   223
grammar   52, 143, 147, 163, 190, 223
  philosophical (*see* philosophical,
    grammar)
Grassmann, Hermann   61, 129
Green, Thomas Hill   67, 69–71, 73
Greifswald Objectivists   151, 156–64
Grundlagen (Frege)   197, 230

Hacohen, Malachi H.   172
Haeckel, Ernst   53
Hager, Paul   87
Hamilton, Elisabeth   69
Hamilton, William R.   129
Hannequin, Arthur   88
Hare, Richard M.   171
Hartmann, Nicolai   22–3
Hegel, Georg W. F., Hegelian   5, 7, 12–13,
    22, 29, 34, 41–55, 59, 61, 63,
    67–70, 73, 75, 81–2, 84–5, 89,
    100, 167, 215, 218
Heidegger, Martin   16, 42–3, 70, 136,
    209, 211, 214, 218
Hempel, Carl Gustav   3
Herbart, Johan Friedrich   7, 68, 73, 84,
    101
Heyde, Erich   157
Hilbert, David   236–7
hinge   134
Hintikka, Jaakko   136, 146
historicism   116
history of philosophy   5–13, 15–27, 41–2,
    47–8, 71, 153, 171, 193, 202,
    206, 211, 214, 226
Hobbes, Thomas   33
Höffding, Harald   74
human being(s)   42, 52, 60, 83, 87, 214

Hume, David 8, 16–8, 23–4, 49, 57, 111–12, 138, 176–7, 204, 211, 220
Husserl, Edmund 4, 12, 16, 23, 49–50, 61, 71, 82, 96–7, 103, 106, 109, 111–41, 145–6, 151, 154–6, 163–5, 170, 183, 202, 204–5, 211, 213–14
Hylton, Peter 46

idealities 86, 92
ideas (*Vorstellungen*) 97, 101–2
identity of indiscernibles 92, 202, 204
ideography 31–2
illusion 39, 217
immanent philosophers 157, 160
indefinables 11, 36, 76, 78, 134, 137–47, 158, 160, 170, 200, 232, 237
individuals 40, 48, 56, 58, 62–4, 87, 92–3, 104–5, 162, 184, 233
induction 169–70, 176
ineffable 80, 105, 139, 145
intentionality 111
Introduction to Mathematical Philosophy (Russell) 118
intuition 145, 244
   eidetic 138, 201
   intellectual 121

Jacobi, Friedrich Heinrich 49
Jacoby, Günther 157, 160
Jacquette, Dale 5
James, William 23, 49, 78, 82, 206
Jevons, William Stanley 61
Jones, Constance 69
Joseph, Horace W. B. 17
Jourdain, Philip E. B. 17
judgment(s) 23, 44, 54–5, 57, 59–60, 71, 77, 85, 90–1, 93–4, 97–107, 120, 127, 131, 158, 163, 168–71, 177–8, 194–5
   affirmation of 100
   ontology of 104
   relational theory of 77, 99
Jungius, Joachim 33

kaleidoscope 97–8
Kant, Immanuel 5–8, 12, 16–9, 22–3, 42, 44, 54, 56, 67–8, 71, 73, 81, 88, 101, 123, 127, 134, 138, 143, 167–8, 171–2, 174, 197, 201, 204, 211–14, 216, 218–20
Kelsen, Hans 173, 177, 210
Keynes, John M. 152
Kneale, William and Martha 70
knowledge 7, 9, 33–4, 38–9, 45, 56, 67, 86–9, 92, 97–8, 101–2, 105, 115–16, 127, 129, 159, 163, 167–70, 174–5, 177, 185–7, 189–90, 202, 204, 213, 222, *see also* acquaintance, knowledge by
   complex 169
   immediate 47, 168–70, 175
Köhler, Wolfgang 223
Kraft, Julius 173–4
Kripke, Saul 11, 206
Kroneker, Leopold 129
Kuhn, Thomas 10
Külpe, Oswald 172
Künne, Wolfgang 155
Kuntz, Paul Grimley 72, 75
Kusch, Martin 151

Lambert, Johann Heinrich 42
language 6, 18, 31–3, 43, 46, 51–2, 54, 57, 60–3, 76, 112, 119–20, 135, 142, 147, 162, 165, 177, 182–3, 196, 199, 203–4, 209–10, 212
   Adamic 33–4
   formal 196
   -games 52, 141, 146
   logically perfect 34–5, 119
   ordinary (*see* ordinary language philosophy)
   private (*see* private language)
   symbolic 92
law(s) 34–5, 38, 49, 56, 61–2, 79, 86, 88, 126–7, 129, 169, 197, 207, 210
Leibniz, Gottfried Wilhelm 31–40, 42, 54–5, 82, 123, 126, 170, 227–9, 237–8
Lie, Sophus 129
life 36, 43–5, 52, 58–60, 62, 74–5, 80, 82, 86, 99, 146, 153, 190, 198, 200, 217–20, *see also* forms of
   meaning of 190, 244
lingua characterica 35, 54, 60–1
linguisticism 189
Linke, Paul 96
local signs 99

Locke, John 17, 33, 42, 49, 55, 168, 202
logic 3, 8–9, 21, 35, 42–5, 48, 51, 54–7, 59, 61–4, 69–70, 73, 80, 82, 84–5, 92, 100–3, 117, 119, 126–30, 133–4, 141–3, 147, 172, 184, 188, 193, 195, 197, 200, 209, 215, 221–2
  apophantic 126–7
  content of 42, 61–2
  empirical 144
  first-order 63, 141
  formal 45, 61, 105, 127, 187
  formalization of 73
  informal 45
  intensional 62–3, 99–100
  language of 45, 182
  mathematical 117–18, 133, 212
  modal 242
  new 62–3, 133, 182–3, 194–5, 241
  philosophical 8–9, 37, 54–5, 57, 59, 69–70, 84–5, 103, 115–16, 120, 134, 147, 155, 188, 197, 200–2, 206, 209, 215, 222, 225, 232, 243
  pure 117, 126
  speculative 42, 45, 215
  symbolic 37, 70, 133–4, 209, 243
  terms of 63
  transcendental 42, 113, 126
logical 7, 19, 24, 26, 47, 51, 56, 60, 76–7, 79, 89–90, 105, 112, 116, 132, 137, 146, 186, 189, 200
  constants 47, 51, 79
  constructions 123, 186–8, 193–5, 200, 203–4, 216, 237, 242
    (see also constructivism)
  forms (see forms, logical)
  geography (see geography, logical)
  Positivists 176, 181–3, 186–7, 191
  scaffolding 231
  skeleton 51
  voluntarism 60
logicism 73, 231
logocentrism 8–10
Lotze, Hermann 4, 7–8, 12, 23–4, 39, 54–5, 59, 61, 65, 67–107, 151, 170, 202

McDowell, John 46
McGuinness, Brain F. 106–7
Mach, Ernst 49, 153, 163

McTaggart, John 41, 69, 81, 90–1, 181
magnitudes 91, 93, 130, 233
manifolds, see theory of
Manser, Anthony 74
map 19–21, 23–4, 26, 152, 200, 203, 207
Marx, Karl 41, 174
materialist 33, 185
mathematics 7–8, 32–4, 37, 42, 45–6, 52, 55–6, 58, 61, 63, 73, 82, 91–2, 113, 117–18, 128–34, 147, 167–70, 175–7, 197, 212, 223
  super- 117, 130
  meta- 236
mathesis universalis 31, 126, 128, 130–2
Mayer, Verena 4, 124
meaning 22, 47, 58, 70, 96–8, 101, 111–12, 165, 190, 192, 196, 198, 219, see also life
mechanism 72, 86, 92, see also philosophy
mediacy (-tion) 48–54, 213
  intermediary 229 (see also analytic, immediacy)
medicine 32, 36, 39, 84
mereology 48, 65, 147, 221, 228, 235
Mersenne, Marin 31
Messer, August 120, 154–5, 163–4
metaphysics (-al) 34, 40, 55, 71, 76–7, 86, 90, 103, 139, 158, 164, 173, 176–7, 181, 184, 209–13
  analytical 222
  consequence (entailment) 189
  old 84, 181
  point 237
method 5, 9–11, 13, 18, 33, 41, 45, 47–9, 52, 68, 86, 100, 115–17, 137, 142–3, 162, 168–9, 171–4, 176, 198, 201–5, 215–18, 221–2
  axiomatic 236–7
  critical 172, 175, 240
  descriptive 115, 138, 140–1, 156, 163, 226, 240, 243
  economic 47, 98, 147, 234
  eliminativist 47, 49, 51, 115, 241
    see also eliminativism
  philosophical 47, 85, 145, 201, 215
  piecemeal 12, 85, 116, 181–2, 232
  Platonic 172
  progressive/regressive 168–9, 235

Socratic   33, 145, 170–2
scientific, in philosophy   194, 215, 232
Michaltschew, Dimitri   151–3, 156–9, 161–5
microcosm   79–80, 83
Mill, John Stuart   22, 53, 70
Misch, Georg   83, 94, 103
Mohanty, Jitendra N.   111
monism   75, 89–90, 93
 epistemological   158
 neutral   113, 239
Moog, Willi   157
Moore, George Edward   5–6, 8–9, 11–12, 14, 16, 18, 20, 23–4, 37–8, 47, 49–52, 67–9, 72, 76–7, 81, 93–5, 111, 120–1, 139–40, 145, 147, 151–66, 177–8, 181–3, 185–92, 208–13, 215, 221
Mulligan, Kevin   5, 99, 114, 211–12, 217, 220, 243
multiplicity   88, 97, 101, 105, 128–9, 134, 158, 163, 175, 184
mystical   42–3, 140, 218
Mysticism and Logic (Russell)   39, 113, 193

names, logically simple   92
naturalism   9, 113, 116, 157
 naturalistic fallacy   234
natural laws   86, 207
Nelson, Leonard   6, 8, 12, 166–78, 221
neo-Friesian(s)   6, 8
neo-Hegelian(s)   7, 12, 41, 46, 53, 67, 69, 73, 93
neo-Kantian(s)   4–6, 18, 41, 54, 70, 82, 160–1, 167, 183–4
 Marburg   4, 6, 8, 183–4, 232
 Southwest   4, 6, 80, 184, 232
Nettleship, Richard L.   67, 69
Neurath, Otto   167
Newton, Isaac   33
Nicholson, Peter   67
Nietzsche, Friedrich   218
noema   111, 113, 121
Normore, Calvin   15–16
Novalis   178
Nozick, Robert   210
numbers   56–7, 64, 93, 123, 126–7, 129–30, 134–5, 139, 144, 146–7, 159, 197, 203, 232
Nuzzo, Angelica   46

objectivism   8, 82–3, 88, 154, 159, 163–4
objects   72, 140, 158, 239
Ogden, Charles   106–7
ontology (-ical)   35, 47–8, 51, 72, 74–5, 81, 83, 92, 98–9, 104, 107, 115, 128, 132, 136–7, 145, 155, 164
 formal   127, 135
 fundamental   115, 136, 214
 glue   48, 50, 98
 logical   204
 nomenclature   214
 Tractarian   36, 135, 146
 ways of   234
Oppenheimer, Franz   174
order   31, 35, 40, 63, 72–73, 75, 81, 83, 86–8, 93, 98, 107, 122, 141–2, 144–5, 198, 233
ordinary language philosophy   17, 41, 44, 46, 171, 197, 203, 215
organicism   44, 55–6, 60
organic unity   49, 58
organism   56–8
Orth, Ernst Wolfgang   6
Our Knowledge (Russell)   37, 112, 121–2, 124, 133, 156, 169, 193

panpsychism   79, 107, 234
paradox   40, 63–4, 82, 117, 230
pasigraphy   31
Passmore, John   17, 22, 68
Peano, Giuseppe   8, 112, 221
Pears, David   106–7, 135, 146, 216, 222
Peckhaus, Volker   54
peirastic   37–8, 100, 143, 145, 171–2, 174, 240, *see also* dialectic
perception   34, 71, 85, 87, 97, 99–101, 120–3, 164, 198
perspectives   122–3, 186
Pfänder, Alexander   113
phenomena   114–15, 117, 120, 122–3, 137–46, 155, 158, 160, 176, 181
 mental   139, 155
phenomenology (-ical)   7, 82, 111, 113, 117–18, 122, 125–6, 128, 136, 138–9, 141, 143–6, 161, 163, 202, 205, 214, 236
 analysis   143, 145, 148
 genetic   113, 123
 reduction   235

philosophical   3, 5, 7–9, 12, 17–22, 24–6,
    33, 39, 47, 49, 54, 61, 69–71, 75,
    83–5, 96, 111, 113, 116–17, 128,
    136, 140, 145–7, 152–3, 161–3,
    167, 170–1, 174, 188, 192,
    195–6, 199–202, 205–6, 208–9,
    214–5, 217, 220–2
  culture, open/close   205
  education   40
  grammar   92
  practice   38, 84, 161, 214
  problem(s)   20–3, 45, 116–17, 162,
    164, 170, 186, 201
  psychology   119, 156, 168–70, 236
  school   49, 151, 161, 210
  training   37–8, 45, 52, 147
Philosophical Investigations (Wittgenstein)
    47, 51, 142, 192, 235
philosophy
  analytic   166, 168, 206, 243
    British vs. American   191, 203
    definition of   208–14, 222
    early   3–9, 11–14, 37, 41–2, 45,
      47–8, 50, 52, 111, 133, 153, 156,
      159–61, 163, 169, 171, 178, 193,
      196, 203, 208, 215, 244
    late   5, 9–10, 48, 213, 217, 222
    middle   9–10
    proto-   6, 8, 211, 243
    two concepts of   180, 191, 196,
      202–3, 207, 214, 244
  anti-speculative   210
  concrete   215
  continental   4, 6, 52, 112, 195, 205,
    211, 214, 217–21, 243
  critical   8, 172
  of education   171
  exact   211–12
  language of   6, 9, 12, 22, 51, 63, 112,
    165, 177, 209–10
  logicalization of   6, 71–2
  mathematics of   91, 168, 175, 233, 240
  mechanic, -istic   33, 42, 55–6, 117
  mind of   72, 114, 119–21, 123, 156,
    222–3
  monstrous   212
  new   9, 16, 24, 42, 73, 140, 154, 178,
    208–9, 211, 213–15, 221–2
  old   218
  revolution in   211–12

  rigorous   37, 137, 213–14
  science of   9–10, 88, 131, 172–5, 177,
    240
  solid results in   195, 199, 201, 207,
    213–14, 216, 218, 225
  speculative   67, 76, 85, 162, 195, 210
  systematic   15, 19–20
  Teutonic   33
  traditional   52, 146, 213, 220
"Philosophy of Logical Atomism"
    (Russell)   113, 121, 140, 153,
    156, 200
physic(s) (-al)   33, 45, 85, 92, 98,
    128, 144, 147, 158–60, 176,
    184, 194
physiognomy   79–80
picture theory   196, 199
Plato   8, 12, 16–17, 22–3, 37–9, 97,
    100, 137, 143, 145, 162, 171,
    211, 216
Plato's Progress (Ryle)   17, 226, 228
play   59, 127, 130, 132, *see also* game
pluralism   89–91
poetry   218–19, 229
Poincaré, Henri   91
political theory   10, 171, 226
Popper, Karl   166–7, 169, 171–8
positivism   176
possibilities, contemplating   144, 238
practice   32, 38–9, 50, 52, 142, 191, 196,
    201, 203, 210, 220
pragmatism   7, 82, 175
Price, Henry   18, 20, 211
Priest, Graham   50
Principia Ethica (Moore)   50, 76, 139,
    152, 155
Principia mathematica (Russell and
    Whitehead)   51, 118, 236, 242
Principles of Mathematics (Russell)   50,
    73, 82, 98, 106, 112, 134, 139,
    152, 154, 187, 221, 239
Prior, Arthur   68
private   88, 122–3, 165, 196
  experience   160
  language   39, 192
Problems of Philosophy (Russell)   16, 23,
    37, 120–1, 152–3, 188, 237
proposition(s)   7, 13, 35, 43, 47, 50–1,
    62, 70, 74, 77–9, 90–4, 101,
    112, 119, 127, 131, 134, 140,

165, 169, 173, 182, 187–9, 192,
    196–7, 207, 209, 214–16
  analysis of   240
  unity of   229
propositional
  approach   163, 168
  attitudes   121
psychologism   9, 73, 113, 116, 151, 157,
    163, 165, 170, 230–1, *see also*
    anti-psychologism
psychology   24, 57, 84, 103, 116, 119–20,
    156, 168–70, 176, 202, 210, 220,
    223, 230
  analytical   120, 321
  descriptive   210
  experimental   168
  of knowledge   175
  philosophical   119, 168, 236

quality   162
quantifier(s) (-cation)   57, 62–3, 112,
    132, 221, 230
quantity   91
Quine, Willard   9–11, 160, 189–90, 203,
    206–7, 215–16
Quinton, Anthony   219

Rawls, John   10, 210
realism   71, 75–6, 90, 92–3, 135, 181,
    188, 213, 216
reality   31, 34, 36, 60, 71–2, 77, 88, 94,
    97–8, 102–3, 117, 134, 174, 181,
    194, 199, 217, 223
Redding, Paul   5, 46
reductionism   49, 160, 194, 207, 228, 241,
    see also eliminativism
regulative idea   219–20
reflective equilibrium   171, *see also*
    peirastic
Rehmke, Johannes   8, 151, 153, 155, 157,
    159–65
Reichenbach, Hans   173
Reinach, Adolf   50, 103–4
relation(s)   3, 5, 22, 48, 50, 58, 61–2,
    70–2, 74, 77, 83, 87, 89, 91,
    98–100, 102, 105–6, 123,
    127, 155–6, 164, 185, 194,
    199, 219
  external/internal   74
  nexus of   99

reciprocal   50, 98, 105–6
  reciproca tantum   106, 234
  spatial   34, 61, 87–8, 154
relationism   69–71, 73–4, 82–3, 86
relativism   116
religion   43, 69, 72, 90, 244
Remarks on the Foundations of Mathematics
    (Wittgenstein)   197
Richardson, Allan   6
Rickert, Heinrich   4, 163
Riemann, Georg   129, 175
Rosado Haddock, Guillermo   4
Rousseau, Jean-Jacques   211
Roy, Jean-Michel   4
Royce, Josiah   7, 23
rule, -following   39, 142–4, 204
Russell, Bertrand, Russellian   5–6, 8–9,
    11–14, 16–17, 20, 22–4, 27,
    37–9, 46–7, 49–53, 60, 63, 67–9,
    71–4, 76–8, 81–3, 85–95, 98,
    106, 111–27, 129, 131, 133–6,
    139–40, 145–7, 152–6, 159–61,
    163–70, 177–8, 181, 183, 185–9,
    191, 193–8, 200–16, 218, 221–2
Ryckman, Thomas   4, 124
Ryle, Gilbert   11, 17, 21–4, 45, 190, 195,
    203, 208–11, 216

Sachverhalt   50, 71, 78, 96, 99, 106–7,
    234, *see also* state of affairs
Santayana, George   75, 106
saturation   58–9, 85, 229
Schelling, Friedrich W. J.   26, 53–4,
    63, 68
Schiller, Ferdinand   175
Schlegel, August Wilhelm   18
Schleiermacher, Friedrich   18, 71
Schlick, Moritz   205
Schoenflies, Arthur   58
Schopenhauer, Arthur   7, 178
Schröder, Ernst   61
Schuppe, Wilhelm   157, 160–1
science   9, 32, 39, 46, 71, 81, 86, 114, 119,
    125, 127, 132, 135, 139, 141,
    144, 159, 167–70, 173, 175–7,
    202, 207, 217–18, 222–3
  empirical   9, 53, 207
  exact   13, 212
  natural   7, 9
Searle, John   223

Sellars, Wilfrid   160, 215
sense-data   23–4, 47, 71, 76, 85, 111–12,
    115, 139, 141, 144–5, 147, 154,
    156–60, 176, 186, 190, 194–5,
    227, 239
series   93
Shakespeare, William   218
Shelly, Percy Bysshe   218
show, showing   32, 80, 105, 134, 137–8,
    140, 143, 196
Sidgwick, Henry   69
Sigwart, Christoph   68, 102
Simons, Peter   205, 217
Smith, Barry   5, 63, 96, 101, 102, 103,
    104, 217
Smith, D. W.   125–6
Snell, Karl   26, 53–4
Soames, Scott   8, 11, 206
society   52, 155, 167, 191, 215, 219
sociology (-ical)   25–6, 220
Socrates   171
solipsism   154, 186, 192
Some Main Problems of Philosophy
    (Moore)   16, 23, 152, 188
space   68, 73–4, 76, 82, 86–91, 93, 123
    empty   87–8
    Euclidean   116, 200 (*see also*
        geometry)
    logical   43, 116
    and time   63, 87, 89–91, 105, 115,
        123, 129, 134, 142
Spengler, Oswald   167
Spiegelberg, Herbert   118
Spinoza, Baruch   16, 62, 211
spirit, spiritual   9, 12, 35, 43, 49, 79, 99,
    166, 178, 181, 219
Sraffa, Pierro   223
state(s) of affairs   23–4, 51, 78–9, 96–101,
    103–4, 106–7, 127–8, 132–3,
    135, 147, 164, 233–4, *see also*
    Sachverhalt
static/dynamic
    data   142, 145
    indefinables   144
    logic   142, 238
Staut, George   68
Stebbing, Susan   177, 181–92, 215, 241
Strawson, Peter   17, 20, 45, 147, 202, 216,
    223
Stumpf, Carl   23, 63, 73, 96–7, 103

subjectivism   88, 154
subject vs. object   83, 155
sub specie aeternitatis   80, 140, 198
substance   58, 62, 72, 77–9, 82, 88, 98–9,
    107, 137, 147
symbolism   34–6, 183, 199
    logical   60, 92
symbols   34–6, 51, 61, 77, 117, 185, 188
    incomplete   159, 188–9, 239
    logical   80
    primitive   36
syntax   92, 119
system   7, 21, 62, 75–6, 85, 90, 99,
    117, 122, 131–2, 142, 187,
    194, 215
    constitutional   194
    encyclopaedic   46
    logical   46, 141, 143
systematic philosophy   15, 19–20

Tarski, Alfred   172, 191
tautology, -ical   57, 196
teleomechanism   85–6
term(s)   23, 43, 47, 50, 55, 58, 60–1,
    63, 67, 70, 74, 76–7, 82–3, 87,
    90–2, 96–7, 102–7, 116, 121–2,
    125, 128–9, 136, 139, 147, 156,
    162, 169, 188, 190, 193–4, 202,
    210–12
    complex   40
    concrete   85, 213
    exact   47
tertium quid   51–2
theory, of
    denoting   235
    descriptions   17, 112, 184, 187, 209,
        244
    everything   126, 131
    forms   11, 38, 116, 126, 129, 135, 227
        logical   112, 209
    judgment   54, 77, 91–2, 94, 103, 231
    manifolds   91–2, 117, 119, 125–7,
        129–34, 141, 237
    mind   122
    order   72, 83
    perception   122
    propositions   90–2, 94
    relations   91, 194
    space   76, 82, 88
        and time   91

theories 126-7, 131-4, 236
truth
　apophantic 137
　identity 165
things 97, 106-7
thinking 32, 40, 43, 52, 54-5, 59, 61, 73, 83-4, 87, 97-8, 102, 117, 127, 130, 132, 147, 166, 182-3, 199, 217-18
　pure 230
thought(s) 5, 8, 12, 19, 31-4, 49, 54, 58-60, 62, 87-8, 98, 100, 102, 117, 130-1, 139, 145, 165, 182-3, 196, 211, 219
　experiments 117
　secondary 97-8, 100, 102
time 16, 54, 61, 74, 82, 89-90, 105, 134, 147, 151, 216
　and space (*see* space)
toolbox 38, 147
Tractatus logico-philosophicus
　(Wittgenstein) 35, 42-3, 52, 134-5, 140-1, 146, 181, 183, 187-8, 191, 199, 205, 207, 210
tradition, philosophical 3, 10, 42, 49, 53-5, 112, 136, 202, 212, 220
　ancient 126
　British 181, 202
　continental 219
　German 126, 230
translation 69, 102-3, 106-7, 120, 196, 204, 207, 215
Trendelenburg, Adolf 7-8, 15, 24, 54-5, 71, 83, 102
truth 37, 43, 45, 59-60, 72, 100-3, 121, 126-7, 137, 147, 158, 165, 170-1, 174, 190, 202, 214, 219, 222
　abstract 115
　analytic/synthetic 206-7
　eternal 204, 206-7
　formal 115
　-making 103, 187, 237, 242
　philosophical 25, 171, 198, 201, 205-6
　sense of 171, 234
truth-value 59-60, 71, 85, 165, 196, 232
Turing, Alan 223
turn
　formal 7
　linguistic 46

logical 71
objectivist 7, 70
propositional 163, 189

Uebel, Thomas 5
Ueberweg, Friedrich 68
unities 48, 50
universals 128, 137, 147
universe 6, 63, 72, 88, 99, 188
Urmson, James O. 17

vague (-ness) 37, 169, 175, 235
value 4, 15, 63, 67, 70-1, 73, 80, 85, 101, 111, 142, 165, 219, 242, *see also* truth-value
van Heijenoort, Jean 62
Vienna Circle 9, 11, 17, 173, 176-7, 181-3, 187, 190-1, 210, 229
von Goethe, Johann Wolfgang 229
von Hartmann, Eduard 75, 178
von Helmholtz, Hermann 73
von Schubert-Soldern, Richard 157, 161

Waismann, Friedrich 39, 209
Wallace, William 67
Wang, Hao 136-7
Ward, James 68-9
Warnock, Geoffrey 17
Weierstrass, Karl 63, 82
will 60, 78-9, 121, 155
　free 59-60
Wilson, J. Cook 69, 139
Windelband, Wilhelm 18, 22, 80, 100
Wisdom, John 189-90, 209, 211, 215-16, 235
Wittgenstein, Ludwig 3, 5-6, 8-9, 11-12, 14, 16-17, 22-3, 35-6, 41-5, 47, 49-52, 57-8, 60, 71-2, 76, 78-80, 91, 96-7, 101, 105-6, 112-13, 125-6, 133-48, 156, 163, 169-71, 177-8, 181-3, 187-202, 204-10, 212-13, 215-16, 221-3
Wolff, Michal 42
Woolf, Virgina 152
world(s), the 34, 36, 42, 46, 59, 61, 63, 80, 86, 98-9, 101, 116, 124, 135, 144, 160, 181, 193, 196, 198, 200, 204-5, 216, 218, 220, 233

conceptual   200
epistemological   204
external   6, 47, 59, 160, 185–7, 193, 222
facts of   51, 135, 146
   basic of   185
logical   193–8, 200–5, 243
phenomena of   160
many   230

objective   88, 156
possible   193, 205, 237, 241
spiritual   99
third   196–8, 200, 202, 207, 222
ultimate constituents of   185
Wundt, Wilhelm   68, 102

Zermelo, Ernst   167
zoology   200

www.ingramcontent.com/pod-product-compliance
Lightning Source LLC
Chambersburg PA
CBHW070019010526
44117CB00011B/1645